Normative
Discourse

PRENTICE-HALL PHILOSOPHY SERIES
Arthur E. Murphy, Ph.D., Editor

PAUL W. TAYLOR

Department of Philosophy, Brooklyn College

Normative

Discourse

PRENTICE-HALL, INC. *Englewood Cliffs, N.J.,* **1961**

To

MARTHA, *my wife*

Preface

The subject of this book is the logic of evaluating and prescribing. I am concerned with the following questions: What is it to evaluate something? What is it to prescribe an act to someone? How can we justify our evaluations and prescriptions? The language in which we express evaluations, prescribe acts, and give reasons for or against evaluations and prescriptions, I call "normative language." When we judge an object to be good or an act to be right, when we tell someone what he ought or ought not to do, and when we try to justify such judgments and prescriptions, we are carrying on normative discourse.

Normative discourse is to be distinguished from scientific, mathematical, and historical discourse, and from any other "universe" of discourse in which language is used for purposes other than the making and justifying of evaluations and prescriptions. What I am doing in this book with regard to the universe of normative discourse may also be done with regard to other universes of discourse. My purpose is, first, to make clear the key concepts used in carrying on normative discourse and, second, to make explicit the rules of reasoning which govern the justification of normative assertions. It is a primary task of philosophy to clarify, by means of an analysis of its key concepts and rules of reasoning, the logic of every universe of discourse in which human beings do their thinking. The aim is to come to a clear understanding of *what it means to be rational,* whether we are pursuing science, mathematics, or history, or are evaluating and prescribing. It is also the task of philosophy to compare one universe of discourse with another and to discover whatever logical connections there are between them. In Chapter 9 of this book I try to accomplish this task with respect to the relation between normative discourse and descriptive discourse.

There are three concepts of normative discourse which comprise its key concepts: the concept of a good thing, the concept of a right act, and the concept of what-one-ought-to-do. We understand the meaning of these concepts insofar as we know how to use correctly the terms "good," "right," and "ought" (and any other terms used in similar ways for similar purposes). "Good" and "right" are the basic evaluative terms of normative language. "Ought" is the basic prescriptive term, although—as I shall point out in Chapter 7—it has some evaluative uses also. A philosophical analysis of normative discourse, then, must elucidate what it means to say that something is good, what it means to say that an act is right, and what it means to say that someone ought to do a certain act.

A philosophical analysis of normative discourse must also include an examination of the rules of reasoning which govern normative discourse. These are the rules we implicitly follow when we try to justify our claim that something is good, that an act is right, or that someone ought to do a certain act. The rules of reasoning tell us, first, what makes a reason *relevant* to such claims and, second, what makes a reason a *good* reason in support of, or in opposition to, such claims. The rules that determine the relevance of reasons, I call "rules of relevance." The rules that determine whether a relevant reason is also a good reason, I call "rules of valid inference." I shall argue in this book that the same rules of relevance and valid inference govern both the justification of value judgments and the justification of prescriptions. (This is why both evaluating and prescribing belong to one universe of discourse.)

There is only one set of rules of valid inference for the entire universe of normative discourse. These rules, along with the key concepts already mentioned, differentiate normative discourse from all other kinds of discourse. But normative discourse itself may be divided into many subordinate universes of discourse. Moral discourse, for example, may be distinguished from aesthetic discourse, even though both are for the most part normative. In addition to moral and aesthetic discourse there are religious discourse, intellectual or logical discourse, political, economic, and legal discourse, the discourse of custom or etiquette, and many other kinds of discourse, all of which consist, at least in part, in the making and justifying of evaluations and prescriptions and, consequently, belong to the universe of normative discourse. If all of these kinds of discourse are normative, what is it that distinguishes each of them from the others? The answer I shall propose (in Chapters 4 and 11) is that each is distinguished by the *rules of relevance* which govern the justification of evaluations and prescriptions within it. Normative discourse as a whole has only one set of rules of valid inference but many sets of rules of relevance.

Corresponding to each of these sets of rules of relevance is a particular *kind* of value judgment and a particular *kind* of prescription. Thus there are moral judgments and moral prescriptions, aesthetic judgments and aesthetic prescriptions, and so on. Furthermore, each subordinate universe of discourse sets the framework of a *point of view* from which evaluations and prescriptions can be made. A moral judgment or prescription is one made from the moral point of view, an aesthetic judgment or prescription is one made from the aesthetic point of view, and so for the other kinds of evaluations and prescriptions. I shall argue in Chapter 11 that when we take a point of view, we adopt a certain *normative language* (the language of morals, the language of aesthetics, etc.) for use in evaluating and prescribing. To say that we adopt a certain normative language is to say that we commit ourselves to following a certain set of rules of relevance in justifying our evaluations and prescriptions.

This way of analyzing the universe of normative discourse enables us to handle with a fair degree of clarity and rigor questions such as: In what respects, if any, are moral judgments like aesthetic judgments? How do moral prescriptions compare with political, economic, or legal prescriptions? Do religious attitudes have anything in common with aesthetic attitudes? On what grounds can we claim that morality takes precedence over custom or etiquette? What differences are involved in evaluating social practices and institutions from a moral point of view, from a legal point of view, from a religious point of view, and from the point of view of custom? In the last chapter of this book I shall indicate how my account of normative discourse clarifies the meaning of the term "realms of value" by providing criteria for distinguishing and comparing different kinds of evaluations and prescriptions.

Although evaluations and prescriptions may be classified according to the rules of relevance which govern their justification and they may be so placed in various universes of discourse, all still belong to the wider universe of normative discourse. A moral judgment and an aesthetic judgment have at least this in common: they are both value judgments. We shall see in Part I that this means they share many important characteristics. It also means that they are justified in accordance with the same rules of valid inference (though not in accordance with the same rules of relevance). In Part II, I shall point out the many characteristics which all prescriptions have in common, whether they be moral, aesthetic, political, religious, or of any other kind. It will be shown that the same rules of valid inference that govern the justification of value judgments also govern the justification of prescriptions. These factors, common to all evaluations and prescriptions, make it possible to place them all within the one universe of normative discourse. Unless there were these common features we could not speak of a "universe" of normative discourse at all. We would always have to speak of the universe of moral discourse, or the universe of aesthetic discourse, or the universe of religious discourse, and so on.

It should now be clear that this book is not an essay in moral philosophy. It is, instead, an essay in general theory of value (or "axiology"). It is simply an attempt to bring the techniques of philosophical analysis to bear upon the problems which traditionally have been grouped under the heading "general theory of value." When these techniques are used, the problems are bound to undergo a certain amount of transformation. Thus, instead of asking "What is the nature of goodness?" I ask "How is the word 'good' used when we evaluate something?" Instead of asking "What is the difference between the right and the good?" I ask "How does evaluating according to standards differ from evaluating according to rules?" Instead of seeking the foundations of values, I try to find out what makes a reason a good reason for or against a value judgment. Instead of examining the place of value in a world of facts, I investigate the logical relations between normative assertions and empirical assertions.

Readers who are already familiar with the two major studies by American philosophers in general theory of value—Ralph Barton Perry's *General Theory of Value* and C. I. Lewis's *An Analysis of Knowledge and Valuation*—should not be surprised, therefore, to find that I put the old questions in a new way and emphasize different problems as the central ones in the field. I do claim to be working in that field, even though my greatest philosophical debt is to those philosophers who have carried out in recent years careful analytic investigations of "informal logic" in the more restricted areas of moral, aesthetic, political, and religious discourse. To my knowledge, this book is the first fullscale attempt to use the "informal logic" approach in general theory of value. There are, no doubt, many weaknesses in this attempt, and I am aware that much more needs to be done to explore its ramifications and to fill out the gaps in it. I can only hope to make a suggestive beginning and perhaps to give a new direction to general theory of value which will prove fruitful for further inquiry in the field.

Acknowledgments

To cite all the books and articles which have aided my thinking about normative discourse would be an impossible task. In the bibliography, I have listed those writings which have been especially enlightening and stimulating to me. The bibliography is divided into two parts, the first being made up of books and articles not wholly restricted to the field of ethics; the second lists books and articles which are so restricted but which contain material directly relevant to the broader problems of general theory of value. I am indebted in varying degrees to the authors of all these works.

Among the people I have known personally who have had an influence on my thinking I must mention Professor Martin Lean, my colleague at Brooklyn College. The meticulous care and rigorous logic with which he carries on philosophical discussion have set an example for me which I am striving to follow in this book. I alone, however, bear full responsibility for the views set forth. Professor Lean would undoubtedly disagree with many of them.

I am grateful to all of the following authors, editors, and publishers who have kindly given me permission to quote directly from their works: Mr. Bernard Mayo for excerpts from his book *Ethics and the Moral Life*; Professor Gilbert Ryle for excerpts from articles published in *Mind*; the editors of *The Philosophical Review* for excerpts from articles published in that journal; Mr. Peter Winch for excerpts from his book *The Idea of a Social Science and Its Relation to Philosophy*; Harvard University Press for an excerpt from *The Structure of a Moral Code* by John Ladd; Cambridge University Press for excerpts from *An Examination of the Place of Reason in Ethics* by S. E. Toulmin; The Clarendon Press, Oxford, for excerpts from *The Language of Morals* by R. M. Hare; Cornell University Press for excerpts from *The Moral Point of View* by Kurt Baier; Basil Blackwell Ltd. and the Macmillan Company for excerpts from *Philosophical Investigations* by Ludwig Wittgenstein; Penguin Books Ltd. for excerpts from *Ethics* by P. H. Nowell-Smith; The Free Press of Glencoe, Illinois for excerpts from *The Logic of Moral Discourse* by Paul Edwards; Appleton-Century-Crofts, Inc. for excerpts from *Readings in Ethical Theory*, edited by Wilfrid Sellars and John Hospers; and Prentice-Hall, Inc. for excerpts from *Ethical Theory* by Richard B. Brandt. It should be noted that in all direct quotations italics are given exactly as they appeared in the original.

PAUL W. TAYLOR

Brooklyn, New York

Contents

Part I • EVALUATING

Part I

EVALUATING

The process of evaluation

1

A. Value judgments and the process of evaluation

The word "evaluate" is subject to the process-product ambiguity. It may refer to the process of carrying out an evaluation, appraisal, or criticism of something, or it may refer to the product of such a process. The process of evaluation consists in trying to determine the value of something. As a product or outcome of that process, an evaluation is a settled opinion that something has a certain value. The aim of the process is to come to a decision; the process terminates when the decision is reached. During the process we are uncertain, trying to make up our minds. When our minds are finally made up, we have arrived at an evaluation (appraisal, criticism). I shall refer to this evaluation, the product of the process, as a value judgment.

A value judgment may be formed without being uttered in an evaluative sentence, but it must always be possible in principle to utter such a sentence. To have come to a decision implies that one can answer the question, "What have you decided?" We may answer this question either by saying "I have decided to do such-and-such" or by saying "I have decided that such-and-such is the case." Only

3

the second sort of answer is pertinent here, since the evaluation process leads to a settled opinion that something is the case; it does not (directly) lead to a decision to act in a certain way. In Chapter 2, I shall examine the nature of a value judgment and its expression in an evaluative utterance. In this chapter my purpose is to make clear what it means to carry out an evaluation. What makes a thought process an evaluative process? If we answer merely that its aim is a value judgment and that it terminates in a value judgment, we have not said what the process itself consists in. We have not answered the question: How do we think when we are evaluating something? This is the question I shall now try to answer.

The process of evaluation is either a process of *grading* something or a process of *ranking* something in comparison with other things. That which is graded or ranked I shall call "the evaluatum." Every grading or ranking process may be analyzed in terms of the following five elements:

1. *A class of comparison* whose members are the evaluatum and all the things in comparison with which the evaluatum is graded or ranked.

2. *A norm or set of norms* according to which the evaluatum is graded or ranked.

3. *A pro-attitude, a con-attitude, or a neutral attitude* on the part of the evaluator.

4. *A set of good-making or bad-making characteristics* possessed by the evaluatum.

5. *A point of view* within the framework of which the grading or ranking is carried out.

The aim of the evaluation process is to arrive at a judgment in which we make the claim that the evaluatum either fulfills or fails to fulfill the norms. The evaluation process is not to be thought of as the psychological way by which we always in fact arrive at value judgments. Rather, it is the logical method which a rational person *would* follow if he were trying to come to a careful, reflective decision about the value of something. Indeed, an appeal to the process of evaluation itself may serve as part of the method by which we justify a value judgment, as we shall see in Chapter 3.

Every process of evaluation and every value judgment contextually implies that the norms being used are appropriate or valid. By "contextually implies" I mean that anyone who understands that an evaluation is being carried out, or that a value judgment is being made, considers it legitimate and proper to question the appropriateness of the norms, and expects the evaluator to be able to give reasons showing that they are appropriate. Because the claim that the norms are appropriate is contextually implied by every value judgment, the *complete* justification of a value judgment requires going beyond a process of evaluation in which certain norms are appealed to. We must, in addition, justify the appeal to those norms. (What constitutes such a justification will be considered in Chapters 3, 5, and 6.)

A double claim is involved whenever we evaluate something. First there is the claim that the evaluatum fulfills or fails to fulfill the given norms, a claim explicitly made when we utter a value judgment. Second there is the (contextually implied) claim that it is valid or appropriate to apply the given norms to the evaluatum. Unless good reasons can be given in support of both of these claims, a value judgment cannot be justified. In order to determine what sort of reasons might be good reasons, the process of evaluation must be examined in detail.

There are two basic kinds of evaluation, depending on whether the norms appealed to are *standards* or *rules*. I shall examine each kind in turn.

B. Evaluation according to standards

1. GRADING AND RANKING

When the norms are standards, the process of evaluation may consist either in grading something or in ranking something as superior, inferior, or equal to something else. (We shall see that this distinction is inapplicable when the norms are rules. In that case, all evaluations are gradings.) We grade something as good or bad, desirable or undesirable, worthwhile or worthless. We rank something when we try to decide whether it is better or worse than another thing, whether it is as good or as bad as another thing, or whether it is the best or worst of a group of things. In both sorts of evaluation a point of view is presupposed. For example, we cannot evaluate a car as good or bad, or as better or worse than another car, unless we know what point of view we are to take. We must know what we are evaluating the car *as*. Is it to be evaluated as a piece of mechanical engineering? As an object of aesthetic contemplation? As a means of family transportation? As a symbol of social prestige? Each point of view we take makes a difference, since different standards (norms) are appropriate to different points of view. (What differentiates one point of view from another is a matter to be considered in Chapters 4 and 11.)

In grading a car as good or bad, the class of comparison is the class of all cars. If the evaluator is concerned only with passenger cars available within a certain price range, the class of comparison is accordingly restricted to all passenger cars in that price range. When a car is ranked as better or worse than, or equally as good or as bad as, another car, the class of comparison is restricted to the two cars being compared. In ranking a car as the best or the worst of a group, the class of comparison includes just those cars that make up the group.

Whether evaluations are gradings or rankings, the class of comparison varies independently of the point of view. Thus the class of comparison of different evaluations may remain constant while their points of view are changed, and the point of view may remain constant while the classes of comparison are changed. This is easily seen in the case of value rankings. One may rank painting A as superior to painting B from the aesthetic point of view, and rank painting B as superior from the economic point of view (that is, considering the paintings as commodities or investments). Here the class of comparison remains the same while the point of view changes. On the other hand, we may rank painting A as aesthetically better than painting B and then, still keeping the aesthetic point of view, rank two other paintings in comparison with each other. In this manner we may change our class of comparison without changing our point of view.

That points of view and classes of comparison are logically independent is as true of value gradings as it is of rankings, although this may not be apparent at first glance. When we grade a painting as good from the aesthetic point of view and then change our point of view and grade it as a poor investment, does not the class of comparison necessarily shift? When we judge the painting aesthetically, the class of comparison is the class of paintings; but from the economic point of view it is compared not only with other paintings but also with other kinds of investments. If the prospective buyer has $1000 to invest and judges the painting as a good (or poor) investment, he is presumably comparing it with other ways of investing $1000. These may include not only the buying of other paintings, but also the buying of many other kinds of things, such as real estate or government bonds. This shift does more than merely broaden the class of comparison (from paintings alone to paintings plus other things). The aesthetic evaluation of the painting may include in its class of comparison many famous paintings in museums and galleries all over the world, whereas the economic evaluation includes in its class of comparison only those paintings currently on the market and priced at $1000 or less. We see that a shift in point of view *may* be accompanied by a shift in class of comparison. But is the shift in class of comparison logically entailed by the shift in point of view? Clearly, it is not. It is quite possible for a person to evaluate a painting from the aesthetic point of view and limit his class of comparison to paintings currently on the market and priced at $1000 or less. Thus in the case of value gradings as well as in the case of value rankings, the class of comparison may remain constant when the point of view changes.

In order to make clear the difference between value gradings and value rankings, it is helpful to begin by considering the difference between two meanings of the word "good." Suppose we are trying to decide whether a certain president of the United States was a good president. Do we mean good as far as presidents usually go? Or do we mean good in an absolute sense, with an ideal president in mind? In the first case, our class of comparison is the thirty-five men who have actually been president. To say that someone was a good president in this sense means that he was *better than average*. It is to claim that he fulfilled certain standards to a higher degree than most of the other men who were president. "Good" is being used as a ranking word. In the second case, our class of comparison is not the class of actual presidents but the class of all possible (imaginable) presidents. To say that a certain president was good in this sense means that he fulfilled to a high degree those standards whose complete fulfillment would define an ideal president. "Good" is here used as a grading word. It is not possible to specify exactly to what degree the standards must be fulfilled for a man to be graded as a good president rather than as mediocre or bad. That depends on what standards one is appealing to (that is, what conception of an ideal president one has in mind), how clearly those standards are defined, to what extent the degrees to which they can be fulfilled are measurable, and how "distant" from reality is one's ideal. The distance between ideal and reality in any evaluation is a reflection of the amount of severity in the evaluator's general outlook on the matter and of the height of his idealism. If one's standards are severe enough or one's ideals high enough, the grading of all actual United States presidents will result in a judgment that *not one* was a good president—that they were all poor or mediocre in varying degrees.

Such a judgment would not be possible in a value ranking. One president must be ranked as the best and one as the worst, unless more than one are equally good (bad) and are equally better (worse) than all the others. At least one will be ranked as average (mediocre, fair, so-so), and the others will be judged good or bad in varying degrees. They cannot all be ranked as bad, for there must be some who are better than average and these are by definition good. When used as ranking words, "good" and "bad" mean *comparatively* good and *comparatively* bad. They can be defined in terms of "better" and "worse," "good" meaning "better than average" and "bad" meaning "worse than average." In order to decide whether one thing is better or worse than another, some standard or set of standards must be appealed to. In order to decide what is average, a certain class of comparison must be given. The average is then definable as what is worse than about half the members of the class of comparison and what is better than about half, when all are judged according to the given standards.

It is possible for the standards of a value ranking to be identical with those of a value grading. A ranking of the presidents of the United States from best to worst may be made according to the very same standards by which they are graded as all mediocre or bad. When that occurs, it is not a contradiction to say that a certain president was both a good one and a bad one *as judged by the same standards*. To say he was a good president is to rank him as being better than most of the presidents, and to grade him as a bad president is to claim he was too far from the ideal to be worthy of a pro-attitude on our part, and so to be worthy of being praised as a good president.

The distinction between value rankings and value gradings is independent of the point of view involved. We may rank as well as grade United States presidents from a moral point of view, a political point of view, an intellectual point of view (were they intelligent, well read, etc.?), a marital point of view (were they good husbands and fathers?), and so on. For each point of view different standards of evaluation would be used, but this would not determine whether the judgment was to be a ranking or a grading. To take another example, we may judge a painting from an aesthetic, an economic, a moral, or some other point of view. But whatever the point of view, when we judge the painting to be good we must ask ourselves: Is the painting good as compared with the paintings I have seen recently and which are still fresh in my mind, or with all the paintings I have ever seen, or with all the paintings in this exhibition, or with all the paintings in the world? Or is it good as compared with what a painting of this type *should* be? If our judgment is of the first kind it is a ranking of the painting (in one of several classes of comparison). If it is of the second kind it is a grading of the painting.

2. THE LOGIC OF THE EVALUATION PROCESS

I shall now set forth the process of evaluation as a process of reasoning. Whether an evaluation consists in ranking something in relation to something else or in grading something in relation to an ideal, it may be analyzed into a series of logical steps. This analysis is not meant to be a psychological account of what happens in our heads when we evaluate something. I am not trying to describe or explain our thought processes as they actually occur. I am trying instead to make explicit the pattern or structure of the logic of our thinking. The steps are as follows:

1. *Adoption of a standard or set of standards* for evaluating (ranking or grading) the evaluatum.

2. *Operational clarification of the standards.* This consists in a set of statements to the effect that if an object O has characteristics C,

it fulfills a certain standard S to a certain degree D; that if O has characteristics C', it fulfills S to a greater (lesser) degree D'; etc.

3. *Specifications of the class of comparison.*

4. *Determining the good-making and bad-making characteristics of the evaluatum.* (In the case of value rankings this would ideally be done for every member of the class of comparison.)

5. *Deducing,* from 2 and 4, *the degree to which the evaluatum on the whole fulfills or fails to fulfill the standards.* (In the case of value rankings this would ideally be done for every member of the class of comparison. The members would then be ranked in order according to the varying degrees to which they fulfilled or failed to fulfill the standards.)

Having completed these five steps, a person would be able to give a direct and unequivocal answer to the question: What is the value of this? His answer would express a value judgment concerning the evaluatum. Thus a value judgment is a decision or verdict, resulting from the process of evaluation, which concludes the evaluation both in a logical and in a temporal sense. It is the logical conclusion of the five steps, and when it is reached the process terminates. To reach such a decision is the very point of carrying out the evaluation.

The characteristics C, C', and so on, in step 2 are what I have called good-making and bad-making characteristics. These characteristics belong to an evaluatum (or any member of a class of comparison); it is by virtue of these characteristics that something is good or bad to some degree or other, as judged by the standards of evaluation. The evaluatum itself may have characteristics of both kinds. There may be respects in which it is desirable (its virtues or merits) and respects in which it is undesirable (its deficiencies or demerits). These may balance each other off, so that *on the whole* the object is neither good nor bad, but more or less indifferent. When it has more virtues than deficiencies, or when its virtues outweigh its deficiencies (in a sense to be explained), it is on the whole good. Under the opposite conditions it is on the whole bad.

Good-making and bad-making characteristics are relative to the standards being used. A characteristic which is good-making according to one standard may be bad-making according to another. For example, if we judge a car according to standards of ample size and seating capacity, the fact that it has a wide wheelbase and can seat six passengers are good-making characteristics. When judged by the standard of convenience in parking, these same characteristics will be bad-making. Since different points of view entail the adoption of different standards, good-making and bad-making characteristics will vary as different points of view are taken in an evaluation. The very feature that makes an advertisement a good one from the economic point of view may make it a bad one from the aesthetic or moral point of view.

Even within the same point of view, different standards may be adopted, with the result that disagreements will arise about whether certain characteristics of an evaluatum are good-making or bad-making. Two literary critics may disagree about the worth of a new novel because they disagree about what is to count in its favor. A feature which one critic believes to be a mark of literary excellence will be considered by the other an aesthetic failure. Both are taking the aesthetic point of view, but they are appealing to different value systems. (The distinction between a point of view and a value system will be dealt with at considerable length in Chapters 4, 5, and 6. Its importance has been overlooked too often in philosophical studies of values.)

In step 2 of the process of evaluation, mention was made of the degree to which an object fulfills or fails to fulfill a standard. What does "degree of fulfillment" mean in this context? The best way to answer this is to consider, first, what we mean when we grade things as excellent, very good, quite good, fair, rather poor, very poor and so on; and second, what we mean when we rank one thing as much better than, slightly better than, or about as good as another thing. In grading football players, for example, a coach might judge that one man is an excellent passer, a fair runner, a good blocker, and a poor kicker. Such judgments may or may not be numerically measurable in terms of some kind of units of goodness or badness. As a measurement of a player's running ability, the coach might use the formula: total yards gained minus total yards lost when the player carried the ball, divided by the number of plays. The coach might then set up a scale of running ability with the following categories—excellent: ten or more yards gained; good: 5-10 yards gained; fair: 0-5 yards gained; poor: 0-5 yards lost; ready-for-the-

JV's: more than five yards lost. On the other hand, the coach might not use any measurement for grading a player's blocking ability. He might simply rely on his *intuitive* judgment, based on careful observations of the player's performance as a blocker in scrimmages and games. These intuitive judgments would be expressed in such phrases as "an outstanding blocker," "a very good blocker," or "a fair blocker," without further refinement in quantitative terms.

Similar considerations hold for value rankings. Suppose we are trying to decide which of two equally priced houses we should buy. With respect to some of the standards we use (such as the distance of the houses from our place of work, or the size of the bedrooms in each house), a quantitative judgment may be made (in terms of distance in miles or volume in cubic feet of space). With respect to other standards (such as pleasantness of appearance and convenience of the arrangement of rooms), we might intuitively judge that one house fulfills them to a greater degree than the other, without being able to say to *how much* greater a degree. This does not mean that the concept of "degree of fulfillment" is inapplicable here. It only means that degree of fulfillment is not measurable. It still makes perfectly good sense to use such ranking terms as "much better than," "slightly better than," and "about as good as" in this context.

Let us now consider what is involved in the claim that an evaluatum may simultaneously have both good-making and bad-making characteristics. This claim may be restated in a less technical way: an object may be good in some respects and bad in others. This is possible because different standards are applied to different features of the object. But what determines whether the object is good or bad *on the whole?* The answer is somewhat different for gradings and for rankings. I shall consider gradings first.

There are two factors that determine whether an object is to be graded as good or bad on the whole: the degree to which the object fulfills (or fails to fulfill) all the standards applied to it, and the relative precedence of those standards. We have seen what degree of fulfillment means. The relative precedence of standards must now be clarified, at least in a preliminary way. (Full consideration of this will be taken up in Chapter 3, in connection with the validation of standards.) When we evaluate an object by appealing to more than one standard, the standards may be organized in a system of relative precedence. To say that one standard S takes precedence over another standard S′ is to say that, when we are making an over-all judgment of its value, greater *weight* is given to the fact that an object fulfills (or fails to fulfill) S than to the fact that it fulfills (or fails to fulfill) S′. (Why this is so will be explained in Chapter 3.) In other words, if we assume that the object fulfills both S and S′ to the same degree, its fulfillment of S adds more to its over-all goodness than its fulfillment of S′. Greater weight is given to a good-making or bad-making characteristic that is determined by S than to one that is determined by S′. An example will help to clarify this. Suppose we are evaluating a vacation we have just spent abroad. We say that there were good and bad things about it. We might include among the good things the nice people we met, the fine works of art we saw, and the pleasant hotels where we stayed. Among the bad things we might count poor roads for driving, bad weather, and our trying to see too much in too short a time. Suppose we then say that, on the whole, the vacation was a very good one. I suggest that the basis for our saying this is that the good aspects of the vacation outweigh the bad. How is it that one aspect can outweigh another? The answer lies in the fact that the standards fulfilled by one aspect are higher than (i.e., take precedence over) the standards fulfilled by the other. In the case at hand, the good-making characteristics of the vacation fulfilled higher standards than those which the bad-making characteristics failed to fulfill, so the former carried more weight than the latter in the final judgment. If the bad-making characteristics had failed to fulfill higher standards than those fulfilled by the good-making ones, the vacation would have been judged, on the whole, to be bad.

The assumption made here is that the vacation fulfills or fails to fulfill each of the standards to the same degree. But if the vacation were to fulfill one standard to a greater degree than another, then the former good-making characteristic would carry more weight than the latter. This determinant of the "weight" of a good-making (or bad-making) characteristic varies independently of the other determinant of "weight," namely the relative precedence of the standards involved. If an object fulfills a lower standard to a greater degree than it fulfills a higher standard there is a counterbalancing of weights. If it fulfills a higher standard to a greater degree than a lower standard there is an increment of weight on one side. No precise measurement can be made of such changes in weight, but we can have an intuitive grasp of them. A vacation which fulfilled to a high degree the relatively low standard of good roads for driving, but did not fulfill to any great extent the relatively high standard of seeing great works of art, would not be as good on the whole as a vacation which fulfilled the second standard to a greater degree than the first. Even though no units of weight can be assigned, it is clear that the over-all judgment is affected by both factors—degree of fulfillment and relative precedence of standards fulfilled.

3. PRO-ATTITUDES AND CON-ATTITUDES

How these two factors operate in the formation of a judgment of something as good or bad on the whole, may be explained by reference to the role played by our pro-attitudes and con-attitudes in the evaluation process. Given a standard which we believe appropriate to apply in evaluating a certain object, we have a pro-attitude toward the object insofar as it fulfills the standard, a con-attitude toward it insofar as it fails to fulfill the standard. Now our pro-attitude or con-attitude *increases in strength* according to the degree to which the object fulfills or fails to fulfill the standard, and according to the relative precedence of the standard. The greater the degree of fulfillment (or failure of fulfillment) and the higher the precedence, the stronger the pro-attitude (or con-attitude). In evaluating our vacation we have a pro-attitude toward each of its good-making features and a con-attitude toward each of its bad-making features. We like, approve of, or favor the vacation in virtue of the good things about it and dislike, disapprove of, or disfavor it in virtue of the bad. If our final judgment is to be positive rather than neutral or negative, the good-making features must outweigh the bad-making, not only according to the degrees to which they fulfill the given standards, but also according to the relative precedence of the standards themselves. We use the word "good" about something when we have a pro-attitude toward it, the word "bad" when we have a con-attitude toward it, and such words as "mediocre," "fair," "all right," "unobjectionable," "so-so," "not bad," and "tolerable" when we have a more or less neutral attitude toward it. If our final judgment of the vacation is that *on the whole* it was a good one, we have a pro-attitude toward it on the whole because the total strength of our pro-attitudes is greater than the total strength of our con-attitudes. If the relative strengths of the two groups of attitudes were about equal, our final judgment would be neutral. What determines the relative strength of our pro-attitudes and con-attitudes? Insofar as we are rational (i.e., insofar as we have *justifiable* pro-attitudes and con-attitudes), the relative strength of these attitudes is determined by the relative precedence of the standards we use and the degree to which the evaluatum fulfills them.

In the case of value rankings, there are three factors that determine whether we have a pro-attitude, a con-attitude, or a neutral attitude toward the evaluatum. The first factor has already been found in value gradings—our pro-attitudes and con-attitudes are directed toward the good-making and bad-making characteristics, respectively, of the evaluatum. Here the relative strength of attitudes, based on degree of fulfillment and relative precedence of standards, plays the same role in determining our over-all attitude toward the evaluatum. But this is not sufficient for our ranking the evaluatum as better or worse than something else, or as good or bad (i.e., as better or worse than average). We must also take into account the good-making and bad-making characteristics of the other member or members of the class of comparison, in relation to which the evaluatum is being ranked. If we evaluate the object by itself, which is simply the process of grading, we may conclude our evaluation with a positive judgment and hence have a pro-attitude toward the object on the whole, only to find that, when compared to most of the other objects in the class of comparison, it is inferior. What appears by itself to be good may turn out to be worse than something else, or even the worst of a group of things. Similarly, what appears by itself to be bad may be better than something else or the best of a group of things. To decide whether the evaluatum is better or worse than something else, or is the best or the worst in the class of comparison, two factors must be taken into account: whether the evaluatum is good on the whole or bad on the whole when *graded* according to the given standards, and whether its over-all goodness or badness outweighs the over-all goodness or badness of each member of the class of comparison. If its over-all goodness outweighs that of every other good member of the class of comparison, the final ranking judgment is that it is the best of the group. If its badness outweighs that of all the over-all bad members, it is finally ranked as the worst of the group. If its over-all goodness outweighs the over-all goodness of the average members of the class of comparison, or if the average members are bad over-all, it is ranked as good (i.e., as better than average). It is also ranked as good if it is bad over-all but its badness is out-weighed by the over-all badness of the average members. Though bad, it is less bad than the average and therefore to be ranked as good.

A third factor becomes important when we want to know whether the final ranking judgment expresses a positive, negative, or neutral attitude. We must know the evaluator's over-all attitude toward the whole class of comparison. It is not enough to say that a positive judgment results when the evaluatum compares favorably with (i.e., has more or stronger good-making characteristics and fewer or weaker bad-making characteristics than) most members of the class of comparison, that a negative judgment results when most members of the class of comparison compare favorably with the evaluatum, or that a neutral judgment results when the evaluatum compares favorably with about half of the class of comparison and compares unfavorably with about half. We must also take into account how the evaluator judges the class of comparison as a whole. In the example of evaluating presidents of the United States, I mentioned the possibility that a person might have such severe standards or such a high ideal of the presidency that all the actual presidents would be graded as mediocre or bad. But even under these conditions some presidents would be better than others, some would be good in the sense of better than average, and one would be the best. In ranking a president as good or as the best, however, the person would not necessarily be expressing a pro-attitude toward that president. He might not admire or approve of him at all, although his attitude would perhaps be softened by the recognition of the inferiority of most of the other presidents.

It is only when "good" is used in a grading judgment that we can be assured it expresses a pro-attitude on the part of the speaker. If it is used in a ranking judgment, it may or may not express a pro-attitude, depending on the speaker's evaluation of the entire class of things with reference to which the evaluatum is being ranked. (We shall see later that there are other uses of "good" which are not essentially connected with a pro-attitude on the part of the speaker. I discuss these in Chapter 2.)

The fact that a value grading or ranking can result in a neutral judgment (the object is neither good nor bad, but fair or mediocre) raises the question of how such a neutral judgment differs from an ordinary statement of fact. Theories of value that define "good" and "bad" in terms of interests, attitudes, desires, and other subjective states or dispositions all emphasize the positive-negative dimension of such states or dispositions. This positive-negative dimension appears to set values off from facts, for when we say that something is good or bad our pro- and con-attitudes are involved in a way they are not when we say that something is round or heavy or green. I have been trying to show how pro- and con-attitudes do have an important place in our evaluations, yet it seems to me that we may have neutral attitudes toward things when their good-making and bad-making characteristics are of approximately equal weight. An object may be in some respects good (and insofar as it is we take a pro-attitude toward it) and in some respects bad (and insofar as it is we take a con-attitude toward it), but *on the whole* neither good nor bad. Our pro- and con-attitudes toward different features of the object cancel each other out, as it were, and leave us with a neutral attitude. We then judge the object as fair, so-so, all right, unobjectionable, and so on. This is altogether different from making a statement of fact about the object.

Neutral value judgments do not indicate that no pro- or con-attitudes have been involved in an evaluation. Indeed, such attitudes must be involved for them to become neutralized. It is the fact that pro- and con-attitudes are always part of an evaluative process that distinguishes the *grading* and *ranking* of things according to *standards* from merely *comparing* or *classifying* them according to *criteria*. We may compare cities with respect to their population, cars with respect to their speed and power, or bombs with respect to their destructive force, without evaluating them as good, bad, or indifferent. To arrange cars in an order of increasing speed and power is not necessarily to arrange them in an order of merit or desirability. A comparison is evaluative only when things are graded or ranked, that is, classified according to their *worth* or *value*. And their worth or value is determined by the degree to which they fulfill standards that one has adopted. When standards are applied in judging an object, a person has a pro-attitude or con-attitude as a consequence of the fact that the object fulfills or fails to fulfill the standards. Thus grading and ranking are very different from merely comparing or classifying.

Suppose that we always ranked apples as excellent, good, fair, or poor according to certain good-making and bad-making characteristics (defined in terms of certain standards). Now suppose that we trained a child to separate correctly all the apples he was given into the four categories *without* letting him have pro-attitudes toward excellent and good apples, a neutral attitude toward fair apples, and a con-attitude toward poor apples. The child would not be able to rank or grade the apples at all. He would know the standards only as criteria of classification. What for us are the good-making and bad-making characteristics of apples would be, for the child, simply different features of apples that tell him whether to put the apples in the box marked "excellent," the box marked "good," the box marked "fair," or the box marked "poor." The child would not understand the meaning of these words, even though he could correctly apply them. If he were to point to an apple and say (correctly) "This is a good one," he would mean "This belongs in the box marked 'good.'" He would not mean what we mean by saying "This is a good one," because his pro-attitudes would not be involved. He would not, in other words, be expressing a value judgment.

The same holds true in the case of a neutral judgment. When the child says "This is a fair apple" he is not expressing a neutral value judgment. For him the apple does not have both good-making and bad-making characteristics that cancel one another out, leaving a neutral attitude. The child has no attitude at all toward the apple. Having a *neutral* attitude is far different from having *no* attitude. In order that something be the object of a neutral attitude, it must be thought to have good-making and bad-making characteristics. What counts as a good-making or bad-making characteristic is not merely that in virtue of which an object satisfies or fails to satisfy certain tests or criteria, but that in virtue of which it fulfills or fails to fulfill certain standards *and consequently is the object of pro-attitudes or con-attitudes.*

One might want to say that evaluating something is nothing but classifying it as calling for a pro- or con-attitude simply because it belongs to one category rather than another. This analysis would be inadequate. It could not account for the logical structure of the steps which make up the evaluative process, nor could it explain the justification of value judgments as a rational process. Our attitudes are not just accidently attached to our standards. They are involved when we *adopt* our standards in the first place. It is more accurate to say that they are entailed by our standards than that they simply accompany them. This does not mean that standards and attitudes can be put in propositional form so that one can be deduced from the other. The relation between attitudes and standards will be explored in later chapters of this book (especially Chapters 3, 4, 5, and 6). For the present, some enlightenment concerning their relation will be gained by examining one of the ways in which standards may be classified.

4. INTRINSIC AND EXTRINSIC VALUE

The standards appealed to in a process of evaluation may be classified as standards of intrinsic value or standards of extrinsic value. Standards of extrinsic value may in turn be subdivided into standards of inherent value, standards of instrumental value, and standards of contributive value. These distinctions were first formulated by professor C. I. Lewis in *An Analysis of Knowledge and Valuation.* I am making a departure from Professor Lewis's position by including standards of intrinsic value among standards of evaluation. It is one of the fundamental principles of Professor Lewis's theory that expressions of intrinsic value are not value judgments. Following R. B. Perry and John Dewey, Professor Lewis holds that intrinsic value results from the act of *valuing,* which is radically different from the process of *evaluating.* I intend to show that judgments of intrinsic value are as much the outcome of a process of evaluation as are judgments of extrinsic value. Professor

Lewis's concept of valuing is identical with what I would call having a pro-attitude. The act of "valuing" an object is any act governed solely by a disposition of liking or favoring the object, of preferring it to other objects, of approving of it, of prizing it, or of having some other pro-attitude toward it. In my view, a statement that something has intrinsic value is not the direct expression of a pro-attitude (or an act of valuing). It is a value judgment, a claim that something fulfills to a certain degree a certain kind of standard —in this case, a standard of intrinsic value. A person has a pro-attitude toward the thing *in consequence of* its being found, by a process of evaluation, to have intrinsic value. The existence of a pro-attitude directed toward it does not *constitute* its value.

I do not mean to deny that the verb "to value" in its ordinary usage means to prize something, to hold something dear or precious. We ordinarily say that something is valuable *to* a person when he values it in this way. To value a book, a friendship, one's health, or a letter from a loved one is to have a certain kind of pro-attitude toward the valued thing. It is to be disposed to care for the thing, to protect it from loss or harm, and to take pleasure in possessing it or in using it. When we come to value something in this way (and when accordingly it comes to have value for us), we may or may not have good reasons for valuing it. We may value something, for instance, simply out of a blind emotional or sentimental attachment to it. Or we may value it because it satisfies a neurotic desire on our part. On the other hand, when there are good reasons for our valuing something we are *justified* in valuing it. I suggest that only one sort of reason may serve as a good reason in this case: the fact that we can justify an *evaluation* (a grading or ranking) of the valued thing as a good thing. We may justify valuing our health because it is a good means to many desirable ends. Or we may justify our valuing it simply on the ground that we enjoy being healthy. (In the latter instance, we shall see, we are evaluating health as having intrinsic value.) But however we happen to evaluate our health, we must go through a process of evaluation if we are to have good reasons for valuing it. Why is this so? Valuing something is having a pro-attitude toward it, and we are justified in having a pro-attitude toward something only when it can be shown to be *worthy* of being liked, approved of, favored, or valued. If we like or value something that can be shown to be undesirable or bad, we are not justified in liking or valuing it. In the same manner, we can justify our having a con-attitude toward something only when we can show, on the basis of an evaluation, that the thing is undesirable or bad. *Evaluating, then, constitutes the rational ground for valuing.*

Here one relation between standards and attitudes becomes clear. Attitudes can be justified only on grounds of evaluations, and evaluations require the adoption of standards. In this respect attitudes are like decisions, actions, and choices. All of these can be justified only on the basis of evaluations. (This point will be considered in greater detail in connection with the justification of value judgments.)

To say that a thing is valued by someone is not to say that it *has value* (i.e., that it is good). Valuing is having a certain kind of pro-attitude toward something and cannot be identified with the claim that the thing has intrinsic value (or any other kind of value), for such a claim is a value judgment and must be established by a process of evaluation. It is by means of this process alone that we can determine whether something is or is not intrinsically good, that is, whether it does or does not have intrinsic value. The standards appealed to in this process are standards of intrinsic value and function in the same way as do any other standards.

For this view of intrinsic value I am partly indebted to Professor C. A. Baylis who, in his essay "Grading, Values, and Choice" (*Mind,* LXVII, 268; 1958, pp. 485-501), modifies the theory of Professor Lewis to some extent in the way I have indicated. According to Professor Baylis, the existence of a pro-attitude is "initial evidence" for the presence of intrinsic value. Under certain conditions we can judge with a high degree of probability that the object of our pro-attitude has intrinsic value.

When we judge things of certain kinds, e.g. pleasant experiences, to be intrinsically good, the best initial evidence for this that we could have, I submit, is that we find ourselves *prizing* things of that kind, i.e. liking, approving, desiring, preferring, and commending them. . . . Such evidence gives us an initial probability that what we thus prize is intrinsically good. We can increase this probability by making repeated examinations of things of the same kind under circumstances which vary just enough to guard against the kinds of cognitive error which might occur. (*Ibid.*, pp. 494-495.)

I am in agreement with Professor Baylis when he states that having a pro-attitude toward something (prizing it, liking it, etc.) is *not* a defining characteristic of intrinsic value.

. . . The relation between the statements 'X is intrinsically good' and 'X has the observed identifying property of being prized for its own sake by Y' is synthetic rather than analytic. Neither entails the other. If the former is true there is some antecedent probability that the latter is true. If the latter is true and reasonable precautions have been taken in guarding the prizing against various possible types of errors, then the former is confirmed to some degree. (*Ibid.*, p. 497.)

Professor Baylis seems to assume, however, that the statement "X is intrinsically good" does not express a value judgment in the way that "X is extrinsically good" expresses a value judgment. I disagree with him here. It seems to me that each statement is the outcome of a process of evaluation. If I am right in this (and I shall try to defend the point below), intrinsic value and extrinsic value do not differ in their relation to pro-attitudes. In both cases there must be a pro-attitude for an evaluation to take place, but the evaluation itself is a matter of *judging* things *according to a standard,* in the one case a standard of intrinsic value and in the other a standard of extrinsic value. In dealing with intrinsic value and the three sub-classes of extrinsic value, I am concerned with a fundamental way of classifying *standards* of evaluation. This classification is "fundamental" only in the sense that it is helpful in understanding what it means to evaluate and as we shall see, in understanding what it means to prescribe. There are, of course, many other ways of classifying standards of evaluation. (I shall consider eight such ways in Chapter 12.)

In order to make clear the basis of the classification at hand, it is best to begin by noting the various sorts of things that can be evaluated. I have up to now used the rather vacuous words "thing" and "object" to cover anything which could possibly serve as an evaluatum or as a member of a class of comparison. This usage was not intended to give the impression that only physical objects can serve in this capacity. Evaluata may be physical objects ("That is a beautiful building"); but they may also be persons ("Titian was a greater painter than Raphael"), acts ("The assassination of Lincoln was a misfortune for the whole nation"), events ("It was a brilliant discovery"), situations ("It is desirable to have a doctor on duty in this plant"), states of affairs ("International peace is a worthy ideal for all nations"), rules ("The no smoking rule on subways is a good rule"), policies ("Economic assistance to underdeveloped countries is a proper use of federal funds"), practices ("Trial by jury is an admirable part of any legal system"), organizations ("That labor union is a benefit to the entire industry"), physical conditions or states ("Good health is a priceless possession"), the states of mind and dispositions of others ("There is a nasty streak of envy in him"), and the immediately felt or perceived qualities of our own experience ("The dry wine tasted just right with the dinner"). In other words, anything toward which it is possible to take a pro-attitude or con-attitude can be an evaluatum or a member of a class of comparison.

The distinction between standards of intrinsic value and standards of extrinsic value can now be made. (I am following the distinctions as they were drawn by Professor Baylis.) Standards of intrinsic value must be, first, standards used only in evaluations of the immediately felt or perceived qualities of our own experience, and must be, second, standards of nonderivative value. If an evaluatum is not a felt or perceived quality of experience, it cannot have intrinsic value. Objects, acts, situations, and persons can have extrinsic value only. A felt or perceived quality of experience may have either intrinsic or extrinsic value. However, we cannot *identify* evaluations of intrinsic value with evaluations of qualities of experience. We must bring in the second criterion: that the quality be evaluated for its nonderivative value only. The essential difference between intrinsic and extrinsic value is the difference between the derivatively good and the nonderivatively good. An object, quality, act, or person has derivative (extrinsic) value when its value is derived from the value of something else. Without the other thing's having (intrinsic or extrinsic) value it would have no value of its own. Thus automobiles have extrinsic value only, for unless people thought it was desirable to get from one place to another more quickly than animals or bicycles could convey them, automobiles would have no value. Intrinsic value, on the other hand, is nonderivative. Nothing else need have value for a thing to have intrinsic value; the thing is good in itself, apart from its leading to or contributing to the value of other things. Thus the experience of listening to music may be valued intrinsically. One has a pro-attitude toward the experience not because one has pro-attitudes toward other things which the experience makes possible, but simply because the qualities of the experience are what they are. But the orchestra, the conductor, the existence of air waves, and the possession of sense organs for hearing all have extrinsic value derived from the intrinsic value of listening to music. Without the latter, no one would evaluate positively the other things which make it possible (unless they made possible some *other* experiences having intrinsic value to someone).

The experience of listening to music may have extrinsic as well as intrinsic value. One might listen to music in order to relax, enjoying both listening and the sensation of being relaxed which results from listening. To take another example, one might enjoy playing tennis but also do it for the exercise. Thus what has intrinsic value may also have extrinsic value. ". . . To say of anything that it is intrinsically good is not to deny that it is extrinsically good. It is rather to affirm that it possesses a value over and above any extrinsic value it may have." (C. A. Baylis, *op. cit.*, p. 491.) It is possible for something to have intrinsic value and yet have extrinsic disvalue. Indeed, four possible combinations of positive and negative value may occur: a quality of experience may be both intrinsically and extrinsically valuable, both intrinsically and extrinsically disvaluable, intrinsically valuable but extrinsically disvaluable, and intrinsically disvaluable but extrinsically valuable. An example of the first would be listening to music for enjoyment and relaxation; an example of the second would be suffering pain when one is ill and incurring medical expenses at the same time; an example of the third would be a child's enjoying too much ice cream so that he becomes ill; an example of the fourth would be having to work at an unpleasant job in order to have the money to spend later.

There is *normally* only one standard of intrinsic value, namely satisfaction in or enjoyment of the quality being experienced. The corresponding standard of intrinsic disvalue is felt dissatisfaction or unpleasantness. One quality of experience is ranked as intrinsically better than another quality of experience when the first is more pleasant on the whole (or less unpleasant on the whole) than the second. In the process of comparison, however, each quality of experience must be judged as pleasant (or unpleasant) on the whole, quite aside from its relation to the known value of other things or qualities. To say that a quality is "pleasant on the whole" means that, if we experience both pleasantness and unpleasantness in connection with it, the pleasantness outweighs the unpleasantness and as a consequence the quality has a generally positive hedonic tone for us. "Unpleasant on the whole" means the opposite, where the over-all hedonic tone is negative. When a *grading* of intrinsic value is made, the evaluator has a pro-attitude toward the evaluatum (a quality of his own experience) insofar as it fulfills the standard of over-all pleasantness, and a con-attitude toward it insofar as it fails to fulfill this standard.

I have said that the *normal* standard of intrinsic value is felt pleasantness in the quality being experienced. There is nothing logically necessary about this. It would be possible in principle (though perhaps not empirically possible for psychological reasons) for a person to have a pro-attitude toward an experience because it was on the whole unpleasant to him and a con-attitude toward an experience which he found on the whole enjoyable. It is logically possible for people to appeal to some other standard of intrinsic evaluation than pleasantness or satisfaction because standards of evaluation are things which people *adopt* (i.e., *decide* to use). It must always make sense to suppose their not adopting a given standard, even if all people do use that standard. This is one respect in which intrinsic value does not differ from extrinsic value.

In light of the foregoing comment we cannot answer the question "What makes a standard of evaluation a standard of intrinsic value?" by saying that the standard is one of pleasantness or satisfaction in the quality of an experience. This particular standard may not be used in an evaluation of intrinsic value. The answer to the question is that one evaluates a quality of experience according to a standard of intrinsic value when one grades it or ranks it regardless of its relation to the value of anything else (except the value of a member of the given class of comparison). *Any* standard may be used as long as it is used to judge a quality of experience without regard to any value it may derive from its relation to other things. The process of evaluation, when concerned with intrinsic value, takes into consideration only the merits and demerits of each quality by itself, entirely disregarding its causes, effects, accompanying conditions, or the wholes of which it forms a part.

It is legitimate to talk of intrinsic value as being "primary" and extrinsic value as being "secondary" only if we mean that extrinsic value is causally dependent upon intrinsic value, while intrinsic value is not causally dependent upon extrinsic value. It is possible for a thing to have extrinsic value because something else has extrinsic value whose value in turn depends on the extrinsic value of a third thing, and so on. But we always arrive finally at something whose value does not depend on the value of anything else, and this is something (a quality of experience) having intrinsic value. The reason for this does not follow necessarily from the definitions of "intrinsic value" and "extrinsic value," since there is nothing inconsistent in supposing a world where intrinsically valuable experiences are not related in any way to extrinsically valuable objects or situations. We could imagine a world where all values were extrinsic, the value of one thing depending on the value of another whose value in turn depends on the value of something else, ad infinitum, although our actual world is not like this. There are causal relations and part-whole relations which hold between intrinsic and extrinsic values, as well as among intrinsic values themselves and among extrinsic values themselves. I shall examine these relations after considering the three kinds of extrinsic value.

5. THE THREE KINDS OF EXTRINSIC VALUE

Inherent Value. The first kind of standard which determines the extrinsic value of something is a standard of inherent value. Inherent value is the capacity of an object, event, situation, process, or any kind of thing *other than* a quality of our own experience, to produce in us when we respond to it (by perceiving it, imagining it, thinking about it, or otherwise apprehending it) a quality of experience which has intrinsic value. Something has inherent disvalue insofar as it can arouse in us a quality of experience which is intrinsically disvaluable. Assuming the normal standard of intrinsic evaluation, which is satisfaction or pleasantness, we grade an evaluatum as inherently good when we find satisfaction in our response to it and as inherently bad when we find our response on the whole unpleasant. The *inherent* goodness of a good thing is its capacity to produce *intrinsic* goodness in the experience of anyone who responds to it. We rank an object according to a standard of inherent value when we compare this capacity of the object with the same capacities of all other objects in the class of comparison. With respect to its inherent value, the good-making characteristics of an object are those which give it the capacity to produce intrinsically valuable experiences in those who respond to it. Similarly, its bad-making characteristics are those which enable it to produce intrinsically disvaluable experiences.

To rank an object as inherently good on the whole is to claim two things—that the object has a greater capacity than most objects in the class of comparison to produce intrinsic value (or a lesser capacity than most to produce intrinsic disvalue); and that the object has the capacity to produce, in a greater number of experiences of a greater number of people, an overbalance of intrinsic goodness rather than of intrinsic badness. Both of these factors are matters which can be determined by straightforward empirical procedures. An example of an evaluation based on a standard of inherent value would be the judgment that a painting is good because, compared to most other paintings in a given class of comparison, it is more frequently pleasant than unpleasant for more people to contemplate aesthetically.

It is quite possible for an object to be inherently good to one person (because it gives him satisfaction) and inherently bad to another (because it gives him dissatisfaction). It is also possible for an object to be inherently good to a person at one time and inherently bad to the same person at another time. An object is inherently good on the whole if it is more often inherently good than inherently bad to those who respond to it.

This definition of "inherent value" implies that there could be no inherent values unless there were intrinsic values, although there could be, in principle, intrinsic values without there being inherent values. It also implies that all inherent values are extrinsic because nothing could have inherent value all by itself. The inherent value of an object depends on the intrinsic value of someone's experience in response to it. If no one ever responded to an object, it could only be said to have *potential* inherent value (or disvalue); if someone *were* to respond to it he would find satisfaction (or dissatisfaction) in the response. If no quality of anyone's actual or possible experience of the object were intrinsically good or bad, the object could not be said to have even potential inherent value or disvalue.

Instrumental Value. The second kind of standard of extrinsic value is that of instrumental value. In *An Analysis of Knowledge and Valuation* (p. 392), Professor Lewis makes a convenient distinction between instrumental value and utility. A thing has utility to the extent that it is effective in bringing about a given end. If the end is not itself intrinsically or extrinsically good or bad the means to it has no instrumental value or disvalue. Something lacks utility when it is not helpful in bringing about a given end, and a thing has "disutility" when it tends to hinder or prevent the bringing about of a given end. The best means to a given end is that which has the greatest utility, and this is the means which is both sufficient to bring about the end and can bring it about most efficiently. What might be termed the "worst means" is that which is both sufficient to prevent the bringing about of the end and can prevent it most efficiently.

Whether something that has utility also has instrumental value or disvalue depends on whether the given end itself has value or disvalue. (This is what makes all instrumental value extrinsic, i.e., derivative.) There are two ways in which an end can have value and two ways in which it can have disvalue. It has value if it consists in the creation, furtherance, preservation, strengthening, or increase of something which is intrinsically or extrinsically valuable, or if it consists in the destruction, hindrance, avoidance, weakening, or decrease of something which is intrinsically or extrinsically disvaluable. An end can have disvalue in two ways, if it is the creation or strengthening of something disvaluable, or if it is the destruction or weakening of something valuable.

Evaluation according to standards of instrumental value is a process of grading or ranking something as a means to a valuable or disvaluable end. When the given end has value, the evaluatum is ranked as instrumentally good insofar as it has greater utility than most of the other members of the class of comparison; it is ranked as instrumentally bad insofar as it has greater disutility than most of the other members of the class of comparison. When the given end has disvalue, the contrary judgments are made. In each case a pro-attitude on the part of the evaluator is taken toward a means which is judged to be instrumentally good and a con-attitude is taken toward a means judged instrumentally bad. A neutral attitude is taken toward means which fall at or near the center of the order (having utility—lacking utility—having disutility) in which all members of the class of comparison are arranged. If most of the members of the class of comparison have disutility for a good end, while the evaluatum merely lacks utility, the evaluatum will be preferred and will be the object of a pro-attitude. As another possibility, the evaluatum may lack utility for a good end, while most members of the class of comparison have utility for that end. In that case the evaluatum will be ranked as instrumentally bad (on the whole), and a con-attitude will be taken toward it.

There is an important difference between instrumental value and inherent value. Qualities of experience (which are the only kind of thing that can have intrinsic value) may have instrumental value but not inherent value. When an immediately felt or perceived quality of our own experience has instrumental value, it is a means to something else which has value for us. For example, the aesthetic emotions experienced in a church may be evaluated positively as a means to the deepening or strengthening of one's religious attitudes. Ordinarily the aesthetic emotions will also have intrinsic value, and their instrumental value is simply additional. But we cannot say that such emotions have inherent value, since it makes no sense to say that the felt quality of an emotion has the capacity to arouse a pleasant response in us when we apprehend it. The emotion either is pleasant, and so has intrinsic value, or it is not. It may be capable of arousing further pleasant emotions in us, but then it would take on instrumental, not inherent, value.

Considering the ways in which things can have positive or negative instrumental value in combination with other kinds of value, sixteen different possibilities emerge. When the evaluatum is a quality of experience we have the following combinations:

1. It has intrinsic value, and it has instrumental value as a means to other intrinsic values (or disvalues).

2. It has intrinsic value, and it has instrumental value as a means to extrinsic values (or disvalues).

3. It has intrinsic value, but it has instrumental disvalue as a means to other intrinsic values (or disvalues).

4. It has intrinsic value, but it has instrumental disvalue as a means to extrinsic values (or disvalues).

5-8. Same as 1-4, except that the first clause reads: "It has intrinsic disvalue."

9-16. Same as 1-8, except that the first clause reads: "It has extrinsic value (disvalue) other than the instrumental value (disvalue) mentioned in the second clause."

When the evaluatum is not a quality of experience, only combinations 9-16 hold, since things that are not qualities of experience can only have extrinsic value or disvalue.

Contributive Value. The third kind of standard of extrinsic evaluation is that of contributive value. Something has contributive value if it is a part of a whole which has intrinsic, inherent, or instrumental value. A thing has contributive disvalue if it is a part of a disvaluable whole. Professor Baylis gives the example of a spark plug which has little or no value by itself, but is a valuable thing as part of a gasoline motor (which in turn has instrumental value). Similarly, we could say that a certain series of musical notes have little or no value by themselves but take on contributive value when played as part of a symphony. Indeed, listening to the notes in isolation may have intrinsic disvalue for a person, while listening to the whole symphony has intrinsic value for him. Contributive value is like instrumental value, in that any kind of evaluatum may possess it. The degree to which something has contributive value is in direct proportion to what it contributes to a good whole. If it is a necessary part of the whole (i.e., a part without which the whole would entirely lose its value) or if it is an important part of the whole (i.e., a part without which the whole would lose much of its value), then it is contributively valuable to a high degree. If it is an unnecessary or unimportant part of a good whole, it is graded as less valuable. Corresponding negative judgments occur for a bad whole.

Sixteen possible combinations of contributive value or disvalue with other types of value can be made:

1. Something has intrinsic value, and it has contributive value as part of an intrinsically valuable whole. (An important instance of this, namely the contribution of intrinsically valuable experience to the good life as a whole, is discussed in detail by Professor Lewis in Chapter XVI of *An Analysis of Knowledge and Valuation*. However, in light of what I shall say in Chapter 6 it will be seen that "the good life" can here mean only one way of life among many.)

2. It has intrinsic value, and it has contributive value as part of an extrinsically valuable whole.

3. It has intrinsic value, but it has contributive disvalue as part of an intrinsically disvaluable whole. (That is, the particular experience is enjoyed although it is part of a complex experience which is on the whole unpleasant.)

4. It has intrinsic value, but it has contributive disvalue as part of an extrinsically disvaluable whole.

5-8. Same as 1-4, except that the first clause reads: "It has intrinsic disvalue."

9-16. Same as 1-8, except that the first clause reads: "It has extrinsic value (disvalue) other than the contributive value (disvalue) mentioned in the second clause."

As was true in the case of the sixteen combinations involving instrumental value, when the evaluatum is not a quality of experience only 9-16 hold, since things that are not qualities of experience can only have extrinsic value or disvalue.

This completes my account of the three kinds of standards of extrinsic value. It can now be seen why all extrinsic values in actual life are ultimately dependent upon intrinsic values. The inherent value of something is its capacity for arousing intrinsic values, so by definition this kind of extrinsic value depends on intrinsic value. Instrumental value and contributive value are dependent on intrinsic value whenever the instrumental value of something is due to its being a means to an inherently or intrinsically valuable end, and whenever its contributive value is due to its being a part of an inherently or intrinsically valuable whole. There are two more complex cases, in which instrumental and contributive value are indirectly dependent on intrinsic value. First, a thing may have instrumental value in virtue of the fact that it is a means to an end which has contributive value as part of a whole. This whole in turn either may have inherent or intrinsic value itself or may have instrumental value as a means to an end which has inherent or intrinsic value. Secondly, a thing may have contributive value in virtue of the fact that it is part of a whole which has instrumental value as a means to an end. This end in turn either may have inherent or intrinsic value itself or may have contributive value as part of a whole which has inherent or intrinsic value. Still more complex cases than these can be constructed.

In spite of these connections between instrumental and contributive values on the one hand and intrinsic values on the other, it is possible to imagine without self-contradiction a world in which instrumental and contributive values did *not* depend on intrinsic value. In such a world, things would be judged as good solely because they were means to ends which were judged to be good solely as parts of wholes which were judged to be good solely as means to ends, and so on indefinitely. It would be a world devoid of inherent and intrinsic value and thus would be very different from our own world. No one would do anything for its own sake, simply because he found personal enjoyment in it. It would be a world of "practical people" who knew how to get things done but had no reason for getting one thing done rather than another. In our world, on the other hand, things are often judged to be good because they make possible, or because they are constituents of, things that we directly enjoy. And sometimes we judge things to be good because *they* are what we directly enjoy. Or we judge our experiences themselves to be good simply because they have the qualities they have. Thus we arrive finally at things which we judge to be desirable in themselves. Their value is intrinsic to them.

C. Evaluation according to rules

So far I have been concerned with the process of evaluation when the norms used in it are standards. There is a second basic type of evaluation in which the norms used are rules. When so used, rules operate as norms for *correct* and *incorrect* behavior or thought. They may be rules governing the use of a language, rules of a game, moral rules, rules of etiquette, laws (legal rules), rules of inference, aesthetic rules (i.e., rules governing what is alleged to be the proper way to create or to appreciate works of art), rules or maxims that guide us in achieving some personal goal (such as health or wealth), rules or regulations which govern a social institution (a club, a political party, a labor union, a university, etc.), or rules which govern practices or procedures (parliamentary procedure, business office procedures, procedures in a court of law, etc.). The typical words which are used to express evaluations according to rules are "right" and "wrong." The typical words used in evaluations according to standards are as we have seen, "good" and "bad." (I shall consider other ways of expressing value judgments in Chapter 2.)

All evaluations according to rules are gradings; none are rankings. This is because there are no degrees of right and wrong as there are degrees of goodness and badness. I have already pointed out that something may fulfill or fail to fulfill a *standard* of evaluation to a certain degree. But an act either complies with or breaks a rule. If we refer two acts to a rule which applies to both, either we find both acts equally right (they are in accordance with the rule), or both equally wrong (they violate the rule), or one right and the other wrong. Of course a right act is better than a wrong act and a wrong act is worse than a right one, but this hardly deserves to be called "ranking" the two acts. What determines degrees of goodness and badness is the extent to which the evaluatum fulfills or fails to fulfill a standard. What determines whether the evaluatum is right or wrong is whether or not it is in accordance with a rule that applies to it. It is to be noted that an act may be neither right nor wrong, relative to a given rule. This would occur when the rule does not "cover" the act, that is, the act is not included in its range of application. The rule "Automobiles are forbidden to park on the bridge" does not apply to a person walking or riding a bicycle across the bridge.

Rules are of three sorts—injunctions or requirements, permissions or options, and prohibitions or forbiddings. That is to say, when a rule includes an act in its range of application the act may be en-

51523

joined by the rule, permitted by the rule, or forbidden by the rule. An example of the first is, "One must have a license to drive a car"; of the second, "Smoking is permitted in this room"; of the third, "No smoking in this room." Sometimes a "right act" is defined as one that is *obligatory*, that is, as one which complies with a rule that enjoins or requires it to be done. (Moral obligation is a special case of this.) At other times it is defined as any act that is not wrong, and a wrong act is defined as an act prohibited or forbidden by a rule. In this second sense, any act which is *either obligatory or permissible* is a right act. I shall not use the word "right" in either of these ways. By saying that an act is right I shall mean simply that it complies with a rule that covers it. Thus an act is right in my sense under any of three conditions: (1) It is in accordance with a rule that requires it to be done. (2) It is in accordance with a rule that permits it to be done. (3) It is in accordance with a rule that forbids it to be done. The third condition may be stated less awkwardly in the following way: When a rule forbids an act to be done, doing the act is wrong and refraining from doing the act is right. An act is wrong in my sense whenever it does not comply with a rule that covers it. Thus refraining from doing an obligatory act is wrong and doing a prohibited act is wrong. No wrong act corresponds to the second type of rule, since the rule permits the doing of an act without forbidding or requiring the doing of any other act. If one does not do the permitted act, one is not breaking the rule and hence no wrong is committed. In these cases I shall say that doing the act is optional, meaning that it is not wrong to do it and that it is not wrong to refrain from doing it. Both alternatives comply with the rule and therefore both are right. In contrast, I shall restrict the phrase "neither right nor wrong" to acts *not covered* by a rule.

Rules of the first and third types (i.e., injunctions and prohibitions) are related in the following way. To require or enjoin the performance of an act is to forbid or prohibit its nonperformance; it is wrong to *refrain* from doing a required act and right to *refrain* from doing a forbidden act. And it is right to *do* a required act and wrong to *do* a forbidden act. It is also possible to define rules of the first and third types as negations of permissions; a rule which requires that an act be done does not permit its not being done. In other words, refraining from doing a required act is not permitted and consequently the rule requiring the performance of the act may be thought of as not permitting its nonperformance. Similarly a rule of the third type, which forbids that an act be done, does not permit its being done. It is a rule not permitting the performance of an act, in contrast to a rule of the first type, which is a rule not permitting the nonperformance of an act.

Professor Bernard Mayo has argued that because there are no degrees of rule-following and rule-breaking and accordingly no degrees of right and wrong, judgments of right and wrong are not evaluations. Such judgments, he says,

. . . are not evaluative, but imperative. To say that an action is wrong is not to apply a scale of preference, since it is not to say that there are other actions which are less wrong. An action is either right or wrong or neutral: it cannot be more or less wrong, as it can be more or less evil. An action is right if it conforms to an accepted principle or rule, wrong if it violates one. Since there are no degrees of rule-breaking—a rule is either observed or it is infringed—there can be no degrees of right and wrong. . . . The logic of the application of principles is thus different from the logic of the application of standards. Standards are fallen short of by greater or lesser degrees, but principles are either conformed to or not. (B. Mayo, *Ethics and the Moral Life*, London: Macmillan & Co., Ltd., 1958, p. 29.)

I would not deny anything that is said here about the use of the terms "right" and "wrong." But I would classify judgments of right and wrong as evaluations, not imperatives (i.e., prescriptives).

Judgments according to rules are similar in certain basic respects to judgments of goodness and badness, the very factors which set the logical pattern of the process of evaluation being common to both. Whether a judgment be concerned with right or wrong, or with goodness or badness, it is the outcome of a process of evaluation in which the following five factors are present: (1) a class of comparison; (2) a norm or set of norms according to which the evaluatum is judged; (3) a pro-attitude, a con-attitude, or a neutral attitude; (4) a set of good-making and bad-making characteristics (now to be referred to as right-making and wrong-making characteristics); and (5) a point of view from which the evaluation is made. Let us examine the place of each of these elements in an evaluation according to rules.

Class of Comparison. In evaluation according to rules, the sorts of things that may serve as members of a class of comparison are the sorts of things that can be judged right or wrong. There are three of these: human decisions, choices, and acts. We speak of making a right or wrong decision or choice, as well as of doing a right or wrong act.

I have already shown how rules can enjoin, permit, or prohibit acts, and hence how acts can be judged according to rules. But do rules enjoin, permit, or prohibit decisions? They do so indirectly. Deciding may be deciding to do something or deciding that something is the case. In both instances we resolve our doubts about something; we make up our mind either to do one thing rather than another, or to claim that something is or is not the case. And we decide either rightly or wrongly, depending on whether the act we decide to do is right or wrong, or on whether the claim we decide to make is justifiable or unjustifiable. Rules of conduct (indirectly) guide the first kind of decision, rules of thought (indirectly) guide the second. A decision is right, then, if it is a decision to do a right act (i.e., a decision to act in accordance with a rule of conduct) or if it is a decision to make a justifiable claim (i.e., a decision to assert or deny something in accordance with rules of valid reasoning). To say "You made the right decision" is to say either "You decided to do the right thing" or "You decided correctly to assert (deny) that such-and-such is so." It is in this way that decisions can be judged according to rules. They can also, of course, be judged according to standards. Thus there may be good or bad decisions as well as right or wrong decisions.

Just as rules may function as norms for decision-making, so they may also function as norms for choice-making. "Choice" has a double meaning in ordinary language. Sometimes it means selecting-one-thing-rather-than-another. In this sense, to choose is to do something, since the selection is an act. Examples would be choosing a lot on which to build a house or choosing a dessert from a list on a menu. In these cases the act of choosing normally consists in a linguistic act, such as saying "I'll take the lot on the corner" or "I'll have apple pie." If a person holds out a pack of cards to us and says "Choose a card," our choice may consist in the nonlinguistic act of taking a card. Since they are acts, choices in this sense may be evaluated as right or wrong choices according to rules that enjoin, permit, or prohibit them.

In a second sense choices are not acts but are either similar to or identical with decisions. Choices are similar to decisions in that a person may choose to do something and then not actually do it (just as a person may decide to do something and then not carry out his decision). A choice in this sense is a preference for doing one thing rather than another. "My choice was to go to the other restaurant but my friends all wanted to eat here." Choosing is not identical with deciding, however, unless one's choice is the outcome of deliberation which resolves a doubt in one's mind. One may choose to do something merely on the basis of one's emotions or moods. Deciding on the other hand contextually implies a process of deliberation; choosing has no such implication. We can say that all decisions are choices (in this second sense of "choice"), but we cannot say that all choices are decisions. Choices can be spontaneous or thoughtless, decisions cannot. Unlike decisions, choices can be based solely on our immediate likes and dislikes. But whether choices are deliberative or spontaneous, they may be evaluated according to rules which (indirectly) apply to them. We have seen that choices in the sense of acts are subject to rules *directly*. In these cases to say "You made the right choice" means "You did the right thing in choosing the way you did." In the second sense, to say "You made the right choice" means "You chose to do the right thing." As in the case of decisions, rules are indirectly applicable here. As a right decision is a decision to do what is right, so a right choice is a choice of (preference for) what is right.

For the sake of simplicity, in all subsequent discussion of evaluation according to rules, I shall refer to acts rather than to decisions and choices when speaking of the evaluatum or the members of a class of comparison. That is, I shall only examine cases in which rules *directly* apply to an evaluatum or a member of a class of comparison.

Appeal to Norms. When we evaluate something according to rules, the rules function as norms in the same way as do standards of evaluation. The process of evaluation according to rules yields a value judgment in which we claim that an act is right or wrong. In order to arrive at such a judgment, we must determine two things: (1) whether a given act falls under (is covered by) a rule and (2) if it does fall under the rule, whether doing the act is in accordance with or violates the rule. If the rule enjoins or requires the act, doing the act is in accordance with the rule and not doing it is a violation of the rule. If the rule permits the act, either doing it or refraining from it is in accordance with the rule. If the rule forbids the act, then doing it violates the rule and refraining from it is in accordance with the rule. A rule includes an act in its range of application (and the act is "covered by" or "falls under" the rule) when the act is of a sort specified in the rule and the performance or nonperformance of the act occurs in circumstances specified in the rule. Thus the rule "No smoking in subways" covers all acts of smoking and all nonperformances of the act of smoking (i.e., all cases of refraining from smoking) by persons while they are in subways. It does not cover acts of smoking done (or not done) by persons outside of subways. To take another instance, the rule "Promises must not be broken" applies only to people who have made promises and only to those acts which could correctly be construed as the keeping or the breaking of promises made.

Pro-Attitudes and Con-Attitudes. The class of acts covered by a rule is the class of comparison for all evaluations made according to the rule. Any act that falls under a rule may be *graded* as right or as wrong, depending on whether the act is in accordance with or violates the rule. When we judge an act to be right according to a rule, we have adopted the rule as the basis (norm) for judging it. In doing so, we commit ourselves to having a pro-attitude toward any act complying with the rule and a con-attitude toward any act violating it. We have a pro-attitude toward a person's doing a required act (or refraining from a forbidden act), and we have a con-attitude toward a person's not doing a required act (or doing a forbidden act). When our rule is a permission we take a neutral attitude toward any act in the specified circumstances, whether it be performance or nonperformance. With regard to acts not covered by a rule we have adopted, we have *no* attitude, not even a neutral one. So far as our commitment goes, such acts are indifferent; they are neither right nor wrong. They become right or wrong, however, the moment we adopt a rule which includes them in its range of application. Thus when a given rule demands, permits, or forbids an act to be done in certain circumstances, the class of comparison is the class of all acts that are correctly describable either as the performance of what is demanded, permitted, or forbidden in the specified circumstances or as the nonperformance of what is demanded, permitted, or forbidden in those circumstances. The rule serves as a norm for judging or grading a given number of the class of comparison (namely the evaluatum). If the evaluatum fulfills the norm, the judgment is positive (or neutral, in the case of permissions); the evaluator accordingly takes a pro-attitude (or neutral attitude) toward the evaluatum. A con-attitude is taken toward the evaluatum when it fails to fulfill the norm, that is, when it violates an injunction or prohibition.

It has been pointed out that there are no degrees of right and wrong in the way that there are degrees of goodness and badness. In the case of evaluations according to standards, an evaluator's pro-attitude or con-attitude varies in strength according to the degree of goodness or badness of the evaluatum. What determines the strength of pro- and con-attitudes in evaluations according to rules? The answer lies in the degree of *stringency* or *importance* of the rule on which the evaluation is based. The more stringent the rule, the stronger is the evaluator's pro-attitude toward an act done in accordance with it, and the stronger is his con-attitude toward a violation of it. The degree of stringency or importance of a rule is determined by an evaluation of the rule according to standards of extrinsic value. A rule itself may function as an evaluatum and be judged according to standards; it may have inherent, instrumental, or contributive value (or disvalue), depending on what standards are used in grading or ranking it. For example, if we judge a rule according to the utilitarian standard, we determine its instrumental value (or disvalue) as a means to the general happiness of mankind. Under such an evaluation the rule "Promises are not to be broken" is seen to be much more stringent or important than the rule "Brush your teeth twice a day." In morals the classic difference between duties of obligation ("perfect" duties) and duties of supererogation ("imperfect" duties) may be understood in this way, the first consisting in acts either enjoined or forbidden by highly stringent moral rules, the second consisting in acts enjoined, permitted, or forbidden by less stringent moral rules. (However, some philosophers would make this a difference not of degree but of kind. Perfect duties would be *right* acts enjoined by moral rules; imperfect duties would be *good* acts which fulfill moral standards.)

Right-making and Wrong-making Characteristics. It is easy to see how right-making and wrong-making characteristics function in evaluations according to rules. A right-making characteristic of an act that falls under a rule is any feature of the act in virtue of which it complies with the rule. The wrong-making characteristics of an act are those features which make it a violation of the rule. Can an act have both right-making and wrong-making characteristics with respect to the same rule? The answer depends on two factors: how complex the act is and how well formed the rule is. A businessman's complex act of carrying on an advertizing campaign for his product can have both right-making and wrong-making characteristics with regard to the vague rule "Be honest." But suppose we adopt a clearly formulated rule, such as: "Whenever a statement made in a public medium of communication will be taken by others as a statement of fact, it must not be a false statement and it must be free from distortion and exaggeration." If we apply this rule to a single statement made in one of the advertisements in the campaign, the act of making the statement will have only right-making or wrong-making characteristics.

Point of View. The final element common to evaluations according to both standards and rules is the presence of a point of view from which the evaluation is carried out. Just as we may judge a painting from an aesthetic point of view, an economic point of view, and a moral point of view, so we may judge an act from many different points of view, only using as our norm of evaluation rules and not standards. We may judge the same act to be right from one point of view (applying its appropriate rules) and wrong from another point of view (applying *its* appropriate rules). For example, the rules of good business practice might require a businessman in times of recession to discharge a number of his employees; such an act would be right from the business point of view. But it might be wrong from the moral point of view, if other economizing measures could be used instead. Similarly, an act which was right from the aesthetic point of view, such as constructing a fine work of architecture as a city's post office, might be wrong from a political or economic point of view. In all cases of this sort an act has both right-making and wrong-making characteristics, but these are determined by different rules. The act is both right and wrong, but right economically and wrong morally, or right aesthetically and wrong politically. Whether the act is right or wrong *on the whole* depends on which rules take precedence over others. (I shall consider the relative precedence of rules along with the relative precedence of standards in Chapter 3.)

I conclude, then, that judgments of right and wrong are sufficiently similar in important respects to judgments of goodness and badness to warrant their being included in the concept of evaluation. The parallel between evaluations according to rules and evaluations according to standards will continue to be drawn in subsequent chapters. That standards and rules have essentially the same function in evaluations is a principal thesis of this book, and I shall also try to show that standards and rules are both subject to the same methods of reasoning when we try to justify our adopting them in practical life.

D. Deliberation

My purpose in the remainder of this chapter is to make clear the relation between the concept of evaluation and the concept of deliberation. There are two sorts of deliberation: deliberation about acts and deliberation about standards and rules. This distinction corresponds to the one which Mr. R. M. Hare has drawn between making decisions, on the basis of given principles, about what we shall do and making "decisions of principle," that is, deciding what principles to adopt as guides to our future decisions. In his discussion of this distinction (in Chapter 4 of *The Language of Morals.* Oxford: The Clarendon Press, 1952) Mr. Hare uses the example of learning to drive a car. Some of our learning process consists in being taught principles of good driving. Having learned these principles, we know what to do to start the car, stop the car, turn around, speed up, slow down, and so forth. The principles guide our decisions about what to do in a certain situation. Unless we had made a decision to adopt these principles as guides to our conduct, they would be no help in learning how to drive. Indeed, we could not learn how to drive at all (or how to do anything else, for that matter) unless we *decided* to use principles as guides to our decisions. But learning how to drive does not consist solely in adopting principles and applying them in practical situations. We are never taught enough principles to guide us in every situation we will meet when we are driving. As we encounter more and more various circumstances, we have to make up our own principles. We set precedents for ourselves by imposing new principles upon our own conduct. We also learn in this manner when to make exceptions to the principles that have been taught us.

Suppose that we have a principle to act in a certain way in certain circumstances. Suppose then that we find ourselves in circumstances which fall under the principle, but which have certain other peculiar features, not met before, which make us ask 'Is the principle really intended to cover cases like this, or is it incompletely specified—is there here a case belonging to a class which should be treated as exceptional?' Our answer to this question will be a decision, but a decision of principle, as is shown by the use of the value-word 'should.' If we decide that this should be an exception, we thereby modify the principle by laying down an exception to it. (R. M. Hare, *op. cit.*, p. 65.)

By functioning as guides to our conduct, principles serve as norms by which we learn what is the right thing to do and what is the wrong thing to do. To break a principle is wrong, unless we can justify making an exception to it or we can justify abandoning it and adopting a new one. In this way we come to judge our conduct and our decisions according to our principles. Such judgments are value judgments, and the principles according to which they are made are what I have called standards and rules. Whether a given decision or act will be a good one or a bad one, a right one or a wrong one, depends on the standard or rule we have adopted as the ground for our evaluation.

Corresponding to this distinction between decisions based on already adopted principles and decisions to adopt principles is a distinction between two kinds of deliberation. In the first kind of deliberation we are trying to make a decision of the first sort. That is, we are trying to decide what to do, what course of action to take from among the alternatives confronting us. We are not questioning the standards and rules which we think are applicable to the situation. In the second kind of deliberation we are uncertain about what standards and rules to apply. We are trying to decide, in Mr. Hare's terms, what principles to adopt, or perhaps whether to make an exception to a principle. I shall consider each kind of deliberation in turn.

When, in a situation of choice, we are deliberating about alternative courses of action, we are trying to decide which course of action is the best. In order to do this we must carry out a series of evaluations in which we *grade* each of the various alternatives and then *rank* all of them in a preferential order from best to worst. Let us consider these two steps of the process of deliberation in detail. (It should be remembered that, like the foregoing account of the process of evaluation, this is not intended to be a psychological description of the way people actually think, but an explication of the logic of their thinking when it is ideally rational.)

1. We carry out an evaluation of each alternative act according to *rules* we have accepted as appropriate or valid in the situation at hand. Our purpose here is to discover which acts are right and which are wrong, as judged according to all the rules we think the acts fall under. If there are rules that cover all the alternatives and if only one alternative can be graded as a right act according to these rules (i.e., all the other acts violate the rules and are therefore wrong), then our deliberation is completed. We know that the one alternative which complies with the rules is not only *a* right act; we also know that it is *the* right act. It is, then, the best thing to do in the circumstances. If on the other hand either our rules do not cover all the alternatives (so that some of them are neither right nor wrong) or more than one act is found to be right, then we must proceed to the second step of deliberation.

2. We carry out an evaluation of each alternative according to *standards* we have accepted, to see which alternative is the most valuable or desirable. The class of comparison of such evaluations is precisely the class of alternative courses of action open to the

evaluator's choice. The aim of this step is to arrange the entire set of alternatives (i.e., the members of the class of comparison) in an order of increasing value or desirability. The act which has the highest place in this order will be the best thing to do, that is, the course of action we ought to choose. Usually this alternative will be an act that was found to be right in our first step of deliberation. But it need not be. If all the acts, when judged according to rules, are wrong, there may still be one which is less *bad* (i.e., whose effects are less undesirable) than the others. Similarly if all the acts are right acts according to our rules, some will be worse than others and one will be better than all the others, when judged according to our standards.

The difference between *a* right thing to do and *the* right thing to do and the difference between *a* wrong thing to do and *the* wrong thing to do may be made clear by reference to the situations in which, respectively, all the alternatives are right acts and all are wrong acts. When all the alternatives are right acts, as judged by our rules, then every act is *a* right thing to do. But only one of the acts is *the* right thing to do, that is, the thing we ought to do. This is the act that is better than any other alternative, when judged according to our standards. This act is the one which not only has value (goodness) in addition to its rightness, but has greater value than any of the other acts. This situation also allows us to distinguish between a required or enjoined act and an obligatory act. (This distinction was disregarded in Section C of this chapter, where I spoke of an obligatory act as a required or enjoined act.) A required or enjoined act is any act which is required or enjoined by a rule. Now it is possible in principle for all the acts in a situation of choice to be enjoined acts. But only one act can be obligatory. That is to say, a person can be obligated to do only one act when he must choose among several. He cannot be obligated to do what is impossible, and presumably it is impossible for him in the given situation to do more than one of the alternatives. An obligatory act, then, is an enjoined act which is *the* right thing to do in a situation of choice. It is the act which is better than any of the alternatives.

With regard to the second case, where all the alternatives are wrong acts, we are tempted to say that the best of these acts is the one which is least wrong. But this is to confuse "least wrong" with "least evil (or bad)." In such a situation our choice is a choice of a lesser evil, not of a lesser wrong. There is no lesser wrong. All the acts are equally wrong, although some are worse (less good or more evil) than others. The best act is that one which, when compared with the others, has the greatest value or the least disvalue according to our standards. Now even though such an act is *a* wrong thing to do, it is not *the* wrong thing to do. In fact in the given situation it is *the* right thing to do (although it is not *a* right thing to do). Every one of the acts in the given situation is *a* wrong thing to do and *all but one* is *the* wrong thing to do. *The* wrong thing to do is any alternative except the best, which is *the* right thing to do. But what is *the* right thing to do in this situation is *a* wrong thing to do. (Sometimes we call a situation of this kind "tragic.")

By means of the second step of deliberation, then, we decide what we ought to do whenever an evaluation of alternatives according to rules yields more than one right act or no right acts. This situation will also occur whenever we find by means of the first step that all the alternatives are permissible and none is enjoined. So far as our rules are concerned, we may do anything we like. Nothing we do will be wrong. But there is nevertheless one act which is *the* right thing to do, and that is simply the *best* thing to do as judged by our standards. We must then enter upon the second step of deliberation in order to arrive at a rational decision about what we ought to do.

Let us now turn to the second sort of deliberation. Here we are not trying to decide what to do in light of our rules and standards; we are trying to decide what rules and standards to adopt. We must evaluate rules and standards according to "higher" standards, that is, according to standards that take precedence over the rules and standards to be evaluated. The class of comparison is the entire group of rules and standards from which we are trying to choose the most valid or appropriate for our evaluations. The overall purpose of our deliberation is to find the best rules and standards to adopt, not only as guides to our decisions and conduct, but also as the norms for our evaluations and prescriptions.

A standard used for evaluating standards and rules might be called a "second-order" standard. When we evaluate rules according to second-order standards, we judge the *effects* of their being followed. We consider what it would be like if one rule rather than another were generally adopted as a norm for right conduct. We then try to determine to what extent the probable consequences of its adoption would fulfill or fail to fulfill the second-order standards. In ethics this system is sometimes called "restricted utilitarianism." Such a system, however, need not operate only for moral rules. A businessman, the head of a corporation, might try in similar fashion to find the best rules for running his company with maximum economy and efficiency. Again, people might decide to change certain rules of etiquette because they have become inconvenient or impracticable under changing conditions of social life. And, of course, legislators may use second-order standards when deliberating about which new laws to enact and which old laws to change or abolish. (Laws are one kind of rules.) The particular second-order standards people will actually use are the standards they consider *appropriate* or *valid* for evaluating different sorts of rules governing different sorts of conduct in different sorts of circumstances. (The grounds for determining the appropriateness or validity of second-order standards will be discussed in Chapter 3.)

When we evaluate *standards* rather than rules, a similar procedure of evaluation is used. We determine what practical consequences are likely to be entailed if this standard or that were generally adopted as a guide to the decisions and conduct of people. We then consider these consequences in the light of our second-order standards, ranking the group of first-order standards in an order of preferability according to the degree to which each one fulfills or fails to fulfill the second-order standards. For example, suppose that in the past our standards for choosing a family car have been its appearance and power. We might come to adopt new standards (say, efficiency of performance and compactness of size) when we find that the cars we bought in the past have not been satisfactory for family use. Or to take another example, a department store buyer might have been using certain standards for buying dresses which did not sell well. He might then change his standards (or the head of the dress department might insist that he change them!) in the hope that dresses selected on the basis of the new standards would appeal to the store's customers.

In both of these examples the unsatisfactory effects of using the old standards constitute their bad-making characteristics. These bad-making characteristics are determined by the second-order standards that are deemed appropriate or valid for judging the old standards. In the second example the buyer's old standards may have been the expression of his personal taste concerning good fabrics and dress designs. On the basis of the second-order standard (increasing the store's sales), the buyer changes his standards for selecting dresses from what he personally likes to what the customers like. The appropriateness or validity of his second-order standard depends on the conditions under which the evaluation of standards takes place, including the purposes for which the evaluation is carried out. Further consideration of this point will be taken up in Chapter 3. We shall find that the utilitarian methods I have mentioned in the preceding two paragraphs are not the only methods for evaluating rules and standards.

To sum up, all deliberating is evaluating. We deliberate on two levels: we try to decide which course of action is best among a set of alternatives, and we try to determine which standards and rules to adopt as guides to our conduct. In the first kind of deliberation our evaluating is done according to first-order standards or rules; in the second kind, according to second-order standards. The two kinds of deliberation differ, then, with respect to their classes of comparison and with respect to the norms which they use. Apart from this, they are similar to each other and to all other processes of evaluation.

Value judgments

2

A. Judging and expressing a judgment

At the beginning of Chapter 1, I distinguished the process of evaluation from the outcome of the process, a value judgment. What a value judgment is can be understood largely in terms of the process of evaluation, since the sole aim of the process is to arrive at such a judgment. In this chapter I shall add, to what has already been said about value judgments, some further considerations that will help make clear what we do when we judge the value of something. I shall also try to clarify the way we use language when we express or pronounce a value judgment.

1. EVALUATIVE CLAIMS AS JUDGMENTS

When we arrive at a judgment as the result of a process of evaluation, we pass a verdict upon the worth or value of something. We make a claim about how good or bad it is, or about whether it is right or wrong. Judging in this sense is not the same as judging in another ordinary sense, that of assessing the empirical properties or the worth of something under less than optimum conditions. In *The Moral Point of View* (Ithaca, N. Y.: Cornell University Press, 1958) Professor Kurt Baier has defined "value judgment" entirely in terms of the latter meaning of judging. He wishes to use the term only in reference to situations in which we must, as we say in common speech, "use our judgment" in making an assertion.

A man may be a good judge of character, or of distance, or of speed. We say that he is a good judge of these things if he can usually judge these things correctly. And we say that he has this power if he can get correct results *under conditions other than optimum;* that is to say, when the pedestrian, reliable methods of verification have not yet been used, as when a person has to judge someone's character after a short acquaintance, or when he has to judge distances without being allowed to use a tape measure, or speeds without a speedometer. Judgment, then, involves giving correct answers under difficult conditions. (K. Baier, *op. cit.*, p. 55.)

Although this is certainly one of the ways we use the word "judgment" in everyday life, it is not of any special philosophical importance when we want to understand what a value judgment is. A value judgment does not cease to be a value judgment when it is made *under optimum conditions.* What we want to know as philosophers is not the difference between judging a person's character after a short acquaintance and assessing that character when we know him well. It is rather the difference between judging (evaluating) a person's character under *either* condition, and judging distance or speed. We do not make *value* judgments when we are estimating ("judging") how far away something is or how fast it is going. But we do make a value judgment of someone's character when we assert that he is dishonest, even if we do not have to use our judgment (in Professor Baier's sense) in making the assertion.

In the sense of the word which I wish to elucidate here, a judgment may or may not be made under optimum conditions. To call an assertion a judgment is, in its wildest sense, to indicate that it is made as a result of a process of weighing the reasons for and against whatever it is that is being asserted. To call it a value judgment is to indicate that the process was one of trying to decide upon the true value or worth of the thing being judged. This is what I have analyzed in Chapter 1 as the process of evaluation. When we begin such a process, we enter upon a course of reasoning for the purpose of coming to a decision about the value of something. We do this when there has been some doubt in our own mind or some dispute with others about the matter. The process of evaluation is thus aimed at deciding an issue, settling a question, or resolving a doubt. The decision which terminates the process consists in making a claim, namely that the evaluatum has a certain value or disvalue. To call this claim a "judgment" is to draw attention to the fact that it is the result of a process of weighing reasons. It is to say that the person who makes the claim is committed in a certain way; if the judgment is challenged, he must be disposed to give reasons in support of it. This is why it is always legitimate to demand that a value judgment be justified. We shall see in the next chapter that the first step in a rational response to this demand consists in retracing the process of evaluation whereby the person arrived at his judgment.

By going through the process of evaluation, one attempts to establish the claim that the evaluatum fulfills (or fails to fulfill) a standard to a certain degree or that it complies with (or violates) a rule. One attempts to justify one's grading or ranking of the evaluatum. But to have successfully established this claim is not to have justified the value judgment completely. For the value judgment not only consists in the claim that the evaluatum has a certain value. It also contextually implies a further claim, the justification of which requires one to go beyond the process of evaluation. This is the claim that the standards or rules used in the evaluation process are appropriate or valid. How this claim can be justified is a question I shall consider in detail in Chapters 3, 4, 5, and 6. Here I only wish to point out that a value judgment *explicitly* claims that something fulfills (or fails to fulfill) a standard or that something is (or is not) in accordance with a rule, and *implicitly* claims that the standard or rule correctly applies to the thing in question.

2. THE EMOTIVE THEORY OF VALUE

This conception of a value judgment contradicts the so-called "emotive" theory of value. According to that theory, any sentence in which an alleged value judgment is stated merely "expresses" (evinces, displays) a pro-attitude or con-attitude on the part of the person who utters the sentence. To utter such a sentence is not to pronounce a judgment, since it is not to make an assertion of any sort; it is simply to express one's attitude toward something. This theory raises important questions about the language of value. What various functions does normative language have? How are we using language when we express value judgments? If my view of value judgments is correct, then evaluative sentences are utterances in which we do make assertions, and assertions which people can affirm or deny on rational grounds.

Suppose we grant that evaluative sentences do express some kind of assertion. Such sentences may still express (in another sense of "express") the attitudes of the speaker. Any evaluative sentence does evince or display the speaker's attitude, if we mean by this that anyone who understands the sentence can infer with some degree of probability the speaker's attitude toward what the sentence is about. But how important is this fact for our understanding of value language? It in no way denies that value judgments can be rationally justified, since an evaluative sentence may express an assertion *as well as* evince an attitude. Moreover, attitudes themselves are not necessarily irrational. We may justify attitudes just as we may justify assertions, although the methods of justification may not be the same.

Nor is the expression of attitudes a *distinctive* function of value language. In the first place, when we say that evaluative sentences express attitudes we must remember that neutral attitudes as well as pro- and con-attitudes may be so expressed. The early emotivists completely overlooked neutral value judgments (that the evaluatum is fair, so-so, unobjectionable, etc.). Neutral judgments are clearly evaluative in that they are one way in which we *grade* things. Therefore we cannot say that the expression of pro- and con-attitudes is the distinctive function of value language. Not all value judgments show that we like or dislike, favor or disfavor something. Neutral value sentences express a different sort of attitude, in which we are neither for nor against a thing, neither like nor dislike it. I would suggest that, because neutral value judgments were overlooked, the expressive quality of value language appeared to the emotivists to have more importance than it does. In the second place, the fact that a sentence evinces an attitude in no way implies that it expresses a value judgment. I evince my attitude when I say in a terrified voice "The house is on fire," but this is not pronouncing a value judgment; I am not making an assertion as a result of a process of evaluation. Similarly I might say "What a terrible noise!" and so give direct expression to my con-attitude toward the noise, without grading or ranking the noise according to a standard. Consequently, the expression of pro-attitudes and con-attitudes is not a distinctive feature of value language. Nor does all value language have this feature. We can, of course, take into account neutral attitudes and say that value language expresses these as well as pro- and con-attitudes; but then have we said anything important about value language?

3. JUDGMENT AND EXPRESSION

Let us consider further the relation between value judgments and the language in which they are expressed. It is possible for a person to judge something to be of value without expressing it in a sentence or other kind of utterance; a value judgment must be capable of being stated but need not actually be stated. We may think of it as a capacity to answer a question. The act of answering is the linguistic act of pronouncing the judgment. The question is "What is the value of this object (act, event, etc.)?" and the answer is the uttering of a value judgment, "The value of this object (act, event, etc.) is V." Now the state of being able to answer the question is the state of having come to a verdict, of having made up one's mind. To be in that state is to have a mental disposition of settled opinion concerning the matter, so that if one were asked the question one would be disposed to give a certain answer. The process of evaluation is the process whereby one acquires such a mental disposition. To arrive at a decision concerning the value of something is to acquire the capacity to answer the question "What is its value?" We say then that we "judge" the thing as having a certain value. And this means either that we actually pronounce judgment upon the thing or that we *would* do so *if* we were asked what its value was.

A value judgment must be distinguished from the act of uttering it. It is perfectly correct to say of someone that he judges something to be good even though he is not actually engaged in stating that it is good. Indeed, in order to say that someone was actually pronouncing judgment on something we would use the present participle: "He is judging." To say "He judges" is normally to say that the person has a certain mental disposition, not that he is performing a linguistic act. The past tense brings out the dispositional use of "judge" even more clearly. Take the sentence: "When he was an art student he judged this to be a good painting." We certainly do not mean by this that during the whole time the person was an art student he continually uttered the statement: "This is a good painting." We mean that he would utter such a statement if the appropriate occasion arose. The noun "judgment" as well as the verb "to judge" has a dispositional use. Thus we say "According to his judgment this is a good painting" or more simply "In his judgment this is a good painting." A bit more stiffly: "His judgment of this painting is that it is a good one." In none of these instances does "judgment" refer to a linguistic act. We specify the act of expressing a judgment by such statements as "He surprised us all by pronouncing the judgment that this is a good painting" or "Yesterday in my presence he expressed the judgment that it is a good painting."

Judging the value of something, then, is not the same as *telling* someone (others or ourselves) what its value is. It includes, however, being able to do so upon demand. A value judgment remains a value judgment even if it is not expressed or asserted, but it must be expressible or assertable. One cannot say "I have made up my mind about the value of this, but I cannot say what its value is." To have made up one's mind is to have the capacity to state how one judges something, and this means to have the capacity to answer the question "What is the value of this?" Judging is in this way like believing, having an opinion, supposing, affirming, and denying. It makes no sense to speak of a person as believing something and at the same time as not being able to say what it is he believes. Of course a person might believe something and not say what he believes. But he must be *able* to say what he believes. The same is true of having an opinion about something, or supposing that something were so, or affirming or denying that something is so. These are all dispositions of an intellectual sort and must therefore be understood in terms of the linguistic acts (as well as the behavioral acts) which give evidence for their existence.

4. THE LANGUAGE OF VALUE JUDGMENTS

Let us now turn to another question. When we pronounce or express a value judgment, is there a particular sort of statement that we make? Are there special "value sentences" or "value expressions" which indicate that a value judgment is being uttered and not some other kind of judgment or belief? If we examine the language which we actually use in everyday circumstances to express value judgments, we find we must answer in the negative. The expression of value judgments cannot be limited to any particular set of words. What makes a statement the expression of a value judgment is not *which words* are used but the ways in which, and the purposes for which, they are used.

Perhaps the simplest way of expressing a (nonneutral) value judgment is by means of a declarative sentence of the form "This is good (bad)" or "This is right (wrong)." These sentences are not restricted in their meaning to one type of value judgment, such as moral judgment or aesthetic judgment. But there are many other typical ways of expressing value judgments in sentences which are not restricted in their meaning to any one type of judgment. A few may be listed: "This is desirable (undesirable)"; "This is valuable (valueless)"; "This is worthwhile, worthy (worthless, unworthy)"; "This is commendable, praiseworthy (reprehensible, blameworthy)"; "This is excellent, fine, splendid (poor, shoddy, shallow)"; "This is satisfactory, adequate (unsatisfactory, inadequate)"; "This is effective, successful (ineffective, unsuccessful)"; "This is helpful, useful (harmful, useless)"; "This is correct, proper (incorrect, improper)." Some of these expressions, of course, are more appropriately used for certain types of value judgments than for others, but they all cut across judgments of more than one type. Do the various predicates used in these sentences have something in common which would identify them as value predicates? The answer is no, for in certain contexts many of these words do not express value judgments at all, and it is perfectly possible to express value judgments without using these words. Let us see how this is so.

There are at least two ways in which it is possible to use these words and not express value judgments by means of them. These uses may be called for convenience the "good-of-its-kind" use and the "conventional" use. The first use occurs when we say that something is a good (fine, excellent, satisfactory, perfect, adequate) example of a certain kind of thing. "I came down with a good cold last night"; "You need a good spanking"; "This is a good torture machine" illustrate this use. In all such cases what is called good is being judged according to standards which the speaker has *not* adopted as standards of true value or worth. To say that something is good-of-its-kind is to say that it fulfills certain standards to a high degree. *But one does not have a pro-attitude toward the thing in consequence of this fact.* Indeed, one may have a con-attitude toward it. A good torture machine may be a bad thing (i.e., a thing toward which we take a con-attitude) *because* it is a good torture machine. To say that it is a good torture machine does not contextually imply either a pro-attitude or a con-attitude toward it. As Professor Baylis has pointed out, to say that something is good-of-its-kind is to say that it is good in a certain respect, and this in no way implies that we consider that particular respect a reason for judging the thing good on the whole.

In labelling something good of its kind, we do not commit ourselves to the assertion that the kind of thing concerned is itself good. In labelling something good in one or more respects we do not thereby label it good on the whole. Consequently it does not follow from 'X is a good thing of kind Y' or 'X is good in respect Y' that 'X is a good thing.' (C. A. Baylis, *op. cit.*, p. 488.)

Professor Baylis proceeds to give two illuminating examples. One is that of a good lie, which for moral reasons might well be judged a worse deed than a bad lie. The other example is the assertion that a gun is a good gun. "Since the uses to which a gun may be put are so varied, some good, some bad, we hesitate to label an object of that kind as in general a good thing or a bad thing." (*Loc. cit.*) These examples help us to see the general rule which underlies good-of-its-kind judgments. Whenever we judge a means to an end purely in respect of its effectiveness as a means, without judging the value or disvalue of the end, we are making such a judgment. Professor C. I. Lewis's distinction between utility and instrumental value, discussed in Chapter 1, can be elucidated by this. The utility of an object depends on how effective it is in bringing about some end, regardless of the value or disvalue of the end. The instrumental value of something, on the other hand, depends on its capacity to serve as a means to a valuable end. (Its instrumental disvalue would be its effectiveness as a means to a disvaluable end.)

Thus the judgment that something has utility is a good-of-its-kind judgment, while a judgment that something has instrumental value or disvalue is a value judgment.

The purely conventional use of so-called "value predicates" is also to be distinguished from the straightforward expression of value judgments. The conventional use, indeed, may become ironic or sarcastic, so that a sentence with a positive value predicate will express a negative value judgment. Mr. Hare calls the conventional use of value words the "inverted commas" use. Thus we might say "It was a very proper party attended by very proper people." The word "proper" is being used almost as if it were in quotation marks, to indicate that the party and the people are not being approved of as proper. In fact the statement expresses a con-attitude. The evaluative meaning of the word "proper," which was originally positive, has now become negative. Mr. Hare offers the following explanation of this linguistic phenomenon:

This procedure is for the word to be gradually emptied of its evaluative meaning through being used more and more in what I shall call a conventional or "inverted commas' way; when it has lost all its evaluative meaning it comes to be used as a purely descriptive word for designating certain characteristics of the object, and, when it is required to commend or condemn objects in this class, some quite different value-word is imported for the purpose. (R. M. Hare, *op. cit.*, p. 120.)

The example which Hare gives to illustrate this process is the word "eligible" as it occurs in the phrase "eligible bachelor."

'Eligible' started off as a value-word, meaning 'such as should be chosen (*sc.* as a husband for one's daughters)'. Then, because the criteria of eligibility came to be fairly rigid, it acquired a descriptive meaning too. . . . In the twentieth century, partly as a reaction from the over-rigid standards of the nineteenth, which resulted in the word 'eligible' lapsing into a conventional use, the second method has been adopted. If now someone said 'He is an eligible bachelor', we could almost feel the inverted commas round the word, and even the irony; we should feel that if that was all that could be said for him, there must be something wrong with him. For commending bachelors, on the other hand, we now use quite different words; we say 'He is likely to make a very *good* husband for Jane'. . . . (*Ibid.*, pp. 120-121.)

The shift described here from a positive evaluative meaning to a primarily descriptive meaning, and from this to a negative evaluative meaning, can easily be interpreted in terms of my analysis of evaluation. When the word has what Mr. Hare calls "evaluative meaning," one normally infers a pro-attitude (if the evaluative meaning is positive) or a con-attitude (if it is negative) on the part of the speaker toward whatever the word is predicated of. This pro- or con-attitude is taken toward the object insofar as the object fulfills or fails to fulfill certain standards, that is, insofar as it has certain good-making or bad-making characteristics. What Mr. Hare calls the "descriptive meaning" of a value word is the set of characteristics which an object must have in order for the word to be applied correctly to it. In a value judgment these characteristics would be precisely the good-making and bad-making characteristics in virtue of which the speaker takes a pro-attitude or con-attitude toward the object. A primarily descriptive word is one whose criteria of application are not standards of evaluation; the characteristics which something must have for the word to be applied to it are not good-making or bad-making characteristics. They do not call forth definite pro-attitudes and con-attitudes on the part of the speaker.

I have been arguing that there is no set of words which provide the distinguishing mark of value judgments because many words that are ordinarily used in certain contexts to express value judgments may be used for other purposes in other contexts. A second reason, I submit, is that value judgments may be expressed in a variety of ways other than by means of declarative sentences using the typical "value predicates."

First, there are simple descriptive or matter-of-fact statements made in certain contexts. The reader's imagination can readily supply situations in which the following express value judgments:

"This apple has a worm in it!"
"It was a clear violation of the rules of the game."
"They're not diamonds; they're rhinestones."
"I get thirty miles to the gallon!"
"People don't do that."
"This is the second time he has been in trouble with the police."

In each of these sentences some good-making or bad-making characteristic is specified. In light of it, we know that the speaker has a pro- or con-attitude toward the object being described. In each case both the class of comparison and the standards (or rules) of evaluation, though implicit, can be inferred from the context (i.e., they are contextually implied). The evaluation process may not have taken place immediately prior to the utterance of the sentence, but this is not necessary for the sentence to express a value judgment. If the speaker were asked for a complete account of the reasons behind his statement and if he were to give such a complete account, he would carry out a process of evaluation leading to the value judgment which is expressed in the sentence (but which could also be expressed by using the typical "value predicates").

Second, there are reports of the speaker's own attitudes. In certain obvious kinds of contexts the following sentences express value judgments as well as propositions that are psychologically true or false:

"I admire that kind of man."
"I am strongly in favor of federal aid to education."
"We fell in love with the house the moment we looked at it."
"I loathe those cigarette ads."

Third, there are exclamations which, when uttered in a certain tone of voice in a certain kind of situation, give expression to value judgments:

"Superb!" "Wonderful!" "Bravo!"
"Thank goodness that's over!"
"He didn't!"
"How could you?"

Fourth, almost all expressions of wishes and hopes contextually imply value judgments:

"May your enterprise succeed."
"If only he would stop shouting for a moment."
"I hope they won't do that again."

Finally, I shall point out in Chapter 7 a number of uses of the word "ought" which are evaluative.

These examples indicate that there is no clearly demarcated class of words or sentences which is appropriate exclusively for the expression of value judgments. Uttering a value judgment is not uttering a sentence of a special kind. Rather, it is using language in a certain way. It is not *which* words are used, but *how* they are used, which is distinctive of the expression of value judgments. Words are used to express a value judgment when we formulate to others or to ourselves a decision we have arrived at by a process of evaluation. Our utterance is then an act of expressing our settled opinion about the value of something. Only then does our use of language constitute the pronouncing of a value judgment.

B. Value judgments and imperatives

Any account of evaluative language should include consideration not only of how words are used to express value judgments, but also of the effect of evaluative language upon the hearer. Some emotivists have distinguished between the "expressive" function of language and the "quasi-imperative" or "dynamic" function of language. The expressive function of language is its capacity to evince or display the psychological state of the speaker. The dynamic function is its capacity as a stimulus to evoke a response in the hearer. As we shall see in Chapter 10, the functions of language are much more complex and multifarious than the foregoing distinction would seem to indicate. Nevertheless, there is a difference between considering language from the point of view of the speaker (or writer) and considering it from that of the hearer (or reader). Since we have been approaching value language primarily from the former point of view, let us now proceed to look at it from the latter.

Here the main issue, it seems to me, is whether the expression of value judgments has the same effect as *imperatives*. Is the purpose of value judgments to guide people's choices? Is uttering a value judgment a way of getting the hearer to do something? In order to answer these questions I shall make a comparison between value judgments on the one hand and orders, commands, and directives on the other. (I am putting aside until Part II a discussion of prescriptions, which might seem at first to be a kind of intermediary between value judgments and imperatives. I shall argue in Chapter 7 that this is not the case.)

There are three basic respects in which value judgments differ from orders, commands, and directives. (1) We can order, command, or direct someone to do something only if it is in his power to do it. If he cannot possibly do the act (or on the other hand if he cannot help but do it) there is no point in ordering, commanding, or directing him to do it. But we do make value judgments of things which people can do nothing about. (2) The very point of imperatives is to get the hearer to do something. This is not the normal purpose of uttering value judgments, although a given judgment may be uttered for this purpose in certain circumstances. (3) It is not legitimate or proper, in the context of receiving orders, commands, or directives, for the hearer to ask "Why should I do what you say?" But it is always legitimate and proper for the hearer of a value judgment to demand reasons for accepting the judgment. Asking for a justification is always out of place in the former case and never out of place in the latter case.

1. IMPERATIVES AND RECOMMENDATIONS

To utter an imperative is simply to tell someone to do something. The purpose of uttering it is to have him do what he is told, and its usual effect is that he does it. To utter a value judgment is to tell someone what the value of something is. There is no distinctive purpose for uttering the judgment, and only in special circumstances is its purpose that of having someone do something. Whether it does have such an effect depends on a number of factors. These include the hearer's respect for the evaluator and the hearer's being in a position of being able to do something about the evaluatum. Perhaps the closest parallel between imperatives and value judgments occurs in the following kind of situation. Someone is trying to decide which among several objects to choose or which among several courses of action to take. That is, he is engaged in a process of deliberation. Unable to make up his mind, he asks someone else "What shall I choose (do)?" The person asked then carries out an evaluation of the various alternatives (that is, he also engages in the process of deliberation). As a result of that evaluation, he utters a value judgment to the effect that one of the alternatives is the best one. The person who raised the question then chooses (does) that alternative.

Now this is an analysis of the situation in which one person *gives advice, offers guidance,* or *makes recommendations* to another, who then follows the advice by doing what is recommended. In this way a value judgment made by one person can directly guide another's choices and acts. We become confused when we think that this situation is the same as that in which one person gives orders, commands, or directives to another, who then obeys by doing what he is commanded to do. We are led into this confusion because it is possible to make recommendations or give advice by means of *imperatives* instead of value statements. When the person who seeks advice asks "What shall I choose (do)?" one might answer him by saying "Choose this" (or "Do this"). By uttering such imperatives, however, one is not ordering, commanding, or giving a directive. One is instead making a recommendation. Whether an imperative expresses a recommendation or a command depends entirely on the circumstances in which it is uttered.

Since not all imperatives are expressions of orders, commands, or directives, a further question arises. In what circumstances *do* they express these things? One person can issue an order, command, or directive to another only if he has authority over the other. Such a practice is understandable only in a social context of authority and subordination. A policeman can give orders to a citizen; a parent can tell a child what he must do; an army officer can command his soldiers; a business executive can issue directives to his subordinates. But we do not say that a person commands, gives orders, or issues directives to his friends, and only a very domineering host can be said to command his guests. (We say that he acts *as if* he had authority over them.) When the relations among people are governed by rules that give one of them authority over the other, the rules define the right of that person to command the others. The others are required by the rules to obey him. If this relationship does not hold among people, some of them can still use language to try to get the others to do certain acts. They can *make a request:* "Would you please close the window?" They can *make a suggestion* or *propose an action:* "Shall we close the window?" "Let's close the window. It's getting cold in here." They can *express a wish:* "I wish someone would close the window." A rather aggressive person could even use an *imperative:* "Close the window, please. It's getting cold in here." But this imperative would not express a command, order, or directive. The person who uttered it would not be in a position of authority; he would not be able to *require* that someone do as he says.

Advising and recommending are distinguished from commanding, ordering, and issuing directives by the fact that a person has a free choice to accept or reject advice, to follow or to decline to follow recommendations, but he does not have a free choice to obey or disobey a command. It makes no sense to say "I command you to do this but you are perfectly free to disobey my command." The person who is commanded must be *capable* of obeying or disobeying, since commanding a person who has no choice at all would be pointless. A person is never commanded to do something which lies beyond his power, or which he has a compulsion to do whether he is commanded to do it or not. In spite of all this, a person is not *free* to choose whether or not to obey. The command comes from an authority having the right to command, as defined by established rules, and these rules can be applied to enforce obedience. No such element of enforcement occurs in giving or receiving advice.

2. VALUE JUDGMENTS AND THE GUIDANCE OF CONDUCT

In discussing the way value judgments can function as advice or recommendations, I have considered only situations in which a person who is deliberating asks for guidance or seeks advice and receives a value judgment in reply. There are many sorts of situation in which it is a mistake to think of value judgments as guiding choice or conduct, or to think that uttering a value judgment is an act of making a recommendation. This holds true for both moral and nonmoral judgments, and for judgments according to both standards and rules. That moral judgments are not always stated for the purpose of guiding choice or conduct can be seen by considering judgments of past events and historical figures. To judge that it was wrong of President Truman to order the atomic bomb dropped on Hiroshima is not to make a recommendation to anyone, since it is about a past event. Can we say that it is an *indirect* recommendation, designed to guide the decisions of future presidents in similar circumstances? Well, it *could* have this function, even though the intention of the person making the judgment was simply to let it be known how he felt about that particular past decision. The *effect* of his utterance may or may not in fact be to guide the decisions of future presidents. Suppose, however, that all nuclear weapons were destroyed by international agreement. Would this mean that there would then be no point in making a moral judgment of President Truman's decision? On the contrary, there would be a number of purposes for uttering such a judgment—to give an example of a decision where moral factors were involved, to have people reflect about crucial decisions in human history, to enlighten people about the responsibilities of leadership, or simply to condemn war. Thus a value judgment does not become pointless when it does not serve directly to guide conduct. Let us take another example. Suppose an historian writes in a history of Western civilization that the Roman Empire at a certain period was a corrupt and degenerate society. Does it make any sense to say that the historian is giving advice or making a recommendation? It makes sense to say this only if the persons to whom the judgment is addressed have a choice about the matter. Is the historian, then, guiding his readers' choices? He might be. Although his readers are not in a position of choosing among alternative kinds of societies (unless they happen to be dictators), they are in a position of being able to exert at least some influence on the moral direction of their own society. The historian, in other words, might be a moralist with a message, offering advice to his readers. But then again he might not. His purpose in making the judgment might simply be to set forth where he stands on the matter. Or he might make the judgment in the context of a certain interpretation of history, without implying that this interpretation is to be used as a guide to the future.

That nonmoral judgments may also be made without serving as advice or recommendations can be seen from the following examples. An art critic might judge a painting to be good even though he knows that his readers or hearers will have no opportunity to see it; it may be in a private collection whose owner will not lend it to galleries or museums for public display. In no sense is the critic trying to guide anyone's choice. Professor Sidney Zink has suggested another case of a value judgment which is certainly not uttered to guide anyone's choice: "During the conversation of a party of elderly persons one of them happens to say that the best time of all was when they were young, and the others meditatively agree." (S. Zink, "Objectivism and Mr. Hare's *Language of Morals*," *Mind,* LXVI, 261; 1957, p. 82.)

Similar considerations hold for value judgments that are made by appeal to rules rather than standards. It is true that we often judge acts to be right or wrong when we are deliberating about what we (or someone else) should do. To utter the judgment that one of the acts open to a person's choice is right is to recommend that the act be done, assuming that no other act is judged to be better. And to say that one of the acts is wrong is to recommend that it not be done, assuming that some acts are not wrong. But it is not necessary that judgments of right and wrong be uttered in the context of guiding a person's conduct. There may be no head-hunters left in the world and yet it makes perfectly good sense to say "It is wrong to keep the shrunken heads of people as trophies." The objection might be raised that, granted such a judgment has no direct application in the world today (assuming that no one is a headhunter or is seriously thinking of becoming one), it neverthe-less appeals to a rule (such as a rule against taking pride in the killing of other human beings) which might well cover the con-duct of some people in the world today. In reply to this objection I would not deny that all moral *rules* have the function of guiding (more accurately, regulating) the conduct of living human beings. But this does not imply that all moral *judgments* are uttered as recommendations, since we can only recommend acts that are open to the choice of living human beings and we might judge an act to be right or wrong which is no longer open to such choice. Some day, one hopes, there will be no occasion when uttering the judg-ment "It is wrong to own slaves" will function as practical advice to a person who is deliberating about what he should do. One might still utter the judgment, however, in reflecting about the past, or in teaching moral principles, or in coming to understand the concept of human rights.

My conclusion is that value judgments, whether they are moral or nonmoral and whether they appeal to standards or to rules, are not uttered for one distinctive or primary purpose. Evaluative language has many functions in everyday use, not only from the speaker's point of view but also from the hearer's point of view.

3. VALUE JUDGMENTS AND JUSTIFICATION

I shall now consider, as a way of introducing the problem to be discussed in the next four chapters, the third point of difference between value judgments and commands. When a person is in the position of receiving a command he cannot rightly demand a justification for his obeying it, whereas one can always rightly demand a justification for a value judgment. It is not legitimate or proper for a soldier, when ordered to stand at attention, to ask "Why?" Nor is it legitimate or proper for him *in that situation* to ask why he should be required to obey anyone else's orders. When he joined the army he committed himself to following certain rules, among which are those giving officers the authority to command him to do certain things. As an active member of an army it is out of place for him to question those rules or to question any particular command given under those rules. As an individual reflecting about the army, however, or as a person deliberating whether or not to join, it is legitimate and proper for him to raise this sort of question. He is then demanding that a certain social institution governed by a whole system of rules be justified. He is, as it were, outside the practice of army life, not engaged in it. This difference need not be temporal. It is a difference of social role, and one who is employed as a soldier can play both roles. But he cannot play both roles *as* soldier. As a soldier he is subject to the rules which define the practice in which he is engaged. As a thinking man he may demand reasons for there being such rules, even though at the time of his thinking he is (employed as) a soldier. The same considerations apply to anyone engaged in a social practice. The employee of a company may not properly demand justification for a policy laid down by the management, in so far as he is functioning as an employee (i.e., doing his job according to the company's rules and regulations). But as an individual human being he can properly demand this, and he can properly demand it as a member of *another* organization, such as a labor union. As a member of a union he can be critical of the rules of the company. But then he cannot, in that role, be critical of the rules of the union. It is only outside a practice that we can criticize the rules by which it is defined. This is part of the logic of having a social role (i.e., of engaging in a social practice). To be engaged in a practice *means* to be in a position where one's behavior is governed by the rules which define the practice. If the rules do not govern one's behavior then *by definition* one is outside the practice. (A more detailed analysis of a social practice and its defining rules will be given in the next chapter.)

In circumstances of receiving advice or recommendations, on the other hand, it is always proper and legitimate for the person being advised to demand reasons for following the advice. By demanding them he is not removing himself from his role as an advisee; it is part of his role to be able to make this demand. (In this respect the role of being an advisee is like that of the student in a college classroom. It is legitimate and proper for the student to ask his teacher to give reasons in support of his statements.) What the advisee, as an advisee, cannot challenge is the rules governing the practice of giving and receiving advice. If he does this, he is by that fact no longer engaged in the practice and hence no longer an advisee.

The right to demand of the adviser a justification for any piece of advice is one of the rules defining the conditions of advice (i.e., defining the social practice of giving and receiving advice.) If the advisee were not granted this right, it would not be the case that he was being advised, but rather that he was being coerced, goaded, persuaded, exhorted, or commanded (ordered, directed). To be advised is to be guided, not goaded. (This distinction will be explored at greater length in Chapter 7.) In short, all advice must be rational, in the sense that it is never out of place for the advisee to demand that reasons be given to justify it. There is something radically wrong with the following two conversations:

    (1) "I recommend that you do X."
        "Why?"
        "Oh I don't know. I have no particular reasons."
    (2) "I recommend that you do X."
        "Why?"
        "Don't be impertinent. Just do as I say."

Clearly a person is not making a recommendation if he tells someone to do something out of mere whim or caprice, or if he tells someone that he must do something just because he is told to do it. To make recommendations is to engage in a rational practice, that is, it presupposes the justifiability of what is being recommended. It should be made clear, however, that this condition does not require either that the adviser actually give reasons whenever he gives advice, or that he be able to give *good* reasons for his advice. It requires only that he recognize the right of the advisee to ask for reasons, and that he be able and willing to reply to the demand. He might not be able to *satisfy* the demand, since the advisee might not consider the reasons which he offers good reasons. Should the advisee not make the demand, the adviser is not under obligation to supply reasons along with his advice. But he must always *have* reasons and must always be able to supply them on demand.

When a recommendation is made by means of expressing a value judgment, the presupposition is that the judge can justify his judgment (at least in his own mind). Indeed, in *any* situation in which a value judgment is uttered, it is always legitimate and proper for the hearer to ask "Why should I accept your judgment?" This does not mean that the judge will be able to give a satisfactory answer, but he must acknowledge the legitimacy of the question. Whether it is done as part of the practice of giving advice or not, uttering a value judgment is always a rational act. It presupposes its own justifiability. The reason for this is that a value judgment contextually implies a reasoning process in which something has been evaluated. To judge the value of something is not merely to have a pro-attitude or con-attitude toward it, nor is it merely a method of getting others to do something. It is an assertion, a claim that something is the case (namely, that an object has a certain value or disvalue). Such an assertion is the outcome of a process of evaluation and may always be challenged. A person who pronounces judgment upon something must have reasons for saying what he does. His position as a judge or evaluator is such that he must try to justify his statement whenever that is demanded. Supposing that he could successfully justify his statement, what would the justification consist in? This is an extremely difficult and complex question. It will be my central concern for the next four chapters.

The justification of value judgments: verification and validation

3

A. What does it mean to justify a judgment?

Up to this point I have tried to make clear what it is to carry out an evaluation of something and what it is to make a judgment of the value of something. I wish now to consider the way we reason for or against value judgments when the reasons which we give are good (legitimate, sound, warranted, valid, intellectually acceptable) reasons.

It is important at the outset to distinguish between justifying a value judgment and justifying our uttering a value judgment. We justify a particular value judgment when we give good reasons for a person's grading or ranking an object in a certain way. But such reasons are not necessarily good reasons for uttering that particular judgment in a given set of circumstances. It might at first be thought that if a value judgment has been justified, then it is always justifiable to utter it. That this is not the case has been argued by Professor Eric Gilman. He states that it is sometimes (morally) unjustifiable to utter a true value judgment and sometimes (morally) justifiable to utter a false value judgment. In support of this he cites the following cases:

> It may be true that one's neighbour is acting immorally, but wrong to publish the fact to the whole neighbourhood. It may be necessary to calm a hysterical delinquent by assuring him for a time, that he has done nothing wrong. One may have performed a noble action but it be wrong to remind oneself of the fact. In other words, the question of whether one ought to express an opinion is different from the question of whether that which one might express is true or false. . . . Distinctions of the kind suggested here are often made in ordinary discourse. For example, it is often maintained that one ought not to express an opinion about the conduct of other people. This is not only because it is so difficult to know enough about other people to form a correct opinion. What is maintained is that we have no right to express such opinions, even when they are correct. (E. Gilman, "The Distinctive Purpose of Moral Judgments," *Mind*, LXI, 243, 1952, pp. 311-312.)

If such cases do show that in some circumstances it is wrong to utter a justified value judgment and right to utter an unjustified one, then the question of whether a given judgment is justified is independent of the question of whether the act of pronouncing it (either to others or to oneself) is justified.

The argument becomes even stronger when we consider pragmatic rather than moral justification of linguistic acts. There are many ways in which expressing unjustified value judgments can be an effective means to an individual's or group's ends (and so be pragmatically justified). An unscrupulous art dealer might succeed in selling a painting which he knows to be a fake by praising it highly in the presence of a customer. A candidate for political office might further his ends by unjustifiably defaming his opponent. The government of a country might find it useful to make exaggerated and unwarranted claims about injustices in another country. On the other hand, pronouncing a true value judgment might well work against a person's ends. A selfish man would certainly frustrate his own desires by expressing publicly an honest evaluation of his character.

In order to justify a value judgment, then, it is not sufficient to justify the act of uttering it. We tend to overlook this when we think that we can justify the judgment that it is wrong to steal, for example, by showing that it furthers the ends of morality to say to a child in a certain tone of voice "It is wrong to steal." But from the cases already cited it is clear that the moral goodness or rightness of an act of pronouncing a judgment has nothing to do with whether there are good reasons for accepting the judgment.

When I speak of justifying value judgments, how is the word "justify" being used? It is correct to say that we do not justify propositions but verify them, and that we do not verify decisions, acts, or dispositions, but justify them. We verify (or confirm) a proposition by showing that it is true, that is, by giving the evidence for it, or by offering reasons in support of it, or by proving it, or by specifying the grounds on which it rests and showing that they are good grounds. We justify a decision, an act, or a disposition by giving reasons for *making* the decision, for *doing* the act, or for *having* the disposition. Or else, if there are good reasons both for and against it, we justify making the decision, doing the act, or having the disposition by showing that the reasons for it outweigh the reasons against it. Thus we speak of justifying (not verifying) one's decision to join the army, to buy a new car, or to follow someone's advice. We say that a person is justified in doing a certain act. ("He is justified in firing that employee.") And we speak of a person's attitudes as being justified. ("He is justified in disapproving of that new law.")

Confusion occurs because we talk (idiomatically) about *assertions* and *beliefs* as being verified as well as being justified. We say "His assertion that there is life on Mars can be verified" or "His belief that there is life on Mars can be verified." But we also say "He is justified in making the assertion that there is life on Mars" or "He is justified in believing that there is life on Mars." Since making an assertion is an act (of uttering a declarative sentence under certain conditions) and since believing is a mental disposition, it is legitimate to use the word "justify" in this way. When we speak of verifying an assertion or belief, however, we are not referring to the *act* of asserting or the *disposition* of believing. We are instead referring to *what* is asserted or believed. We are saying that what is asserted or believed can be shown to be true. What we assert is a proposition (namely that something is or is not so), and the same proposition can be asserted in many different ways (i.e., by means of many different sentences). The proposition is what is true or false, not the act of asserting it. Similarly it is a proposition that is believed, and to believe it may or may not be justified.

There is no logical connection between the verification of a proposition and the justification of an assertion or belief. "That p is true" does not entail, and is not entailed by, "It is justified to assert that p" or "It is justified to believe that p." Let us first consider cases of asserting that p.

A person is justified in asserting that p only when there are good reasons for him to utter the sentence "p" (or some equivalent sentence). These reasons may be good reasons from the moral point of view, from the point of view of prudence, from the point of view of etiquette, or from the logical or intellectual point of view. That is to say, the person's asserting that p may be justified in any one of these ways, even when p is false. Similarly, a person may not be justified in any of these ways in asserting that p, even when p is true.

Examples may be found, taking each of these points of view. Someone who has promised to keep a secret is not morally justified in making the secret known, even if what he makes known is true. On the other hand, a doctor may be morally justified in making false assertions to a patient whose chances for recovery would be greatly diminished if he were told the truth about his condition. From the point of view of prudence, it may be to a man's self-interest to assert what he knows to be false (as in lying to someone about his accomplishments) and it may go against his self-interest to tell the truth. From the point of view of etiquette, it may be impolite to make a true remark in front of someone, and sometimes etiquette demands that we assert what is false (e.g., saying that we enjoyed ourselves at a party when in fact we did not). There is nothing puzzling about these cases. But how is it possible from the *logical* point of view to be justified in saying what is false and not justified in saying what is true? The answer becomes clear when we realize that a person may assert what is false because he has been misled by the evidence, and that a person may assert what is true as a result of a lucky guess. A jury, for example, is logically (as well as morally) justified in giving a verdict of "not guilty" when there is insufficient evidence for the guilt of the accused or when the circumstantial evidence points to his innocence, even if he did in fact commit the crime. And a fortune teller who used tea leaves to make predictions is not logically justified in telling a woman that she will marry a dark, handsome man, even if this turns out to be the case.

Turning from asserting that p to believing that p, I shall only consider cases of being justified or unjustified from the logical point of view. Here again we have two possibilities: a person may not be logically justified in believing what is true, and may be logically justified in believing what is false. A person is not logically justified in believing a true proposition when he is not in a position to *know* that it is true, that is, to have good reasons for believing it to be true. A man who believes that a certain horse will win a race is not justified in believing it if his belief is based on a hunch, or on the fact that the first letter of the horse's name is the same as the first letter of his own name. His belief might well be true; the horse might in fact win the race. But he is justified in believing this only if he has *good* reasons to think it will win, such as reliable knowledge that the race has been fixed. Circumstances in which a person is justified in believing a false proposition are more unusual, but they do occur. A child who has always been told by his parents in a serious tone of voice that there is a Santa Claus is justified in believing that there is a Santa Claus (assuming his parents generally tell him the truth when they speak in a serious tone of voice).

Let us now turn to the use of the word "justify" in reference to value judgments. I have said that there are three kinds of things which we can justify: decisions, acts, and dispositions. (I have just been considering one sort of act, that of making an assertion, and one sort of disposition, that of belief.) A value judgment may be thought of either as a decision or as a disposition. As a decision it is a mental act. (It differs, of course, from behavioral or public acts.) Since it is a mental act of grading or ranking something as a result of a process of evaluation, it is not to be identified with the act of pronouncing or expressing a judgment. We have just seen that it may be justified when the act of uttering it is not justified, and vice versa. But what does it mean to say that a value judgment itself is justified? To say that the judgment ascribing a certain value V to something X is justified, is to say that either the *decision* or the *disposition* to make such a judgment is justified. It is to claim that

the evaluator or judge has good reasons for *deciding* that X has V
or for *believing* that X has V; or that, if he has good reasons for
and also good reasons against such a decision or disposition, the
reasons for outweigh the reasons against.

Can value judgments be said to be true or false as well as justified or unjustified? It might be thought that there is the same relation between a value judgment and its content as there is between
a belief and a proposition. Indeed, I have just used the phrase "believing that X has V" to refer to a value judgment as a disposition.
Why not draw a parallel here and speak of a judgment (a decision
or belief-disposition) as being justified or unjustified, and the content of a judgment (*what* is decided or believed) as being true or
false, verified or falsified? We are tempted to speak in this way for
two reasons. One is the fact that value judgments are expressible in
declarative sentences. The other is the fact that "true" and "false" are
often used in ordinary language simply as words of assent and
dissent. I shall consider each of these reasons in turn.

When we apply the words "true" and "false" to nonvalue assertions, meaning thereby that what is being asserted is or is not intellectually acceptable, we contextually imply a method of verifying
or falsifying the assertions. (Other meanings of the words "true"
and "false" will be considered shortly.) When we ask "Is what he
said true?" we expect that anyone who answers definitely in the
affirmative or negative can show that what he said is or is not true
(or at least can point to someone who can show this). Otherwise we
do not think one is justified in giving a definite answer to our question. Now it is perfectly idiomatic to use the same phrasing about
the utterance of a value judgment in a declarative sentence. When a
person says "Object X has value V" we can ask whether what he
says is true. What we mean by our question is, "Does the object X
really have value V, as he says?" And this appears contextually to
imply that anyone who answers our question definitely one way or
the other can verify or falsify the statement, that is, can show that
X does have V or does not have V (or can point to someone who
can show this). In both cases we appear to be concerned with a
correspondence between what a person says (asserts, claims) to be
the case and what is the case. If there is a correspondence then
what he says is true; if not, then it is false. The conclusion drawn

from this parallel is that value judgments are factual or assertive. As a result, the only difference between value and nonvalue assertions will lie in the *procedures* of verification and falsification. We do not verify or falsify the two sorts of assertion in the same way. But this, it is said, is not a difference in their logical grammar. In both cases words are being used to make an assertion that something is or is not so; in one case we are asserting that an object has value or disvalue, in the other we are asserting something else about an object. In both cases, the argument runs, we can distinguish what is being asserted (the proposition) from the act of asserting it or from the disposition to assert it. We distinguish between the content of a value judgment and the act of judging or the disposition to judge. This, it is claimed, is correlative with the distinction in nonevaluative assertions between what is believed and believing it. In short, the conclusion is drawn that the content of a value judgment can be verified or falsified just as a nonvaluative proposition can be verified or falsified.

What is wrong with this argument? There is no fallacy in it; it is rather a matter of a mistaken emphasis that can be seriously misleading. These similarities between evaluative and nonevaluative assertions tend to make us overlook the differences between them. Once we begin to think of value judgments as a special kind of factual assertion, certain questions seem inevitably to arise. What property is attributed to an object or act when it is judged to be good or right? How can this property be known? Granted that it is not perceivable, can it be inferred from sense perceptions? What is it in the real world to which a value judgment must correspond in order to be true? Is there a realm of values as well as a realm of facts? When philosophers discuss value judgments in this way, they become entangled in the fruitless disputes carried on by intuitionists, naturalists, and nonnaturalists. Their mistake is to have overlooked certain crucial differences between value judgments and nonevaluative assertions. These differences are precisely those which make it misleading to speak of a value judgment as "true" or "false" and consequently as "verified" or "falsified." We shall see that *one* step in the justification of a value judgment is empirical verification. But because there are other essential steps, it is in the interest of clarity to speak of value judgments as justified or unjustified rather than as true or false.

The second reason why philosophers have thought it proper to apply the terms "true" and "false" to value judgments is that these are the words we use for expressing assent and dissent. Under assent I include all of the following uses of the word "true." (They were originally distinguished by Professor P. F. Strawson in "Truth," *Analysis*, X, 1949, and in "Truth," *Proceedings of the Aristotelian Society*, Supplementary Volume XXIV, 1950. Professor Morris Weitz has summarized them in "Oxford Philosophy," *Philosophical Review*, LXII, 1953.) 1. The confirmatory use: *A* utters a value judgment and *B* says "That's true," confirming *A*'s statement by adding the weight of his own opinion. 2. The admissive use: *A* utters a value judgment in a context in which *B*'s statement "That's true" means "I admit it." Such a context would occur when *A* and *B* were disputing a point and *A* gave a convincing argument to *B*. 3. The concessive use: *A* utters a value judgment and *B* replies "That's true, but . . ." meaning "I concede what you say, but there are other things to be taken into account." 4. The agreeing use: *A* utters a value judgment, and *B* says "That's true," thereby indicating to *A* that he shares *A*'s judgment. 5. The novelty use: *A* utters a value judgment which is surprising or new to *B*. *B* says "That's *true*," registering the fact that he had not thought of this before and that he agrees with *A*.

None of these instances of *B*'s statement, "That's true," is an assertion that there is a correspondence between *A*'s value judgment and an actual state of affairs in the world. What has led some philosophers to think that value judgments are true, and that consequently it makes good sense to talk about verifying them, is that we do use the word "true" in all these ways in reference to someone's uttering a value judgment. But in so using the word "true," we are merely expressing our assent. We are saying in different ways that we are in agreement with the value judgment that has been expressed. If the word "false" were used in similar contexts, we would be expressing our dissent or disagreement with what was being said. The words "true" and "false" are not being used here to claim that an assertion is verified or falsified, not even that it *could* be verified or falsified, and still less that the method by which the assertion is to be verified is an empirical method.

What may be called the verification use of the word "true" has, as its criterion of application to any statement, the *intellectual or rational acceptability* of what is stated. And it is just in this sense that it is less confusing to speak of value judgments as being justified or unjustified than as being true or false. For there is a basic difference between what makes a value judgment intellectually or rationally acceptable and what makes an empirical assertion intellectually or rationally acceptable. The latter is intellectually acceptable (or true) if it can be empirically verified. The former is intellectually acceptable if there are good reasons for judging something to have a certain value. These good reasons do not consist in empirical evidence alone. A person can justify his decision or disposition to judge that something has a certain value only by a complex process of reasoning fundamentally different from empirical verification. If in establishing a value judgment as intellectually acceptable, we keep in mind how different this is from establishing the intellectual acceptability of nonevaluative assertions, then whether we call the value judgment "true" (in the verification use of the word, not merely in its assent use) is purely a verbal matter.

B. The process of verification

I come now to the central problem of this and the following three chapters. What sorts of reasons are good reasons in justifying value judgments? My purpose is to bring out the over-all logical structure of the justification of value judgments. Since I am here dealing with all types of judgments (moral, aesthetic, political, religious, matters of etiquette, and so on) and since I include both judgments according to standards and judgments according to rules, my discussion is bound to appear in some respects superficial. However, one specific point I wish to defend is that there are certain ways of reasoning which constitute a unified pattern of thought for justifying *all* value judgments. I am not interested in the particular points of difference that can be shown between, say, justifying moral judgments and justifying the judgments of art criticism. I shall indicate later what I think is the *locus* of such points of difference, but this will only be done in order to throw light on the principles common to all justifications of value judgments.

I distinguish four general phases in the over-all process of justifying value judgments: verification, validation, vindication, and rational choice. We *verify* value judgments by appeal either to standards or to rules which we have adopted. We *validate* standards or rules (i.e., we justify our adopting certain standards or rules) by appeal to higher standards or rules. The adoption of standards or rules which themselves cannot be validated by appeal to any higher standards or rules results from our decision to accept a whole value system. We *vindicate* our accepting a whole value system by appeal to the way of life to which we are committed. Our commitment to a way of life can be justified in terms of a *rational choice* among different ways of life. It is because the three essential steps of validation, vindication, and rational choice must follow the first step of verification that I have not been willing to use the term "verification" to cover the entire process of justifying a value judgment. To use the term "verification" for the first step, however, will not lead to difficulties if my foregoing remarks about verifying and justifying are kept in mind.

I adopt the terms "verification" and "validation" from Professor Kurt Baier's, *The Moral Point of View.* In Chapter 2 of that book, Professor Baier argues convincingly that, once we have adopted certain standards, our value judgments can be verified empirically. The statement that something fulfills or fails to fulfill a clearly defined standard is an empirical statement. The same thing is true of value judgments according to rules, since the statement that an act is in accordance with or violates a clearly defined rule (as distinct from the statement of the rule itself) is an empirical statement.

For both types of value judgment *the process of verification is identical with the process of evaluation* which I have described in Chapter 1. The only difference between verifying a value judgment and carrying out an evaluation in order to arrive at a value judgment lies in the circumstances in which the process takes place. The process itself remains the same. We speak of verifying a value judgment when someone has already arrived at a judgment and is asked to give reasons for it, or when the person himself becomes doubtful of his own judgment and wants to see whether, on reflection, he is right in holding it. We speak of evaluating something when we are trying to come to a decision about its value, that is, when we are trying to arrive at a justified value judgment. In the first case we are trying to decide whether it is reasonable to accept what someone has offered as a correct opinion; in the second we are trying to form an opinion which it would be reasonable to offer as correct. In both cases we are trying to determine the correct opinion on a given matter (the value or disvalue of something). The process by which a judgment is verified is identical with the process of evaluation leading to that judgment because both are procedures of *reasoning* concerning the same judgment. To verify the judgment is to go through a procedure of reasoning which, if the judgment were not yet decided upon, would lead anyone validly to the judgment as its conclusion. To evaluate is to go through the same procedure for the purpose of arriving at a judgment which has not yet been decided upon.

The relation between the processes of evaluation and verification is like the relation between a student's proving a theorem and a teacher's correcting his proof. Professor Bernard Mayo's analysis of this situation is particularly instructive:

Let us suppose that the candidate is asked to prove a certain theorem of which he has not yet been given the proof, but he knows enough to work out the proof. Now it might be supposed that the reasoning is done by the candidate, who does the actual thinking out and writing down of the theorem; what the examiner does is merely to check the reasoning. But this would be a mistake. Reasoning is not the same thing as thinking or writing: it is the application of certain universal standards to the thinking and the writing: in this case, the principles of valid deduction. Obviously this is what the examiner does: he asks whether this proposition follows from that, whether there is a contradiction or inconsistency somewhere, whether what is claimed as a proof really is a proof. But this is not just what the examiner does. It is what the candidate does too. . . . The examiner judges someone else's performance; the candidate judges his own; and that is the only difference there is. That is why it would make sense for the examiner to say 'The right answer is the one which I should have given if I were doing the paper', and for the candidate to say 'The right answer is the one I should mark correct if I were examining the paper' and similarly for the wrong answer. (B. Mayo, *op. cit.*, p. 61.)

The relation between the evaluator and the verifier of a value judgment is parallel to this relation between candidate and examiner. The evaluator's purpose is to come to a conclusion about the value of something which can stand up under critical scrutiny. He is trying to arrive at a justifiable judgment. The verifier's purpose is to decide whether the judgment of the evaluator is justified. Both must appeal to the same rules of reasoning. These rules are the ordinary rules governing empirical verification.

When we verify a value judgment the process of reasoning is that outlined in Chapter 1. It consists in finding out whether the evaluatum does fulfill or fail to fulfill the *given* standards of evaluation to the degree stated in the judgment. Or, if the evaluation is according to rules, it consists in finding out whether the act, choice, or decision being evaluated is in fact required by, permitted by, or forbidden by the *given* rule. In the former case one must determine by empirical tests the good-making and bad-making characteristics of the evaluatum (and, in the case of a ranking, the good-making and bad-making characteristics of the other members of the class of comparison). Then one must grade the evaluatum according to the given standards (or one must rank the members of the class of comparison and decide where the evaluatum falls in the resulting order of preference). In the case of evaluations according to rules one must determine by empirical tests whether the evaluatum does come under the rule, and if it does, whether it complies with or violates the rule.

It is important to realize that, since no question is being raised here about the appropriateness of judging the evaluatum by the given standards or rules, the *verifier's* pro-attitudes and con-attitudes need not be involved in the process of verification. Here is one point at which verification differs from evaluation. (This difference, be it noted, is not a difference in the rules of reasoning, which are still common to both processes.) Since the verifier *must* accept the given standards or rules in order to carry out his verification and since he is not concerned with the validation of such standards or rules, his own attitudes are irrelevant. But the evaluator has *chosen* to apply those particular standards or rules whose fulfillment is something he approves of, likes, or favors and whose nonfulfillment is something he disapproves of, dislikes, or disfavors. Whether his pro-attitudes and con-attitudes are justified depends on whether the standards or rules are appropriate, that is, on whether they can be validated. But this is of no interest to the verifier.

C. The process of validation

If the foregoing were a complete account of the justification of value judgments, one could say that all value judgments are empirically verifiable and hence true or false in the same sense as non-evaluative assertions. But it is clear that we have not succeeded in justifying a value judgment merely by showing that the evaluatum does or does not fulfill certain standards or rules. Another question immediately arises. Are those standards or rules appropriate ones for judging an evaluatum of that sort? We must not only justify the claim that, given the standards or rules, the evaluatum has a certain value. We must also justify the application of those standards or rules in the given circumstances. This is where validation comes in. As Professor Baier puts it:

We have seen that value judgments can be verified just like factual claims, but that in value judgments we make claims that give rise to a further question, namely, whether the criteria employed are the right ones. Factual judgments are decisively confirmed if they are empirically verified. Value judgments, on the other hand, must be not only verified but also validated. It is not enough to show that, *if* certain criteria *are* employed, then a thing must be said to have a certain degree of 'goodness'; we must also show that these criteria *ought* to be employed. . . . A remark ceases to be a value judgment and turns into a factual claim as soon as the question of *the appropriateness of the criteria* is rejected as unnecessary or irrelevant. (K. Baier, *op. cit.,* pp. 75-76.)

What does the process of validation consist in? By way of a preface, let us notice that the standard or rule which is being validated is universal; it must apply to a given class of things. We cannot say that an object X is good according to a standard S unless all objects which are similar to X in the relevant respects are good. (The relevant respects are those features of an object in virtue of which it fulfills S, in other words, its good-making characteristics.) Similarly we cannot say that doing an act A in circumstances C is right according to a rule R unless all acts of type A done in circumstances C are right. The class of all objects which are good (or bad) according to a standard S defines the *scope* or *range of application* of S. The class of all acts which are right (or wrong) according to a rule R likewise defines the *scope* or *range of application* of R. In accordance with what was said in Chapter 1, the scope or range of application of R is the class of all acts "falling under" or "covered by" R.

1. THE DEMAND FOR VALIDATION

In order to understand the various ways in which validation can be carried out, let us first see how the demand for validation arises. I shall consider in turn the validation of a standard and the validation of a rule. Suppose someone claims that a painting he is looking at is a good painting because (among other things) its colors are harmonious. The following dialogue represents schematically how the demand for validation of a standard may arise:

A: This is a good painting.

B: Why?

A: Because, for one thing, its colors are harmonious.

B: Why does that make the painting a good one?

A: Because having harmonious colors is a good reason for judging this to be a good painting.

B: Why is it a good reason for judging this to be a good painting?

A: Because having harmonious colors is a good reason for judging paintings of kind K to be good, and this painting is of kind K.

B: I admit that this painting is of kind K and that its colors are harmonious, but why is having harmonious colors a good reason for judging paintings of kind K to be good?

B's last question may be stated in another way—why is having harmonious colors a valid or appropriate standard for judging paintings of kind K? To answer this question satisfactorily, A must show not only that he, but that anyone (and therefore B), is justified in adopting the given standard for judging paintings of kind K. That is, he must give good reasons why paintings of kind K are correctly included in the range of application of the standard.

This goes beyond the verification of A's value judgment "This is a good painting." The demand for verification only requires A to show that this painting fulfills the standard of having harmonious colors. When we verify (or falsify) the value judgment, we *assume* that the standard of having harmonious colors correctly applies to the *K* class of paintings. This assumption is precisely what is in question when we demand a complete justification of A's value judgment. In order to justify the judgment completely it is necessary to justify this assumption. And this requires that we validate the standard.

It should be noted that the same argument holds for those aestheticians and art critics who claim that each work of art is unique and can be judged only in terms of standards peculiar to it. If the appropriateness of these standards is challenged, the evaluator must give reasons to justify his appealing to them rather than to other standards (unless he is willing to say that his appeal to them is purely a matter of personal taste which he cannot defend as objectively valid). To say that a certain standard is peculiar to one object is to say that it is not appropriate or valid to use that standard when judging any other object. The class of things to which the standard validly applies is a "unit class" (a class having only one member). Now the claim that a given standard applies uniquely to one object is still a claim that must be justified. How can that be done? I submit that there are only two possible methods a person can use, if he is to be fully rational in justifying his claim. He can appeal to a higher standard (or rule) in terms of which he can *validate* the standard in question as applicable to only one object. Or (the more likely method in this situation) he can *vindicate* his use of the standard in terms of his whole way of life. In the latter case he must show that the adoption of the given standard is part of a way of life in which works of art are appreciated in a certain way. The standard would then be shown to be an outward expression of personal aesthetic taste, that is, it would be shown to be the standard a person *would* apply to a work of art, and to that work of art alone, if he had a certain aesthetic taste. A *full* justification of the standard would require, as we shall see, that the whole way of life which includes that aesthetic taste be shown to be a *rational* way of life.

I should like to add, however, that I do not think the claim that *all* aesthetic standards apply uniquely to single works of art can finally be defended. Surely there are standards that apply, say, to (the class of) representational paintings but do not apply to (the

class of) nonobjective or abstractionist paintings. One such standard could be that we see nature in a new light, or learn to look at
things in a new way, once we come to understand fully how the
artist himself has "represented" nature in his painting. In the case
of pure abstractions, this standard would not be appropriate. But
there are standards that do not apply to such broad classes of
comparison as all representational paintings or all abstractionist
paintings. There are standards that may apply only to representational paintings of a certain period. Thus we may apply a certain
standard only to works of the High Renaissance; for example, the degree to which the artist presents to us an idealistic vision of human
dignity or nobility within a Christian framework. There are standards
that may apply only to the works of one artist—for example, how
developed are the "painterly" qualities of Titian's works, or how
free from sentimentality are the "mystical" aspects of Tintoretto's
works. That is to say, we might make our class of comparison *only*
the works of Titian or *only* the works of Tintoretto and apply standards that we claim to be appropriate to one of these classes of
comparison and not to the other. (Standards of freedom from
sentimentality might themselves differ when we judge Tintorettos
and when we judge, say, Renoirs.) Furthermore, if an artist has
painted different versions of one subject matter (e.g., the Annun-
ciation) we might use standards in judging these paintings that
apply validly only to the particular subject matter in question. In
such arts as music, drama, and the dance, we can narrow the range
of application of a standard still further, without yet reaching a
"unit class" of application. We might use standards which we hold
to be appropriate for judging the various performances of one work.
We might apply certain standards to, say, Handel's oratorio, "The
Messiah," and then judge all the known performances of that work
by appeal to those standards. Finally we *may* use certain standards
as applicable to a single performance of one work (or to a single
painting, sculpture, poem, or building). In this last case alone would
a standard be considered uniquely applicable to a particular object.
Whether there are such standards is a question requiring detailed
investigation in aesthetics and so beyond the scope of my present
discussion. I only maintain here that not *all* aesthetic standards are
of this sort.

The demand for validation of a *rule* may be represented as follows:

A: This act is wrong.

B: Why?

A: Because it violates rule *R*.

B: Why is the fact that it violates rule *R* a reason for condemning it?

A: Because rule *R* forbids any act of kind *K*, and this act is of kind *K*.

B: I admit that rule *R* forbids acts of kind *K*, that this act is of kind *K*, and therefore that rule *R* forbids this act. But why is that a reason for condemning the act?

A: Because rule *R* is a valid or appropriate rule for judging acts of kind *K*. (Or: Because acts of kind *K* are correctly included in the range of application of rule *R*.)

B: Why?

This last question demands that *A* validate rule *R*. *A* is asked to give good reasons for anyone's adopting *R* as a rule covering acts of kind *K*. If the rule is validated, then it is shown to be a reason for *condemning* acts of kind *K*, which violate it. Similarly it is shown to be a reason for praising (admiring, liking, or having any other pro-attitude toward) acts of a kind which are covered by the rule and which fulfill it. (There is a parallel in the case of standards. Validating a standard is justifying anyone's adopting it as a basis for evaluating objects of a certain kind. Hence the standard becomes a basis for taking a pro-attitude or con-attitude toward a given object of that kind.)

As in the case of standards, giving a complete justification of a value judgment made according to a rule must go beyond the verification of it. In order to verify it one must *assume* that the rule correctly includes the class of comparison in its range of application. One can then verify the judgment by seeing whether the act in question (the evaluatum) complies with or violates the rule. In order to justify the judgment completely, however, one must justify making this assumption; one must *validate* the rule.

2. THE THREE STEPS OF VALIDATION

How is a standard or rule to be validated? Its complete validation requires three logical steps. 1. We must show (by methods to be discussed below) that the standard or rule is *relevant*. That is, its scope or range of application must include the class of comparison of the given value judgment. As a consequence of this first step, the evaluatum is shown to belong to a *class* of things which are correctly judged by the standard or rule. 2. We must show that neither the circumstances in which the evaluatum occurs nor anything out of the ordinary about the evaluatum (i.e., anything which distinguishes the evaluatum from the other members of the class of comparison) permits us to make an *exception* to the general application of the standard or rule determined in step 1. As a consequence of this second step, the evaluatum itself, not merely a class of things to which it belongs, is shown to be correctly judged by the standard or rule. 3. We must show either (a) that no other valid standard or rule conflicts with the one being applied, or (b) that, if there is a conflict, the one being applied takes precedence over all those in conflict with it.

If we fail in any of these three tasks, our validation of the standard or rule is not complete. When we successfully accomplish step 1 there is a certain presumption that the standard or rule is valid for judging the evaluatum. When we successfully accomplish step 2 there is a greater presumption that the standard or rule is valid. But we have conclusive reasons for believing that the standard or rule is valid only when we have completed all three tasks. Only then do we *know* that the standard or rule is valid.

If someone should ask on what grounds such a claim to knowledge can be made, my answer would be that no other way of reasoning could yield better reasons for accepting a standard or rule as valid. I am merely trying to explicate the pattern of reasoning which would yield the *best* results for justifying a value judgment, taking into consideration only the nature of evaluation and the *point* of demanding such a justification in everyday life. I am not trying to set up a special method which will lend support to a particular theory of value (such as intuitionism or naturalism), nor am I selecting a method which will make a certain predetermined set of value judgments turn out to be true. *Whatever* value judgments are considered to be true by *anyone* (in any culture or in any period of history), good reasons for accepting the standards or rules on which they are based must be put forward. What better reasons could there be for accepting a standard or rule than the successful accomplishment of the three steps of validation I have outlined? If someone is not satisfied that such reasons would logically be the best reasons, he must show that an alternative method would constitute a better way of validating a standard or rule. I submit that this cannot be done, if I am right in my foregoing analysis of evaluation and value judgments. (For further consideration of this question, see Chapter 4, Section B.)

I have not yet made clear, however, in what way the three steps of validation can be carried out, and this must be done before the reasonableness of the entire process of validation can be fully demonstrated. By what methods can the three tasks listed above be accomplished? There are three possible methods. The first and second are alternative methods for carrying out step 1, and the third must be used for carrying out steps 2 and 3. Let us designate the standard to be validated as S and the rule to be validated as R. The three methods may then be summarized as follows:

Method I: Appeal to standards or rules which are more general than S or R and from which S or R can be deduced.

Method II: Appeal to standards for judging the consequences of fulfilling or of not fulfilling S or R.

Method III: Appeal to standards or rules for deciding whether it is better to make an exception to S or R than to follow S or R, and for deciding the relative precedence of any standards or rules which are in conflict with S or R.

I shall now consider how the first two methods can be used to accomplish the task of step 1 and how the third method can be used to accomplish the tasks of steps 2 and 3.

STEP 1. One way to show that S is relevant—that it is correct to include a given class of comparison and hence a particular evaluatum in the range of application of S—is to appeal to a more general standard S' from which S can be deduced. (The relevance of S' would itself have eventually to be validated by Methods I or II.) When do we say that one standard can be deduced from a second? The statement that an object fulfills the second standard in certain circumstances must logically entail the statement that that object fulfills the first standard in those circumstances (though not necessarily in *all* circumstances). An example or two will clarify this.

Consider the relation between the standard of benevolence and the standard of liberality in giving to charity. A person fulfills the standard of benevolence when, in certain circumstances, he is liberal in giving to charity. But he also fulfills the standard of benevolence when, in other circumstances, he helps a person in distress (as in an automobile accident), and when, in a third set of circumstances, he joins a movement for racial equality, and when, in a fourth set of circumstances, he goes out of his way to speak up in behalf of a man being unjustly defamed. This may be put in the form of a simple diagram:

$$
\begin{matrix}
\text{Fulfilling} \\
\text{standard } S' \\
\text{(being benevolent)}
\end{matrix}
\left\{
\begin{matrix}
\text{In } C_1, \text{ fulfilling standard } S_1 \text{ (being liberal)} \\
\text{In } C_2, \text{ fulfilling standard } S_2 \text{ (being helpful)} \\
\text{In } C_3, \text{ fulfilling standard } S_3 \text{ (participating in po-} \\
\text{litical action)} \\
\text{In } C_4, \text{ fulfilling standard } S_4 \text{ (protecting the in-} \\
\text{nocent)}
\end{matrix}
\right.
$$

If we adopt standard S' as validly applicable to an object X (say, any human being), then the statement "X fulfills S'" entails the statements "X fulfills S_1 in C_1"; "X fulfills S_2 in C_2"; and so on. When this relationship between S' and S_1, S_2, . . . S_n holds, I shall say that S_1, S_2, . . . S_n are *deducible* from S'. Of course, if S_1 is deducible from S', then the fact that an object X fails to fulfill S_1 in C_1 entails its failure to fulfill S'. However, the failure of X to fulfill S_1 in circumstances *other than* C_1 does not entail such a failure. In a given set of circumstances to be benevolent requires one to be liberal in giving to charity; in a different set of circumstances (say, when the individual himself is destitute), it does not. In these circumstances, failure to be liberal does not mean failure to be benevolent.

It is to be noted that the deducibility of S_1, S_2, . . . S_n from S' depends on the adoption of S' as a *valid* standard for judging a class of objects K of which X is an instance. If the validity of S' were brought into question a new process of validation would be necessary. In the given case perhaps the standard of benevolence as applied to all human beings (class K) could itself be deduced from a more general standard, such as the principle of brotherly love. Thus we might have the following logical pattern:

$$\text{Fulfilling } S'' \text{ (brotherly love)} \begin{cases} \text{Fulfilling } S_1' \text{ (being benevolent)} \\ \text{Fulfilling } S_2' \text{ (being honest)} \\ \text{Fulfilling } S_3' \text{ (being just)} \\ \text{Fulfilling } S_4' \text{ (being conscientious)} \end{cases} \begin{cases} \text{In } C_1, \text{ fulfilling } S_1 \\ \text{In } C_2, \text{ fulfilling } S_2 \\ \vdots \\ \text{In } C_n, \text{ fulfilling } S_n \end{cases}$$

Here the logical relation between S'' and S_1', S_2', . . . S_n' would be the same as that between S_1' and S_1, S_2, . . . S_n. The applicability of S'' would have to be assumed, just as the applicability of S' was assumed before. If this assumption were questioned, a still higher stage of validation would have to be carried out, and so on, until we reached the supreme norms of the value system we have adopted. (As we shall see later, any further justification would require that we shift from validation to vindication.) To sum up, if a man is judged to be morally good because he gives liberally to charity, one can justify the relevance of the standard used, by showing that it follows from the more general standard of benevolence as a sign of good character. The claim that benevolence is a standard relevant to a moral judgment of good character is itself in need of justification; *if* it is justified, then it follows that being liberal in giving to charity is also validated as a relevant standard.

Let us take another example. We can show that having harmonious colors is a valid standard for judging paintings of a certain kind (say, European paintings of the seventeenth and eighteenth centuries), by deducing it from a more general standard which is appropriate to paintings of that kind. Such a general standard might be the "integration" or "organic unity" of all the formal and qualitative elements in the composition of a painting. *If* we accept this standard as relevant, and *if* color harmony is one of the conditions necessary for a certain kind of painting to fulfill the standard, then we have established that color harmony is a relevant standard.

The relevance or applicability of a standard may also be established by Method II. One might argue, for instance, that liberality in giving to charity is a relevant standard for judging a man's character, because the over-all effects of people's acts are *better* when it is fulfilled than when it is not. In other words, the more widely the standard is adopted in a society, and the more completely it is fulfilled by those who adopt it, the *more ideal* the society will be. (Method II would not normally be used to validate aesthetic standards.) The judgment that the effects are better or that the society is more ideal is itself a value judgment made according to some *other* standard. This other standard may be the maximizing of happiness for as many people as possible, or the prevention of social conflict, or the attainment of economic security, or the like. Whatever it is, the original standard in question has not been shown relevant by Method II until this other standard has been established (by Method I or II). However, assuming that this standard is relevant (for judging the social consequences of adopting and fulfilling other standards), the relevance of the original standard is established.

Methods I and II may also be employed to validate a rule. The methods must show that a given act is legitimately included in the range of application of the rule. Suppose we judge an act to be wrong because it violates the rule: always pay the bills you have incurred as a result of your purchases. On what grounds can we show that it is correct to apply this rule to a person when he does not pay his bills? It is not sufficient merely to say that he had a charge account at the store and charged things when he purchased them. This is to *assume* the relevance of the rule that one must pay for things one has charged. Method I may be used to establish the relevance of the rule as follows. The rule in question is a particular case of a more general rule (that of keeping one's promises). To incur a debt contextually implies that one promises to repay it—unless this promise were made, there would be no debt. To be in debt *means* to be obligated by one's implicit or explicit promise to repay it. Now when one opens a charge account at a store, by that very act one promises to pay one's bills in the future. (This is part of what the social practice of opening a charge account means. One does not have to *say* that he promises to pay his bills.) By Method I it is correct to condemn a person's act on the ground that it violates a rule if that rule can be deduced from a more general rule which covers the act. In the present example the given act violates the rule: one must pay one's bills. There is a more general rule which covers the act in question and from which the aforementioned rule can be deduced, namely: one must keep one's promises. Therefore it is correct to condemn the act as a violation of the more particular rule.

To argue the case by Method II, we would imagine what it would be like if people in general did not repay their debts, and then to predict (infer) what consequences would probably result from this practice. We then judge these consequences to be bad according to a certain standard, such as the standard of maximizing happiness. Again, we would assume that this standard is itself relevant to the case. If this assumption were challenged, the validation of the standard would have to be carried out by using Method I or II.

The use of Methods I and II in validating a rule reveals how a social practice as a whole can be justified. A social practice is a way of behaving according to a set of rules. These rules define the practice, so that to follow the rules is to engage in the practice. This has been pointed out by Professor John Rawls. "It is the mark of a practice," he says, "that being taught how to engage in it involves being instructed in the rules which define it, and that appeal is made to those rules to correct the behavior of those engaged in it." (J. Rawls, "Two Concepts of Rules," *The Philosophical Review,* LXIV, 1; 1955, p. 24.) In these cases, an act of a certain sort would not even be described as an act of that sort unless it fell under the rules which define a practice. A person could not be said to be voting in a political election, for example, unless he placed a proper kind of mark on an official ballot at the appropriate time (between certain specified hours on Election Day) in the authorized place (the district election center), unless he was registered in a recognized party, unless the person he voted for was a candidate running for a definite office and had been duly nominated for that office, and so on. To *describe* an act of checking a piece of paper as an act of voting, we must understand the act as part of a practice defined by a particular set of rules. "To engage in a practice, to perform those actions specified by a practice, means to follow the appropriate rules. If one wants to do an action which a certain practice specifies then there is no way to do it except to follow the rules which define it." (Rawls, *op. cit.,* p. 26.)

It is important to notice that one might violate the rules and still be engaged in the practice. Indeed, if the act is correctly described as a violation of the rules, one *must* be engaged in the practice. To be engaged in the practice only means that one's acts fall under the rules and are describable in terms of the rules, not that they are always in accordance with the rules. In order to say that a person keeps a promise (or repays a debt), we have to presuppose that the person is engaged in the practice of making promises (or incurring debts). The same holds true when we say that he breaks a promise (or does not repay his debts). He must still be engaged in the practice of making promises (or incurring debts), otherwise his acts do not fall under the rules defining the practice.

Now the fact that the rules are needed to describe the practice does not of itself imply that they are validated or that the acts are *correctly* judged according to them. To engage in a practice is to have one's acts fall under certain rules and consequently to make it possible to judge one's acts by the rules. But having one's acts fall under the rules still needs to be justified, and justifying it requires that the rules be shown to be relevant in judging the acts. To show that the rules are relevant is *to justify the entire social practice.* Let us see why this is so.

When an act is judged according to rules which define a practice, the judgment is verified (but not validated) when the practice is specified and the act is correctly described as one that complies with or violates a rule of the practice. The judgment "That act is wrong" is verified when the practice of promising, for instance, is specified, and when the act is correctly described as breaking a promise. This does not fully justify the judgment, however; one might ask why the practice of promising should be engaged in at all. This is a demand for the justification of a social practice. In order to justify engaging in it (and so acting under and being judged by certain rules) it is necessary to validate the rules which define it. That is, it is necessary to justify *adopting* those rules in the first place and so *making* one's acts fall under them. When Methods I and II are used to validate practice-defining rules, then Methods I and II are used to justify social practices. To validate such a rule by Method I as that one must repay his debts, we must show that the social practice defined (in part) by that rule is included in a wider or more general social practice (say, making promises) which is itself justified. A social practice P is included in a wider or more general social practice P' when every act which is describable in terms of P is also describable in terms of P', but not all acts describable in terms of P' are describable in terms of P. (That is, to engage in P is always to engage in P' also, but not vice versa.)

Use of Method I in justifying a social practice is most familiar to us in the field of ethics, where it constitutes the basic idea of restricted utilitarianism. We validate the rules defining a certain social practice by means of Method II when we give a moral justification for the practice by appealing to the principle of utility (or the greatest happiness principle. In such a case the rules defining the practice are themselves evaluata. They are judged as having instrumental value or disvalue to an inherently valuable end (the greatest happiness of all sentient beings). In Chapter 1 I mentioned the case of judging rules themselves with regard to their stringency or importance, according to their instrumental value. Validating practice-defining rules by Method II is an instance of this.

Professor Stephen Toulmin's, *An Examination of the Place of Reason in Ethics* (Cambridge, England: Cambridge University Press, 1950), contains an excellent account of this distinction between justifying a particular act falling under a social practice and justifying a social practice as a whole. Professor Toulmin gives the following example. I have borrowed a book from someone and I am asked why I ought to return it.

. . . I may reply that I ought to take it back to him, 'because I promised to let him have it back before midday'—so classifying my position as one of type S_1. 'But ought you *really?*', you may repeat. If you do, I can relate S_1 to a more general S_2, explaining, 'I ought to, because I promised to let him have it back.' And if you continue to ask, 'But why ought you really?', I can answer, in succession, 'Because I ought to do whatever I promise him to do' (S_3), 'Because I ought to do whatever I promise anyone to do' (S_4), and 'Because anyone ought to do whatever he promises anyone else that he will do' or 'Because it was a promise' (S_5). (S. Toulmin, *op. cit.*, p. 146.)

Professor Toulmin then adds that beyond this point we cannot raise the question, "Why ought I (you) to do this particular act in these circumstances?" because "there is no more general 'reason' to be given beyond one which relates the action in question to an accepted social practice." (*Ibid.*, p. 146.)

Suppose, however, that the circumstances are changed, so that I seem to be justified in making an exception to the social practice. Then a second sort of reason must be introduced. I cannot merely appeal to the social practice to justify my action. Professor Toulmin gives this example:

. . . If I have a critically ill relative in the house, who cannot be left, the issue is complicated. The situation is not sufficiently unambiguous for reasoning from the practice of promise-keeping to be conclusive: I may therefore argue, 'That's all very well in the ordinary way, but not when I've got my grandmother to look after: whoever heard of risking someone else's life just to return a borrowed book?' (*Ibid.*, p. 147.)

There is yet a third kind of reason in ethics. One can reply to a demand for justification, not of an exception to a social practice, but of the social practice itself. Suppose I know that, *given* the practice of promise-keeping, I am obligated to return the book; I want to know, however, why such a practice *ought* to be accepted. I am no longer asking for justification of a particular act of promise-keeping. I am asking for a justification of promise-keeping itself.

To question the rightness of a particular action is one thing: to question the justice of a practice *as a practice* is another. (*Ibid.*, p. 149.)

How would such a question arise? Professor Toulmin contends that it would arise under changing economic, social, political, or psychological conditions.

If a society has a developing moral code, changes in the economic, social, political or psychological situation may lead people to regard the existing practices as unnecessarily restrictive, or as dangerously lax. If this happens, they may come to ask, for instance, 'Is it right that women should be debarred from smoking in public?', or 'Would it not be better if there were no mixed bathing after dark?', in each case questioning the practice concerned *as a whole*. (*Ibid.*, p. 149.)

The kind of reason which would then become appropriate, according to Professor Toulmin, is the kind of reason I have placed under Method II. It consists in using a standard for making a value judgment of the consequences of the social practices involved. Here is where the principle of restricted utilitarianism occurs in ethics.

> The answer to be given will . . . be reached by estimating the probable consequences
> (i) of retaining the present practice, and
> (ii) of adopting the suggested alternative.
> If, as a matter of fact, there is good reason to suppose that the sole consequences of making the proposed change would be to avoid some existing distresses, then, as a matter of ethics, there is certainly a good reason for making the change. (*Ibid.*, pp. 149-150.)

This distinction between moral reasons for doing a particular act and moral reasons for adopting a social practice is by no means a recent discovery in ethics. Professor Toulmin himself points out that Socrates, in the *Crito,* was making this very point.

> It was this distinction between the 'reasons' for an individual action and the 'reasons' for a social practice which Socrates made as he waited for the hemlock: he was ready to die rather than repudiate it—refusing, when given the chance, to escape from the prison and so avoid execution. As an Athenian citizen, he saw that it was his duty (regardless of the actual consequences in his particular case) to respect the verdict and sentence of the court. To have escaped would have been to ignore this duty. By doing so, he would not merely have questioned the justice of the verdict in his case: he would have renounced the Athenian constitution and moral code as a whole. This he was not prepared to do. (*Ibid.*, p. 151.)

The conclusion I wish to draw from Professor Toulmin's discussion is this. When Method II is used to validate rules which define a social practice, validating the rules is the same as justifying the social practice as a whole. This may readily be distinguished from justifying a particular act falling under the social practice. We justify a particular act by verifying a value judgment of the act according to the practice-defining rules. When we shift from verification to validation in justifying that judgment, we shift from justifying an act falling under a social practice to justifying the social practice itself. (It will be shown in Chapter 5 that social practices may also be justified by a process of vindication.)

Throughout this account of validating a standard or rule by

Methods I and II, I have been making two assumptions. First, that the evaluatum of the value judgment which is being justified does not constitute an exception to the standard or rule. And second, that there are no other standards or rules which conflict with the one being validated, or that if there are, the one being validated takes precedence over them. A consideration of the second and third steps of validation brings these assumptions into question.

STEP 2. An act may be a case of breaking a promise, but that is not a *conclusive* reason for our judging it to be wrong. This is so even though we realize that the agent himself must be engaged in the practice of making promises in order to be said to break a promise, and even though we believe that the practice of making promises is a justified practice. The given act might be a legitimate exception to the rule that we must keep our promises. Although the rule *generally* covers acts of that kind, the *given* act may be distinctive in a relevant respect. An example of this is to be found in a passage I have quoted from Professor Toulmin. A person is excused from returning a borrowed book because he must look after his critically ill grandmother. If keeping his promise to return the book involves risking his grandmother's life, we say it is right for him to make an exception to the rule: Always keep your promises. The range of application of the rule ordinarily includes promise-breaking acts. But because of the circumstances, this particular promise-breaking act becomes permissible, even obligatory. The judgment that the act is wrong cannot be justified; the evaluatum, in those circumstances, does not fall under the rule according to which the judgment is made.

How do we know when the violation of a rule (or the nonfulfillment of a standard) can be counted as a legitimate exception? On what grounds do we justify making such an exception? The answer is to be found in the use of Method III. We must appeal to a standard or rule which permits such an exception to be made. *Assuming* the validity of *this* standard or rule, it is possible to decide the question. A full justification of the resulting value judgment, however, would necessitate the justification of that assumption. We would have to validate (or vindicate) the standard or rule appealed to in making the exception. Validation of this standard or rule would be made by further use of Methods I, II, and III.

It is easy to see how a standard can function as a ground for making an exception to another standard (S) or to a rule (R). If, according to the standard, it is *better* to make the exception than to fulfill S or R, then making the exception is justified. We are dealing here with a value ranking whose class of comparison is composed of 1 anything that fulfills S or R and 2 something which, in the given circumstances, would constitute a failure to fulfill S or a violation of R. When the result of evaluating the members of this class of comparison is such that the evaluatum in 2 is judged to have more value or less disvalue than instances of 1, then it is legitimate to make an exception to S or R. Let us consider an example of justifying in this way an exception to S, and then an exception to R.

Suppose a new library building is being planned for a city. One of the architectural principles (standards) accepted by the city officials is that of functionalism—the best building is the one that most effectively serves the purposes for which it is to be used. According to this standard, good-making characteristics of a library would include such things as spaciousness of stacks and reading rooms, quietness, efficiently organized offices, easy availability of books, and so on. Let us suppose, furthermore, that the best library building as judged by the standard of functionalism would cost so much to build that the city would have to take funds allotted to another project (say, slum clearance) to pay for it. The choice becomes: fulfill the standard of functionalism and damage the slum clearance project, or fail to fulfill the standard and preserve the project. An evaluation is then made of these two alternatives *according to a standard,* such as the welfare of the people of the city. An evaluation according to this standard might result in ranking the second alternative as better than the first. An exception would then be made to the standard of functionalism in architecture. If an architect were to present two plans for the library building, one of which was clearly better than the other according to the standard of functionalism, the better one would *not* be chosen. It would not be considered really better in the given circumstances. Hence an exception to a standard is justified on the basis of the circumstances in which the evaluatum occurs. The standard of what is "really better" is the standard of the public welfare. If this standard were itself to be challenged, the process of validating *it* by Methods I, II, and III would have to take place. (Or else it would have to be vindicated.) In this example I am assuming that this standard is not challenged.

The most familiar case of making an exception to a rule on the basis of a standard occurs when we judge that the *effects* of following the rule will be worse in a given set of circumstances than the effects of violating it. Thus we sometimes make exception to a moral rule, such as the rule forbidding lying, on grounds of a moral standard, such as that of minimizing suffering. Exceptions to rules of etiquette or of custom are quite frequently made on such grounds. In all instances of this sort an evaluation is being made which results in the (ranking) judgment that violating a rule is better than following it. Whenever this occurs, making an exception to the rule is justified (assuming, of course, the validity of the standard according to which the evaluation is made).

How can a *rule* be used to justify an exception to a standard (S) or to another rule (R)? The pattern of reasoning is essentially the same as in the preceding cases. We carry out an evaluation to see whether it is better not to fulfill S or to violate R than to fulfill S or comply with R. But here the evaluation is made according to a rule, not a standard. Justifying an exception to a standard on the basis of a rule might occur as follows. Suppose a businessman has set an ideal standard of efficiency for his company. He usually judges to be good whatever fulfills this ideal, bad whatever fails to fulfill it. Sometimes in order to fulfill his ideal most completely he might well have to break a law (e.g., the minimum wage law). From the point of view of his ideal, it would be better to break the law than to obey it. In these circumstances, however, he makes an exception to his standard. If he is to follow the rule which requires him to obey the law, he must do certain things which work against his ideal. Assuming the rule to be valid, he is justified in making such exceptions to his standard.

Making an exception to a rule R is justified on grounds of another rule whenever the other rule takes precedence over R and requires an act which is forbidden by R (or forbids an act enjoined or permitted by R). For example, when we think that obeying a certain law is a serious violation of our moral code, we may believe that we are justified in breaking the law. We do not have to condemn the law *as* a law on moral grounds, as a conscientious objector would condemn a military draft law as a law. We might generally approve of the law and yet in unusual circumstances believe it is right to break it. The moral rule "Always help a person in distress" might require our breaking a traffic law (say, going through a red light in order to get a critically injured person to a hospital).

It is worth repeating that in all these ways of justifying exceptions to standards and rules, some other standard or rule is presupposed. One can always challenge a person's claim that he is justified in making an exception by demanding that the presupposed standard or rule itself be justified. Such a justification process may consist either in validating the standard or rule by further use of Methods I, II, and III, or in vindicating its adoption. How it can be vindicated will be discussed in Chapter 5.

Having shown how an exception can be justified, I have also shown what it means to say that making an exception is *not* justified. Making an exception to S or R is not justified when doing so has less value or greater disvalue than fulfilling S or R. Making the exception must be ranked in relation to not making the exception. Such a ranking must appeal to some standard or rule other than S or R, which in turn must be either validated or vindicated.

STEP 3. So far we have analyzed the first two steps of the process of validation. In step 1, we show that in ordinary circumstances a given evaluatum is correctly included in the range of application of a standard S or a rule R. In step 2, we show that the evaluatum does not occur in such unusual circumstances, or differ in such a way from other members of the class of comparison, that it constitutes a legitimate exception to S or R. Now a third step is necessary if the validation of S or R is to be complete; for there might be other standards and rules which are in conflict with S or R and which take precedence over them.

What does it mean to say that standards and rules may be in conflict? Two standards conflict with each other when something which is good according to one is bad according to the other. Two rules are in conflict when an act which is in accordance with one violates the other. There is a conflict between a rule and a standard when an act which fulfills the standard violates the rule, or when an act which is in accordance with the rule fails to fulfill the standard.

In order to resolve a conflict between standards or rules logically, one must decide which standard or rule takes precedence over the other. There are two ways in which this can be done: by appeal to a second-order standard and by appeal to a second-order rule. Let us examine first the appeal to a second-order standard S'. A first-order standard S_1 takes precedence over another first-order standard S_2 if and only if something which completely fulfills S_1 is *better* (according to S') than something which completely fulfills S_2. Similarly a rule R_1 takes precedence over another rule R_2, if and only if an act done in accordance with R_1 is better (according to S') than an act done in accordance with R_2. In the case of a conflict between a rule R and a standard S, R takes precedence over S when an act done in accordance with R is better (according to S') than an act which completely fulfills S. If an act which completely fulfills S is better than an act done in accordance with R, then S takes precedence over R. In each instance we determine whether one thing is *better* than another by ranking the two things according to a second-order standard (S').

There is a parallel situation when the relative precedence of standards and rules is decided by appeal to a second-order *rule* rather than a second-order standard. In this case, the act in accordance with the standard or rule taking precedence is said to be *right*, while the act in accordance with the other standard or rule is *wrong*. The rightness and wrongness of the act are determined by an evaluation according to a second-order rule R'.

It should be noted that when one rule R_1 is found to take precedence over another rule R_2 (whether by appeal to a second-order standard or by appeal to a second-order rule), we can say that R_1 makes a "higher claim" upon us, lays down a "heavier obligation," or imposes a "more stringent duty" than R_2. (Which of these phrases is most appropriate depends on whether the type of rules concerned are moral, legal, etiquette, and so on.) We might also say it is better that our conduct be guided or regulated by R_1 than by R_2. Similarly when a standard S_1 is shown to take precedence over another standard S_2, we can say it is better for someone to try to fulfill S_1 than S_2. For the sake of simplicity I have given definitions only of conflicts between two standards, between two rules, and between a standard and a rule. Conflicts may occur, however, among a great number of standards and rules. In these cases all the standards and rules can theoretically be arranged in a hierarchy, each one (except the lowest) taking precedence over another. Whether the actual set of standards and rules accepted by an individual ever constitutes such a neat "value system" is a matter I shall deal with shortly.

The standard by which we judge whether something which fulfills S_1 or R_1 is better than something which fulfills S_2 or R_2 (and accordingly whether S_1 or R_1 takes precedence) I have called a second-order standard. By a second-order rule, we judge that an act which fulfills S_1 or R_1 is right and an act which fulfills S_2 or R_2 is wrong (and accordingly we determine that S_1 or R_1 takes precedence over S_2 or R_2). A standard or rule is second-order simply in virtue of the fact that it is used for judging the relative precedence of other (first-order) standards or rules. Such second-order standards and rules function exactly like first-order standards and rules in a process of evaluation. For any second-order evaluation, the members of the class of comparison are *ideals* of S_1 and S_2 (i.e., things which perfectly fulfill S_1 and S_2) or ideals of R_1 and R_2 (i.e., acts which are in perfect accordance with R_1 and R_2). If the conflict holds between S_1 and S_2, then the class of comparison of the second-order ranking has two members: the ideal of S_1 and the ideal of S_2; if the conflict is between S_1 and R_1, the class of comparison is the ideal of S_1 and the ideal of R_1; and so on. When many standards and rules are in conflict, the class of comparison is composed of the ideals of all these standards and rules.

When a second-order evaluation is made according to a standard, its purpose is to arrange the ideals of all the first-order standards and rules in an order of preference depending on their good-making and bad-making characteristics. The first-order standards and rules that are in conflict do not determine the good-making and bad-making characteristics. For according to each of them there is one member of the class of comparison which is *ideal* in comparison with which all the others are in varying degrees bad. It is the second-order standard that determines the good-making and bad-making characteristics on the basis of which some of these ideals are judged to be better than others. When a second-order evaluation is made according to a rule, the class of comparison is always composed of acts, decisions, or choices that have been judged as ideal according to the first-order standards or rules (whose relative precedence is being decided). The second-order evaluation is a process of judging the rightness or wrongness of each act, decision, or choice in the class of comparison by appeal to the second-order rule.

A person's second-order standards and rules reflect his general outlook on life. If we know that a man lives according to the second-order rule "Whenever there is a conflict between moral rules and the rules of long range self-interest (prudence), do what is prudent, not what is moral," we know something fundamental about the person. His second-order rule reveals to a great extent his "philosophy of life." If a man's basic goal in life is to become wealthy, he will judge the various ideals of his first-order standards and rules according to their instrumental value in realizing that goal. He will subordinate such ideals as obeying the law, enjoying a happy married life, and being well liked to the more fundamental ideal of gaining wealth. The latter standard takes precedence over all other standards and rules in his life.

Two further points should be noted about second-order standards and rules. In the first place, they are the logical, not necessarily the psychological, basis on which an individual organizes his life. They are the standards and rules which an individual *would* specify as his basic principles or "values" *if* he were thoroughly honest and *if* he reflected objectively about his own life. In the second place, it is only the unusual person who integrates all his standards and rules in an order of relative precedence. Most people do not have such organized views of life. At any one time they might have several second-order standards or rules which themselves conflict; according to one, S_1 takes precedence over S_2, and according to another S_2 takes precedence over S_1. These second-order standards or rules might also shift from time to time, so that a person gives up some life goals and adopts others as his situation in life changes. It is perfectly possible, indeed, for a person to live entirely without second-order standards or rules. In that case when his first-order standards and rules come into conflict with each other (as they are bound to do in the everyday affairs of life) he will act in an inconsistent manner. At one time he will try to fulfill one standard, at another time a conflicting one. Today he will follow rule R_1 at the cost of violating R_2; tomorrow he will (in similar circumstances) follow R_2 at the cost of violating R_1.

The clearest examples of second-order standards and rules are to be found in the lives of those "integrated" persons who have dedicated themselves to a fundamental ideal. I have mentioned the case of the man who seeks wealth above all things. Other examples might include a deeply committed religious man, a political fanatic, a thoroughgoing militarist, a professional athlete in training, a creative musical genius, and a dedicated scholar or scientist. At the core of such individuals' lives are certain integrating second-order standards and rules according to which at least some, if not all, of their first-order standards and rules are arranged into a hierarchy. If such a person were asked to justify his (implicit or explicit) belief that one first-order standard or rule takes precedence over another, he would cite certain second-order standards (e.g., standards of total commitment in advancing a political cause, or standards of impartiality and logical rigor in the pursuit of truth) and certain second-order rules (e.g., I must always obey the will of God, or I must never do anything detrimental to my development as a tennis player).

Are there third-order standards and rules by which to resolve conflicts among second-order standards and rules? Theoretically, there are. They would be appealed to if a validation of a second-order standard or rule were demanded and if that validation included the use of Method III. Probably very few people actually organize their lives on the basis of such third-order standards or rules, however.

So far I have discussed the use of second-order standards and rules in the life of an individual. They also have an important place in the functioning of a social group, whether that functioning be organized (as in the case of an army waging a battle, a company producing, distributing, and selling goods, or a university carrying on its academic functions) or relatively unorganized (as in the case of a cocktail party or a race riot). Sometimes the functioning of a group is so organized as to constitute a social practice. The first-order rules which define a social practice may be arranged hierarchically according to second-order rules (which are then as much a part of the definition of the practice as are the first-order rules). When the first-order rules of a practice conflict with each other, it is necessary to decide their relative precedence. If a social group is to be able to function at all, there must be an established way of resolving conflicts among its rules and this requires an appeal to second-order rules. Suppose an army unit has the two rules: "Always obey the commands of a superior officer," and "No one is to enter this building without a special pass." If an officer without a special pass commands the soldier on duty to let him enter the building, which rule ought the soldier obey?" A well-run army unit will specify the relative precedence of such conflicting rules by means of a second-order rule. After the statement of the rule requiring a special pass, there might be added the second-order rule, "Absolutely no personnel of any rank will be exempted from this requirement."

The third step in validation, to conclude, is accomplished by Method III. Here the task is to show that the standard or rule to be validated is not in conflict with any other validated standards or rules, or if it is, that it takes precedence over them. The relative precedence of conflicting standards and rules is found by ranking them according to second-order standards or rules. These second-order standards or rules themselves must be assumed to be validated (or vindicated) if the original value judgment is to be justified. Should this assumption be challenged, the second-order standards or rules would have to be validated by Methods I, II, and III (or they would have to be vindicated by the method to be discussed in Chapter 5).

D. On the argument for radical skepticism

If we disregard for the moment the possibility of vindicating standards and rules and consider the justification of value judgments only in terms of verification and validation, then the following argument arises. In order to justify a value judgment we must not only verify it by appeal to standards and rules but we must also validate those standards and rules. Since such validation itself depends on the justifiability of higher standards and rules, then the latter must also be validated. This would require our accepting still higher standards and rules, whose validation in turn would presuppose still higher standards and rules, and so on. Now either this process goes on to infinity or it stops somewhere. In the former case, since the ultimate grounds on which a value judgment is based can never be reached, no value judgment can ever really be shown to be justified. In the latter case, the point at which validation stops must be arbitrarily chosen, since it cannot itself be validated. The conclusion of radical skepticism is then drawn: we cannot legitimately claim to *know* what is good or bad, right or wrong.

The force of this argument derives from viewing evaluative reasoning on the model of mathematical deduction. Value judgments are thought of as theorems that are strictly entailed by statements of standards and rules. The latter in turn are thought of as theorems strictly entailed by statements of higher standards and rules, until we arrive at axioms, that is, statements of *ultimate* standards and rules. Since these axioms are not themselves entailed by any higher statements, they are held to be pure postulates, arbitrarily chosen. For this reason all value judgments are claimed to be equally absurd.

This argument does not claim that value judgments are matters of taste, about which there is no disputing. In matters of taste we do not even *attempt* to argue for or against a person's statements. If value judgments were considered to be matters of taste, no claim would be made that a value judgment is justified or that a standard or rule has rational grounds. As soon as the question "Why should I accept the standards and rules you appeal to?" is raised, we are no longer concerned with a matter of taste. The radical skeptic is not denying that we raise such questions about value judgments. He grants that they can be as rationally grounded as mathematical theorems. But, he says, *finally* they are absurd because they rest on axioms, which are decision-statements, not claims-to-truth. As a result, they are beyond the boundaries of rational discourse. One "value system" (a set of standards and rules arranged hierarchically according to their relative precedence) is no more justified than another.

An attempt is made to preclude this kind of skepticism by those who claim that one set of axioms is intuitively certain. Such a claim rests, I think, on the following line of reasoning. Since the axioms are statements of standards or rules, they are not tautologies—they are not true by definition or by the law of noncontradiction. On the other hand they are not empirical statements. They are normative, not descriptive. Now because they are not tautologies, they must be synthetic statements. And because they are not empirical, they are not true a posteriori but must be true a priori. Therefore they are synthetic a priori statements. How then do we know whether they are true? Since axioms by definition are not deducible from any higher premises, they are not known to be true because other statements are known to be true. And we have just seen that they are not known to be true on the basis of evidence provided by our senses. They must therefore be known to be true by an immediate intuition, yielding a unique sort of knowledge that is totally independent of all other knowledge. It is knowledge of what ought to be, not knowledge of what is. Consequently value judgments *can* be justified. Their justification consists in three things—verification by reference to standards or rules, validation of these standards or rules by reference to higher standards and rules (finally by reference to ultimate or highest standards and rules), and synthetic a priori intuition of the truth of these ultimate standards and rules. Accordingly we do have knowledge of what is good or bad, right or wrong. There is nothing arbitrary, irrational, or absurd about our value judgments.

I shall be brief in my criticism of these arguments. Their basic error is to misconstrue the nature of our reasoning about value judgments. They do this for two reasons. They consider verification and validation purely in terms of reasoning in the empirical sciences and in mathematics, respectively. And they do not take into account the two further stages of justifying value judgments: vindication and rational choice.

Both the argument for and the argument against radical skepticism rest on the false assumption that there are only two ways of reasoning about anything—the way we reason in mathematics and the way we reason in the empirical sciences. Both arguments accept the fact that, unlike empirical assertions, value judgments must be validated as well as verified. But it is assumed that the only alternative to empirical verification is deductive inference from axioms. Since validation is different from empirical verification, it must consist in a final appeal to axioms. As a result, two questions arise which both the skeptic and his opponent are trying to answer. What are the axioms from which value judgments are deduced and on which they ultimately depend for their justification? Are these axioms such that we can claim knowledge on behalf of our value judgments?

The analysis of validation which I have given in this chapter lends some support to this way of looking at the problem. I have emphasized how the validation of any standard or rule depends on our accepting a higher standard or rule. And it is perfectly true that, in this relation of a given standard or rule to a higher one, the first is deducible from the second (in just the ways I have been describing under Methods I, II, and III). It would seem, then, that if we are not to go on to infinity we must arrive at standards or rules that are ultimate. What is there left but to say that these ultimate standards or rules are either arbitrary (and hence are accepted without reason) or are knowable only by a synthetic a priori intuition?

A fundamental mistake is being made here. Certainly there is a deductive element in justifying value judgments, just as there are deductive elements in establishing scientific theories and laws. But this does not mean that evaluative reasoning is like mathematical reasoning in *all* respects. We are overlooking what is *distinctive* about evaluative reasoning. We are trying to fit it into some preconceived logical pattern, such as the analtyic-synthetic dichotomy. If we look at the way we actually do reason about what is good or bad, right or wrong, we find that there is an important difference. Just as such reasoning does not stop at verification of a value judgment but goes on to the validation of standards and rules, so it does not stop at validation. There are two further steps which are *essential* in the complete justification of any value judgment. These are the vindication of whole value systems and the rational choice of a way of life. The next three chapters are concerned with these steps in the justification of value judgments.

Value systems and
points of view

4

A. The concept of a point of view

In order to understand the third and fourth steps in the justification of value judgments, namely vindication and rational choice, it is first necessary to distinguish two concepts and see how they are related to each other. These are the concept of a value system and that of a point of view. A value system is a set of standards and rules *of a certain kind* arranged according to the place they have in the verification and validation of value judgments (and prescriptions) *of that kind*. Thus a *moral* value system is a set of moral standards and moral rules that are appealed to in verifying moral judgments and moral prescriptions, and that are arranged in an order of relative precedence corresponding to the hierarchy implicit in their validation. An *aesthetic* value system is a set of aesthetic standards and aesthetic rules that are appealed to and validated in the justification of aesthetic judgments and aesthetic prescriptions. In like manner there are political value systems, economic value systems, religious value systems, etiquette value systems, prudential value systems, and so on. In each case, the structure of the system is logically determined by the justification of value judgments and prescriptions of a particular kind. (We shall see in Part II that prescriptions are justified in the same way that value judgments are justified. A value system includes the standards and rules used in justifying both evaluations and prescriptions, but for the sake of simplicity I shall assume that prescriptions are included whenever value judgments are mentioned in this chapter.)

When value systems are said to be of different kinds, what criterion of classification is being used? The answer lies in the concept of a point of view. If we understand what it means to take a certain point of view, such as the moral or the aesthetic point of view, we will understand what makes a value system a moral or an aesthetic one. What differentiates a moral value system from any other kind is the moral point of view; what differentiates an aesthetic value system is the aesthetic point of view, and so for the other kinds of value systems. Belonging to each point of view are many value systems, often opposed to each other. There is only one moral point of view, for example, but there are many moral value systems. This is reflected in our speech. We talk of *the* moral point of view, but *a* moral system, or *the* aesthetic point of view, but *an* aesthetic system, and so forth. The concept of a point of view, moreover, is a cross-cultural concept, while that of a value system is culture-bound. One point of view may be found in different societies and at different periods of history, even though the value systems belonging to that point of view are composed of different standards and rules organized in different ways. Similarly a point of view shared by different social groups or by different individuals may retain its identity, no matter how varied are the actual value judgments, standards, and rules accepted by them. We identify certain judgments, standards, and rules accepted by an ancient Egyptian as moral ones, for instance, according to the same criteria that we use to identify certain judgments, standards, and rules accepted by an American Indian, or an Australian bushman, or a contemporary Englishman, as moral. Value systems vary from culture to culture, from epoch to epoch, from group to group, and from individual to individual; points of view do not. In order to account for this difference, we must see what it means to take a point of view.

Whenever someone attempts to justify a value judgment by the methods of verification and validation, he is offering reasons in support of the judgment. We may ask two questions about them. Are they relevant reasons? Are they good reasons? All good reasons, of course, must be relevant reasons. But the converse does not hold; what makes a reason a relevant reason is not the same as what makes it a good reason. We must distinguish the *rules of relevance,* which are implicitly or explicitly followed in justifying value judgments, from the *rules of valid inference.* Rules of relevance provide the criteria by which we determine whether a reason offered by someone in justifying a given value judgment is relevant. Rules of valid inference provide the criteria which determine whether a reason we have already found to be relevant is good (warranted, legitimate, valid, logically sound, intellectually acceptable). These two sets of rules together comprise the *canons of reasoning* which constitute the framework of the verification and validation of value judgments.

Taking a certain point of view is nothing but adopting certain canons of reasoning as the framework within which value judgments are to be justified; the canons of reasoning define the point of view. When we verify and validate our judgments from that point of view, we cite reasons which are good (and *a fortiori* relevant) according to the particular canons which define that point of view. We have already said that a value judgment is a moral judgment if it is made from the moral point of view. This means precisely that the judge or evaluator has adopted a set of rules of relevance and valid inference that recognize only certain reasons as relevant and good. It is not my task here to specify what the particular canons of reasoning are which define the moral or any other point of view; I am concerned only with elucidating the concept of a point of view in general. To give a detailed account of what particular canons of reasoning differentiate the moral, the aesthetic, the political, and other points of view is not necessary for distinguishing any point of view from the value systems that belong to it. It is essential to notice, however, that the concept of a point of view covers more than evaluative or normative points of view. There are also such nonnormative points of view as the scientific, the mathematical, and the historical. In each case, what defines the point of view is the canons of reasoning that govern the justification of the assertions made from it. Thus the scientific point of view is defined by the canons of scientific reasoning ("the scientific method"), the mathematical point of view by the canons of mathematical reasoning, and the historical point of view by the canons of reasoning used by historians. There is an important difference between what distinguishes a normative from a nonnormative point of view and what distinguishes one normative point of view from another. In the first case, both rules of relevance and rules of valid inference together constitute the differentiae; in the second, only rules of relevance have this function. The methods of science differ from the methods of justifying value judgments not only with regard to the sort of feature which makes a reason relevant, but also with regard to what makes a reason a good reason. A rule in virtue of which a reason is good in scientific justification is not always applicable in the justification of value judgments. In particular, the validation of standards and rules, which is essential to the justification of value judgments, is not a part of scientific reasoning. The rules of valid inference for the empirical sciences differ in this respect from those for normative reasoning. Scientific and normative reasoning also differ in their rules of relevance. What makes a reason relevant to the confirmation of an empirical hypothesis, a causal law, or a theory in the sciences is not the same sort of feature that makes a reason relevant to the verification and validation of a value judgment. It is relevant to the justification of a causal law, for example, that certain phenomena can be explained by it. But a moral rule does not function as an explanation of the particular acts which fall under it. To cite instances in which a moral rule is being followed or in which it is being violated is not relevant to its justification. The capacity of a scientific law to account for particular cases, on the other hand, is just what is relevant to its justification. Nonnormative points of view differ from normative points of view, then, in respect of both rules of relevance and rules of valid inference.

The situation is quite different when we compare one normative point of view with another (say, the moral with the aesthetic). Here the rules of valid inference are the *same* for both points of view. They are the rules which define the processes of verification and validation as these were analyzed in the last chapter. No matter what the different points of view from which value judgments are made, they are always justified in the same way (i.e., according to the same rules of valid inference). We shall see in the following two chapters that this is also true of the third and fourth steps in the justification of value judgments. The rules of valid inference which govern the processes of vindication and rational choice remain identical for moral judgments, aesthetic judgments, and all other kinds of value judgments.

What, then, differentiates one normative point of view from another? The answer lies in the rules of relevance which are appropriate to each. To take one point of view rather than another is to decide to follow one set of rules of relevance rather than another. The canons of reasoning which define the two points of view do not vary in their rules of valid inference, but only in their rules of relevance. What makes a reason good in justifying a moral judgment is the same thing that does so in justifying an aesthetic judgment, *assuming that both reasons have already been found to be relevant to their respective judgments.* But if we ask what makes each reason relevant, we find that different features are appealed to. What makes a reason relevant to the justification of a value judgment is very different in the case of a moral and of an aesthetic judgment. When we justify our judgment that a certain novel is good on the ground that it inspires the reader to become a morally better person, our judgment is moral and not aesthetic. The standard referred to is one typically used in justifying moral judgments; we are judging the novel from the moral point of view. If on the other hand we judge it to be a good novel because its style is appropriate to its subject matter, our judgment is made from the aesthetic point of view. Exactly why one reason is a moral reason and the other aesthetic is a question I shall not attempt to answer, since it involves specifying the rules of relevance that define these particular points of view. What I do wish to make clear is that the difference between the two points of view lies in the relevance of the reasons accepted in justification of a given value judgment, not in the goodness of the reasons. We shall see in Part III that the ground for saying this is the fact that *all normative languages are used in fundamentally the same ways for the same purposes, but different normative languages are being used in these ways for these purposes.*

Before I examine the relation between a point of view and the various value systems which may be said to belong to it, one further consideration about the relations among points of view should be brought out. This is the fact that points of view overlap and shade into one another. I was over-simplifying when I spoke as if one point of view can be sharply separated from all others. It is important to see that this is not always the case. Generally a rule of relevance which is included in the canons of reasoning that define one point of view is not included in the canons that define another point of view, but sometimes this does occur. When it does, the two points of view may be said to "overlap." The rule of relevance is common to both points of view. For example, it is relevant to justifying (validating) a rule from the moral point of view to consider its effects upon the welfare of people. This is also relevant to justifying a civil law from the political point of view. Here the moral and political points of view overlap. (The overlapping of points of view will be considered further in Chapter 11.)

To say that two points of view shade into one another is to say that one cannot always tell when a given instance of justifying a value judgment belongs to one point of view or the other (and hence cannot tell what sort of value judgment it is). For any two points of view P_1 and P_2, there will be clear-cut cases of reasoning that belong in P_1 and clear-cut cases that belong in P_2. But there may be cases of reasoning which we are not sure about placing in either P_1 or P_2, although we may be confident that they do not belong in any other points of view P_3, P_4, . . . P_n. For example, we might justify saying that a child acted wrongly in an unprovoked attack on another child on the ground that "people don't do that." This is clearly not an aesthetic or religious judgment. But is it a judgment from the moral point of view or from the point of view of etiquette or custom? There is no sharp division between the latter points of view in this situation; we must simply acknowledge that the judgment could be classified either way. All points of view are in this sense vague. We can *draw* dividing boundaries if we like, but it is doubtful whether doing so will serve any useful purpose. And in any case we would not be justified in criticizing others for drawing different boundaries. It is important to notice those respects in which two points of view are clearly distinct and those respects in which they shade into one another. But it is not necessary for the clarity or accuracy of our thinking to force a sharp distinction between points of view by stipulating what reasons shall definitely be included in one and excluded from the other.

I come now to the relation between points of view and value systems. What does it mean to say that a given value system "belongs to" a particular point of view? It means that the standards and rules which constitute the value system are, first of all, the standards and rules appealed to when value judgments are *verified* in accordance with a certain set of rules of relevance, and are secondly themselves *validated* in accordance with the same set of rules of relevance. Thus a value system is a moral value system (i.e., a system of moral standards and moral rules) when the rules of relevance that define the moral point of view govern the verifying process that appeals to those standards and rules, and the validation of those standards and rules themselves. It is rules of relevance (or more generally, the canons of reasoning) that define a point of view, not any specific standards or rules of conduct. As a result, it is perfectly possible for various systems of standards and rules of conduct to belong to one point of view. In such a case the same canons of reasoning would govern the justification of judgments, standards, and rules within each of the value systems concerned.

It is for this reason that it makes sense to speak of the moralities or moral codes of different societies. Each moral code is made up of different standards and rules arranged in different hierarchies of relative precedence. But each is a *moral* code, nonetheless. In each code value judgments are made and justified from the moral point of view. And this means that the framework within which verification and validation take place is determined by the canons of reasoning which define the moral point of view. To take the moral point of view is not to adopt a specific moral code. It is to be disposed to carry on normative reasoning or normative discourse in a certain way, according to certain rules of relevance and by using a certain normative language (as analyzed in Part III). Hence, we cannot say that some one standard, such as the greatest happiness principle, or some one rule, such as the Golden Rule, is *defining* of morality. We must be willing to speak (as we ordinarily do in our nonphilosophical moments, and as anthropologists and sociologists do) of the moral codes of headhunting societies and of juvenile street gangs, of the Greek moral code and of the Christian moral code, of slave-morality and master-morality, of a liberal moral system and of a conservative moral system.

In a similar manner, there are many systems of aesthetic norms, many sets of political principles, many religions with different standards for the sacred, the holy, and the divine. What makes each of them value systems of a certain kind (aesthetic, political, or religious) is the canons of reasoning which govern the justification of the particular standards or rules of which they are composed. Theoretically, *any* standard for evaluating objects could serve as an aesthetic standard, *any* rule of conduct could be a moral rule. It is an empirical matter, not a matter of definition, that certain standards or rules are never moral but always aesthetic, or are never aesthetic but always moral, or are sometimes both aesthetic and moral. There is no inherent characteristic of a standard or rule which prevents it from belonging to a certain sort of value system or which necessitates that it belong to a certain sort. (This point will be explored further in Chapter 12.) The only thing that counts is the relevance of the standard or rule in the justification of value judgments and the sorts of reasons that are relevant to its validation. These are empirical matters in virtue of the fact that the rules of relevance involved are the rules implicitly or explicitly followed by people when they use a certain normative language, that is, when they actually carry on moral discourse, or aesthetic discourse, or political discourse.

B. In what sense can points of view be justified?

To show that a particular value system is a moral one (or an aesthetic one) is not to justify it in any way. It is only to classify it descriptively. This also holds for an individual standard or rule. To show that a standard is a moral standard is to contrast it with *nonmoral* standards. It is not to justify it as being moral (i.e., morally good) rather than *immoral* (i.e., morally bad.) The statement that any standard, rule, or value system belongs to one point of view rather than another never constitutes a reason for adopting the standard, rule, or system. We must not confuse specifying the *kind* of justification which is appropriate to something with actually justifying it. When we say that a standard, rule, or value system belongs to a certain point of view, we are saying that certain reasons and not others will be relevant to its justification. We are not *giving* such relevant reasons. In like manner, to justify a standard or rule is not to classify it as belonging to a certain point of view, even though we cannot justify it without presupposing a certain point of view (i.e., without having committed ourselves to following a set of canons of reasoning). We justify a standard or rule, as we saw in Chapter 3, by *validating* it. We justify a whole value system, as we shall see in Chapter 5, by *vindicating* it. The process of validation is always carried out within the framework of a point of view, but it is not part of that process to *state* that the standard or rule belongs to a certain point of view. (We shall see in Chapter 5 that vindication is not carried out within the framework of a point of view.)

It should be remarked that we never validate a point of view; it is not the sort of thing that can be validated. This is so because validating something presupposes a point of view. We can validate something only by following the canons of reasoning that set the framework of validation, and such canons are precisely what constitute a point of view. We validate standards and rules of a certain kind, not the criteria that determine what kind they are. We validate moral standards and rules, for instance, by appeal to other (higher) standards and rules in a moral value system. The canons of reasoning that govern the entire process define both the method of validation itself (through the rules of valid inference) and the point of view which tells us (through the rules of relevance) that the value system is a moral one. Without the canons of reasoning validation cannot occur. Consequently they cannot themselves be validated.

Can a point of view be justified in *any* sense? This question requires us to distinguish carefully four things.

1. Stating the canons of reasoning which define a point of view.
2. Deciding to adopt the canons of reasoning of a point of view (i.e., deciding to take the point of view).
3. Justifying the statements made in 1.
4. Justifying the decision made in 2.

It might at first appear that the task of 1 is simply to describe the rules which govern the way people think about a certain matter. But this is not quite accurate. The canons of reasoning which define a point of view do have an empirical base in the way people actually carry on their reasoning. But these canons are normative: they establish norms for *correct* reasoning; they are *guides* for people to follow in their reasoning. Our task in 1 is *the explication of an ideal* which is only implicit in the reasoning of people. Consider the parallel between explicating the canons of reasoning implicit in a normative point of view and explicating those implicit in a non-normative point of view, such as the scientific.

To explicate the canons of scientific thinking is to state the rules of inference according to which scientists justify their assertions. This is not simply to describe how any particular scientist actually thinks; any particular scientist might make a mistake in his thinking. Nor is it to describe how all scientists or a statistically large majority of scientists actually think. For the rules of inference which we want to explicate are prescriptive rules, not generalizations. Their function is to *regulate* thought, not simply to express *regularities* in the way thinking is in fact done. No doubt these rules originally emerged from the patterns of thought actually present in the thinking of physicists, chemists, astronomers, and other scientists. But they now serve to guide that thinking, in the sense that they are the very rules by which scientists determine whether a mistake has been made, and whether a given argument is to be accepted as confirming a hypothesis. The canons of scientific reasoning are the rules which scientists themselves appeal to in *judging* (*evaluating*) the logical soundness, the warrantability, the intellectual acceptability, of the reasons they give as scientists in justifying their assertions. (We might call such judging "logical evaluation," that is, making value judgments from the logical point of view.) We might say that the canons of scientific reasoning are the rules of thinking which an *ideal* scientist would follow in justifying his assertions. They are the rules which anyone must follow *if he is to be fully rational* in his thinking about scientific matters. To explicate such rules is to state clearly and in specific detail how a scientist would reason if he never made a mistake, that is, if he always gave good reasons for his assertions. The same considerations would apply to explicating the canons of mathematical reasoning and of historical reasoning. (This defines, it seems to me, one of the main tasks of philosophy; the tasks, specifically, of the philosophy of science, the philosophy of mathematics, and the philosophy of history.)

It is in this sense that the task of 1, namely the statement of the canons of normative reasoning, consists in explicating an ideal. To state the canons of reasoning that define a normative point of view is to specify the rules of relevance and of valid inference which anyone would follow, *if he were fully rational,* in verifying and validating value judgments of a certain kind. They are the rules a person would follow if he were always to give good (and *a fortiori* relevant) reasons in justifying his judgments and in arguing against the judgments of others. It is the task of explicating the rules of valid inference that I am trying to accomplish in Chapters 3, 5, and 6 of this book. The steps of verification, validation, vindication, and rational choice, which make up the entire process of justifying value judgments, are all ideal procedures of reasoning. They are the procedures that must be followed if we wish to discover the most well founded value judgments there can be.

What, then, is the difference between 1 and 2, that is, between stating the canons of reasoning which define a point of view and deciding to adopt such canons? We are now in a position to locate precisely the respects in which they differ. To state the canons of reasoning is to *explicate* an ideal in the sense just explained. To decide to adopt such canons of reasoning is to *commit oneself* to an ideal. It is to decide to follow, to the best of our ability, the rules of relevance and valid inference specified in 1. For moral reasoning, the distinction may be stated as follows. To explicate the canons of moral reasoning (i.e., the canons of reasoning which define the moral point of view) is the task of the moral philosopher. To decide to justify one's moral judgments according to such canons is to adopt the role of the moral judge. The moral philosopher tells us what the moral point of view is; the moral judge takes that point of view. (A third role is that of the moral agent. His task is to live a moral life, i.e., to live in such a way that his conduct and character fulfill moral standards and rules.) The moral philosopher tries to state what makes a reason a good reason in moral argument. The moral judge tries to *give* good reasons in moral argument. It is the moral judge, not the moral philosopher, who carries on moral discourse. The moral philosopher carries on second-order (philosophical) discourse about moral discourse.

Now let us turn to the distinction between 3 (justifying the statements made in 1, and 4 (justifying the decisions made in 2). The phrase "to justify a point of view" might mean either of these two things. It might mean "to justify an explication of the canons defining a point of view," or it might mean "to justify the decision to take a point of view." These two activities of justification, although logically connected, are not identical. And they are both to be distinguished from the justification of value judgments. Focussing our attention upon the moral point of view again, we can see immediately that the task of justifying value judgments is the task of the moral judge, and that this is very different from the task of justifying a person's decision to *become* a moral judge, that is, his decision to adopt the moral point of view. The moral judge has, by definition, already adopted the moral point of view. He is thinking *within* its framework. The person who must justify a decision to adopt the moral point of view is *outside* that framework. He is trying to decide whether there are good reasons to place himself within it. Hence the rules of reasoning which define that framework cannot serve to guide his decision. In short, the decision to adopt the moral point of view is not a moral decision.

The question we must answer concerning 3 is this: How is it possible—if it is possible at all—to justify the explication of the canons of reasoning which define a point of view? The canons of reasoning which would have to govern such a justification could not be the canons of reasoning which are explicated. The canons governing the explication of a point of view may be called the canons of *philosophical* reasoning. They are the rules and methods of reasoning which the philosopher (ideally) follows when he attempts to explicate the canons of all types or ways of reasoning (including his own). When the philosopher attempts to explicate the canons of scientific reasoning, mathematical reasoning, historical reasoning, or normative reasoning (including the moral, aesthetic, political, and so on), his method of explication is itself governed by canons of reasoning. These are the canons by reference to which one can decide whether a given explication is justified. What are these canons of philosophical reasoning?

This is by no means an easy question to answer, but I should like to offer the following account as at least a first step toward doing so. We might say that an explication is justified when it is shown to be correct or accurate. The test for correctness or accuracy would be this—any person in any culture at any time in history, who understood what the statements expressing the explication asserted, on reflecting about the conditions under which he was willing to apply such terms as "sound," "warranted," "legitimate," "valid," "relevant," and "good" (or their equivalents in his own language) to reasons given for or against value judgments, would be disposed to admit that the explicated rules would govern the normative reasoning of a fully rational mind. Such an opinion would always be subject to correction in light of further reflection by others or by the person himself. I would add, as a further condition, that during his reflection the person maintain a high degree of objectivity. By this I mean that he exert every effort to prevent his own value judgments, standards, and rules from influencing his opinion. The key to this method is critical reflection concerning the conditions under which a person would be willing to claim that reasons offered in support of a value judgment were sound, warranted, legitimate, valid, relevant, or good, and, on the other hand, the conditions under which the person would reject offered reasons as unsound, unwarranted, illegitimate, invalid, irrelevant, or bad.

This method for determining the accuracy or correctness of an explication may be thought of as providing criteria which are endlessly corrigible. We might say that an explication is accurate or correct *to the extent that* (i) more persons, (ii) from more varied cultural and historical backgrounds, (iii) upon longer and more careful reflection, (iv) exercising greater and greater objectivity, (v) tend more and more to agree that the explicated rules do define what they would mean by a well established justification of a value judgment. Thus philosophers might gradually arrive at closer approximations to an ideal concept of rationality in the universe of normative discourse. (In this book I am offering my own conception of this ideal. It is expressed in the canons of reasoning set fourth as the fourfold process of verification, validation, vindication, and rational choice. I am claiming that this process is an accurate or correct explication of rational thinking when we try to justify our value judgments and prescriptions. This claim is open to the sort of correction which I have just indicated as being appropriate in philosophical discussion.)

It should be noted that even the most accurate explication of the canons of reasoning which define a point of view does not provide a justification of the value judgments made from that point of view. The explication states what an ideally rational justification of those value judgments consists in; it does not involve the actual justifying of the judgments. To explicate certain canons of reasoning is not to use those canons of reasoning in our thinking. To state what makes a reason a good reason for a value judgment is not to *give* a good reason for the judgment. What is more, the ability or inability to state correctly what makes a reason a good reason is neither causally nor logically connected with the ability or inability to give good reasons. We may, as moral judges, be unable always to follow the canons of reasoning which moral philosophers have correctly explicated. The correctness of the explication is no guarantee that moral judges will never make mistakes. Similarly we can be mistaken, as moral philosophers, about the canons of moral reasoning and still, as moral judges, be able to give good reasons for our judgments. In such a case the moral philosopher would simply not have a correct understanding of what makes the moral judge's good reasons good. Thus the accuracy or inaccuracy of an explication is irrelevant to the logical soundness of a justification for a value judgment. The fact that a person may be able to give a sound justification and not be able to state accurately what canons of reasoning he is following shows that philosophical acumen is not necessary for practical wisdom. (The parallel with regard to scientific reasoning makes the point even clearer, a good scientist need not be a good philosopher of science.)

Is there a similar independence between justifying an explication of a point of view and justifying the decision to take a point of view? That is, is there any logical connection between 3 and 4? We must not confuse 4 (justifying the decision to take a point of view) with justifying value judgments within the framework of a point of view. I have pointed out that the decision to take a point of view cannot be justified in terms of the canons of reasoning that define the point of view, since the decision to take the point of view is made outside its framework. We are still confronted with the question of how such a decision can be justified. An answer to this question can be found by considering the relation between 3 and 4. I shall argue that 3 (an accurate explication of the canons of reasoning that define a point of view), does provide 4 (the justification for a decision to take that point of view.) In other words, although the justification of value judgments (within the framework of an already adopted point of view) is independent of 3, the justification of the decision to take a point of view is not independent of 3.

Deciding to take a point of view is deciding to reason in a certain way, namely according to the canons which define the point of view. How does one find out what these canons are? By means of the philosopher's explication of them. When the philosopher's explication is accurate, it tells us how we must think if we are to take the point of view. It tells us the rules of valid inference (common to all normative points of view) and the rules of relevance (unique to each point of view) which we must follow if we have decided to adopt the point of view. But as my analysis of 1 showed, the philosopher's explication is not merely a description of how people do think when they have adopted a point of view. It is the explication of an *ideal* way of thinking. It tells us how we would think (upon adopting a point of view) if we were fully rational. The canons of reasoning explicated by the philosopher guarantee that, if a person carries on his reasoning in accordance with them, his reasoning will always be logically sound. Now we can see why the decision to adopt a point of view is *always* justified. It is the decision to commit oneself to an ideal of rationality. Deciding to adopt a point of view is deciding to follow the canons of reasoning which define what it means to reason in the best (i.e., the most rational) way possible.

Another way to put this is as follows. What an accurate explication explicates is the ideal to which everyone who takes a certain point of view is committed in the act of taking it. To take the moral point of view, for example, is to commit oneself to the ideal of always giving good and relevant reasons when justifying moral judgments, moral prescriptions, moral standards, and moral rules. One might not be able to fulfill this ideal, but to have adopted the moral point of view is to have placed oneself in the position of striving to realize it and of having one's reasoning subject to correction in light of it. The decision to take the moral point of view is simply the decision to be as rational as one can concerning moral matters. Such a decision is justified precisely because this is what the decision consists in. To decide *not* to take the moral point of view would be to decide not to be as rational as possible in moral matters. It would be a decision to be less than rational and hence would be an irrational decision.

The parallel with scientific reasoning will again be of help. To take the scientific point of view, we have seen, is to have our thinking about the world guided by the canons of scientific method. These canons define the ideal of scientific reasoning. They are the canons which anyone who does science must follow if his reasons are to be good reasons and if his inferences are to be valid inferences. Now what would it mean to *justify* the decision to take the scientific point of view? It would mean simply to give good reasons for deciding to follow the canons of scientific method. But once we see that these canons themselves define the ideal of rationality in science, we also see that the decision to follow these canons must by its very nature be justified. For if a person were to decide not to follow these canons, his decision would be a *paradigm* of what we mean by irrationality in empirical matters. To decide to adopt the scientific point of view is nothing else but to decide to be as rational as possible in gaining empirical knowledge about the world. What decision could be more rational, and hence more justified, than this? The same argument holds in the parallel case of normative reasoning. Deciding to adopt a normative point of view is nothing else but deciding to be as rational as possible about our value judgments and prescriptions. To decide not to adopt such a point of view is the very thing we *mean* by being irrational. Such a decision, in other words, would be a paradigm of an unjustified decision.

The demand for a justification of the decision to take a point of view is a peculiar demand. Once we understand the nature of the decision, *we see that it is not necessary to justify it.* We might express this by saying that the justification of the decision follows from its nature. Or we might prefer to say that such a decision *cannot* be justified, because we are unable to find any reasons outside of the nature of the decision itself to justify it. However, this does not mean that the decision is not justified; for no such justification is necessary. To demand justifying reasons here is to demand reasons for being rational, and this is a meaningless demand. If a rational decision is a justified decision and a decision to be rational is a rational decision, then the decision at hand is as justified as it can ever be, simply because it is a decision to be rational. No further reasons (than the fact that it is a decision to be rational) can be given to justify it, but no further reasons need be given. To have shown that it is a decision to be rational is to have justified it in the only way it can be justified.

To take a point of view, then, is to adopt canons of reasoning as guides to the verification of value judgments and the validation of standards and rules. It is justified simply because it is a rational way of thinking. But we must draw a sharp contrast between justifying a point of view in this sense and justifying (vindicating) a value system. To vindicate a value system is not to justify canons of reasoning, but to use those canons in justifying the value system itself. The canons so used are rules of valid inference only. Rules of relevance do not apply, since in order to justify a particular value system (which belongs to a point of view) we must step *outside* the point of view. We justify a moral system, for example, by reference to a whole way of life, and a whole way of life includes all kinds of value systems, nonmoral as well as moral. The justification of a moral system as a whole is not a moral justification since it goes beyond the moral point of view. That point of view governs the verification of moral judgments by appeal to moral standards and rules, and the validation of those standards and rules by appeal to higher standards and rules. But to attempt to justify the entire set of standards and rules requires that we go beyond validation (and hence go beyond the moral point of view) to a different sort of process, namely vindication. I shall explain the nature of this shift from validation to vindication in the next chapter. For the present I only want to point out that vindication, the third step in normative justification, is a reasoning process that must transcend any given point of view, including the point of view of the value system which is being vindicated. In vindicating the value system, we must consider a whole way of life which cuts across many points of view. Consequently the canons of reasoning that define the process of vindication are the rules of inference which differentiate normative from nonnormative reasoning. They are not the rules of relevance which differentiate one normative point of view from another.

We are dealing here with two social practices, each defined by its own set of rules. There is the social practice of a value system and there is the social practice of normative reasoning. The rules defining a value system are rules of conduct; the rules defining normative reasoning are rules of thought (or rules of inference). The latter rules are those which we *use* in justifying the former rules. The rules so used are themselves justified by means of a correct philosophical explication which shows that they embody an ideal of rationality. The difference between the two sets of rules is reflected in the different methods of justifying them: vindication in the one case and explication in the other. Both methods are practiced outside the framework of a point of view. When I discuss the process of vindication in the next chapter, it should be remembered that I am trying to explicate the rules of reasoning which govern our justification of a whole value system. I am not trying to justify the act of taking a point of view, nor am I engaging in the practice of vindication itself.

The justification of value judgments: vindication

5

A. Validation and vindication

I take the distinction between validation and vindication from Professor Herbert Feigl's essay, "Validation and Vindication: An Analysis of the Nature and the Limits of Ethical Arguments" (in Wilfred Sellars and John Hospers, eds., *Readings in Ethical Theory*. New York: Appleton-Century-Crofts, Inc., 1952, pp. 667-680). Professor Feigl makes the distinction in the following way. We can validate our claims to knowledge, he says, only by referring to the basic rules of deductive and inductive logic. Similarly we can validate our moral judgments only by referring to the supreme norms of a given ethical system. The rules of logic and the supreme norms are the "validating principles" which constitute the "frame of validation" within which all validation must take place. Now suppose there is disagreement about these validating principles. How can such a disagreement be resolved? Not by rational argument, Feigl claims, because rational argument presupposes agreement on a set of validating principles. Feigl suggests three possible ways in which such disagreement can be "removed":

This can occur either through the disclosure and explication of a hitherto unrecognized common set of standards, i.e. still more fundamental validating principles to which implicit appeal is made in argument, or it can be achieved through the pragmatic justification of the adoption of an alternative frame, or finally, through sheer persuasion by means of emotive appeals. (H. Feigl, *op. cit.*, p. 675.)

It is the second method which Feigl calls "vindication."

Validation terminates with the exhibition of the norms that govern the realm of argument concerned. If any further question can be raised at all, it must be the question concerning the pragmatic justification (vindication) of the (act of) adoption of the validating principles. (*Ibid.*)

Assuming that we have reached the ultimate standards and rules appealed to in validating other standards and rules in a value system, the only way we can argue rationally (instead of resorting to "sheer persuasion by means of emotive appeals") is by vindicating the value system as a whole.

It should be noted that Professor Feigl does not distinguish between a value system and a point of view. Indeed, he appears to confuse them when he compares the supreme moral norms of an ethical system with the rules of deductive and inductive logic. He refers to both of these as "justifying principles":

The justifying principles . . . for the establishment of knowledge-claims have been retraced to their ultimate foundations in the rules of inference and substitution in deductive logic. We cannot without vicious circularity disclose any more ultimate grounds of validation here. Similarly the rules of maximal probability in inductive inference form the ultimate validating basis of all empirical reasoning. Correspondingly the supreme norms of a given ethical system provide the ultimate ground for the validation of moral judgments. No matter how long or short the chain of validating inferences, the final court of appeal will consist in one or the other type of justifying principles. (*Ibid.*)

The term "justifying principles" covers both rules of logic and the supreme norms of value systems. These rules and norms, according to Feigl, can be justified only pragmatically, that is, by the method of vindication. In light of the argument which I gave in the last chapter, however, the rules of logic should be compared with the canons of reasoning that define a point of view, not with the supreme norms (standards and rules) of a value system. Those canons are rules of thought which govern the processes of verification and validation. As such they are comparable to the rules of deductive logic which govern the validation of theorems in a proof, and to the rules of inductive logic governing the confirmation of empirical hypotheses. Indeed, the rules of deductive and inductive logic define nonnormative points of view just as the canons of normative reasoning define normative points of view. The validation of value judgments consists in the *appeal to* the supreme norms of a value system, but is done *in accordance with* rules of relevance and rules of valid inference. In a parallel way the validation of theorems in a deductive system consists in the *appeal to* axioms and proved theorems, but is done *in accordance with* the rules of deductive inference; and the confirmation of empirical hypotheses consists in the *appeal to* sense experience but is done *in accordance with* the rules of inductive inference.

In the last chapter, I argued that we justify the adoption of a point of view (i.e., a set of canons of reasoning) by the method of philosophical explication. That is, we show that the canons of reasoning in question are those that would be followed if a person carried on his thinking in an ideally rational way. This applies both to canons of reasoning that define normative points of view (such as the moral and the aesthetic) and to those that define nonnormative points of view (such as the mathematical, the scientific, and the historical). Accordingly I shall not claim, as Feigl does, that we justify the "validating principles" (canons of reasoning) of deductive and inductive logic by the method of vindication. It may be possible to do this, although I am inclined to believe that the method of explication is both adequate and appropriate for this purpose. When it comes to normative points of view, I claim that we justify the adoption of them by way of a correct explication of the canons of reasoning involved. But such explication does not provide a justification of the supreme norms of all the different value systems which belong to a point of view being explicated. Indeed, the supreme norms of different value systems may be in conflict, even when they belong to the same point of view. In order to justify our adoption of a given set of supreme norms we must use the method of vindication.

It is one thing to explicate the rules of relevance and the rules of valid inference that define the moral point of view; it is quite another to vindicate a particular moral system. In the first case we are justifying a way of thinking; in the second case we are justifying a way of behaving. In order to justify a way of thinking we must show that it is rational; in order to justify a way of behaving (along with the standards and rules that govern such behaving) we must vindicate it. We show that a way of thinking is rational when we give a correct explication of the canons of reasoning that set the ideal for it. When we vindicate a way of behaving (or a value system), we are *following* certain canons of reasoning, which must in turn be justified by the method of explication. A correct explication of the entire process of justifying value judgments, I maintain, would include explicating the method of vindication as the rational way to justify whole value systems (including their supreme norms).

In order to see what is involved in the method of vindication, let us first contrast it with the method of validation. Validation always takes place *within* a value system. We validate standards and rules by referring to higher standards and rules within the same value system; we validate these higher standards and rules in turn by referring to still higher standards and rules within the system. Finally we must come to a set of highest standards and rules— standards and rules for which we can offer no further validation. These are the supreme norms of the given system. Just as value systems will vary from individual to individual, from society to society, and from one period of history to another, so also will these supreme norms. But at any given time, for any given person, there will be some norms that are for him supreme. What makes them supreme? Simply the fact that the person *accepts* them as supreme whenever he is asked to justify the standards and rules he has adopted. Implicit in his thinking when he justifies his value judgments (or argues against the value judgments of others) is a set of canons of reasoning which require that certain standards and rules are not validated by appeal to any higher standards and rules.

Now suppose the person is asked to justify his supreme standards and rules. What is he to do? He cannot validate them, since they are supreme. He is being asked to justify the whole value system within which he validates all his other standards and rules. The jump from validating norms within the framework of a value system to justifying the value system as a whole is as great as the jump from justifying an act within the framework of a social practice to justifying the social practice as a whole. We saw in Chapter 3 that we may justify an act by appeal to the rules that define a social practice under which the act falls. The entire social practice may in turn be justified by validating its defining rules. In doing this, however, other (higher) standards or rules must be appealed to. Thus justifying a social practice by validating its defining rules always takes place within the framework of a value system. We must assume the justifiability of the value system in order to justify the social practice. If the justifiability of the value system as a whole is brought into question, we cannot continue to use the method of validation. We must use some fundamentally different method, just as we had to use a fundamentally different method when we were asked to justify, not a particular act, but a whole social practice. We must, in short, make the shift from validation to vindication.

B. The process of vindication

The standards and rules that make up a value system have a double function. They are the norms a person appeals to in validating other (lower) standards and rules, and they guide a person's conduct. When a person adopts a value system, he decides to accept certain standards and rules as the basis for justifying his value judgments. But he also decides to place his conduct under the regulation of all the standards and rules of the value system. He commits himself to trying to fulfill the standards and to acting in accordance with the rules. This in turn involves his attitudes. He comes to have a pro-attitude toward whatever fulfills the standard or complies with the rules, and a con-attitude toward whatever is not in accordance with them. When a person has adopted a value system, then, he is not only disposed to *reason* in a certain way (by appealing to its constituent standards and rules), but he is also disposed to *live* in a certain way (by trying to realize the ideals it proposes).

When I speak of vindicating a value system I speak in an abbreviated form. What we vindicate is not a value system itself but a person's act of adopting it and a person's state of being committed to it (in the double way just mentioned). The act of adopting a value system may or may not be the result of a conscious decision on the person's part. A person might have been brought up under a value system, or conditioned in some other way to accept it, and so never have made a conscious decision to adopt it. But as long as he does not deliberately reject it and as long as he tries (consciously or unconsciously) to live in accordance with it, he is committed to it. He lives *as if* he has adopted it. To vindicate a value system means to justify either the *act* of adopting its standards and rules or the *disposition* to be guided by its standards and rules. This disposition is the state of being committed to the value system and presupposes an (implicit) act of having adopted it. For convenience I shall continue to speak of vindicating value systems. But it is to be understood in every case that vindication applies to the adoption of, or commitment to, a value system, not to the standards and rules which make up the system.

Following Professor Feigl I use the term "vindication" as a synonym for "pragmatic justification." But I include in pragmatic justification standards of both instrumental value and contributive value. We can vindicate something in two ways. We can show that it is a necessary, effective, or sufficient means to bringing about or furthering an end, and we can show that it contributes to the value of a whole of which it is a part. Vindication is thus the outcome of two sorts of evaluation—evaluation according to a standard of instrumental value and evaluation according to a standard of contributive value. When the evaluatum which is judged according to this twofold standard is the act of adopting (or the disposition of being committed to) a whole value system, a positive conclusion which has been justified would express a vindication of the value system in question. Thus to vindicate a value system is to grade it as a good value system according to a standard of instrumental value and a standard of contributive value. The class of comparison consists of acts of adopting (or commitments to) other actual or possible value systems which have instrumental and contributive value (or disvalue) when judged by the same standards. We are immediately confronted with two questions. What is the end with reference to which the members of the class of comparison are being judged to have instrumental value or disvalue? What is the whole with reference to which they are being judged to have contributive value or disvalue? I submit that the answer to both of these questions is "a way of life." I shall define the concept of a way of life later in this chapter. At this point I wish to consider a possible objection to the method of vindication just outlined.

It might be objected that we cannot possibly vindicate a value system by evaluating its instrumental and contributive value, for in so doing we appeal to a standard, namely a way of life. Are we not merely continuing the process of validation? By vindication, we are supposed to justify a value system as a whole, and this includes the highest standards and rules in terms of which all other standards and rules are validated. There should be no higher standards for grading a value system as a whole, since a whole value system contains *ultimate* or *supreme* standards. How then can we appeal to a standard of instrumental or contributive value in justifying a whole value system? To appeal to such a standard would show that we are operating within the framework of a value system, instead of justifying a value system from without. Indeed, by referring to a standard of instrumental value as a higher standard for judging other standards and rules, would we not be using Method II in the first step of validation? (See Chapter 3). If this were so, then we would not truly be vindicating the highest standards to which a person appeals in justifying his value judgments. We would be appealing to at least one standard higher than these, namely the end in relation to which their instrumental value is judged.

This objection is based on a misconception of the nature of vindication. To subscribe to the objector's criticisms as they stand is to lose touch with the reality of normative reasoning. We must keep in mind what occurs in everyday life when we try to justify our value judgments fully and consistently. Let us review what happens in such a practical context. We start with uttering a value judgment. It is then challenged by someone or we come to doubt it ourselves. We respond by verifying it, appealing to certain standards or rules. If it is then demanded that we justify our acceptance of these standards or rules, we proceed to go through the three steps of validation, using Methods I, II, and III. We complete the validation process when we appeal to standards or rules which are ultimate, that is, to the standards or rules which we are unwilling or unable to validate by appeal to higher standards or rules. We simply do not have any higher standards or rules to appeal to. Now let us suppose someone still challenges our original value judgment. He says: "I admit that your judgment is true (verified) *if* we accept standard S or rule R, and I admit that S or R is valid *if* we accept the ultimate standard S' or the ultimate rule R'. But why should I accept S' or R'?" He is challenging the validation process *as a whole*. He wants us to justify the decision to adopt S' or R' as the validating grounds for S or R. He does not want us to *validate* S' or R', since he is not questioning the fact that we accept S' or R' as an ultimate norm. What he is demanding is a good reason for *him* to accept S' or R' as an ultimate norm, and hence a good reason for *his* carrying out the validation of S or R as we did.

What sort of reply would we make to this challenge, if we were trying to be thoroughly rational in justifying our original value judgment? We would shift our ground. We have no higher standards or rules to appeal to, so we acknowledge that validation has come to an end. No further reasoning can be done within the framework of the value system. In order to justify S' or R' (our ultimate standard or rule) we must get outside that framework. Our whole method of reasoning undergoes a fundamental change—the change from validation to vindication. Instead of assuming the value system has already been adopted and proceeding to justify our judgment on the basis of it, we now attempt to justify our adopting the system in the first place. And we attempt to do this in such a way that adopting the value system will also be justified to our opponent. How is this accomplished?

All we can do to justify anyone's adopting a value system as a whole is to ask (invite) him to adopt it. We then ask him, first, whether the consequences of his doing so do not further certain ideals which, on reflection, he really wants to see realized in the world, and second, whether living in accordance with that system is not part of a whole way of life which, on reflection, he really wants to live. This is a general summary of what is involved in vindication. Now for the details.

What does it mean to invite a person to adopt a value system in his own life? It means two things. First, it means inviting him to take a certain point of view, namely the point of view to which the value system belongs. If it is a moral value system, to adopt the system is to take the moral point of view, that is, to be disposed to reason in accordance with the canons of reasoning which define the moral point of view. Second, it means inviting him to try to make his conduct conform to the standards and rules which constitute the value system. Adopting a value system psychologically involves the whole person—his thinking, his feelings, his attitudes, his behavior. It is not only to decide to have certain canons of reasoning govern the way we justify value judgments, standards, and rules. It is also to decide to live in a certain way, to endeavor to fulfill the standards and to follow the rules that have been adopted. (It is for this reason that a person might not be able to adopt a value system without some preparatory training or education. In order to learn how to live in accordance with the value system of an established religion, for example, it may be necessary to be trained in certain disciplines and to be educated in a certain way.)

The first essential condition, then, for vindicating a value system is that a person must be willing to *commit* himself to the standards and rules of conduct which make up the value system and commit himself to the canons of reasoning which define the point of view to which the system belongs. The second essential condition for vindicating a value system to a person is that he *freely choose* to adopt the system in his own life. A value system cannot be vindicated to a person who is forced (by threats, intimidations, or other forms of coercion) to adopt it. He must be invited to adopt it, and this implies his right to decline the invitation. Of course if he does decline it, he precludes the possibility of the value system being vindicated to him. Hence vindication presupposes acceptance of the invitation. Acceptance of the invitation, however, does not entail vindication. It only makes vindication possible. Unless a person freely makes up his own mind to place himself under the direction of the standards and rules of the system and to have his thinking guided by the canons of reasoning of the point of view involved, he is not in a position to see whether the system is pragmatically justified. We might sum up this second condition for vindication by saying that a person's adoption of the value system must result from a voluntary decision on his part so to commit himself.

It should be noticed in this connection that the value system in which a person has been brought up as a child cannot be vindicated to him in childhood, since in childhood he cannot be said to have freely chosen to adopt the system. A child is not invited to adopt a system, he is brought up within one and automatically (unthinkingly) accepts it. This does not mean that he is compelled or forced to accept it. Being compelled or forced implies that something is being done against one's will (or would be done against one's will if one wanted to resist), and the child has no will to exert against his upbringing. The child's will is being formed in the very process of bringing him up within the value system. Can the value system ever be vindicated to that individual, even after he has grown up? The answer is yes, since he can place himself as it were outside his own value system (and so suspend his judgment and critically reflect about the system). He can put himself in the position of anyone who questions the justifiability of the system. Indeed, he must do this if he wants to find out whether the system in which he was brought up is or is not justified. To this end he "invites" himself to adopt the system and to put it on trial. And this means that for the moment he *supposes* that he is living in accordance with it as a result of his having voluntarily decided to do so.

The third essential condition for vindication to take place is that there be some end or ends with reference to which the value system in question can be judged as having passed or failed the pragmatic test. A value system is vindicated when it is shown to have instrumental and contributive value. It is shown to have instrumental value when it is shown to be pragmatically successful in furthering certain ends, after a person has freely chosen to adopt it. A vindicated value system is one that "works" in practical life. But to decide whether something "works," we must specify the ends which are to be achieved in the successful "working" of the thing. Unless such ends are specified, we would not be able to tell whether it works successfully or not, since we would not know what to look for when it is put into practice.

These features of vindication bring to the fore its fundamental difference from the processes of verification and validation. Unlike these processes, vindicating is not a method of convincing someone by means of argument. The person to whom a value system is vindicated must *see for himself*. He cannot merely reason according to certain rules of logic. He must make a decision to live in a certain way, actually live that way, and then experience the results to find out whether the decision he made was justified. No person convinces him; experience "convinces" him. To claim that a value system can be vindicated to someone is to claim that, as a result of his adopting it, he will discover that his adopting it was pragmatically justified. It is the practical consequences of his voluntary decision that must convince him one way or the other. That his value system "works" or that it fails to "work" is something he must come to realize in his own experience of trying to live by it. And this means that when he conducts his life according to the standards and rules that make up the value system, he will find his life either in discord or in harmony with a whole way of life which embodies his conception of the *summum bonum*.

I have said that a value system is vindicated when it is shown to have instrumental and contributive value toward a way of life. This must now be explained in light of the foregoing remarks on the general nature of the vindicating process. I define a way of life as *a set of value systems each of which belongs to a different point of view and all of which are arranged in an order of relative precedence*. A way of life may include a moral system, an aesthetic system, a political system, a system of etiquette, and so on. Each system is made up of standards and rules arranged hierarchically, and all the systems together are arranged hierarchically.

We have already seen what it means to say that one standard or rule takes precedence over another within a given value system. What does it mean to say that one value system takes precedence over another? A full answer to this question will be given in the next chapter. For our present purposes the following account will suffice. Consider any given situation of choice in which a person has several courses of action open to him. His way of life will tell him, first, which value systems are *relevant* to that situation of choice, and second, which among the relevant value systems *take precedence over* the others. To say that one value system takes precedence over another is to say that, when the two systems conflict with regard to the courses of action open to choice, the first system makes a higher claim upon the person than the second. Suppose, for example, that someone is in a situation in which he has the choice of helping or not helping others. Their lives are in great danger; but if he helps them, he endangers his own life. Now his whole way of life may determine that an aesthetic value system and an etiquette value system are irrelevant to this situation of choice. Neither course of action is to be evaluated according to aesthetic standards or according to standards of etiquette. Let us assume, however, that his way of life is such that both a moral value system and a prudential value system are relevant, and that the moral system takes precedence over the prudential. In that case, the person is required to choose the course of action demanded (enjoined) by morality rather than the opposite course of action demanded (enjoined) by prudence. Of course he may not so choose, but he knows that he ought to do so if he is to live in accordance with his way of life.

When I say that a value system is vindicated because it has instrumental value toward a way of life, I mean that if a person, in putting that value system into practice, finds that he brings about or furthers the ideals of his way of life, then to that extent the value system is vindicated to him. The ideals of his way of life consist in the total fulfillment of the supreme norms in the various value systems that make up his way of life. The supreme norms must be fulfilled according to the relative precedence of the value systems in which they occur. Thus in the example cited above, a person would be furthering the ideals of his way of life only if he chose the course of action demanded by his moral system, even though the supreme norms of his prudential system are also relevant to the situation. Let us suppose he does choose the course of action demanded by his moral system. He thereby lives up to his moral system and furthers the ideals of his way of life. To that extent his commitment to the moral system is vindicated to him. Since a person will further the ideals of his way of life in so far as he is committed to the value systems that constitute it, those are the value systems that will be vindicated *to him* (and to any others who have chosen the same way of life). Whether his way of life is itself justified is a further question which must be answered in terms of a rational choice among ways of life. A value system is vindicated *to everyone* only if the way of life toward which it has instrumental value is a rationally chosen way of life. (I shall explain in the next chapter what it means to say that a way of life is rationally chosen.)

A value system is not fully vindicated unless it is shown to have contributive as well as instrumental value toward a way of life. It has contributive value when its adoption is an essential part of living a way of life. In other words, a value system is vindicated to a person if, by acting in accordance with its rules and by fulfilling its standards, he is actually living the way of life he has chosen. Any value system that is a constituent element in a person's way of life has contributive value toward that way of life, since it is an essential part of it. It follows then that any value system that is a constituent element in a person's way of life is vindicated *to him,* simply by virtue of the fact that it is a constituent of his way of life. For the same reason it is vindicated to anyone who has chosen a way of life of which it is a part. The value system is vindicated *to everyone,* however, only if the way of life toward which it has contributive value (i.e., of which it is a part) is rationally chosen.

In short, a value system is vindicated absolutely in so far as actually living in accordance with it is a means to, and a part of, a rationally chosen way of life. The judgments of instrumental and contributive value that establish this must be verified in actual practice. A person must experience the consequences of trying to live in accordance with the value system and see for himself whether the standards of evaluation are fulfilled. These standards are the ideals of a rationally chosen way of life.

Two points may now be made about these standards. First, they cannot themselves be validated. To validate them would require higher standards or rules to appeal to. But there are none, because the value systems which make up a way of life contain the supreme norms of any validation process. The way of life itself determines the framework in which validation takes place. Indeed, since it includes many different value systems, it encompasses many different frameworks of validation. The ideals of a way of life are the standards according to which whole value systems are vindicated. These ideals are themselves defined by the supreme norms of the various value systems which make up the way of life. How then can they be justified? Taken together, they form an integrated concept of the *summum bonum* and can be justified only by a rational choice. Taken separately, each ideal may be vindicated as part of the value system in which it is a supreme norm. In neither case is the method of validation applicable.

Secondly, these ideals do not all belong to one point of view, but to as many points of view as there are value systems in the way of life. Now every value system that is part of a way of life belongs to a different point of view. Consequently, the ideals of a way of life, defined by the supreme norms of its constituent value systems, are of many different types—moral, aesthetic, religious, intellectual, and so on. The standards and rules that make up one value system all belong to one point of view; the ideals that make up a way of life do not. This fact brings out a major difference between verification and validation on the one hand and vindication on the other. Verification and validation always take place *within* a point of view. The point of view determines the canons of reasoning that govern the processes of verification and validation in a given value system. To vindicate a value system as a whole is always to vindicate something which *belongs to* one point of view, since a value system is determined by the point of view to which it belongs. But vindicating a value system is done *by reference to* the ideals of a way of life that includes many value systems belonging to many different points of view. The ideals of a way of life, which constitute the standards of instrumental and contributive value referred to when a value system is vindicated, cut across many points of view. Unlike verification and validation, therefore, vindication does not take place within the framework of one point of view. It takes place within the framework of one way of life, which covers a variety of points of view. If the demand is made that we justify this framework, we must use the method of rational choice. Before examining this further stage of justification, I wish to consider two examples of vindication in recent philosophy. One example is in the field of aesthetics and the other is in the field of ethics.

C. Two examples from recent philosophy

The first example is taken from William E. Kennick's article, "Does Traditional Aesthetics Rest on a Mistake?" (*Mind*, LXVII, 267; 1958). Professor Kennick argues that we must think of the standards by which we evaluate works of art in terms of the various purposes for which works of art are used. Now all works of art do not serve the same purpose. We may evaluate works of art from the aesthetic point of view but within the framework of different aesthetic value systems. Our value judgments may then differ because we appeal to different aesthetic standards. And when the value systems belong to different points of view, the resultant judgments may exhibit even greater variation. Different points of view govern our evaluation of works of art when they are used for different purposes.

We can use novels and poems and symphonies to put us to sleep or wake us up; we can use pictures to cover spots on the wall, vases to hold flowers, and sculptures for paper weights or door stops. This is what lends point to the distinction between judging something *as* a work of art and judging it *as* a sedative, stimulant, or paper weight; but we cannot conclude from this that Art has some special function or purpose in addition to the purpose to which it can be put. (*Ibid.*, p. 329.)

Even when we judge something *as* a work of art, we must not think that we are judging it according to *the* function of art. We are taking one point of view toward it—the aesthetic—but even this point of view includes many different value systems with varying standards. There is no one purpose for which art is used which is common to all aesthetic value systems. Consequently there are many different ways of judging a work of art *as* a work of art, that is, of judging it aesthetically.

There is no special aesthetic use of works of art, even though it may make sense, and even be true, to say that a person who uses a statue as a door stop is not using it as a work of art; he is not doing one of the things we normally do with works of art; he is not treating it properly, we might say. But the proper treatment of works of art varies from time to time and from place to place. It was quite proper for a cave man to hurl his spear at the drawing of a bison, just as it was quite proper for the Egyptian to seal up paintings and sculptures in a tomb. Such treatment does not render the object thus treated not a work of art. (*Ibid.*, pp. 329-330.)

One might say that a work of art has different functions in different value systems (whether in the same culture or in different cultures), even though these are all aesthetic value systems, that is, proper or normal ways of viewing it *as* a work of art and not *as* an object to be used for a special purpose in unusual circumstances. Therefore when we make a value judgment of a work of art *as* a work of art, we cannot validate our standards of judgment by referring to one universal function of art which constitutes its proper purpose. How then can we justify our standards? Kennick recognizes that this question is quite different from the question of how we can verify our judgment.

We are confronted, I think, with a problem that is really two problems: there is the problem of saying why a given work of art is good or bad, and there is the problem of saying why our reasons are good or bad, or even relevant. We may praise a picture, say, for its subtle balance, colour contrast, and draughtsmanship; this is saying why the picture is good. We may now go on to raise the more 'philosophical' question of what makes balance, or this sort of colour contrast, or this kind of draughtsmanship an artistic virtue. (*Ibid.*, pp. 332-333.)

The second question, according to Kennick, can be answered in either of two ways: by appeal to custom or by a decision. "We either simply praise what is customarily praised and condemn what is customarily condemned or we *decide* what the criteria shall be." (*Ibid.*, p. 333.) The appeal to custom, however, cannot be used to *justify* a value judgment. One can always demand why the standards accepted by custom are valid or relevant. It is the second answer which brings out the fact that Kennick is here concerned with *adopting* a value system which *sets* the standards of aesthetic evaluation. The problem of justifying standards becomes that of justifying our decision to adopt a certain value system. Different standards are *made* relevant when different value systems are adopted.

Only an aesthete ignores, or tries to ignore, the many relations of a poem or picture to life and concentrates on what are called the purely 'formal' values of the work at hand; but in doing so he *determines* what he will accept as a reason for a work of art's being good or bad. That a work of art assists the cause of the proletariat in the class struggle *is* a reason for its being a good work of art to a convinced Marxist, but it is not a reason, let alone a good reason, to the bourgeois aesthete. That a picture contains nude figures is a reason, to the puritan and the prude, for condemning it, though no enlightened man can be brought to accept it. (*Ibid.*, p. 333.)

In judging a given work of art, then, different people will apply different standards according to the value systems they have adopted, and their value systems will reflect their ways of life.

Suppose we then ask which value system is the most justified. Kennick's position here appears to direct us to consider the different value systems in light of our general interest in works of art and the needs that works of art gratify. In some circumstances a person will be interested in art for certain reasons; in others he will be interested in it for different reasons.

Different reasons are persuasive at different times and in different contexts. The same explanation is operative: the needs and interests that art gratifies are different from time to time and, to a lesser extent perhaps, from person to person. But as the needs and interests vary, so also will the criteria and the weight we place on them. (*Ibid.*, p. 334.)

In what context do these "needs and interests" arise? Kennick does not discuss this question. But his reference to variation in the aesthetic standards used by the Marxist, the bourgeois aesthete, and the puritan reveals that he has in mind something like the concept of a whole way of life. The standards which people appeal to in their aesthetic judgments are part of their aesthetic value systems. They adopt their value systems in accordance with the "needs and interests" which art satisfies for them. What are these needs and interests but the basic aims and ideals of whole ways of life? For the Marxist, they will be the interests and needs of the class struggle, in furthering the overthrow of capitalism and the establishment of a classless society. For the bourgeois aesthete they will be the ideals of pure aesthetic delight, of the depth of aesthetic contemplation, or the satisfaction of aesthetic tension. For the puritan they will be the ideals of godliness and righteousness on the strait and narrow path to salvation. Thus the needs and interests which art serves to gratify are not themselves the aesthetic *standards* which a given person uses in judging art. They are outside his aesthetic system, at the core of his whole way of life. They are the fundamental ideals to which the person is committed and which determine what aesthetic system he will adopt. In justifying a person's value judgments of works of art, the final appeal must be to his way of life rather than to the standards that constitute his aesthetic value system.

The second example of the idea of vindication in recent philosophy is from Professor Baier's book, *The Moral Point of View*. In the last chapter of that book Baier offers an answer to the question "Why should we be moral?" Baier is here concerned with justifying a moral value system, not the moral point of view. He is trying to answer the question "Why should we do what is right?" This is to demand a justification for adopting a moral value system, since it demands reasons for *acting* morally, not for *reasoning* according to the canons which define the moral point of view. To ask "Why ought I to be moral?" is not to ask "Why ought I to take the moral point of view?" The answer to the latter question is: "Because taking the moral point of view consists in being *rational* about moral judgments, standards, and rules." To adopt it is to carry on moral discourse according to those canons of reasoning which define the ideal of rationality in these matters. If taking the moral point of view is challenged, we need only reply that *if* anyone wants to give good reasons in justifying his moral judgments, standards, and rules, he must follow the rules of relevance and the rules of valid inference which define the moral point of view. Not to follow such rules would not be justified because, by definition, it would not be thinking in the most rational manner possible.

But the question "Why should we *do* what is (morally) right?" is a demand for reasons which would justify our trying to live a moral life, that is, trying to fulfill the moral standards and to follow the moral rules which we have adopted as our moral system. This question presupposes that we already know what is morally right. Baier himself clearly distinguishes the two questions: "How do we know what is right?" and "Why should we do what is right?" The first question is answered by stating the methods by which a fully rational man would justify his value judgments. It is the philosophical (epistemological) question which must be answered by a correct explication of the canons of reasoning implicit in the way we carry on normative discourse. The second question makes the assumption that the first question has been answered successfully. It means, "Granted that we know what is right, why ought we to *do* what we know to be right?"

Now this is a very peculiar question. I think there are at least four ways it can be interpreted. (It is the last of these interpretations which Baier is concerned with.)

1. The question can be interpreted as a request for motivating reasons. Under this interpretation it means something like, "Get me to do what is morally right." The person who asks it wants to be persuaded verbally *to adopt a moral value system.* He wants to be inspired to fulfill moral standards and follow moral rules. He wants the person he asks to exert an influence on him, to get him to commit himself to a moral system. In this sense it would be very difficult, if at all possible, to answer the question. As Aristotle says, we must be *trained* to be disposed to live a moral life. We must be brought up morally. Good habits must be developed in us. We must be given a conscience. Our moral character must be developed by moral education. All this cannot be done by answering a question.

2. The question may mean, "Give me moral reasons for doing what is morally right." When interpreted this way the question is clearly not a request for the justification of a moral judgment. When a person asks this question, he is not asking for moral reasons for doing a particular act, or for doing acts of a certain kind, that are not already known to be morally right. If he were making this request, he would not ask "Why should I be moral?" but "Why (morally) should I do this?" or "Why are acts of this sort morally right?" What he is asking is "Why (morally) should I do this which I already know to be morally right?" Or else he is asking the more general question "Why (morally) should anyone do anything which is known to be morally right?" And this means "Why should I (or anyone) act according to what I (or anyone) know to be morally right?"

Now this question rests on a confusion. Anyone who asks it has not made the distinction between justifying something *within* a value system and justifying a value system from *without.* By asking for *moral* reasons for being moral, he is asking the question within the framework of a value system which belongs to the moral point of view. Hence he cannot demand a justification, in terms of these reasons, for adopting a moral system. But this is just what he does demand, since he is asking for moral reasons to justify *being moral at all*. To be moral at all is to adopt any value system belonging to the moral point of view. It is to be disposed to fulfill moral standards and to follow moral rules. "Why be moral?" means "Why be moral at all?", and this means: "Why adopt any moral system?" Hence the person is asking the question *outside* the moral point of view. But then he cannot expect to be given *moral* reasons in reply, since these reasons are acceptable only *from* that point of view.

Once this confusion is dispelled, however, the person might shift his ground and ask the question again. He realizes that "Why be moral?" cannot be answered by giving moral reasons for being moral. He sees that one way to justify being moral is to show that moral standards and rules make a higher claim upon us than, say, the standards and rules of self-interest. If the moral reasons for doing something outweigh the prudential reasons against doing it, or if the moral reasons against doing something outweigh the prudential reasons for doing it, then acting morally will have been shown to be justified. Here we have a third interpretation of the question "Why be moral?"

3. Why should moral reasons outweigh other kinds of reasons? The question can be answered only by showing that moral standards and rules make a higher claim upon us than other (conflicting) standards and rules. The situation in which such a question would arise is one to which two conflicting value systems, a moral one and a nonmoral one, are both relevant. The standards and rules of the moral system tell us to do one thing and the standards and rules of the nonmoral system tell us to do something else. To act in accordance with one system is to act in opposition to the other. Now how do we determine what we ought to do? We must decide what value system *takes precedence over* the other. To decide this, we must appeal to a whole way of life, for the relative precedence of value systems is determined by the principles of a way of life.

The question "Why be moral?" interpreted in this way means "Why should I commit myself to a way of life in which a moral system takes precedence over any nonmoral system?" The answer to this question, I submit, must be based on the concept of a rational choice among ways of life. If it can be shown that, when people make a rational choice among ways of life, they prefer a way of life in which a moral system is supreme, then this provides the justification for being moral whenever we must decide whether to act morally or not. What it means to make a rational choice among ways of life will be discussed in the next chapter.

4. There is a fourth interpretation of the question "Why be moral?", namely, that it requests a *vindication* of a moral system. This is how Professor Baier interprets the question. For in offering an answer to it, he appeals to the *consequences* which would result if people were actually to live their lives according to the particular moral system which he calls "the moral point of view." He then compares these consequences with what would result if people lived their lives according to a value system of self-interest. Thus he presents us with two different states of affairs or "two alternative worlds."

> The universal supremacy of the rules of self-interest must lead to what Hobbes called the state of nature. At the same time, it will be clear to everyone that universal obedience to certain rules overriding self-interest would produce a state of affairs which serves everyone's interest much better than his unaided pursuit of it in a state where everyone does the same. Moral rules are universal rules designed to override those of self-interest when following the latter is harmful to others. (*Ibid.*, p. 309.)

Baier does not tell us exactly how the adoption of a moral system on everyone's part actually will result in *everyone's* interest being served. (One might object that it would not serve a dictator's interests, or the interests of a sadist.) But the *kind* of reasoning which he uses is that of vindication, not validation. He appeals to our preference for one of two different sets of consequences.

> . . . We are examining two alternative worlds, one in which moral reasons are always treated by everyone as superior to reasons of self-interest and one in which the reverse is the practice. And we can see that the first world is the better world, because we can see that the second world would be the sort which Hobbes describes as the state of nature. (*Ibid.*, p. 310.)

It is important to notice that this argument rests on the assumption that the ideals of our own way of life are furthered when everyone adopts the system of morality rather than the system of self-interest. The only sense in which the first of the two alternative worlds is "better" than the second is that it is in basic harmony with our whole way of life while the second is in conflict with it. If our whole way of life were to be one in which we gloried in struggling with others, in fearing and distrusting them, and in having them fear and distrust one another, then the second world would be better to us than the first. Baier would reply to this by claiming that he is concerned only with justifying a moral system ("the moral point of view") to those who want to be rational in their lives. Being rational involves wanting to maximize our own satisfactions and minimize our own frustrations. And in a world where people generally followed their self-interest, they would not be able to satisfy their desires to as great an extent as would be possible if everyone in the world adopted the moral system in question.

Thus Baier justifies our adopting a moral system by vindicating it. He argues that it is justified because our adopting it brings about a greater fulfillment of our ideals than would our adopting some other moral (or nonmoral) system. I do not agree with Baier that a value system is vindicated only when we see that the consequences of everyone's adopting it are such as to maximize everyone's satisfactions and minimize everyone's frustrations. For this presupposes that *everyone's* interests should be taken into account in judging the consequences of a value system. Now the ideal of satisfying *everyone's* interests is the ideal of one way of life, but there are other ways of life with conflicting ideals. Unless we can show that the first way of life is more justified than the others, we cannot merely assume that its ideal is a valid standard for judging the consequences of adopting a value system. Baier at one point admits that a prudential value system can be vindicated to a particular person at a particular time. But he adds that such a system cannot be vindicated to *everyone*.

. . . A person might do better for himself by following enlightened self-interest rather than morality. It is not possible, however, that *everyone* should do better for himself by following enlightened self-interest rather than morality. The best possible life *for everyone* is possible only by everyone's following the rules of morality, that is, rules which quite frequently may require individuals to make genuine sacrifices. (*Ibid.*, pp. 314-315.)

It seems to me that Baier is begging the question here. He is assuming "the moral point of view" while he is trying to justify "the moral point of view." One could consistently say, "I admit that it is in the interest of everyone (including myself) for everyone to live morally rather than for everyone to live for his self-interest. But I also claim that it is *more* to my interest for everyone *except myself* to live morally." The person who says this may accordingly vindicate his own value system of self-interest without claiming that everyone's adopting such a value system is vindicated. If it were objected that the person could not then vindicate his value system of self-interest to others (or to everyone), he could reply: "Of course not. But I do not claim that my system of self-interest can be vindicated to others. It is vindicated to me because it furthers the ideal of my whole way of life (namely, to have others act morally while I act for my self-interest and take advantage of others). I disregard the fact that such a way of life (with its constituent value systems) is not in the interest of others." We cannot condemn this person for disregarding the interests of others *without ourselves taking "the moral point of view"* (i.e., without ourselves adopting Baier's moral system). To condemn him would be to assume that he ought to take "the moral point of view." But this is the very thing at issue. All the person would have to do is to repeat the original question: "Why should I be moral?" That is, "Why should I consider the interests of others as well as my own?" The only adequate reply to this question lies in our showing that *his* adopting Baier's moral system would be vindicated *to him*, not in our showing that it is vindicated to us or even to everyone except him.

We might grant the point that if it were to the interest of every individual to adopt a certain moral system, then that system would be vindicated to everyone. But Baier admits in the passage quoted above that it is sometimes to the interest of a person to adopt a prudential value system. Hence the prudential system rather than the moral system may sometimes be vindicated to a person. Baier then argues that this cannot be the case for everyone. Everyone's interests are better served by everyone's adopting the moral system. By "everyone's interests" Baier must mean the interests of all *taken together as a whole,* not the interests of each individual taken separately. For he has admitted that at least one individual's interest, taken separately, is not served by *his* adopting the moral system. Therefore the fact that it is to the interest of everyone as a group that every individual adopt the moral system is not a reason which successfully vindicates the moral system to every individual.

Let us grant Baier's point: a world in which everyone adopted the moral system would be one in which more interests (including the ideals and ways of life) of more people are satisfied than a world in which *everyone* adopted a value system of self-interest. We admit that it is to everyone's advantage (as a group) that everyone adopt the moral system instead of the system of self-interest. But there might well be one person or several persons who would choose a different way of life in which it was to *their interest* to have everyone adopt the system of self-interest. In that case, everyone's adopting the moral system would not be more advantageous to *them* than everyone's adopting the system of self-interest. If this appears far-fetched, we can cite the much more plausible case of a world where all the people in a highly privileged social and economic class adopt a value system in which the interests of their class take precedence over the interests of everyone outside the class. It is likely that such an arrangement would be more to their interest than an arrangement in which everyone, including themselves, adopted the impartial moral system which Baier calls "the moral point of view." In such a case the impartial system would not be vindicated to an entire class of individuals.

I submit that an impartial morality can be vindicated to everyone in only one way. We have to show that every individual, when faced with the choice of conducting his life either in accordance with that morality or in accordance with some other value system, would be justified in deciding in favor of the former. In order to do this, it is necessary to go one step beyond Baier's argument. If one is to vindicate a value system, one must show not only that living in accordance with it is part of, and tends to further the ideals of, an individual's way of life. One must also show that *this way of life can be rationally chosen.* More accurately, one must show that

the individual's commitment to a whole way of life can be justified
by a rational choice among alternative ways of life. Let us suppose
that in every situation in which a person can conduct his life either
in accordance with the moral system in question or in accordance
with some other value system, conducting his life in accordance
with the moral system would have instrumental and contributive
value toward a way of life W_1 and corresponding disvalue toward
another way of life W_2. Let us also suppose that conducting his life
in accordance with any other value system than the moral one
would have disvalue toward W_1 and value toward W_2. If we found
that, whenever a rational choice (to be described in the following
chapter) was made between W_1 and W_2, W_1 was preferred to W_2,
then adopting the moral system (and so living in accordance with
it) would be vindicated to every individual. If the same conditions
held for all possible ways of life (i.e., W_1 was always preferred to
another way of life on the basis of a rational choice between them)
and in all situations where an individual had to choose between
adopting the moral system and adopting some other value system,
then the moral system would be vindicated to everyone as far as it
could be.

Throughout our account of vindicating value systems in this
chapter, we have presupposed a higher stage of justification, namely
a rational choice, which justifies the way of life in terms of which
a value system is vindicated. We have stressed the fact that a value
system can be vindicated only as part of a way of life (its contributive value) and as a means to its ideals (its instrumental
value). It is vindicated in so far as someone's adopting it, and so
trying to live in accordance with it, has contributive and instrumental value toward his way of life, *if* his way of life can itself be
justified. Now it is always legitimate to ask why this way of life
should be accepted as a standard of evaluation and hence as the
ground for the entire logical structure of verification, validation,
and vindication. Accordingly there remains one further step before
the process of justifying a value judgment can be completed. This
is the task of giving good reasons for a person's ultimate commitment to a way of life as a whole. If good reasons can be given, and
if the way of life so justified provides a standard on the basis of

which the contributive and instrumental value of a value system can be established, and if adopting that value system allows for the validation of the standard or rule appealed to in verifying a value judgment, then that value judgment is *finally and completely* justified. My next task is to examine what it means to make a rational choice among whole ways of life.

The justification of value judgments: rational choice

6

A. *The concept of a way of life*

I have defined a way of life as a hierarchy of value systems in which each system belongs to a different point of view. Since a value system is nothing but a set of standards and rules arranged according to their relative precedence, it follows that a way of life is simply an organization of different sets of standards and rules. These sets (value systems) are in turn arranged according to *their* relative precedence. How is their relative precedence determined? In order to answer this question we must first consider what it means for a value system to be relevant to a situation and to be in conflict with another value system. It is only when two value systems are both relevant to a situation and are in conflict with each other that one can be said to take precedence over the other.

In Chapter 5 I gave as an example a situation to which an aesthetic value system and an etiquette value system are irrelevant and to which a moral value system and a prudential value system are both relevant. It was a situation in which one's own life and the lives of others are in danger and one is confronted with the choice of whether to risk one's life to help others. Now the fact that aesthetic considerations and considerations of etiquette are not relevant to such a situation is a fact about a person's way of life. Another person with a different way of life might hold that they are. In the act of committing himself to a way of life, a person subscribed to the principle that, if his own life and the lives of others were in danger, it would be irrelevant to use the standards and rules of aesthetics or of etiquette in deciding what to do. Another person, in committing himself to a way of life, may have subscribed to the opposite principle. We cannot say whether such value systems "really" are relevant or irrelevant to the situation. We can only decide the question on the basis of a given way of life, and different ways of life will yield different answers.

What, then, does it mean to say that a value system is relevant to a situation? It is to say that, according to a certain way of life, the standards and rules of that system are to be used to guide the choices and regulate the conduct of those in the situation. And this means simply that the standards and rules in question include the situation in their range of application. According to the given way of life, it is legitimate and proper to judge the choices and conduct of people in the situation by the standards and rules of the value system. Conversely a value system is irrelevant when its standards and rules do not cover the situation in their range of application, and so cannot be used to judge choices or conduct in the situation.

It is possible for two value systems, each belonging to a different point of view, to be relevant to a situation but not to be in conflict. They do not conflict when it is possible for a person's choice and conduct to be in accordance with the standards and rules of both systems. Two relevant value systems are in conflict, on the other hand, when a person's adopting one system in the situation prevents him from adopting the other, that is, when the standards or rules of one system are in conflict with those of the other. From Chapter 3 we know that one standard conflicts with another when a feature of something which is good-making according to one will be bad-making according to the other. That is, in so far as an object fulfills one standard it fails to fulfill the other. And we know that one rule conflicts with another when acts which are right according to one are wrong according to the other. There are different degrees to which two value systems may be in conflict, depending on how many of the standards and rules of one are in conflict with those of the other.

That two different value systems can be relevant to a situation and not in conflict may be illustrated as follows. Suppose we are judging a painting from two points of view, the aesthetic and the economic. When we judge it aesthetically, we apply the standards of a certain aesthetic value system we have adopted. When we judge it economically, we are interested in its worth as an investment and we apply the standards of an economic value system we have adopted. The painting may be aesthetically good and also a good investment; it may be aesthetically bad but a good investment; it may be aesthetically good but a bad investment; or it may be both aesthetically bad and a bad investment. The two value systems are thus logically independent of each other. They may be said to be divergent, but not to be in conflict. Even when they diverge (i.e., when the painting is judged as aesthetically good and economically bad, or vice versa) that which *makes* the painting aesthetically good is not that which *makes* it economically bad. In other words, the features of the painting which are good-making characteristics from the aesthetic point of view are not the same features which are bad-making characteristics from the economic point of view. As a result, our judgment that the painting is beautiful does not entail that we buy it, and our judgment that it is a bad investment does not entail that we find it aesthetically displeasing. Since the aesthetic system and the economic system are not logically connected, to increase (or decrease) the aesthetic value of something is not *eo ipso* to increase (or decrease) its economic value, although there may be a causal relation between the two. Therefore they cannot be in conflict. For an example of two value systems in conflict, I would cite the case discussed above, where one's own life and the lives of others are in danger. Here a moral value system may indeed conflict with a value system of self-interest, since to act from self-interest would *involve* acting immorally (i.e., violating a moral rule), and acting morally would *involve* sacrificing one's own interests.

It should be noted that the decision as to whether two value systems conflict in a given situation does not depend on a way of life, but on the nature of the value systems themselves. They conflict when their constituent standards and rules conflict, regardless of the way of life that contains them. It is true that conflict does not arise unless the way of life allows the two value systems to be relevant to the same situation. But once this is so, then whether or not they conflict is not determined by a way of life.

Let us now suppose that two value systems are in conflict. If we ask which system takes precedence over the other, it is to the principles of a way of life that we must refer for an answer. Different ways of life will entail different answers. According to one, value system V will take precedence over value system V'; according to another, V' will take precedence over V. There is nothing in the value systems themselves which renders them superior (or inferior) to others. We cannot show that a moral value system always or necessarily takes precedence over a prudential value system, for example, merely by examining the value systems themselves. We cannot even show this by analyzing the two points of view to which the value systems belong. The canons of reasoning which define one point of view do not stipulate that any value system which is guided by them shall be superior to any value system guided by another set of canons. Such a stipulation can only be made outside all points of view, as a principle to which one subscribes as part of one's way of life. Thus we cannot say that the moral point of view takes precedence over the prudential point of view unless we have committed ourselves to a way of life in which a moral value system takes precedence over a prudential value system whenever the two conflict. The mere fact that the one system is moral does not *make* it take precedence over another system. Indeed, there is at least one way of life, actually practiced by a culture, which does not claim superiority on behalf of its moral system over the value system of prudence or self-interest. This is the culture of the Navaho Indians. (This has been argued by John Ladd in *The Structure of a Moral Code*. Cambridge, Mass.: Harvard University Press, 1957, esp. pp. 212-213 and pp. 292-296.) However, for the Navaho there is perhaps no conceivable conflict between morality and prudence, in light of "the general Navaho presumption that the welfare of others is a necessary condition of one's own welfare." (*Ibid.*, p. 296.)

The commitment to a way of life involves the decision to *make* one value system take precedence over another when they are in conflict. Since each value system that is part of a way of life belongs to a different point of view, it may be thought that the commitment to a way of life also decides which *point of view* shall take precedence over another. But the most we can say is that a way of life determines indirectly the relative precedence of points of view. We can speak of one point of view (say, the moral) taking precedence over another point of view (say, the prudential), but only in the sense that, given a situation in which a person must decide between acting morally and acting in his self-interest, the person's way of life determines that the moral system takes precedence over the prudential system. In another situation, or with another way of life, it might be the case that self-interest will take precedence over morality. Thus we cannot ask, "Does one point of view in general take precedence over another?" We can only ask "Does this particular value system belonging to one point of view take precedence over that particular value system belonging to another point of view?" And this question can be answered only relatively to a way of life. However, under special conditions it would be possible to make a generalization, albeit a somewhat misleading one, concerning the relative precedence of points of view. Suppose, for example, that there is one way of life which is always preferred to every other way of life on the basis of a rational choice. And suppose that, according to this way of life, whenever a moral value system conflicts with a prudential value system the moral system takes precedence. We might then say, still somewhat misleadingly, that the moral point of view takes precedence over the point of view of self-interest. (The relative precedence of points of view is discussed further in Section B of Chapter 11.)

In summary, to commit oneself to a way of life is to subscribe to certain principles. These principles are of two types: principles of relevance and principles of relative precedence. When we subscribe to a principle of the first type, we *decide* which value systems shall be relevant to a certain kind of situation and which shall not. In choosing a way of life we *make* a given system relevant or not relevant to a given situation. Similarly, when we subscribe to a principle of the second type, we *decide* that one value system shall take precedence over another in a situation where they conflict and to which they are both relevant. In choosing a way of life we stipulate the relative precedence of our value systems. Thus we cannot answer the question why a certain value system is relevant or why it takes precedence over another. We can only say that these simply are the principles to which we subscribe in virtue of the fact that we are committed to a particular way of life. In the very act of committing ourselves, we make value system V relevant to situation S and we make value system V take precedence over value system V'. We cannot give reasons for claiming that V is relevant to S or that V takes precedence over V'. We can only say we have chosen that way of life. Such a choice is our *ultimate normative commitment*. The only kind of reasons which can be given to justify the principles of a way of life are reasons which justify the way of life as a whole. As we shall see, such reasons consist in showing that the way of life is rationally chosen.

Variation in ways of life depends on the particular principles of relevance and relative precedence which define each. From this variation in ways of life themselves, we can distinguish another kind of variation—a variation in *commitments* to a way of life. Thus we may classify varying commitments according to (a) their degree of coherence and stability, (b) their degree of depth, (c) their degree of conventionality or unconventionality, and (d) their degree of explicitness.

(a) I have been speaking up to now as if everyone commits himself to just one way of life, striving to live by its principles and to realize its ideals throughout his life. The fact is, however, that individuals vary widely in the coherence and stability of their ultimate commitments. In a society at large, there will always be a more or less definite way of life to which most members of the society have been committed by being brought up within it. They have not committed themselves as a matter of choice, but have been committed by others. If they remain uncritical and conventional in their outlook, they will have a coherent and stable way of life. But there will be individuals who for one reason or another will come to doubt the way of life in which they have been brought up. They might then choose a new way of life which will be just as coherent and stable as the way of life of their society. On the other hand, they might become disillusioned with their new way of life. They might shortly find themselves committed to another, which again might turn out to be unsatisfactory to them. To the extent that a person's commitments are in this way temporary and constantly changing, to that extent they lack coherence and stability. The extreme of incoherence and instability is reached when an individual has no way of life of his own. He lives without principles or ideals. Whatever standards and rules he does follow are not organized into unified value systems. He lacks second-order norms by which to determine the relative precedence of other norms. And he applies his norms inconsistently, sometimes having pro-attitudes toward the very same things which at other times are the objects of his con-attitudes. From this extreme there is a continuum of commitments of increasing coherence and stability until we arrive at a single, all-embracing, permanent way of life, in which the value systems of all points of view are integrated in a consistent hierarchy.

(b) Commitments to ways of life may vary not only in degree of coherence and stability, but also in degree of depth or thoroughness. A strong-minded, deeply convinced, thoroughly committed person will strive to live according to his way of life under all circumstances. He will exert every effort to fulfill its ideals, even at great cost to his own comfort or safety. A person who is not deeply committed to a way of life will be only weakly motivated to live by its principles and ideals, and will frequently fail to adhere to the standards and rules involved in it when it is not to his immediate advantage. (I shall consider depth of commitment further in Chapter 12.)

(c) Commitments to ways of life also vary in degree of conventionality or unconventionality, according to their agreement or disagreement with the way of life of the general culture or times. An individual's way of life is conventional to the extent that it agrees with the way of life of his family, of his religious background, of his economic and social class, and of the various groups to which he belongs. (We shall see that the conventionality or unconventionality of a way of life has nothing to do with whether it can be rationally chosen.)

(d) Another dimension in which commitments to ways of life vary is in their degree of explicitness. A person might live fully in accordance with the ideals and principles of a way of life and yet not be able to *tell* someone what they are. Such a person would be unable to make his way of life explicit; he could not articulate, either to himself or to others, his basic beliefs and "values." We might say of him that he lives *as if* he believed in certain ideals and principles. His commitment is implicit, not explicit. Another person might be able to state clearly and coherently what his way of life is. If he is of a certain bent and has certain abilities, he might even write out his "philosophy of life" in a book. He might also preach it to others and try to get them to become committed to it. He might accordingly be proclaimed a prophet or wise man, or else (depending on the social conditions of his time and on the nature of his way of life) a fanatic, a crank, a reformer, or a demagogue.

B. *Absolutism and relativism*

Having considered what it means to be committed to a way of life, we are now prepared to continue our inquiry into the justification of value judgments. We have reached the fourth and final stage of such justification: the rational choice of a way of life. We have seen that the commitment to a way of life is an ultimate commitment. If we ask someone to justify his value judgments and he appeals to standards or rules, and if we ask him for reasons for accepting his standards or rules and he validates them, and if we then ask him to justify his entire value system and he vindicates it, he must finally refer to his whole way of life. There he takes his final stand. The question now before us is: How can this ultimate commitment itself be justified? This question, it seems to me, lies at the heart of the controversy between absolutism and relativism in values.

No one has brought out more clearly the fact that commitment to a way of life is an ultimate commitment than R. M. Hare. In the following passage Mr. Hare gives his account of the justification of decisions and principles. (The term "principles" covers not only what I have referred to as standards and rules, but also what I have called the ideals and principles of a way of life.)

. . . A complete justification of a decision would consist of a complete account of its effects, together with a complete account of the principles which it observed, and the effects of observing those principles. . . . Thus, if pressed to justify a decision completely, we have to give a complete specification of the way of life of which it is a part. This complete specification it is impossible in practice to give; the nearest attempts are those given by the great religions, especially those which can point to historical persons who carried out the way of life in practice. Suppose, however, that we can give it. If the inquirer still goes on asking 'But why *should* I live like that?' then there is no further answer to give him, because we have already, *ex hypothesi*, said everything that could be included in this further answer. We can only ask him to make up his own mind which way he ought to live; for in the end everything rests upon such a decision of principle. He has to decide whether to accept that way of life or not; if he accepts it, then we can proceed to justify the decisions that are based upon it; if he does not accept it, then let him accept some other, and try to live by it. (R. M. Hare, *The Language of Morals*, p. 69.)

We have considered a somewhat parallel situation with regard to the vindication of value systems. There, however, an appeal is made to "principles" in a wider context, for we found that a value system can be vindicated in terms of the ideals of a whole way of life. But there is no such wider context to refer to when we are asked to justify a way of life itself. Hare says that we can only ask the person to try to live by it. But is there no way to show that one person's choice of a way of life is more *intelligent* or *enlightened* than another's? Hare himself argues that the choice of a way of life is not an *arbitrary* decision.

To describe such ultimate decisions as arbitrary, because *ex hypothesi* everything which could be used to justify them has already been included in the decision, would be like saying that a complete description of the universe was utterly unfounded, because no further fact could be called upon in corroboration of it. This is not how we use the words 'arbitrary' and 'unfounded.' Far from being arbitrary, such a decision would be the most well-founded of decisions, because it would be based upon a consideration of everything upon which it could possibly be founded. (*Ibid.*, p. 69.)

In light of these remarks, it would seem that there is at least one condition for rationality in making a "decision of principle" to commit oneself to a whole way of life, namely the condition that one *know* what is involved in all the alternative ways of life among which one is choosing. I shall later specify what I consider to be the necessary and sufficient conditions for a rational choice among ways of life, and this condition will be included among them. Before doing this, however, it is important to clarify the general nature of a rational choice.

The context in which I am dealing with such a choice is the context of justifying a value judgment. My purpose is to make clear the logic of our reasoning when our value judgments are consistently challenged. In setting forth the conditions of a rational choice among ways of life, I shall not be trying to describe a situation of choice which would actually confront someone in everyday life. I shall be constructing a concept of a rational choice in the abstract. This concept is designed to answer the question, "What sort of commitment to a way of life would anyone on reflection be willing to call a justified one?" The question is not, "How do people actually come to commit themselves to a way of life?" Nor is it, "What would be the psychological grounds (causes) for a person's choice if he actually were confronted with alternative ways of life among which he were asked to choose?"

The philosophical question with which we are concerned arises only when we try to push back our defense or support of a value judgment as far as it will go—to its ultimate foundations, as it were. The logic of our thinking moves step by step from the judgment to a standard or rule, from a standard or rule to higher standards or rules, from those to the highest standards or rules within the framework of validation, from there to the whole value system which sets that framework, and from there to the whole way of life in terms of which the value system is vindicated. Here we stop, until we notice that there are many different and conflicting ways of life. We see that if we commit ourselves to one we will be able to justify our value judgment, but that if we commit ourselves to another we will be able to show that our value judgment is unjustified. It is then that we ask ourselves if all ways of life are equally justified. Is it not possible to give good reason for accepting one way of life rather than another?

The issue raised here is that which many philosophers call the issue between relativism and absolutism. Are values relative or absolute? If we can trace the logical foundations of our value judgments back to our commitment to a certain way of life but cannot justify this commitment itself, then all values are said to be relative. They are relative to our way of life. (More accurately, they are relative to our value systems, and our value systems are themselves relative to our way of life.) This relativistic position holds that, if we find (as we do) that different societies and cultures have conflicting ways of life, then the struggle between them is a matter of brute force, unless they voluntarily decide to tolerate each other's differences. No rational choice can be made between them. If one has a moral code (i.e., a moral value system) which contradicts the moral code of the other—so that acts of a certain sort are right in the one culture and wrong in the other—we cannot talk about acts of that sort being "really" right or "really" wrong. They *are* right (not merely believed to be right) in one culture and wrong in the other. Good reasons can be given *for* doing the acts, if one accepts the supreme norms of the value systems as vindicated by the way of life of the first culture. Similarly, good reasons can be given *against* doing the same acts in the framework of the way of life of the second culture. Since good reasons cannot be given in support of one whole way of life rather than the other, any "good reasons" are relative to value systems and finally to ways of life. They are valid only in so far as one adopts a certain value system and with it a certain way of life.

We cannot escape this kind of relativism by arguing that the canons of reasoning which define normative points of view are equally as rational as the canons of reasoning which define the scientific, the mathematical, and the historical points of view. It is true that just as we can explicate the canons of reasoning that govern the latter and thereby reveal the ideal of rationality implicit in those ways of thinking, so we can explicate the canons of reasoning which govern the various normative points of view and thereby disclose the ideal of rationality implicit in them. The relativist can grant this and still claim that our inability to justify a whole way of life opens the way for skepticism, and destroys the rationality of normative thinking *as a whole*. His argument is based on the fact that the canons of reasoning which govern the scientific, the mathematical, and the historical points of view are independent of whatever way of life a scientist, a mathematician, or a historian may be committed to. A physicist will appeal to the same sort of evidence to confirm a hypothesis whether he be a Hindu or a Christian, a Communist or a Capitalist. But the reasons which he appeals to in trying to justify his *value judgments* will vary according to the way of life he is committed to. Unless his way of life can itself be justified, the reasons which he gives will not make a universal claim on all men. The relativist would have to admit that, on the levels of verification and validation, taking a certain point of view would entail the same rules of valid inference and relevance for everyone, no matter what his way of life may be. Hence *to this extent* a person can claim rationality on behalf of his way of justifying value judgments. It is only when we reach the level of vindicating a whole value system that the skeptical power of relativism is felt. At this level we can no longer appeal to the universality of our canons of reasoning as a sufficient ground for claiming that the justification of value judgments is a rational process. The universal canons at this level are the rules of valid inference which define the process of vindication itself. That is, they are the rules according to which we justify a value system by showing that it has contributive and instrumental value to a way of life. *But such rules allow for the same value system to be both justified and unjustified,* since a value system which has contributive and instrumental value to one way of life can have contributive and instrumental disvalue to another.

Under the relativist's assumption that ways of life cannot rationally be justified, it seems we must make an important, indeed a damaging, qualification in our claim to *know* what is good or bad, right or wrong. We must admit that such knowledge varies from way of life to way of life, whereas scientific, mathematical, and historical knowledge do not. This difference is sufficient to make us doubtful about using the word "knowledge" at all in connection with value judgments. A similar doubt arises concerning our use of the words "true" and "false." A value system may be vindicated in one culture and an opposite or conflicting value system may be vindicated in another culture, since each culture embodies a different way of life. This seems to imply that a given value judgment may be true in one culture and false in another. Indeed, it is possible to define valuational relativism as the view that no value judgment is simply true or simply false, but is only true *for* someone (or *for* some group or culture), and false *for* someone else (or *for* some other group or culture). Nobody would say this about scientific, mathematical, or historical statements. A scientific, mathematical, or historical statement is simply (absolutely, genuinely) true or false. To say that it is true *for* someone means only that someone believes it or *thinks* it is true. Value judgments may also be said to be true for someone in this sense. But this is not what the relativist is getting at when he makes such a claim. He means that the truth of a value judgment is relative to someone's (or some group's or culture's) way of life in such a way that the same judgment will be false relative to another person's (or group's or culture's) way of life.

Valuational absolutism, on the other hand, claims that a value judgment is simply true or false, not true or false *for* someone. It is true when it can be shown to be justified, false when it can be shown to be unjustified. It is shown to be justified when it is verified by appeal to a standard or rule which can be validated within a value system, which in turn is vindicated by reference to a way of life, *and this way of life can rationally be preferred to all others.* If the way of life which vindicates the value system can rationally be shown not to be preferable to some other way of life, then the value judgment is false. To say that the judgment is true or false is to say that it is *really* true or false, quite aside from whether or not people think so. Of course its truth or falsity does depend on a given value system, but not all value systems are equally justified. Some may be vindicated in terms of a nonrational way of life. Hence value systems do not fully provide a justification for a value judgment. A value judgment is *completely* justified (i.e., it is as justified as it can be) when the value system within the framework of which it is verified and validated is itself vindicated by reference to a *rational* way of life. Only such a value judgment can be claimed to be really true. Its truth in some respects will be different from scientific and mathematical truth, although, like the latter, it will be independent of cultural variation. A value judgment will be true even though its truth is not recognized by a whole culture (just as "The earth is a globe" was true even when people thought that the earth was flat).

For the valuational absolutist, what is the difference between the truth of value judgments and the truth of scientific or mathematical statements? The answer lies in how they are justified. Scientific and mathematical statements are completely justified in terms of the canons of valid reasoning set by the scientific and mathematical points of view. To decide to take such a point of view is to decide to reason in a certain way, that is, according to certain rules of inference. What is found to be intellectually acceptable according to these rules will be designated as true; what is found, under the same rules, to be intellectually unacceptable will be false. The canons of reasoning which govern the complete justification of a value judgment, on the other hand, require the steps of vindication and rational choice. These latter do not correspond to any steps used in verifying scientific statements or in proving mathematical statements. The verification and validation of value judgments are carried out within the framework of a value system according to the canons of reasoning which define a normative point of view; they may be compared generally with empirical verification and deductive reasoning in nonnormative points of view. But as we have seen, the value system referred to in the verification and validation of value judgments must itself be justified. The method used is that of a pragmatic test, which in turn makes reference to a way of life. There is no similar test and no similar reference in scientific and mathematical reasoning.

C. The concept of a rational choice

I shall now proceed to give the argument for valuational absolutism. To do so, I shall try to explicate the concept of a rational choice among ways of life, and thereby show that the preference for one way of life rather than another is not arbitrary. This is the fourth and final stage in the total justification of a value judgment. It can be accomplished by showing that whenever anyone is confronted with a situation in which he is to choose between a given way of life and other ways of life, and whenever that situation satisfies the necessary conditions for a rational choice, the given way of life will be chosen in preference to any other.

The necessary conditions for a rational choice among ways of life must be specified. I suggest that these conditions may be grouped under three general headings: conditions of freedom, conditions of enlightenment, and conditions of impartiality. I shall say that a choice is rational *to the extent that* it is free, enlightened, and impartial. Each of these conditions sets up an ideal. No actual choice can ever be completely free, completely enlightened, or completely impartial. Hence no choice actually made among alternative ways of life can be fully rational. As I have already pointed out, the concept of a rational choice is the concept of an ideal. In describing it, I am trying to explicate one of the canons of rationality—to state what *would* be considered by anyone to be a rational choice, *if* such a choice were ever to occur under ideal conditions. I am not trying to describe any actual choice made by someone. All that is necessary for ultimately justifying a value judgment is that a *meaning* be given to the concept of rational choice that will make explicit the assumptions underlying the way a fully rational person would think in the given context. My claim here is that *to the extent that* any actual choice fulfills the conditions of rationality which I shall state, *to that extent* it justifies the way of life chosen and consequently can be used to justify a value judgment. I shall now specify the conditions of rationality under the three headings mentioned.

1. *Conditions of freedom.* A choice is free to the extent that:

(a) *The choice is not decisively determined by unconscious motives.* That is, if unconscious motives do have a role as psychological determinants of the person's choice, their role is not decisive. What *is* decisive will be given in the fourth condition of freedom, stated below under (d).

(b) *The choice is not at all determined by internal constraint.* That is, the person who makes the choice is under no element of compulsion, whether of irresistible impulse or extreme desire. He is calm and collected, in complete control of himself.

(c) *The choice is not at all determined by external constraint.* That is, there is nothing in the physical or social environment of the person to compel him to make a choice. So far as the physical environment is concerned, the person is not in any immediate physical danger and does not have to suffer any immediate physical harm when he makes his choice. (Some of the ways of life among which he is choosing, however, might entail more physical danger and suffering than others.) So far as the social environment is concerned, no social pressure is being brought to bear on him to choose one alternative rather than another. No one is goading him, threatening him, or trying to intimidate him. He is not under any form of coercion or duress.

(d) *The choice is decisively determined by the person's own preference.* That is, his choice follows upon his preference, though in order that his choice be rational *his preference must be enlightened and impartial* (as spelled out below). To say that a choice is free is not to say that it is uncaused or undetermined. It is rather to say that the choice is the result of, and hence determined by, the individual's making up his own mind about the matter. I do not call this process *deliberation,* however. Deliberation is evaluation, and all evaluation is made according to standards or rules. We are concerned here with a preference, not an evaluation. There are no standards or rules to appeal to, since we are dealing with a choice among whole ways of life and all standards and rules are included in these. If we were to appeal to a standard or rule, we would be presupposing a way of life in making the choice, and therefore our choice would not be a choice among ways of life.

2. *Conditions of enlightenment.* A choice is enlightened to the extent that:

(a) *The nature of each way of life is fully known.*
(b) *The probable effects of living each way of life are fully known.*
(c) *The means necessary to bring about each way of life* (i.e., what is required to enable a person to live each way of life) *are fully known.*

There are three kinds of knowledge involved in *each* of these conditions: intellectual knowledge, imaginative knowledge, and practical knowledge. Intellectual knowledge of a way of life includes all the empirical knowledge necessary for a complete and accurate *description* of the way of life itself, of the probable effects of living according to it, and of the necessary means for bringing it about. Such knowledge must provide us with answers to a whole series of questions. What is it like for a person (or group, or culture) to live the way of life? What are the ideals of the way of life; what vision of the *summum bonum* does it embody? What value systems are relevant to different sorts of situations and what value systems take precedence over others in those situations? What would be the psychological and social consequences of a person's (or group's, or culture's) living that way of life? What physical, social, and psychological conditions must be realized before a person (or group, or culture) would be able to live the way of life?

In addition to the knowledge that the empirical sciences must provide, intellectual knowledge of the *nature* of a way of life must also include philosophical knowledge. We must know the canons of reasoning that constitute the point of view to which any value system in the way of life belongs. What are the rules of relevance and the rules of valid inference which govern the justification of judgments, standards and rules within the framework of each value system? That is, according to what criteria is a reason a relevant reason or a good reason in such justification?

Intellectual knowledge of a way of life, in short, consists of all the scientific and philosophical knowledge that can possibly enlighten us concerning the value systems and the points of view which constitute it. A person does not make a rational choice among ways of life, however, if he merely has intellectual knowledge of them. Imaginative knowledge is also necessary. He must be able to *envisage* what it is like to live each way of life. He must be able, by imagination, to convey himself into each way of life and experience it vicariously. Short of actually having lived a way of life, there are four particularly effective means for developing this imaginative knowledge: through personal contact with people who live the way of life, through the reading of history, biography, and to a lesser extent anthropology and sociology, through the study of religion, and through appreciation of the fine arts.

When one has personal friends or acquaintances who live a certain way of life, or better, lives among people who follow it, one's imaginative insight into it is increased, even if one does not share that way of life with them. Constant contact with people makes us subtly aware of their interests, attitudes, points of view, and aspirations, so that we can sense intuitively the way they look upon the world. The closer we get to people and the better we come to know them, the deeper becomes our understanding of their way of life.

We can also increase our ability to envisage a way of life by reading the history of peoples who have embodied it in their culture, or by reading a biography of an individual whose life exemplifies it to a high degree. This is especially helpful when the historian or biographer is sympathetic to the way of life. If an individual's letters, essays, and speeches have been published, reading these will also help to convey to us his way of life. Anthropological and sociological studies of whole cultures or of subcultural groups sometimes can be used to the same effect. Thus Margaret Mead's writings on Samoa can help us to imagine the Samoan way of life, and sociological studies of New York City's juvenile gangs can make us vividly aware of their way of life.

Each of the established religions of a society is itself a total way of life and a sensitive reading of its sacred texts and other scriptures will to some extent enable a person who does not practice it to imagine what it is like to practice it. The detailed investigations of scholars in comparative religion can also help a nonbeliever envisage what it is like to have a particular religion and to experience life from its point of view. Of course one can have *full* knowledge of a religion only if he himself practices it, that is, actually lives the way of life which is the religion. This is what I have called "practical knowledge," and I shall consider it more fully below. My only claim here is that the sensitive reading of the literature of a religion can *aid* us in coming to an imaginative grasp of its meaning, even if we do not practice it or believe in it. It is necessary in addition to purely scientific and philosophical knowledge about the practices and beliefs of the religion if a rational preference for the religion over another way of life (or for another way of life over the religion) is to be made.

The critical analysis and appreciation of art has long been recognized as a way to deepen our understanding not only of an artist's personal outlook but also of the whole spirit of an age or the general world view of a culture. The music, the painting and sculpture, the dance, the architecture, the drama, and the literature of a culture all present to us the way of life of the culture. A thorough understanding of works of art in these various forms brings us to an imaginative awareness of a way of life which no scientific or philosophical knowledge, however complete, could yield. One of the most interesting aspects of a great novel, poem, or drama, for example, is the way its author creates a world in which certain fundamental attitudes, points of view, and ways of life are expressed. A novelist, poet, or dramatist does not necessarily attempt to persuade us to accept *his* world outlook or way of life. He confronts us with one, or sometimes several, for our imaginative contemplation. And his work often reflects the entire world view which underlies his social milieu and cultural background. Reading a novel or poem, watching a drama or ballet, listening to music, looking at painting, sculpture, and architecture all can give us a direct insight, an intuitive grasp, of a way of life. Thus we gain an envisagement of what it is like to live a way of life which we ourselves may never have lived.

The third kind of knowledge which we must have if our choice among ways of life is to be ideally enlightened is knowledge by acquaintance, or what I have designated "practical knowledge." A person has this kind of knowledge of a way of life when he actually has lived it. This means that he has been inspired by the ideals of the way of life and that he has adopted the appropriate value systems relevant to given situations. We recall that adopting a value system involves both reasoning in a certain way and living in a certain way. To have practical knowledge of a way of life is to know what it is like to live it because one has conducted his thinking and his behavior in accordance with the value systems of which it is comprised. In the case of a religion, one has practical knowledge of it when one has been a believer, has practiced it, has actively and sincerely participated in its form of worship. Although such knowledge by acquaintance can be one of the best means of enlightening ourselves about ways of life, it should be noted that a person who lives a way of life might not be able intellectually or imaginatively to see it as a unified whole. He may be too involved in it to have the kind of detached understanding which can come from an outsider's intellectual or imaginative knowledge of it. A second limitation of practical knowledge is that we can come to know very few ways of life by means of it. One cannot just decide to "try out" a way of life as an experiment and live it for a few months or even a few years. A person must be educated in a certain way, and sometimes must receive special training, to come to the point where he can accept a way of life and commit himself wholly to it. It should further be noted that, at the time of the rational choice itself, the person who makes the choice must not be committed to any of the ways of life among which he is choosing. But this brings us to the third set of conditions for a rational choice.

3. *Conditions of impartiality.* A choice is impartial to the extent that:

(a) *The choice is disinterested.* That is, the choice is not at all determined by bribes, by exercise of favoritism, by desire to protect one's privileges (or those of one's family, friends, or class), or by any emotional prejudices on the part of the person who makes the choice. For example, if a person is influenced by anti-Semitism he cannot possibly make a rational choice between the way of life of Judaism and some other way of life. And this holds regardless of how much intellectual or imaginative knowledge he might possess of Judaism.

There is one condition that can *guarantee* the complete disinterestedness of the choice, and I therefore include it among the conditions of a rational choice. (It was suggested to me by Professor John Hospers.) We can eliminate entirely the element of self-interest in a choice by stipulating that the person who makes the choice *not* know what position he himself would have in any chosen way of life, if it were to be realized on earth. Like the souls in Book X of Plato's *Republic,* his future destiny would be *decided by lot.* Thus there would be no possibility that the person was influenced by desire for personal advantage or protection of special privileges in making his choice. For he would have no idea which way of life would be more in his self-interest to choose.

(b) *The choice is detached or objective.* By this I mean that it is a choice among ways of life other than that in which the person who makes the choice was brought up and other than that to which he is committed at the time of choice. The latter condition must be included for the obvious reason that we are asking a person to state his preference for one way of life over others. If he is already committed to a way of life and yet (under the second set of conditions) knows about other ways of life, his preference is set in advance. He will prefer his own way of life to the others. Such a person is not in a position to make a choice at all, to say nothing of a rational choice.

The first qualification, however, deserves to be examined at greater length. A rational choice among certain ways of life can be made only by those who were not brought up within the framework of any one of those ways of life. For it is impossible entirely to escape the influence of early childhood, when we were given rules to follow and standards to fulfill and all the pro-attitudes and con-attitudes that go with success or failure in doing this. Although, as we shall see when we come to the third condition of impartiality, a person need not be *biased* as a result of his being brought up in one way of life, he will always be under its influence. Consequently his choice among ways of life which included that one will never be truly impartial. In order to insure the maximum degree of impartiality, then, the following conditions of "detachment" or "objectivity" must hold. Let us assume that a person was brought up in a way of life, A, so that he is not qualified to make a rational choice between way of life A and way of life B, or between way of life A and way of life C. But (*if all other conditions of a rational choice are satisfied*) he is qualified to make a rational choice between B and C. Similarly, a person brought up in B cannot make a rational choice between A and B or between B and C, but he can between A and C. And one brought up in C can choose between A and B, but not between A and C or B and C. Now suppose all persons who were brought up in ways of life C, D, E, F, G . . . etc., were to make a rational choice between A and B, and suppose that they all preferred A to B. Then, under the assumption that *in each case all the conditions of rationality were satisfied*, we may conclude that way of life A is more justified than way of life B. This judgment is strengthened to the extent that ways of life C, D, E, F, G, etc., are very different from one another and from both A and B. The judgment is strengthened even more if persons brought up in B, upon satisfying all the other conditions of a rational choice but this one, were to prefer A to B.

It might be objected that, no matter how free and enlightened the choice is, and no matter how disinterested are the persons making the choice, it is still not a truly impartial choice. For a person brought up in C will prefer A to B because A is more *similar* to C than is B. And the same for those brought up in D, E, F, G, etc. In each case A is more similar and B is less similar to the way of life in which the person was brought up, and for that reason the person always has a slight bias toward A and away from B. The influence of early childhood is ever-present and therefore impartiality is never attained. Indeed, it is unattainable. In order to face this objection, I set one additional condition of impartiality.

(c) *The choice is unbiased.* In order to minimize the impact of early childhood environment upon a rational choice, I stipulate not only that the person making the choice must not have been brought up in one of the ways of life among which he is choosing (the condition of detachment), but I also stipulate that the person was not *indoctrinated into* or *conditioned blindly* to accept the way of life in which he was brought up. To put it positively, a choice is unbiased to the extent that (i) the person's upbringing was nonauthoritarian, (ii) the person's education was liberal, and (iii) the person's experience of life up to the time of choice was of considerable variety, richness, and depth.

All children are brought up within the framework of some standards and rules. But there is a great difference between being conditioned to an unuqestioning acceptance of standards and rules and being brought to see the reasons behind such standards and rules. When the standards are imposed and the rules laid down in an authoritarian manner by the parents, the child learns blind obedience and rigid conformity. When the parents impose standards and lay down rules in a nonauthoritarian manner (and they must impose *some* standards, lay down *some* rules, or else the child will have no guidance), the parents encourage the child to question the standards and rules and to ask that they be justified. The parents' answers will at first, of course, be given in a relatively simple way, for instance, in terms of the usefulness of the standards and rules in accomplishing this or that specific purpose. Nonauthoritarian parents will also try to develop in the child, as he grows older, an ability to make "decisions of principle," that is, to make up his own mind whether to follow a rule or standard or to make an exception to it in a given situation, or to decide to reject the rule or standard entirely. A nonauthoritarian upbringing enables a child as he grows older to justify his value judgments and his standards and rules, and finally to choose his own way of life (which may or may not be the same as that of his parents). As a mature person he will be able to change his way of life when social, economic, political, domestic and other conditions of his life demand such a change.

A similar contrast can be found in the difference between indoctrination and education. To be *educated within* the framework of a society's way of life is not necessarily to be *indoctrinated into* that way of life. Indoctrination is a deliberate manipulation of the mind of a child, an attempt to produce unquestioned belief in one way of life and a blind rejection of all others. Education, on the other hand, is a process of giving the child tools of criticism as well as of adjustment. As the child matures, his education becomes more liberal, presenting him with value systems and ways of life which are foreign to his own. At the same time his mind is trained to think critically about his own way of life, so that he is forced to make up his own mind about issues on which he finds he must take a stand, or about controversies on which he finds he must take sides. The society which not only permits, but encourages, its members to criticize its own foundations (value systems) is in no sense a society which indoctrinates its members.

Finally, we may contrast the life of a person who has been brought up in a uniform culture, where he meets only people who have the same outlook and opinions as he does and whose value systems are the same as his, where he remains in one occupation all his life, never travels either to foreign countries or to other areas of his native land, reads no books, remains protected from any great suffering, and never goes through any deeply emotional experiences —we may contrast such a life with that of a person who meets and gets to know people of varied backgrounds and from all walks of life, who travels widely, reads a great deal, and has a generally varied and rich experience of life. Although both of these persons are, in some very general sense, "children of their culture," the latter is much less a child of his culture than the former. In the same way, an educated person is much less a child of his culture than an indoctrinated person, and a person with a nonauthoritarian upbringing than one with an authoritarian upbringing.

To the extent that a person in these various ways is *not* a child of his culture, to that extent he is better able to make an impartial choice among ways of life which exclude the one he was brought up in. And to that extent he will not automatically prefer the way of life which is most similar to that of his childhood. Thus, although total absence of bias cannot be guaranteed, we can in this way minimize it.

These, then, are the conditions which define an ideal rational choice among ways of life. It is a choice which is totally free, totally enlightened, and totally impartial. No one is ever in a situation where he can actually make such a choice. We are never confronted with alternative ways of life under these ideal conditions. But that is not to the point. The real question is this. What *would* make a reason for committing ourselves to a way of life a *good* reason? My answer, in sum, is that such a reason is to be found in the situation I have described—where we find that more and more people brought up in a variety of ways of life tend more and more to prefer one particular way of life to all others, when their preference results from a free, enlightened, and impartial choice. What better reason *could* there be for committing ourselves to a way of life?

I have tried only to show that it makes sense to talk about a rational choice among ways of life, and that therefore the relativist's position is not tenable. In justifying our value systems we can go beyond vindicating them in terms of a way of life. We can ask that the way of life itself be justified. It will always be impossible *in practice* to know with certainty which way of life is more justified than any other, since the conditions of an ideal rational choice are such that it is difficult even to approximate them. But it is *theoretically* possible to do so, and therefore *meaningful* to speak of a rationally chosen way of life. Although we can never be certain whether one way of life is rationally preferable to another, we can reach a probable knowledge of this in the following way. We can say that, to the extent that choices become more and more rational and to the extent that more and more people who make such choices tend to prefer a way of life A to a way of life B, then *to that extent it is reasonable for anyone to accept* A *as preferable to* B. Such acceptance must remain tentative only. It must be open to revision in the light of further choices under conditions which more closely approximate those of an ideal rational choice. But it provides the best *available* way of knowing whether A really is preferable to B.

It might be objected that no such agreement could ever be

reached, even if all the conditions of a rational choice were fully realized. For it is always possible that variations in temperament among people will result in variations in their preference for ways of life. Thus even choices made under ideal conditions of rationality will be subject to the disagreements among romanticists and classicists, doers and thinkers, rationalists and mystics, dogmatists and skeptics, optimists and pessimists, conservatives and radicals, seekers of happiness and doers of duty. This possibility must be admitted, but it does not destroy the concept of a rational choice as such. It merely leaves open the question—which would have to be left open even without this consideration—whether increase in rationality of choice leads to agreement among the choosers. All that we can say is that, *if* under the conditions of a rational choice there was a tendency among choosers to agree that way of life A is preferable to way of life B (whether or not the choosers were of the same temperament), then we would have just that much reason to conclude that A is more justified than B. That such a tendency would be made manifest as ideal conditions of rational choice were more and more closely approximated must remain an open question.

D. Why be rational?

There is one difficulty involved in this attempt to define a rational choice among ways of life which, if not satisfactorily met, undercuts the entire project. Have I not imposed *my own* way of life upon the concept of a rationally preferable way of life by stipulating just these conditions of rationality and not others? In other words, am I not begging the question by giving conditions for a rational choice which are themselves part of a way of life? Am I not merely presupposing a way of life and working within its framework, rather than taking a standpoint outside all ways of life? And in that case how do I know that the way of life I am presupposing is itself preferable to all others? Until I have shown that it is so, I cannot claim that the conditions which I specify for a rational choice really do justify one way of life rather than another. On the other hand, if I try to establish the preferability of this presupposed way of life by appeal to a rational choice, I am arguing in a circle, for the conditions of a rational choice are part of that way of life itself.

My answer is to deny that the conditions of a rational choice are part of a way of life. For they are the conditions which I presume *anyone*, in *any* way of life, would accept as defining a rational choice, in the ordinary sense of the word "rational." If people on reflection would not be willing to accept these conditions, I would not say they were making a mistake. Nor would I continue to impose my conditions upon them. I would ask them what conditions *they* would give for defining a rational choice. If they offered some which I had not thought of and which did seem (to me and to them) to elucidate further our ordinary meaning of being rational in making choices, then these new conditions would go into the definition. Would they not then be imposing *their* way of life upon the concept of rational choice? The answer is no, because the concept of a rational choice is independent of all ways of life. Even if two persons were committed to very different ways of life, both would have to admit that, *if* a rational choice *were* to be made between their two ways of life, it would have to be a free, enlightened, and impartial choice. Or else it would have to be a choice under other conditions which better elucidate what a rational choice means.

But whatever the conditions, they cannot change when the way of life being judged changes. This follows from the very meaning of the word "rational." If the choice is to be a rational one, it must at least have properties of rationality which do not vary with the ways of life among which the choice is being made. Thus it must always be possible for a person to admit that a rational choice was made and yet another way of life was preferred to his own. To test the preferability of one's own way of life by the method of rational choice always presupposes the possibility that the test will turn out negative. For otherwise it is no test at all. One would have set up the conditions of a "rational choice" (the test conditions) in such a way that one's own way of life would always come out on top. To vary the conditions so that they always bring about this result is a sign that the choice is *not* rational. For it is an essential part of the meaning of rationality that its conditions not vary with what is being judged.

In specifying the conditions of a rational choice, then, no particular way of life is involved. All that is involved is an attempt to make explicit the idea which we all have (no matter what may be our way of life) when we reflect about what an ideally rational choice among ways of life would be. I have spelled out what I think it would be. It is for others to challenge my account and to improve upon it. The conditions I have specified are, I think, an accurate explication of the meaning of the word "rational" in this context. Consequently I believe that any person would have to admit that this is what a rational choice consists in, even if making such a choice would result in other ways of life being preferred to his own.

Furthermore, if my explication of rational choice is correct, then any person would have to agree with it, even though his own way of life denied freedom of choice to people, prevented enlightened choices from being made, and did not develop impartiality in people. It does not follow, however, that his way of life would never be preferred to others when a rational choice among them was made. We do not know what actual ways of life would be preferred when rational choices were made, and *there is no necessity that the preferred ways of life have the same characteristics as the rational choice itself*. The concept of a rational choice is not logically connected with the *content* of any particular way of life. I am not imposing the content of my own way of life upon others when I explicate the conditions of rationality in terms of freedom, enlightenment, and impartiality. If one should ask me, "Why ought I to accept your conditions of rationality?", my answer would be, "They are not *my* conditions of rationality, but yours too. Is this not what *you* would mean by an ideally rational choice?" If the reply is negative, then the way is open for further explication of a rational ideal common to both of us, with both of us trying to make our explication correct.

Perhaps behind the foregoing objection is a deeper (but more confused) one. Suppose a person grants that, as far as he is concerned, my explication of a rational choice is correct. He admits that I have shown what being ideally rational means in the context of choosing among ways of life. But he then raises the following objection. "Let us assume way of life A is rationally preferred to way of life B, that is, A is rationally chosen—in the sense you have specified—over B. Why does it follow that I should live according to A rather than B? I grant that A is rationally *preferred* to B. But why is the way of life which *is* preferred the way of life which *ought to be* preferred? Do not answer that it is because the preference is based on a rational choice. I already know it is based on a rational choice. I am asking why I ought to follow a rational choice. My question concerns the claim that a rational choice has upon me. Why ought I to live the way of life that is rationally chosen? To put it all in a nutshell, why be rational?"

This is a huge muddle. The confusion becomes apparent when we ask ourselves what sort of answer the person wants. What reply could possibly satisfy him? I shall try to disentangle this confusion by discussing four points:

1. The distinction between (a) giving a correct explication of a rational choice among ways of life and (b) giving reasons for trying to be rational in explicating a rational choice.

2. The distinction between (a) and (b) on the one hand, and, on the other, (c) giving reasons for the validity of the argument that "*A* ought to be preferred to *B*" follows from "*A* is preferred to *B* on the basis of a rational choice."

3. The distinction between (c) and (d) giving reasons for the validity of the argument that "One ought to live according to way of life *A*" follows from "Way of life *A* is rationally chosen over all others."

4. The distinction between (c) and (d) on the one hand, and, on the other, (e) giving reasons for committing oneself to try to discover which way of life is rationally chosen over all others.

1. If someone asks why he *should* live the way of life that is rationally chosen, one possible reply is that the question is beside the point. In defining (explicating) the conditions of a rational choice I am not trying to argue that people ought to live the rationally chosen way of life. I am only trying to state what a rational choice *means,* regardless of whether or not people actually want to live a rationally chosen way of life. I am not saying they ought to want to do this. If people do want to live according to the most justified way of life, they must first know which way of life is most justified. In my explication of a rational choice I am trying to state how we find out what that way of life is. My explication will be of little interest to those who do not want to discover the most justified

way of life. But if my explication is a correct explication, it will be of help to those who have such an aim. The aim is to find out how to discover what it means to live rationally, that is, according to the most justified way of life. But in carrying out my explication I am not imposing this aim or this further purpose upon anyone. Nor am I claiming that anyone ought to have such an aim or purpose. So the question "Why be rational?" is simply irrelevant to the attempt to explicate the method for finding the most justified way of life.

But this reply might not satisfy the objector. He might make the following rejoinder. "My question 'Why be rational?' is not entirely irrelevant, for I can ask it about your explication itself. If you are trying to give a rational account of the method for finding the most justified way of life, as you say you are, then what reasons are there for accepting your account? Suppose I do not accept it. You may claim that in that case I would not be rational. But why be rational here?"

There is a confusion in this rejoinder which stems from a failure to distinguish between the demand for reasons for preferring a way of life and the demand for reasons for accepting an account of such reasons. The first demand is expressed in the question: (a) What are good reasons for preferring one way of life to another? The answer to this question lies in the attempt to *explicate* what it means to be ideally rational in preferring one way of life to another. Let us suppose an answer is offered, such as the answer I have proposed in the concept of a rational choice. Then the second question is asked: (b) Why should the canons of reasoning governing this answer be accepted? Let us see how this question arises.

It may be that the concept of a rational choice as I have defined it does not provide a correct or accurate explication of justifying a way of life. I may have failed in my attempt to answer question (a) and I am perfectly willing to be criticized on that account. But any such criticism must itself be governed by the canons of reasoning that govern correct explication. The person who makes the criticism is seeking a correct explication and therefore must accept the canons of reasoning which define the philosophical point of view (as distinct from the scientific, the mathematical, and the various normative points of view). *Within* that point of view he may carry on arguments concerning the acceptability of answers to question a. But the question "Why be rational?" does not arise within such a rational framework.

How, then, does it arise? The questioner may explain that he means as follows: "When I ask 'Why be rational?' I am demanding reasons for anyone's placing himself within a rational framework, like that of the philosophical point of view. I am not asking for reasons within a rational framework. I am outside a point of view and am asking why I should take the point of view and so have my thinking governed by its canons of reasoning. 'Why be rational?' means 'Why take the philosophical point of view (or any point of view, for that matter)?' "

Here the questioner wants to be given reasons for accepting the canons of reasoning which govern a proposed explication. These are the canons of the philosophical point of view. What sort of reasons could we give? I submit that only one sort of reason can be given: *If* we want to live the most justified way of life, or *if* we want to answer question a, then taking the philosophical point of view is indispensable. If a person did not care to live the most justified way of life, or if he were not interested in trying to find out what that way of life is, or if he did not want a valid procedure for finding out what that way of life is, then it would be pointless (in the present context) to take the philosophical point of view. Taking that point of view is a necessary means to the three ends just mentioned. Unless a person takes that point of view he cannot achieve any of them. But if he does not seek them, no reasons can be given for his taking the point of view. We cannot argue that he *ought* to seek those ends without assuming the canons of reasoning of some point of view which the objector is also willing to assume. Since he has stated his unwillingness to be placed within any point of view, no argument can be given that will make a claim to his assent. In short, if his question "Why be rational?" is a demand for reasons for taking *any* point of view, then it is logically impossible to answer his question. In order to answer the question "Why?" we must give reasons, and giving reasons is a process of thought governed by canons of reasoning that define some point of view. Since no such canons are accepted, no reasons can be given.

Further reflection on this situation makes us doubtful about just what the difficulty is. If it is logically impossible to give an answer to a question, is there actually any question to be answered? In the present case an answer to the question is logically impossible because the questioner has deliberately refused to accept the conditions required for giving an answer. It is the questioner himself who has made his question unanswerable. It is hardly surprising, then, to discover that we cannot give any answer that will satisfy him. Indeed, must we not conclude that no genuine question is being asked? For the words "Why be rational?" can have meaning only if reasons can be given for being rational. But no such reasons are allowed under the conditions set by the questioner. Thus in asking the question he is demanding reasons and at the same time making it impossible to satisfy the demand. The conclusion we are forced to draw is that he does not know what he is saying. He is merely pronouncing words in an interrogative form outside of any possible context for their use.

On the other hand, suppose the questioner does want to live the most justified way of life, or wants to find out what such a life would be. In these circumstances he has very good reasons for taking the philosophical point of view. For only by doing so will he be able to discover which way of life (if any) is the most justified. We might call this a pragmatic justification (vindication) of the philosophical point of view, although this must not be confused with vindicating value systems which belong to normative points of view.

2. But perhaps the foregoing discussion has missed the principal point of the objection. What is being objected to is our saying that a person *ought* to prefer a way of life because it has been shown to be rationally chosen over other ways of life. Would we not be falling into the naturalistic fallacy? (A full account of the naturalistic fallacy will be given in Chapter 9.) From the fact that people rationally prefer one way of life to another we infer that we ought to prefer it. Is this not going from "is" to "ought"? We might reply that if a person does not prefer what is rationally preferred, he is not rational. The question then pops up, "Why be rational?" Here the challenge means, "Why ought one to prefer a way of life which, under conditions of a rational choice, actually is preferred over other ways of life?"

A reply would have to provide good reasons for going from "A is rationally preferred to B" to "A ought to be preferred to B." Is there not a fallacy in this inference? I do not think so, for the following reason. When we say that A is rationally preferred to B, we mean that whenever the conditions of a rational choice hold, A is preferred to B. Let us assume that the conditions as I have specified them do correctly explicate the justification of a way of life (and this assumption is not now in question). Then it would follow that A is more justified than B. This means that there are better reasons for choosing A than for choosing B. If a person, knowing this, were still to prefer B to A, his preference would be a paradigm of an irrational choice. The person might want to persist in his choice nevertheless, claiming that he honestly does prefer B to A. There is no logical error in his doing this, so long as he does not claim that he has good reasons, or is being rational, in doing it. He is saying in effect that he does not care to be rational about this matter. But then he must not ask "Why be rational?" For as soon as he asks "Why?" he is demanding reasons and thus presupposing rationality. To ask such a question is to speak as if only a rational answer will be acceptable. But in the present situation he already knows what a rational preference is (namely, the preference of A over B) and that his own preference runs counter to the rational one. What more does he need to know? Again his question appears to be outside any contexts for its possible use.

3. We may further distinguish between the question (c) "What are good reasons for going from 'A is rationally preferred to B' to 'A ought to be preferred to B'?" and a very similar question (d) "What are good reasons for going from 'A is rationally preferred to all other ways of life' to 'Everyone ought to live in accordance with A'?" Question (d) is, I think, the basic question that is in the back of many people's minds when they ask "Why be rational?" In asking this they want to know why anyone ought to do what he already knows to be rationally justified. Why should one's action be motivated by one's knowledge of the good? I shall now try to show that this is an empty question.

To say that someone already knows that an act, X, is rationally justified is to say that he knows there are good reasons for doing X. Thus he already has good reasons for doing X. Why, then, should he ask for such reasons? He might say that he knows X is the rational thing to do but he wants to know why he ought to do the rational thing. He wants to know, in other words, by what rule of logic we can go from "X is the rational thing to do" to "X ought to be done." The answer is that both statements mean the same thing, namely that there are good reasons for doing X. As I shall point out in Part II, the word "ought" is here being used prescriptively, and this contextually implies that there are good reasons for doing the act prescribed. To prescribe act X by saying "X ought to be done" is contextually to imply that there are good reasons for doing X. Now if a person wants to know why he ought to do X, he is asking for good reasons for doing X. But in the case at hand he acknowledges that he has good reasons for doing X. Hence his question is empty. It can only be "answered" by uttering a tautology: "There are good reasons for doing an act which you have good reasons for doing." Or: "It is rational to do what is rationally justified." Or: "It is rational to be rational."

The same considerations apply if we demand good reasons for living a way of life which is acknowledged to be rationally justified. If a person knows that a way of life is rationally chosen and is therefore as justified as it can be, then he knows why he ought to live it. Indeed, he already has the very best reasons for living it. This renders the demand for good reasons otiose. No further reasons can be given for him to live the way of life, since *ex hypothesi* he already has the best reasons for living it. But then he does not *need* any further reasons.

4. It was mentioned under point 1 that when a person *wants* to know how a way of life can be justified, he must assume that taking a rational point of view toward the problem is itself justified. Canons of reasoning (in this case canons of philosophical reasoning) must be accepted in any attempt to solve the problem. So if he seeks an answer to his problem, he cannot demand reasons for taking the philosophical point of view. He cannot ask "Why be rational?" since he already presupposes the justification of being rational in seeking an answer to his problem. Now he might seek an answer to his problem purely from intellectual curiosity. He might not be interested in justifying his own way of life. He might simply want to know whether anyone's way of life can be justified and if so, how. It

would then be perfectly consistent for him to find out how a way of life can be justified and then not try to justify his own nor try to live in accordance with a justified one.

Suppose, on the other hand, that a person wants to know how a way of life can be justified in order to discover whether his own is justified and in order to live in accordance with a justified one. And let us suppose that such a person, on learning of the method of rational choice, accepts it as a correct explication of how a way of life can be justified. Then suppose he asks "Why ought I to try to live in accordance with the rationally chosen way of life?" We must now be puzzled about what his question can mean. Can he be serious in asking it? For he is already committed to trying to live in accordance with a justified way of life. And his question cannot mean "What makes a way of life justified?", since he accepts the concept of a rational choice as providing a correct answer to this. His question is rather, "Granted that a rationally chosen way of life is a justified one, why ought I to try to live in accordance with it?" But if he is interested in finding out how a way of life can be justified in order to live in accordance with a justified one, then he knows he is committed to living a rationally chosen one, since this makes it justified. Hence he cannot be serious in demanding reasons for living such a way of life. He is already trying to do so.

The person might then make the following move, in explaining his question. He might say, "It is true that I am already committed to living a rationally chosen way of life because I want to live in accordance with a justified one. But it seems to me that my commitment is without reason. I am asking if there are any reasons for committing myself in the way that I have. It is true that I am now trying to live rationally, but I want to know what reasons can be given for my (or anyone's) decision to try to live rationally."

This question is quite different from the one discussed under point 1. For the person is not demanding reasons for taking the philosophical point of view. He already knows that taking this point of view is necessary if he is to find out how a way of life can be justified and so find out which way of life to try to live in accordance with. His question is rather about his end of trying to live in accordance with a justified way of life. He wants to know if any reasons can be given for seeking such an end. Moreover, his question is not the question discussed under point 3. He is not asking why he should live a rationally chosen way of life. He knows why—because it is rationally chosen. He sees that this is an empty demand, since he acknowledges that a person who knows that his way of life is rationally chosen already has all the reasons he can possibly have for living that way of life. The question he is concerned with is not why a person should live a justified way of life, but why a person should try to find out what way of life is justified in the first place, and why he should seek a justified way of life in order to try to live in accordance with it. In other words, why not simply disregard the problem, or seek some other end?

How can such a question be answered? It would seem that if a person did not care about finding a rational way of life or did not want to try to live in accordance with one, nothing could be said to show that he was unjustified in his attitudes. It would seem that no reasons could be given *against* his lack of commitment to seeking a rational way of life, and also that no reasons could be given *for* such a commitment. Either a person cares about such things or he does not, and that is all there is to be said on the matter.

Yet something more can be said. In the first place, we can point out that a person who is not interested in finding a rational way of life or in trying to live in accordance with it cannot give reasons *for* his lack of commitment (or for his commitment to other ends). Nor can he give reasons *against* the commitment of a man who does want to find out which way of life is most justified and who does care about living in accordance with it. In the second place, it is possible to interpret the question, "Why try to find a rational way of life, and why have the purpose of trying to live in accordance with it?" as a way of asking to be *convinced* or *persuaded* that one is right in making these commitments. Like the person who asks "Why be moral?" and wants as an answer to be inspired to fulfill moral standards and to follow moral rules (i.e., to adopt a moral value system), the questioner here wants to be moved to be more deeply committed to his basic goals. He wants to have his attitudes strengthened, to be encouraged, to be given support in his endeavors. Can such a demand be satisfied? I think there are two general methods which can be used. We might try to convince him intellectually or we might try to persuade him emotionally. It must be understood that the first method is not a matter of proof. We cannot give reasons from which it follows that a person is right in being committed to seeking a rational way of life. We can, however, ask him to review his commitment in light of alternative commitments. We can ask him to think what a justified way of life is—that it is the way of life which a person would have the best reasons for living. If he says he already knows this (as we acknowledge that he does), we can only invite him to think about it more deeply, to pay more attention to what it is he is seeking when he seeks a rational way of life, and to be fully aware of what it means not to care about seeking a rational way of life. Finally, however, we must leave it up to him. He must *choose* whether to seek a rational way of life or not. He makes no logical error in choosing not to seek it, but if he chooses not to, he must not expect to find a way of life which he can justify when it is challenged. If, on the other hand, he does want to find that way of life which can best be defended rationally against attack, then in the very fact that he wants to do this lies his commitment. He has made his choice, for to try to find such a way of life is already to seek the end he now wishes to be encouraged to seek.

This is about all we can do in an intellectual way to answer his question. What can we do in the way of emotional appeals? In order to persuade the person emotionally that he is right in seeking his end we must use techniques (such as praise, rewards, pointing at inspiring examples, and so on) which would be effective in strengthening his motivation to seek the end. This is not, strictly speaking, to *answer* his question. But it is to respond to his question in such a way (if we are successful) as to satisfy him. The outcome of this process is that he no longer asks the question. And this is not because we have silenced him. Our procedure does not involve preventing him from *uttering* a question that is still in his mind. Rather, we put to rest the inner doubt. He no longer asks the question *to himself*. He has come to have a strong, stable disposition to try to find a rational way of life in order to live in accordance with it. He no longer demands that he be justified in having this disposition.

This completes my account of the justification of value judgments. Throughout the discussion I have taken the philosophical point of view and so committed myself to approaching the question as rationally as I could. But this commitment to rationality was not my *ultimate commitment*, for one can always give reasons for taking the philosophical point of view. These reasons would constitute a pragmatic justification (vindication) of taking that point of view. They would point out that it is a necessary means to a certain end we have chosen. If our end is to learn as much as we can about what it means to be rational in justifying value judgments, then taking the philosophical point of view is indispensable for achieving our end. The *ultimate* commitment is our deciding to seek this end. Throughout my discussion of the justification of value judgments, I have assumed that the reader shares with me not only this commitment, but also the acceptance of the philosophical point of view which such a commitment requires. Within the framework set by the canons of reasoning of that point of view, the reader may wish to criticize what I have to say about the justification of value judgments. But he cannot criticize me for taking that point of view on the grounds that when I state what it is to be rational in justifying value judgments I am assuming canons of rationality and therefore arguing in a circle. For the canons of the philosophical point of view only govern the correctness of an *explication* of the rules of reasoning used in justifying value judgments. Those canons are not themselves *used* in justifying value judgments. (The canons of normative points of view, however, are so used.) My explication of the justification of value judgments may well be incorrect at many points and I am open to criticism on that account. But whatever criticism is made, it must be made from within the framework of the philosophical point of view. And the one who offers such criticism is ultimately committed to the same ideal as that to which I am committed—to learn as much as possible about what it means to be rational in justifying value judgments.

We must distinguish this philosophical ideal from the practical ideal of actually trying to live a rational life. The philosophical ideal requires only that we be rational in our intellectual inquiry into what it means to live a rational life (including what it means to be rational in the justification of our value judgments). The practical ideal requires that we be rational in all of life. The philosophical ideal is to find out *whether* value judgments can be justified and, if so, *how*. The practical ideal is to find out *which* value judgments are justified and to live in accordance with them. This means trying to fulfill the standards and follow the rules that verify our value judgments and that constitute the value systems of a rationally chosen way of life. Is the commitment to live this way of life an ultimate commitment? Yes, if we mean by "ultimate" that no further justificatory reasons can be given for making the commitment.

Someone might now triumphantly conclude, "You see, it is all *ultimately* absurd. We finally come to the point where we must commit ourselves without reason. Push reason far enough and you will arrive at unreason. All our ultimate commitments, being ultimate, are arbitrary. Thus we might as well toss a coin to decide whether to live a rational or a nonrational way of life. In the end they are equally nonrational. No reasons can be given for deciding in favor of a rational life rather than a nonrational life. It is impossible to answer the question 'Why not live a nonrational life?' So both rational and nonrational ways of life are on an equal footing. The choice between them is arbitrary, unfounded, and absurd."

The reply to this objection should now be obvious. It is the very reply I have made (under point 3 above) to the person who demands that reasons be given for living a rational life. No reasons *can* be given, it is true. But no reasons *need* be given. For knowing that a certain way of life is rational is knowing that one is wholly justified in committing oneself to it. To know that it is rational is already to have all the reasons one could possibly have for living it. As Mr. Hare pointed out in a passage I have quoted, the decision to commit oneself to a way of life which is rationally chosen over other ways of life (each of which must be fully known for the choice to be enlightened and hence rational) is the most reasonable, least arbitrary, and best founded decision of all. It is the decision to live the way of life one is most justified in living, all things considered.

Part II

PRESCRIBING

The concept of prescribing

7

A. *"Ought" sentences*

We carry on normative discourse when we use language for the purposes of evaluating and prescribing and when we give reasons for or against our evaluations and prescriptions. In Part I of this book I have been concerned with evaluative discourse; in Part II I shall be concerned mainly with prescriptive discourse. The basic concepts of evaluative discourse are *good* and *right* (corresponding to evaluations according to standards and evaluations according to rules, respectively). The basic concept of prescriptive discourse is *ought*, although the word "ought" also has evaluative uses. The precise differences between evaluating and prescribing will be the subject of the next chapter. In this chapter I shall try to make clear what an act of prescribing is. Throughout the two chapters I shall center my attention on the evaluative and prescriptive uses of the word "ought." These are to be contrasted with another use of the word, which I shall call its predictive or inferential use. (In ordinary talk the word "should" is perhaps more frequently used than the more severe and formal "ought." Both words have the same variety of uses I shall distinguish in this chapter.)

1. THE INFERENTIAL USE OF "OUGHT"

The predictive or inferential use of "ought" occurs in a context in which we have asserted (or assumed) a set of facts and are expressing a prediction or inference based on these facts. Thus in demonstrating an experiment a physicist might say, "When I throw the switch a spark ought to jump from one electrode to the other." The physicist is not prescribing that the spark jump but predicting that it will. The same use of "ought" occurs when we make an inference. Thus a detective might say, "Judging from his footprint, the man ought to weigh about 150 pounds." This is not like a doctor's saying that someone ought to weigh about 150 pounds. The detective's statement is not evaluative, the doctor's is. The man who guesses people's weight at a carnival is *making an inference* when he says to us, "You ought to weigh about 150 pounds." When a doctor says this, he is *prescribing* to us.

One major difference between predicting and inferring, on the one hand, and prescribing, on the other, is that we predict and infer that conditions ought to occur which are beyond human control, whereas we never prescribe that someone do something which it is beyond his power to do. On looking at a sunset, a person may predict, "It ought to be clear tomorrow." A scientist might infer that there ought to be life on a certain planet. In neither case is an "ought" sentence being used to exert an influence on someone's behavior to bring about that which is predicted or inferred. Nor are we expressing any kind of evaluation of the predicted event or the inferred condition. Indeed, sometimes what is predicted or inferred may be negatively evaluated, so that what ought to happen (in the predictive-inferential sense of "ought") ought not to happen (in the evaluative sense of "ought"). Similarly, what ought not to happen (in the predictive-inferential sense) may be positively evaluated as something that ought to happen. In these instances there is no contradiction in saying that what ought to be the case is bad and that what ought not to be the case is good. Examples of the first are: "My political opponent ought to win in this district." "The hurricane ought to hit this city about midnight tonight." "This student ought to do rather poorly in mathematics." Examples of the second are: "With all these delays the ski lift ought not to be completed before the season is over." "We ought not to have many bright days this winter." "At this rate he ought not to live until morning." It should be noted that when we make statements of the second sort we are not asserting that it is good that something ought not to happen. In fact, if we were going to evaluate the state of affairs the sentences are concerned with, we would say that what ought not to happen is a good thing. That is, the event whose non-occurrence is predicted or inferred is something which, if it were to occur, would be positively evaluated.

Not only is there the possibility of this sort of divergence between the predictive-inferential and the prescriptive-evaluative meanings of "ought," there is also the possibility of the convergence of the two meanings in one sentence. Thus a doctor might say cheerfully, "The penicillin ought to fix him up in no time." The basic meaning here is a prediction that the patient will get well. But there is also the clear evaluative connotation that what is predicted (i.e., what ought to happen) is a good thing. In the following statement, not only is evidence given on the basis of which a prediction is made, but a pro-attitude toward the predicted event is also being expressed: "The thief ought to be caught this time because the police have increased their watch on the area." A more complex case of ambiguity occurs when we say, "In light of its past performance, our team ought to have won the game." This expresses an inference based on the statistical probability that there was a better chance that the team would win the game than lose it. But there might be expressed simultaneously a negative evaluation concerning the team's losing the game. That is, the speaker might be blaming the team for not having come up to expectations based on its past performance. His tone of voice would indicate whether or not he was making such a value judgment.

In all these uses of "ought," however ambiguous they may be, it is always possible to separate in our minds the predictive-inferential element from whatever prescriptive or evaluative connotations are involved. Any of these statements is *true* if the thing that we say ought to happen is a probable event. In other words, the prediction or inference, based on the facts contextually implied by (or explicitly stated in) the sentence, is justified. Whether the prediction or inference is justified is entirely independent of the justifiability of any value judgments the speaker might be making about the predicted or inferred event. In addition to these predictive-inferential "ought" sentences, however, there are sentences, in which the word "ought" is used unambiguously in a purely evaluative or prescriptive way. No prediction or inference need be involved. From this point on, I shall be concerned exclusively with these uses of "ought."

2. CLASSIFICATION OF "OUGHT" SENTENCES

All "ought" sentences, whether evaluative or prescriptive, may be classified as follows:

I. Particular sentences
   A. *Ante eventum* sentences
      1. First person ("I, we ought to do X.")
      2. Second person ("You ought to do X.")
      3. Third person ("He, she, they, or those named or described in some specific way, ought to do X.")
   B. *Post eventum* sentences
      1. First person ("I, we ought to have done X.")
      2. Second person ("You ought to have done X.")
      3. Third person ("He, she, they, or those named or described in some specific way, ought to have done X.")
II. Universal sentences
   A. Active ("One ought to do X in circumstances C.")
   B. Passive ("X ought to be done in circumstances C.")

In order to make clear the criteria of classification I am using here, I distinguish the following four aspects or elements of any given "ought" sentence:

1. The speaker (the one who utters—speaks or writes—the sentence)
2. The addressee (the one who is addressed by the speaker when he utters the sentence)
3. The agent (the person designated in the sentence as the one who ought to do the act)
4. The act (in each case, the act referred to by X)

I classify an "ought" sentence as particular or universal according to whether the agent is specified or not specified in the sentence. In a universal sentence the nature of the act and the circumstances in which it ought to be done are specified, but the person or persons who ought to do the act are not. The agent is *anyone* in those circumstances who can do the act. In a particular sentence, on the other hand, the agent is referred to by a proper name, by a personal pronoun, or by a definite description. In each case something more about the agent is specified (or contextually implied) than merely that he is an agent.

Whether an "ought" sentence is *ante eventum* or *post eventum* depends on the temporal relation between the act of uttering the sentence and the act designated in the sentence. (The terms *ante eventum* and *post eventum* are from R. M. Hare's *The Language of Morals*, p. 157.) If the act of uttering the sentence occurs before the act designated in the sentence, the sentence is *ante eventum*. When the sentence is uttered after the designated act, it is *post eventum*. We shall see that this distinction is important for understanding the difference between prescribing and evaluating. For the uttering of a *post eventum* "ought" sentence is never an act of prescribing but is instead the expression of a value judgment. *Ante eventum* sentences, however, may be either prescriptive or evaluative, depending on the circumstances in which they are uttered and on whether they are in the first, second, or third person.

The classification of particular "ought" sentences according to their person may be explained in the following way. A first person singular "ought" sentence (whether *ante eventum* or *post eventum*) is one in which the speaker and the agent are the same person. The addressee, however, may or may not be the same person as the speaker (or agent). He is the same person if the speaker is talking to himself; if he is talking to others, then they are the addressee. In the case of first person plural sentences, the agent is a group which includes the speaker as one of its members. The addressee may be identical with the agent, a part of the agent, different from the agent, or overlap with the agent. Thus one may address the sentence "We ought to do *X*" only to the group which is designated by "we," or only to a part of that group (which may be the speaker alone, if he is talking to himself), or only to persons who are not members of the group (where "we" takes on the meaning, "the group of which you know me to be a member"), or to an aggregate of persons, some of whom are members of the group and some of whom are not. Second person "ought" sentences (whether singular or plural, *ante eventum* or *post eventum*) are those in which the addressee and the agent are always the same person or persons. The speaker of such a sentence is not the addressee (or agent), except in the somewhat peculiar case in which a person is talking in the second person to himself. In this case, as in the case of the speaker's uttering a first person sentence to himself, the addressee, the agent, and the speaker are all one and the same person. A third person "ought" sentence (whether singular or plural, *ante eventum* or *post eventum*) is only used in situations in which the agent is different from the addressee. Moreover, the speaker is always different from the agent and is usually different from the addressee. (He is identical with the addressee only when he is talking to himself.)

We have seen that for universal "ought" sentences the agent is anyone in the specified circumstances (i.e., circumstances *C*) who can do the specified act (i.e., act *X*). If either the speaker or the addressee of such a sentence happens to be in circumstances *C* and happens to be able to do *X*, he is included in the agent (i.e., the sentence applies to him as well as to others). If either the speaker or the addressee is not in circumstances *C*, or if he is in circumstances *C* but is unable to do *X*, then he is not included in the agent. As in the case of particular "ought" sentences, when the speaker of a universal sentence is talking to himself, he is identical with the addressee. If in this case he is also in circumstances *C* and able to do *X*, he is included in the agent as well as being the speaker and the addressee. That is, the sentence (like a first person or second person sentence spoken to oneself) is uttered *by* him, is uttered *to* him, and *applies* to him.

I shall now attempt to show that, with two exceptions to be noted later, all these various kinds of "ought" sentences have one of two functions in ordinary discourse—either to express value judgments (the evaluative function) or to prescribe an act to someone (the prescriptive function). Whether any given "ought" sentence is evaluative or prescriptive depends first on what kind of sentence it is according to the foregoing classification, and second on the conditions under which it is uttered. We shall find that only certain kinds of "ought" sentences can be prescriptive, and that they are prescriptive only when uttered under certain conditions.

3. POST EVENTUM "OUGHT" SENTENCES

Let us first consider *post eventum* "ought" sentences. These sentences make sense only under two conditions—when the agent has been confronted with the choice of doing either the act specified or some alternative act, and the situation of choice has ceased to exist by the time the sentence is uttered. (The sentence is uttered *post eventum*.) Even in the case of a second person sentence, where the agent is the same person as the addressee, the addressee is no longer in the position of an agent with respect to the particular act in question. To say "You ought to have done X" is to refer to a past situation in which the addressee had a choice of doing or not doing X. The statement contextually implies (first) that the addressee chose not to do X, (second) that the addressee was wrong in so choosing, and (third) that the situation of choice is now past. The second implication is a negative value judgment which is ambiguous with regard to its evaluatum. What is negatively evaluated may be the act which the agent did or it may be the agent himself as well as his act. As we shall see below, to say that an agent ought to do (or ought to have done) an act is to judge the act as the best alternative open to the agent. It is a value ranking whose class of comparison is made up of all the alternatives in the given situation of choice. Similarly, to say that an agent ought not to do (or ought not to have done) an act is to judge or rank the act as less-than-the-best in the situation of choice. Thus when we say to a person that he ought to have done X (and so imply that he did not do X), we indirectly express a negative value judgment of the act which he *did* do, and we directly express a positive evaluation of act X, which he did not do. However, in negatively evaluating the act chosen by the agent we are not necessarily negatively evaluating the agent for having chosen it. This depends on whether we (the speaker) believe the agent was blameworthy or culpable. If he was, then "You ought to have done X" not only condemns the act done by the agent but also condemns the agent for having done it. The act is condemned as not being the best thing for the agent to have done in his situation of choice. The agent is condemned (blamed) for not having done the best thing (namely act X).

The conditions under which an agent is held to be blameworthy or culpable are complex and need not be considered in detail here. (Almost any book in ethics includes a discussion of the point.) Suffice it to say that we tend not to blame a person for doing what he ought not to have done, when he honestly believed he was doing what he ought to do and when he could not have been expected to have known that there was a better alternative.

It is to be noted that ordinarily both positive and negative *post eventum* sentences express negative value judgments. Whether we say "You ought to have done X" or "You ought not to have done X," we are condemning the act which the agent did and we are condemning the agent if he was blameworthy. In the first sentence we blame the agent for not having done X, in the second for having done it. The first, in other words, contextually implies a "wrong of omission," the second a "wrong of commission." In the first case, act X was the best of the alternatives in the situation of choice. In the second case act X was not the best of the alternatives (though it was not necessarily the worst of the alternatives). To say "You ought to have done X" is to blame the addressee because act X, which he did not do, was the best thing for him to do. To say "You ought not to have done X" is to blame the addressee because he did X, which was not the best thing for him to do. Can a *post eventum* "ought" sentence ever express a positive evaluation of the act or the agent? Such sentences are almost never used for this purpose. In order to do this one would have to make the awkward statement, "You ought to have acted just as you did." It is much more natural to use an evaluative sentence with the predicate "right" to make the point— "It was right of you to have acted as you did," or more simply, "You did the right thing."

Before passing on to first person and third person *post eventum* sentences, it should be pointed out that there is one use of second person *post eventum* "ought" sentences which may be neither evaluative nor prescriptive. This is the utterance of such sentences simply for purposes of emphasis. When we exclaim "You ought to have seen the expression on his face" or "You ought to have seen it rain," we are not expressing any value judgments. It is as if we said "How surprised he was!" or "How hard it rained!" Such "emphasis-oughts," however, may be uttered in contexts where they serve to express evaluations. Thus if we have been praising an actress we might say, "You ought to have seen her performance in——" Here we not only continue our praise of the actress, but also express the value judgment that it would have been desirable, a good thing, or fitting if the person to whom we are speaking had seen the play referred to. No reference is made to a past situation of choice and there is no implication that the addressee's seeing the play was the best alternative open to him.

When a first person *post eventum* "ought" sentence is uttered, the speaker is expressing a negative value judgment of his own past act and (if he is blameworthy) of himself for having done it. When I say "I ought to have done X," I am condemning myself for not having chosen to do X in a past situation of choice. This negative evaluation of myself is based on a negative evaluation of my past act. The act is evaluated as a member of the class of comparison made up of the alternatives open to my choice. By saying "I ought to have done X" I am acknowledging the fact that I chose not to do the best act open to me, which was act X, and *for that reason* I am blaming myself. I also blame myself when I utter the negative sentence "I ought not to have done X." But this time I blame myself for what I did, not for what I did not do. It is an acknowledgement of a "wrong of commission" rather than of a "wrong of omission." The sentence contextually implies, not that an act *not* done *was* the best thing for me to do, but that the act *done* was *not* the best thing for me to do. The same analysis applies to first person plural sentences ("We ought—or ought not—to have done X"), except that the agent being blamed is not the speaker alone but the whole group of which the speaker is a member.

Third person *post eventum* sentences also express negative evaluations of the agent or his act. However, they do not prescribe an act to the agent. This can only be done when the agent is the addressee, since prescribing is *telling* the agent what *he* ought to do. It is the mark of third person "ought" sentences that the agent is never the addressee. We may *indirectly* guide our own or others' choices by uttering a sentence of the type, "He, she, they ought (ought not) to have done X." We would then be giving examples of acts which ought (or ought not) to have been done. Prescribing an act to someone, however, is not merely giving him examples of what he ought to do in various sorts of circumstances. It is to tell him what he ought to do when he has (or will have) the choice of doing or not doing what he is told. It is to provide a direct and unequivocal answer to the question "What should I do?" Such an answer cannot be provided by a sentence of the form "He, she, they ought to have done X," since it only states how *others* should have acted in the *past*, not how the person himself should act in the present or future.

Throughout this discussion of *post eventum* "ought" sentences I have spoken as if the negative value judgment in which we blame or condemn the agent (when he is culpable) is a harsh or severe one. I now wish to emphasize that the negative judgment need not be strong at all. It may run from severe condemnation to mild regret. Nor is it necessary that it be a *moral* condemnation. An art critic might sharply blame a gallery owner by saying "You ought never to have exhibited these paintings." Since he would appeal to aesthetic standards to support his statement, the "ought" sentence is an aesthetic one, not a moral one. A mild reproof from the aesthetic point of view would be illustrated if the gallery owner's friend said to him, "You ought to have made the lighting in this room a bit brighter."

The strength of the condemnation is also diminished when the agent is not believed to be culpable, and only his act is negatively judged. Thus we might say to a child, "You ought not to have taken things that do not belong to you." We are not blaming him (for he did not know better), but trying to teach him that it is wrong to steal. An example of a nonmoral expression of mild regret would occur when we said to a guest who has arrived late, "You ought to have turned left at the traffic light." Here we are not blaming the person, since it was his first visit to our home and he did not know the best way to come. Our statement is about equivalent to saying "It is too bad you did not turn left at—" or "It would have been better if you had turned left at——"

So far I have been considering *post eventum* "ought" sentences in which the grammatical subject refers to an agent who had the choice of doing or not doing the act mentioned in the sentence. But there are *post eventum* sentences in which this is not the case. Such sentences express negative value judgments of persons not explicitly referred to. Consider, for example, a doctor's saying "He ought not to have died." Here the doctor is not blaming the person who died, but those who did not take proper care of him. An example of a second person sentence used in this way would be, "You ought not to have been treated so unfairly." The speaker is blaming an agent not mentioned in the sentence. An example of a first person sentence would be, "I ought to have been allowed to eat in the restaurant where white people eat." In all cases of this sort, the agent who is being negatively evaluated for having done the act mentioned in the sentence is someone other than the person referred to by the subject of the sentence.

4. ANTE EVENTUM "OUGHT" SENTENCES

All *post eventum* "ought" sentences (except some "emphasis-oughts") have an evaluative function. They are never used to prescribe an act to someone. Let us now turn to *ante eventum* sentences. Are they not all prescriptive rather than evaluative? If we begin with third person sentences, we see at once that they cannot be prescriptive for the same reason that third person *post eventum* sentences cannot be prescriptive; they are never addressed to the agent and so can never provide a direct answer to the question "What should I do?" I suggest, then, that third person *ante eventum* sentences are evaluative. They differ from *post eventum* sentences on two counts. First, they express value judgments only of the act, never of the agent. And second, positive sentences express positive judgments and negative sentences express negative judgments (instead of both expressing negative judgments, as is the case with *post eventum* sentences).

When we say of a person, "He ought to do X," we mean that X is the best thing for the person to do in a situation of choice which now confronts him or which will confront him in the future. It is to make a value judgment of X, based on a process of evaluation in which X is compared with all the other acts open to the agent in his present or future situation of choice. This evaluation, which may be made according to rules or according to standards, results in a ranking of X as the best member of the class of comparison. Act X is superior to all other acts in the order of preferability resulting from the evaluation, and as such it is judged to be the act which the agent ought to do. Unlike the sentence "He ought to have done X," which expresses a condemnation of the agent (or his act) on the ground that he did not do X in the past, the sentence "He ought to do X" neither praises the agent for doing X nor condemns him for not doing it. How could it, since at the time of uttering the sentence the agent has neither done nor omitted doing X? He is still confronted with the choice of doing or not doing it, either in the present or in the future. In saying that someone ought to do a certain act X, we are not evaluating *him* at all. Nor are we evaluating his past act. We are instead evaluating only the act X itself (as the best thing for him to do).

But the act, in being evaluated, is not being prescribed. Although the sentence tells what the agent ought to do, it does not tell it *to him*. The agent is not the addressee. The sentence is being addressed to someone else, who is being told what the agent ought to do. From the standpoint of the addressee, *he* is not being told what to do; he is only being told what someone else ought to do. We can also look at the sentence from the standpoint of the speaker. In saying, "He ought to do X," the speaker is stating what he thinks a certain person ought to do. He is not *telling* that person what he ought to do. But prescribing is, at least, telling a person what he ought to do. Therefore the uttering of a third person *ante eventum* "ought" sentence is not an act of prescribing.

Just as the positive sentence "He ought to do X" expresses the positive value judgment that X is the best thing for the agent to do in the presupposed situation of choice, so the negative sentence "He ought not to do X" expresses the value judgment that X is not the best alternative in the situation of choice. Act X may be *a* right act (as judged according to a rule) or a good act (as judged according to a standard), but it is not, in comparison with the other acts, the very best (or *the* right) thing to do. Hence it is judged negatively, as being less than the best. Similarly, when we utter the positive sentence "He ought to do X," act X may be a wrong act or a bad act, but when compared with the alternatives it is the *least* bad. It is the best of the alternatives and consequently is the act that ought to be done.

Let us next consider first person *ante eventum* sentences. Here I shall discuss singular and plural sentences separately, since there are some pertinent differences between them. First person singular *ante eventum* sentences ("I ought to do X") are evaluative, not prescriptive. They are, in fact, ordinarily used in the context of the speaker's deliberation, and deliberation (as I showed in Chapter 1) is a form of evaluation. Professor P. H. Nowell-Smith has pointed out that, unlike "You ought" and "He ought," "I ought" contextually implies that the speaker has decided, or is trying to decide, what he ought to do. (*Ethics.* Harmondsworth, England: Penguin Books Ltd., 1954, pp. 261-262.) The sentence "I ought to do *X*" either sums up a deliberative process and informs the addressee that the speaker has come to a final decision, or it is uttered before deliberation has terminated. In the former case, the speaker has carried out an evaluation of all the alternatives open to him (or has accepted some-one else's evaluation of them) and has made up his mind concern-ing which alternative is best. In saying "I ought to do *X*" he is expressing a value judgment which results from that deliberative (evaluative) process. In the latter case, in which the speaker has not completed his deliberation (or has not accepted another's deliberation), he may say "I ought to do *X*" as a tentative decision, not a final decision. In moral deliberations (i.e., when the delibera-tive process appeals to moral rules and standards for evaluating the alternatives), the speaker is then in the situation analyzed by Nowell-Smith as follows.

. . . 'I ought' is also used, not to express a decision, but in the course of making up one's mind before a decision has been reached. A man may hesitate between two moral principles and say to himself at one time 'I ought to do X' and at another 'But on the other hand I ought to do Y' or he may contrast 'I ought' with 'I should like to.' In the first of these cases he is hesitating between two moral principles, in the second be-tween acting on a moral principle and acting on some other motive. But in neither case has he arrived at a verdict. (*Ibid.*, p. 261.)

In both of these instances the "ought" sentence is evaluative, not prescriptive. We deliberate about what we ought to do when we are (or will be) in a situation of choice, and are trying to decide on the best course of action open to us. When we come to a decision, however momentary or tentative, we arrive at a judgment about what is the best thing for us to do. To arrive at such a judgment is the very purpose for which we deliberate.

When a first person singular *ante eventum* sentence is spoken to oneself (in which case the speaker, the addressee, and the agent are all one and the same person) it is tempting to say that the speaker is prescribing an act to himself. On the face of it, the speaker seems to be telling himself what he ought to do, and to tell someone what he ought to do is to prescribe. Indeed, the parallel with ordinary prescribing is so strong that there is a point in saying that in this situation "I ought" really functions as an internalized "You ought" (which, as we shall see, is the phrase we normally use to prescribe an act to someone). Professor Nowell-Smith makes this suggestion in his analysis of cases in which a person involved in moral deliberation hesitates between two moral principles ("I ought to do X but on the other hand I ought to do Y"), or between acting on a principle and acting on some other motive ("I ought to do X but I should like to do Y").

In the first case it is quite natural to represent the two 'oughts' as being spoken by internal moral authorities advising or telling him what to do; and in the second to represent the conflict as one between the Voice of Conscience and Desire. But these are the voices of advocates, not of judges; and what they say is, not 'I ought,' but 'you ought.' (*Ibid.*, pp. 261-262.)

Being an advocate and being a judge are the roles we take, respectively, when we prescribe and when we evaluate. And it is not incorrect to think of ourselves as advocating (prescribing) that we do one thing rather than another, when we tentatively reach decisions during a deliberative process. But a caution must be interposed. Although reaching decisions during deliberation is like prescribing in some respects, in other respects it is not.

First, we are using the word "prescribe" out of its normal context. (The same is true of Professor Nowell-Smith's use of "You ought" in the above passage.) Granted that prescribing consists in telling someone what he ought to do, it typically consists in doing this in a social context in which one person is offering guidance, making recommendations, or giving advice to another. Second, we must realize that in uttering the "ought" sentence to himself, the speaker is not merely prescribing to himself. He is also pronouncing a value judgment that is the outcome of his (or another's) evaluation of various acts open to him. It is only on the basis of the judgment "X is the best thing for me to do" that he then concludes, "I ought to do X." Third, if the latter sentence is taken to be an act of prescribing to oneself, the four necessary conditions for prescribing, which I shall consider shortly, must be fulfilled. (When we utter such a sentence seriously to ourselves these four conditions in fact will usually be fulfilled.)

First person plural *ante eventum* sentences have more varied uses than any of the "ought" sentences so far considered. They may be deliberative (and hence evaluative); they may be evaluative but not deliberative; or they may be prescriptive. When the sentence "We ought to do X" is deliberative (i.e., when it is uttered in a context of deliberation), it functions in the same way as "I ought to do X." The only difference is that in the plural sentence the speaker is a member of a group (referred to by "we") and the sentence is uttered as part of, or as the outcome of, the group's deliberation. As in the case of "I ought to do X," the sentence may be uttered privately, addressed by the speaker to himself. When its utterance is public, it is addressed either to the group as a whole or to individual members of the group.

But "We ought to do X" may not be uttered in a context of deliberation at all. Furthermore, the addressee may be neither the group as a whole nor any member of the group. The sentence may be addressed to an outside party, and in that case the speaker is simply uttering a value judgment of act X as the best thing for the group to do. He is telling someone who is not in the group what the group ought to do. He is not telling the group what *it* ought to do. The sentence in this case is evaluative, but not deliberative and not prescriptive.

Suppose, in a third kind of context, the group is the addressee but, as in the second kind of context, it is not involved in deliberation. Then the speaker as a member of the group is telling the group what *it* ought to do. It is in this case that the speaker is *prescribing* the doing of act X to the group (assuming that the four necessary conditions for prescribing, to be stated below, are fulfilled).

In second person *ante eventum* "ought" sentences, the addressee is always the agent. To utter the sentence "You ought to do X" is always to tell someone directly what *he* as an agent ought to do. When such a sentence is uttered under the following conditions, its utterance is an act of prescribing:

1. The sentence is uttered in earnest and is affirmed by the speaker.

2. The addressee is an agent in a present situation of choice (or will be an agent in a future situation of choice) in which doing X is one of the alternatives.

3. The agent (or addressee) has (or will have) the freedom to choose to do or not to do X.

4. It is considered by the speaker legitimate and proper for the addressee to demand reasons of the speaker as to why he, the addressee, ought to do X.

Whenever the addressee and the agent of an *ante eventum* "ought" sentence are identical, the act of uttering the sentence under the four conditions above is an act of prescribing. Thus all second person *ante eventum* sentences are prescriptive when uttered under them. First person plural sentences are prescriptive under these conditions if they are addressed to the group designated by "we" in the sentence. And, with the qualifications that were set forth above, all first person sentences, singular or plural, are prescriptive when addressed by the speaker to himself. We shall see later that there are other kinds of sentences than "ought" sentences which may be used prescriptively, but in every instance the four conditions listed must hold. I shall examine each condition in turn.

1. We would not say that uttering an "ought" sentence was an act of prescribing unless the speaker uttered the sentence in earnest and also affirmed what it said. By saying that a sentence is uttered "in earnest" I mean to exclude not only its being uttered in jest, but also its being uttered simply to frighten, amuse, annoy, bewilder, shock, or have some other emotional effect upon the addressee. Unless a sentence were normally used "in earnest," it would not have the capacity to bring about such effects. These emotional functions of a sentence are consequently secondary or derivative. What, then, is the primary or nonderivative use of a sentence? It is the use of the sentence "in earnest," that is to say, when the speaker's main intention in uttering it is to have the addressee give his sincere assent to what is being said. He is not merely letting the addressee

know what he thinks about something. His intention is to have the addressee accept what he says and act accordingly. When the statement is a prescription (i.e., when uttering the sentence is an act of prescribing), the addressee's acceptance of it will involve at least setting himself to do the prescribed act and having a pro-attitude toward doing it. Giving one's sincere assent to a prescription involves being *disposed* to perform the act and to approve of its being performed, even if one fails actually to perform it.

To utter a sentence in earnest, in this sense, precludes its being uttered in certain special contexts. For example, a sentence is not uttered in earnest when it occurs in the context of poetry or fiction, or when we are interested only in setting forth a proposition for consideration or as a supposition. We do not utter a sentence in earnest when we are "mentioning" it but not "using" it, or when our sole purpose is to let the addressee know what we think about something, without expecting him to agree with us.

Now it is possible to utter a sentence in earnest and yet not affirm what it says. For example, we may not ourselves believe what we are saying, although we want and expect the addressee to believe it. This would be the case whenever we are lying to the addressee, or whenever we are trying to conceal from him our true thoughts and feelings. An "ought" sentence is prescriptive, then, only if it is both uttered in earnest and affirmed by the speaker. (Throughout this book I am assuming that sentences are being uttered in earnest and are being affirmed by the speaker.)

2. The second condition, that the addressee be an agent in a situation of choice, is clear from what has been said earlier. To prescribe is to tell someone what he ought to do, and what he ought to do is the act which is the best alternative open to him. His situation of choice need not occur at the time when the act is prescribed, since it makes perfectly good sense to tell a person that he ought to do a certain act in the future. There must be, however, a specific expectation that a future situation of choice will occur. Thus if we say "You ought to return the book you have borrowed," the addressee must either be in a situation where he can choose to return the book or not, or else there must be a specific future situation in which it is foreseen that he will have such a choice. Otherwise there would be no reason for our addressing the sentence to him. If, for

example, he replies, "The book is lost. I have looked everywhere and can't find it," we shift our prescription, and say, "Then you ought to replace it." We do not continue to prescribe his returning the particular copy of the book which has been lost, on the mere chance that it might be found in the unforeseeable future.

Sometimes second person *ante eventum* "ought" sentences are addressed to persons who are not in a present situation of choice with regard to the proposed act and there is no specific expectation that they ever will be in such a situation in the future. In these cases the sentences are not used for prescribing but for expressing a value judgment. Thus after a trip out West we might say to our friends who have never been there, "You ought to see the Grand Canyon!" This is simply another way of saying "The Grand Canyon is a wonderful sight!" The "ought" sentence would be an act of prescribing only if our friends were planning a trip out West and going to see the Grand Canyon was a possibility open to them.

3. The third condition for an "ought" sentence to be an act of prescribing is that the agent be *free* to choose to do or not to do the act mentioned in the sentence. This condition, in conjunction with the second condition, may be summarized in the familiar statement: "Ought" implies "can." The third condition itself may be analyzed into two requirements: (a) The agent will not do X unless he chooses to do X; (b) The agent will only choose to do X as a result either of his own deliberation or of his freely given decision to follow another's deliberation. Both of these requirements presuppose that there are genuine alternatives open to the agent. This means first, that the agent has the physical ability and the psychological (intellectual and emotional) capacity to do any of the acts in question; second, that the agent is not under external constraint (coercion, duress) to do one thing rather than another; and third, that the agent is not under the influence of any internal compulsion to do one thing rather than another. It makes no sense to say that someone ought to do something when he either cannot possibly do it or cannot help but do it. This is also true of *post eventum* "ought" sentences. To say that a person ought to have done X contextually implies that he did not do X but that he could have done X if he had so chosen and that he could have so chosen. Similarly, to say that a person ought not to have done Y contextually implies that he

did Y but that he would have done otherwise if he had so chosen and that he could have so chosen.

To prescribe an act to someone is not to force or compel him to do it. Indeed, prescribing can occur only if the person is free to choose not to do the act prescribed. This condition derives from the fact that prescribing is one way of giving advice, making a recommendation, or offering guidance. In Chapter 2, I contrasted these activities with commanding, ordering, and issuing directives. There I argued that it is of the essence of giving advice, making a recommendation, or offering guidance that the person who receives the advice, recommendation, or guidance be free to choose not to follow it. This is just what a person is not free to do when he is in a position to be commanded. He must obey a command (under penalty of punishment). A person does not *obey* a prescription. He *decides* to follow it or carry it out; he *adopts* it as a guide to his conduct.

4. Because an act of prescribing is always an act of guiding someone (or making a recommendation, or giving a piece of advice), the fourth condition must hold whenever prescribing takes place. It must always be legitimate and proper for the person to whom one prescribes (i.e., the addressee) to demand reasons for his doing the prescribed act. In my discussion of advising and commanding in Chapter 2, I pointed out that not only must the person who is being advised be free to choose not to follow the advice, he must also be acknowledged to have the right to ask why he should follow it. Prescribing, like all advising, is a rational act. It presupposes its own justifiability. The person who prescribes may not be able to give a justification for his prescription and the addressee may not *in fact* demand that he do so. But he who prescribes must acknowledge the *right* of the addressee to make such a demand. The person who is commanded to do something, on the other hand, is not in the position to ask why he should obey. He is engaged in a social practice whose defining rules are such that the person who commands him has authority over him. To demand a justification for obeying the commands is to place oneself *outside* that social practice and ask that it be justified *as a whole*. But a person may be engaged in the social practice of receiving advice and *within* the practice demand that the advice which he receives be justified. This is part of what it means to engage in such a practice.

A cogent and detailed argument has been given by Professor W. D. Falk to show that all advising or guiding is in this sense rational. In his article "Goading and Guiding" (*Mind*, LXII, 246, 1953, pp. 145-171) he points out that imperatives may not always express commands. We may use imperatives in giving advice (guiding), but when we do, we presuppose their justifiability.

'Do this' may be used in the sense of 'my advice to you is, do this'; it may express a *recommendation*. . . . It is . . . logically assured here that none but rational methods will be used in support. Advice can be 'good' or 'bad'; it has an implicit canon of achievement, defined in terms of what it is understood to set out to do. And this is purely to 'guide,' to make people act as they would have valid and sufficient reasons for acting and not otherwise. (*Ibid.*, pp. 168-169.)

Thus the whole point of giving advice, guiding, or making a recommendation, is to tell a person what it would be rational for *him* to do. To engage in this social practice (as the giver of advice) presupposes that one has good reasons to give the addressee for doing the act which one recommends. Professor Falk argues that one can consistently say "My advice is, do this" only if one has

. . . formed an opinion concerning the facts of the situation all round, as well as concerning their relevance as reasons for the hearer. In fact, 'Do this,' as advice, may also be treated as the stating of an opinion to this effect. One can say 'my opinion is, do this' as if one were saying, 'my opinion is that you have the best of reasons for doing this, the facts all round being so and so'; and one disarms advice by challenging either the facts or their alleged force as reasons. (*Ibid.*, p. 169.)

The person who is being advised can always challenge the advice by challenging the reasons presupposed by the adviser in giving the advice. Whatever reasons are good reasons for the adviser must also be good reasons for the advisee. This follows from the feature of prescriptive speech which Falk calls its "other-regarding orientation."

Whenever guiding is used as a method, persuasion has an other-regarding orientation: looking at actions from other people's point of view, trying to make others do what they would want, or would have an incentive to do, if they were not ignorant or obtuse. And where one is guiding to goad one is still trying to make them act as one wants *oneself* only by means of trying to make them act as they would want *themselves*. Surely then not all prescriptive speech aims purely and typically at bending the hearer's attitudes to those of the speaker. . . . It can serve both to make others favour what we favour; and to aid them in learning to favour what *they* do not favour but would, or might, for independent and acknowledged reasons of their own. (*Ibid.*, p. 161.)

Concerning the use of "ought," Professor Falk points out that to say that a person ought to do something is not to give him a reason for doing it. Prescribing is not giving reasons, even though it presupposes (contextually implied) that reasons can be given for doing what is prescribed. To utter a prescriptive "ought" sentence is to claim that an act ought to be done in light of (or as a consequence of) the supporting reasons. We might say that prescribing is a rational act but not an act of reasoning. The "ought" sentence which expresses a prescription does not itself state any of the reasons for doing the prescribed act.

The fact is 'you ought to' is not used to *replace* or *supplement* any of the features of the situation ordinarily put forward in persuasion by rational methods. On the contrary, it only works in *conjunction* with them. 'You ought to go now' is incompletely persuasive by itself. It needs support from 'your bus is leaving,' or 'you are expected for dinner,' or any other natural feature of the situation which may count as a reason for going. . . . (*Ibid.*, p. 166.)

What, then, is the function of an "ought" sentence if it is not to give a reason for doing what is prescribed? Its purpose is simply to *prescribe* the doing of the act. It is to exert an influence on an agent's behavior or choice. But a rational influence, not any influence. To prescribe the doing of an act is to tell someone that he ought to do it in light of such-and-such reasons for doing it.

Professor Falk never tells us *why* prescribing an act does not consist in giving a reason for it. I should like to offer the following as a possible explanation. In any prescription we must distinguish the act of prescribing from the act prescribed. Why is the act of prescribing itself not a way of justifying the act prescribed? The answer lies in the fact that the relation between the act of prescribing and the act prescribed is the relation between the act of uttering a sentence and what the sentence is about. The act prescribed is part of the content of a prescription; it belongs to what is being said, not to the saying of it. The act of prescribing, on the other hand, is a linguistic act; to prescribe is to utter a certain sort of sentence under certain conditions. *What* is prescribed, however, may or may not be a linguistic act. ("You ought to tell him you are sorry" and "You ought to repay the debt" are cases in which the act prescribed is, respectively, a linguistic act and a nonlinguistic act.) Now the uttering of a sentence is seldom the giving of a reason for believing what is said. It is only in unusual circumstances that our uttering a sentence provides evidence for the truth of what we assert by means of the sentence. Examples would be: "I am alive." "I can speak English." "I am not asleep." It is clear that a sentence of the form "You ought to do *X*" is not of this sort. To utter this kind of sentence gives no evidence for its truth and hence no justification for doing act *X*. So an act of prescribing is not giving a reason for doing the act prescribed. The act of prescribing tells a person what he is to do; it does not tell him why he is to do it.

It may now be seen why making a statement of empirical fact is not an act of prescribing, even when it is done to exert a rational influence on the addressee's behavior. It gives the addressee a *reason* for doing something, and an act of prescribing never does this. To say to someone "You ought to go now" is not to give him a reason for going now. But this is precisely what we do when we say "Your bus is leaving" or "You are expected for dinner." When we add to such statements of fact the remark "You ought to go now," we are not giving an *additional reason* for the person to go. We are drawing a (practical) conclusion. We are telling the person what he should do in light of the reasons already given. This is the act of prescribing. To give the reasons themselves is to justify the act prescribed, not to prescribe it.

Perhaps the point at which making a statement of empirical fact comes closest to being an act of prescribing is the point at which we assert that an act is or is not in accordance with a rule. If we are watching a game and suddenly say to one of the players "That is against the rules," we are making an assertion which is empirically true or false. Such an assertion may well have the same effect as the prescription "You ought not to do that." Similarly, to assert that a certain act is morally obligatory (i.e., that it is required by a moral rule) is to make a statement of fact in a context where a moral value system is accepted. This assertion may be made under the same conditions and for the same purpose as the prescription "You ought to do that." But neither of these factual statements is a prescription, since each supplies a reason for (or against) doing something. To say that an act is in accordance with or violates a rule is not exactly the same as saying *that* a person ought or ought not to do it. It is to say *why* a person ought or ought not to do it. It is to express a value judgment of the act, namely, that the act is right or wrong. A person might then conclude that *therefore* it ought or ought not to be done. Prescribing, however, is not evaluating. (In the next chapter I shall give an account of the differences between prescribing and evaluating.)

B. *Prescriptions and rules*

So far I have discussed only *particular* "ought" sentences. I have now to consider the one remaining type of "ought" sentences— universal sentences. These sentences may take either an active form ("One ought to do X in circumstances C") or a passive form ("X ought to be done in circumstances C"). The two forms are equivalent in meaning. To say "One ought to keep one's promises" is to say "Promises ought to be kept." Whatever assertions I make about universal sentences, therefore, will apply equally to both forms.

In universal sentences no particular agent is specified although an act is specified (act X) and the circumstances in which the act ought to be done are specified (circumstances C). We may then consider as the *agent* anyone in circumstances C who can do X. When such a sentence is uttered, however, the *addressee* may or may not be the agent. If the addressee is not in circumstances C, or if he cannot do X, the sentence does not apply to him. That is, it does not function as a guide to his conduct. Consequently it is not prescriptive. Uttering a universal "ought" sentence is an act of prescribing only if either of the following conditions holds. 1. The addressee is in circumstances C and has the choice of doing or not doing X at the time when the sentence is uttered. 2. There is a specific expectation that the addressee will be in circumstances C and will have the choice of doing or not doing X in the foreseeable future. Since condition 1 here is the same as the second of the four conditions for prescribing listed previously, we may conclude that a total of *five* conditions must hold if the uttering of a universal "ought" sentence is to be an act of prescribing: the four conditions listed previously plus the condition that either the addressee is now in circumstances C or will be in circumstances C in the foreseeable future.

Suppose a universal "ought" sentence is addressed to someone when he is not in circumstances C and when there is no expectation that he ever will be in circumstances C. Or suppose the sentence is addressed to someone when he has no choice about doing the act and when there is no expectation that he will have such a choice. The speaker would not then be telling a person what *he* ought to do. He would instead be telling a person what *anyone* ought to do in certain circumstances. The speaker, in short, would not be prescribing but *stating a general rule of conduct*. It is necessary at this point to distinguish the following things—prescribing, laying down a rule, adopting a rule, and justifying a prescription by appeal to a rule.

A rule tells us how people in general ought to act in certain circumstances. The function of a rule is to regulate or govern people's conduct by stating what they are or are not to do. Thus a rule, as we saw in Part I, may be used as a norm by which to evaluate people's conduct. Every rule requires, permits, or forbids an act *of a certain kind* to be done in circumstances *of a certain kind*. When we express a *rule* by means of a universal "ought" sentence, the sentence should be in the form "One ought to do acts of kind K in circumstances of kind C," rather than in the form "One ought to do this particular act X in these particular circumstances C." A rule applies to anyone who has the choice of doing or not doing what it enjoins. Now to state a rule may or may not be an act of prescribing. Whether or not it is depends on whether the addressee is (or will be) in the specified kind of circumstance and whether the addressee has (or will have) the choice of doing the specified kind of act. When uttering a rule is an act of prescribing, the speaker is *laying down the rule as a guide to the addressee's choice*. When uttering a rule is not an act of prescribing, the speaker may be doing either or both of two things. He may be *laying down the rule for others to follow (though not for the addressee to follow)*, or he may be *adopting the rule for himself.* In the latter case, uttering the rule expresses his decision to try to follow it whenever *he* is in the circumstances specified by the rule, and whenever *he* has the choice of following the rule or violating it. To lay down a rule is to place the conduct of people in general (including oneself) under its regulation. To adopt a rule is to decide to place one's own conduct, not that of others, under its regulation.

Sometimes rules of conduct are called "universal prescriptions." One of the dictionary definitions of "prescribe" is "to lay down a rule." I concede that common usage of the terms "prescribe" and "prescription" allow for their being applied to rules. I should not dispute with someone who wishes to call a rule a prescription and the act of laying down a rule an act of prescribing. Nevertheless I should want to make clear the difference between making a statement about how people in general ought to act and telling a person how *he* ought to act. We may use a rule for the latter purpose only if the person we address is or will be in a situation to which the rule applies. Whether we want to speak of "prescribing" when these conditions do not hold is purely a verbal matter. For my purposes it is convenient to restrict the term "prescribe" to telling a person what *he* ought to do. It is only in this sense that all acts of prescribing are cases of giving advice, making recommendations, or offering guidance.

If we think of a rule as a "universal prescription" and the utterance of a particular "ought" sentence (under the four necessary conditions I have discussed) as a "particular prescription," we may view the justification of an act of prescribing as follows. We show that the act in question is a particular instance of a universal prescription. The reasoning process may be presented thus:

A: "You ought to do X."
B: "Why?"
A: "Because anyone in circumstances C ought to do acts of kind K, you are in circumstances C, and act X is an act of kind K."

Here A justifies his particular prescription by citing a rule and by claiming that the act which he has prescribed is required by the rule. He is assuming in his reply that B, in addition to being in circumstances C, has the choice of doing or not doing X. (If B did not have such a choice, A would not have prescribed that he do X in the first place.) When B demands a justification for A's prescription, A must show three things: that B is in circumstances C (a matter of empirical verification), that act X is of kind K (a matter of definition and of empirical verification), and that the rule "One ought to do acts of kind K in circumstances C" is a justified rule (a matter of validation, vindication, and rational choice). To justify an act of prescribing in this way is to use a form of argument similar to Aristotle's "practical syllogism," in which a universal principle (rule) is the major premise, a specification of an act that falls under the principle is the minor premise, and a prescription of the act is the conclusion.

If we want to call this a case of justifying a "particular prescription" by showing that it is an instance of a "universal prescription," no harm is done so long as we do not forget the differences between stating rules and prescribing acts, and so long as we do not think that this is the only way in which "particular prescriptions" can be justified. We may justify prescriptions by appeal to standards as well as to rules. Suppose a football coach says to his quarterback "You ought to call more pass plays." His prescription is justified not by reference to the *rules* of the game, but to the *standard* of instrumental value toward the end of winning the game at hand. (I shall examine the justification of prescriptions at greater length in the next chapter.)

The difference between stating a rule and stating that an act is or is not in accordance with a rule can be understood in terms of the justification of each kind of statement. We justify the first by the complex process of validation, vindication, and rational choice. We justify the second by simple empirical procedures, once the act has been shown to fall under the rule. (To show that the act falls under the rule involves the various procedures of validation outlined in Chapter 3.) Both types of statement may be expressed in sentences having the predicates "right" and "wrong." Thus the same rule may be stated in the sentence "One ought (ought not) to do acts of kind K in circumstances C" and in the sentence "It is right (wrong) to do acts of kind K in circumstances C." When we use "right" and "wrong" to state that an act is or is not in accordance with a rule which we have adopted, we use sentences of the form "It is right (wrong) to do act X" or "Act X is right (wrong)." In these cases the sentence expresses a value judgment (based on an evaluation according to rules).

C. *Prescriptions and "ought" sentences*

Both of the following generalizations are false: All utterances of "ought" sentences are acts of prescribing. All acts of prescribing are utterances of "ought" sentences. I shall now attempt to enumerate the various exceptions which render these statements false.

There are many kinds of "ought" sentences that are not used as prescriptions. In the first place there are all *post eventum* sentences, all first person singular *ante eventum* sentences, all third person *ante eventum* sentences, and those first person plural *ante eventum* sentences which are not addressed to the group referred to in the sentence. As we saw in Section A of this chapter, these "ought" sentences are evaluative, not prescriptive. In the second place, there are those universal "ought" sentences which express rules that do not apply to the addressee. As we saw in Section B, these sentences are not used to *tell* a person what *he* ought to do and therefore are not prescriptive. In the third place there are certain "ought" sentences I have not yet discussed which are neither prescriptive nor evaluative. In the fourth place there are what may be called "ought-to-be" sentences as distinct from "ought-to-do" sentences. I shall now examine these last two groups of "ought" sentences and show why they are not prescriptive.

"Ought" sentences are neither prescriptive nor evaluative when the sole justification of the act proposed is pure utility. In Chapter 1, the distinction was drawn between pure utility and instrumental value. Something has instrumental value when it is a means to a valuable (good, desirable) end. If an end has no value or if we disregard its value, we might still judge that something is an effective means to it. Such a judgment is a judgment of pure utility; it has no evaluative connotations. Similar considerations hold for pure utility "ought" sentences, in which we say that a person ought to do a certain act *if* he wants to achieve a certain result. We make no evaluation of the result to be achieved. We might say that a murderer ought to have used a silencer on his gun (under the assumption that he did not want to be caught), without thereby claiming that it would have been a good thing if he had used a silencer. Pure utility "ought" sentences may be particular or universal, and particular sentences may be of any person or tense. In no case are they prescriptive, even when they are in the form of second person *ante eventum* sentences. One of the four necessary conditions of prescribing is absent, namely that the addressee have the right to demand reasons for his doing the act mentioned in the sentence and that the speaker be disposed to give such reasons. In the case of pure utility sentences there is no presupposition that the speaker considers the act to be justified. When he says "You ought to do *X*" he always assumes, if he does not explicitly state, "If you want *Y*," and he makes no judgment about the value of *Y*. Accordingly he is not recommending that the addressee do *X* and his utterance of the sentence is not an act of prescribing.

Throughout this chapter I have been concerned only with "ought-to-do" sentences. An exhaustive analysis of the meanings (uses) of the word "ought" requires that the three types of "ought-to-be" sentences also be discussed. I shall argue that all sentences of these types may be uttered in earnest and affirmed by a speaker without the speaker's thereby prescribing an act to an agent.

The first type of "ought-to-be" sentence may be either *ante eventum* or *post eventum* and may be in the first, second, or third person. It is a sentence in which we say that someone ought to have (or have had) a certain feeling or disposition, rather than that he ought to do (or have done) a certain act. Consider the following examples. "I ought to feel grateful, but I'm afraid that I don't" (first person *ante eventum*). "You ought to be glad you escaped without injury" (second person *ante eventum*). "He ought to feel sorrow about his father's death" (third person *ante eventum*). "They ought to have had more understanding and less indignation about the child's prank" (third person *post eventum*). In all cases of this sort, we use an "ought" sentence to express a *value judgment* concerning someone's feelings or dispositions. We are not prescribing that someone do an act. Even in the case of second person *ante eventum* sentences, the speaker is not prescribing to the addressee. The addressee is not confronted with the choice of having or not having the feeling or disposition in question, since a feeling or a disposition is not the sort of thing we can choose to have or not to have. A person who says that we ought to have a certain feeling or disposition is not *recommending* that we have it, nor is he *guiding* our choice. He is instead judging that it would be appropriate, fitting, or desirable that we have it. Thus a particular "ought-to-be" sentence expresses a value judgment. Of course if a person accepts such a value judgment, he will *try* to develop his character and personality in such a way that in future situations similar to those referred to by the sentence, he will have the appropriate, fitting, or desirable feeling or disposition. The value judgment will exert an influence on his behavior. But it would not be correct to call this doing what someone had prescribed. The first type of "ought-to-be" sentences, then, are not prescriptive.

The second type of "ought-to-be" sentences assert that some state of affairs which does not now exist ought to exist, or that some existing state of affairs ought not to exist. Consider these examples. "There ought to be a world government." "Racial discrimination ought not to exist." "Automobiles ought to have air-pollution filters over their exhausts." "This room ought not to have red walls." "There ought to be a law against that kind of advertising." "A doctor ought to be here at a time like this." "We ought to have more honest local politicians." How are these sentences to be construed? In the first place, the phrases "There ought to be a," "A . . . ought to exist," and "We ought to have a" (where the "we" stands for some group or for some society, or for all mankind) are approximately equivalent in meaning. Similarly, "Object *O* ought to have" is about equivalent to "There ought to be a . . . for object *O*." Thus all these sentences can be reduced to a sentence of the form, "There ought (ought not) to be a . . . ." The second point to notice is that all of these "ought-to-be" sentences can be restated as "ought-to-be-done" sentences. For each of the examples above, an equivalent can be given as follows. "A world government ought to be established." "Racial discrimination ought to be eliminated." "Air-pollution filters ought to be placed on all automobile exhausts." "The walls of this room ought to be painted a different color." "A law against that kind of advertising ought to be passed." "A doctor ought to be called at a time like this." "More honest local politicians ought to be voted in." Each of these "ought-to-be-done" sentences is of the form "X ought to be done in circumstances C." But this is just the passive form of a universal "ought-to-do" sentence, which has already been analyzed. Its active form is, "One ought to do X in circumstances C." Therefore the second type of "ought-to-be" sentence introduces no new problems. Like all universal "ought" sentences, they may be used either prescriptively or to express a rule. In the latter case we have another instance of an "ought" sentence not being used for the purpose of prescribing.

The third type of "ought-to-be" sentence that is not prescriptive is one in which we assert that some object, event, or situation is as it ought to be. For example, we might say "Their new house is just what a house for an elderly couple ought to be." Or we might say that the circus this year is "everything a circus ought to be." What we are saying is that the house or the circus is *ideal*. "Ought-to-be" sentences of this type are always evaluative. They are used for stating that something completely fulfills the standards which we deem appropriate for judging the thing. If we say that something is not as it ought to be, we are stating that it fails to fulfill the standards appropriate for judging it. An example would be, "This student's paper is not what it ought to be." Sometimes "ought-to-be" sentences of this type are used to assert that something is (or is not) good-of-its-kind. Concerning a timid lion we might say, "He doesn't behave as a lion ought to behave." In none of these cases are we prescribing when we utter an "ought" sentence.

Not all utterances of "ought" sentences, then, are acts of prescribing. But are all acts of prescribing utterances of "ought" sentences? In investigating the nature of prescribing, I have so far been concerned only with "ought" sentences. May not other kinds of sentences be used for this purpose? I think the answer to this is clearly in the affirmative. There are a number of other linguistic forms ordinarily used for giving a direct and unequivocal answer to the question "What should (ought, shall) I do?"

In the first place there are imperatives. To claim that imperatives may function as prescriptions is to deny that all imperatives express commands. Prescribing is done in the context of giving advice, making recommendations, or offering guidance, and I have shown that these activities are fundamentally different from commanding, ordering, or issuing directives. That sentences in the imperative mood can be used for prescribing is clear from the fact that it is perfectly proper to answer the question "What should I do?" with such sentences as: "Do X." "Be sure to do X." "Do not fail to do X." Whether imperatives express prescriptions or commands depends on the conditions under which they are uttered. They express prescriptions only when they are uttered under the four conditions I have stated as necessary for an "ought" sentence to be prescriptive. To utter an imperative sentence under these conditions is to tell a person what he is to do when he has (or will have) the *choice* of doing or not doing what he is told. Such an utterance is then an act of prescribing.

In addition to their prescriptive use and their use as commands, imperatives may also be used to state rules. Thus the rule "One ought to do acts of kind K in circumstances C" may be expressed in the imperative: "In circumstances C, do acts of kind K." It is for this reason that rules are sometimes defined as "universal imperatives." This definition may be quite misleading, since we may think that rules can only be stated in sentences in the imperative mood and that stating rules is the same thing as commanding. We have already seen that rules can be stated in "ought" sentences and in sentences using the predicates "right" and "wrong." And stating a rule may or may not be an act of commanding someone to do something. It is a command only when the person who states the rule is in a position of *authority* and is *laying down* the rule for others to follow (as distinct from adopting it for himself).

A second way to prescribe without using an "ought" sentence is by means of what may be called "necessity" words. Thus we may answer the question "What should I do?" by saying: "You must do X." "You are to do X." "You are obliged to do X." When such sentences are uttered in the context of giving advice, making recommendations, or offering guidance, they function like second person *ante eventum* "ought" sentences. Uttering such a sentence in that sort of context is an act of prescribing whenever the four necessary conditions of prescribing are fulfilled. (In such a context, the four conditions normally *will* be fulfilled.) It is also possible to state a rule by using "necessity" words. The rule "One ought to do acts of kind K in circumstances C" may be stated in the form "One must do acts of kind K in circumstances C." This would not be a prescription unless the rule was stated under the four necessary conditions of prescribing and under the additional conditions that the addressee be in circumstances C either in the present or in the foreseeable future.

Thirdly, there are a variety of expressions that are milder in their feeling-tone than "ought" sentences, imperatives, and "necessity" sentences, and yet which may be used prescriptively. "I suggest that you do X." "My advice is, do X." "I recommend that you do X." "If I were you, I should do X." All these utterances are prescriptive whenever they are made under the four necessary conditions of prescribing, and they are always made in the context of advising, recommending, or guiding.

I conclude, then, that not all acts of prescribing are utterances of "ought" sentences. It should be noted that the nature of prescribing as I have tried to elucidate it in this chapter is common to all kinds of prescriptions. I wish to emphasize that *moral* prescriptions have no special status among prescriptions in general. The concept of prescribing does, of course, apply to moral prescriptions, such as "You ought to keep your promises." But it also applies in equal measure to all of the following nonmoral prescriptions. "You ought to change the frame on that picture" (aesthetic). "You ought to build the new factory in this city" (economic). "You ought to repeat the experiment under more careful controls" (intellectual). "You ought to kneel during prayer" (religious). "You ought to reinforce the steel on that bridge" (technological). "You ought to put the fork on the left side of the plate" (etiquette or custom). "You ought to throw a pass on the next play" (playing a game). The nature of prescribing does not change as the point of view from which a prescription is made changes. What makes the uttering of a sentence an act of prescribing is not the point of view taken by the speaker, but the kind of sentence it is and the conditions under which it is uttered. In this chapter I have tried to show what kinds of sentences are prescriptive and what conditions must be fulfilled if the uttering of such a sentence is to be an act of prescribing.

Prescribing and evaluating

8

A. *Prescriptions and value judgments compared*

The purpose of this chapter is twofold: to examine the similarities and differences between prescriptions and value judgments, and to understand how they are logically related to each other. My principal thesis will be that prescriptions are justified in the same way that value judgments are justified. I intend to show that the justification of a prescription is nothing but the justification of a set of value judgments.

What precisely is the difference between prescribing an act to someone and judging the value of something? There are three major points of difference: 1. An act of prescribing is a linguistic act, whereas a value judgment is a mental disposition. 2. All prescribing is done for the purpose of guiding conduct, but most evaluating is not done for this purpose. 3. Prescribing an act is not giving a reason for doing it, while on the contrary evaluating an act is giving a reason for (or against) doing it. I shall consider each point in turn.

1. To prescribe an act to someone is always to *tell* him that he ought to do the act, but we may judge something to have a certain value without telling anyone about it. When, as the result of a

process of evaluation, we make up our minds about an object's value, we acquire a disposition to answer in a certain way the question "What is the value of the object?" This disposition is a settled opinion, as distinct from the linguistic occurrences in which we express that opinion to others or to ourselves. Uttering an evaluative sentence is not itself an act of judging the value of something. It is the expression of a judgment already formed. Uttering a prescriptive sentence, on the other hand, is itself an act of prescribing (so long as it occurs under the four conditions necessary for prescribing). We cannot prescribe that someone do an act unless we utter a sentence in which we say that he ought to do it. And we must address our sentence to the person himself. Every prescription is a form of direct address. He to whom one prescribes must be in the position of an addressee and he who prescribes must be in the position of a speaker (or writer). A value judgment, on the contrary, need not be addressed to anyone, and the evaluator need not be in the position of a speaker (or writer).

Suppose we compare a prescription not with a value judgment itself, but with the *expression* of a value judgment. How would these two kinds of linguistic act differ? Their basic differences lie in points 2 and 3 already stated, and I shall consider these points in detail below. For the moment, let us see how close a parallel can be drawn between an act of prescribing and an act of uttering or expressing a value judgment.

A person prescribes when he utters a prescriptive sentence in earnest and affirms what it says. A person expresses a value judgment when he utters an evaluative sentence in earnest and affirms what it says. Each act of uttering a sentence must have been preceded by an evaluation process. In the case of a prescriptive sentence, the evaluation process was a process of deliberation in which the alternatives open to the addressee in his situation of choice were evaluated and ranked in relation to one another. In the case of an evaluative sentence, the evaluation process was the process whereby the speaker arrived at the judgment he is expressing in the sentence. Common to both cases are the following five elements: (a) a *pro-attitude or con-attitude* on the part of the speaker toward what is being prescribed or judged; (b) a *point of view* from which the prescription or judgment is being made; (c) a *standard or rule* according to which the prescribed act or judged object has been evaluated; (d) a set of *good-making and bad-making characteristics* possessed by the prescribed act or judged object; and (e) a *class of comparison* within which the prescribed act or judged object has been evaluated.

Just as uttering in earnest and affirming the sentence "X is good" contextually implies a pro-attitude on the part of the speaker toward object X, so prescribing by means of the sentence "You ought to do X" contextually implies a pro-attitude on the part of the speaker toward the addressee's doing act X. Similarly, negative evaluative sentences ("X is bad") and negative prescriptions ("You ought not to do X") contextually imply con-attitudes. The parallel between evaluative sentences and prescriptions also holds with regard to points of view. At the end of the last chapter I mentioned various kinds of prescriptions, classified according to the points of view from which they are made. Thus there is a moral "ought" and an aesthetic "ought," a religious "ought" and an intellectual "ought," an "ought" of etiquette and an "ought" of prudence, and so on. The distinction between these various "oughts" is based on *the different kinds of standards and rules used in the evaluation of the prescribed act.* A moral "ought" (or moral prescription) is a prescription in which the prescribed act has been evaluated (in the process of deliberation) according to moral standards or rules. An aesthetic "ought" is a prescription in which aesthetic standards or rules have been appealed to. And so on for the other kinds of "oughts." The distinction among different kinds of standards and rules is based on the concept of a point of view, as explained in Chapter 4. Consequently different "oughts" correspond to different points of view. The same is true of evaluative expressions. Whenever we express a value judgment, the value judgment is either a moral judgment, an aesthetic judgment, or a judgment of some other kind. Different kinds of judgments are distinguished according to the different kinds of standards and rules appealed to in the evaluation processes from which they arise, and different kinds of standards and rules are distinguished according to the points of view to which they belong. The fact that both prescriptions and expressions of value judgments presuppose an evaluation process entails that they both presuppose an appeal to standards or rules. It also entails that prescribed acts as well as evaluated objects have good-making and bad-making characteristics. Finally, it entails that there is a class of comparison contextually implied by every prescription and by every expression of a value judgment. In the case of prescriptions, the class of comparison is always the class of alternative acts open to the addressee in his situation of choice. There is no parallel on this point in the case of expressions of value judgments. That is, while both prescriptions and expressions of value judgments presuppose classes of comparison, there is no single class of comparison for evaluative expressions comparable to the class of comparison of all prescriptions. The reason for this lies in one of the differences between prescribing an act and expressing a value judgment, to which I now turn.

2. An act of prescribing always takes place in the context of giving advice, making recommendations, or offering guidance, in which a person is told which act to do among the alternatives open to him. He may not be seeking advice or guidance, nor even be asking himself or someone else which one of the alternatives he should do. A child, for example, may be given moral instruction without his seeking it. But whenever prescribing occurs, it is done for the purpose of guiding conduct. Prescribing is *essentially* and not merely *incidentally* a way of exerting an influence on someone's behavior. Expressing a value judgment, on the other hand, only incidentally has this function in most cases. It was shown in Section B of Chapter 2 that those to whom we express our value judgments are not always confronted with a choice among alternative courses of action. Furthermore it was shown that the classes of comparison of value judgments may not be human acts at all. We may express value judgments of events, objects, and situations which have no connection with the addressee's conduct. (An example given in Chapter 2 was a historian's judgment that the Roman Empire was a corrupt society.) It is only in contexts of giving advice, making recommendations, or offering guidance that our evaluative utterances function as guides to conduct. But prescribing always occurs in a context of that sort. As a result, the class of comparison contextually implied by a prescription is always the class of alternative acts open to the addressee's choice. When a certain act is prescribed to the addressee, it is contextually implied that it is the *best* of the alterna-

tives confronting him. This claim is, of course, a value judgment, based on a ranking of all the alternatives in comparison with each other. The class of comparison of such a ranking is precisely the class of alternatives themselves.

This difference between evaluative and prescriptive discourse may be brought out in another way. Suppose we attempt to construct a parallel, in the case of evaluative sentences, to the four aspects or elements of every prescriptive sentence which I distinguished in the last chapter. These were the speaker, the addressee, the agent, and the prescribed act. With regard to them, let us compare the evaluative sentence "Abraham Lincoln was a good man" with the prescriptive sentence "You ought to repay the debt." Corresponding to the speaker of the prescription would be the evaluator or judge (i.e., the one who utters the evaluative sentence in earnest and affirms what it says). Corresponding to the addressee of the prescription would be the addressee of the evaluative sentence (i.e., anyone to whom the sentence is addressed). Now what would correspond to the agent designated by "You" in the prescriptive sentence? Would it be the man, Abraham Lincoln? At first sight this might appear to be so, since the agent in the case of the prescription is the person referred to by the grammatical subject of the sentence, and Lincoln is that person in the case of the evaluative sentence. But on reflection we see that Lincoln corresponds to the fourth element of the prescription, namely the prescribed act, rather than the third element, the agent. Lincoln is the object being evaluated and hence corresponds to the act being prescribed. In one sentence we evaluate a man, in the other we prescribe an act. In applying the word "good" to the man we express our pro-attitude toward him; in applying the word "ought" to the act we likewise express our pro-attitude toward it. What we evaluate thus corresponds to what we prescribe. We must not be misled by the grammar of the two sentences. The things designated by the grammatical subjects of the two sentences have a different logical status. Lincoln the man has no correspondence with the person referred to by "You" in the prescriptive sentence. This becomes unmistakably clear when we notice that "You" refers not only to the agent but also to the addressee. (As in every case of a prescription, the addressee is identical with the agent.) But it hardly needs saying that Abraham Lincoln is not the addressee of the sentence "Abraham Lincoln was a good man." So far, then, we have the following parallels.

For a prescriptive sentence:

1. The speaker (the one who prescribes the act)
2. The addressee (the one to whom the sentence is uttered)
3. The act (that which is prescribed)

For an evaluative sentence:

1. The speaker (the one who evaluates the evaluatum)
2. The addressee (the one to whom the sentence is uttered)
3. The evaluatum (that which is evaluated)

A complete parallel between the two kinds of sentences cannot be drawn, however. For the addressee of every prescriptive sentence is also an *agent* who has the choice of doing or not doing the act. But the addressee of every evaluative sentence is not an agent who has a choice with reference to the evaluatum. Only when an evaluative sentence is uttered as advice to a person in a situation of choice is there anyone in a role corresponding to the role of the agent of a prescription. But an evaluative sentence need not be uttered in such a context. Although there must always be an agent for a prescriptive sentence, this is not true for evaluative sentences. This follows from the fact that we always prescribe an act to someone who has the choice of doing or not doing the act, whereas we may express our value judgments to those who are not in a position to make a choice with regard to what we are evaluating.

There would be no chance of our confusing the person referred to by the subject of an evaluative sentence (the evaluatum) with the person referred to by the subject of a prescriptive sentence (the agent) if we took as our example not an evaluation of a person but an evaluation of some other kind of object. It would then be clear that the subject of the evaluative sentence referred to what is evaluated and hence corresponded to the grammatical object rather than the grammatical subject of the prescriptive sentence. If we say "That painting is an excellent abstraction," it is clear that the subject of the sentence does not correspond to the subject of the sentence "You ought to repay the debt." What we evaluate (the painting) corresponds to what we prescribe (repaying the debt); it does not correspond to the one to whom we prescribe (the person referred to by "You"). In order to make a prescriptive sentence correspond *grammatically* to an evaluative sentence, we would have to change it from the active to the passive voice. Thus a sentence of the form "*X* is good" would correspond to a sentence of the form "*Y* ought to be done" (and "*X* is bad" to "*Y* ought not to be done"). Here the grammatical subject of one sentence refers to that which is evaluated and the grammatical subject of the other refers to that which is prescribed. It is still not possible to draw a complete parallel, however, since an agent is implicitly referred to in the prescriptive sentence but not in the evaluative sentence.

There is a sharp distinction, then, between prescribing and expressing a value judgment when the latter does not take place in the context of a person's making a choice with regard to the evaluatum. But what is the difference between them when this context does occur? In that case an evaluative sentence functions as a piece of advice or as a recommendation, which is the way a prescription always functions. Although value judgments are not always expressed in the context of an agent's situation of choice and are not always expressed for the purpose of guiding the agent's conduct, they sometimes are. On these occasions how are they to be differentiated from acts of prescribing? The answer to this question lies in the third major difference between prescribing and evaluating.

3. It may at first be thought that we can differentiate between the utterance of a prescriptive sentence and the utterance of an evaluative sentence (when the addressee of both sentences is an agent in a situation of choice and when the sentences are both uttered for the purpose of guiding the addressee's conduct) on the following basis. We might want to say that prescribing an act is a way of getting the addressee to do the act, whereas evaluating the act is not. In expressing a value judgment we remain somewhat aloof and detached, merely telling the addressee what we think of the alternatives confronting him without advocating that he choose one rather than another. In prescribing an act, on the other hand, we are actively engaged in the making of the choice. But this method of differentiating prescriptive and evaluative utterances will not do. For in the particular context in question, to express a value judgment about one of the alternatives confronting the addressee *is* to advocate that he choose (or not choose) it. In such a context our purpose as

evaluators is not merely to have the addressee give intellectual assent to our judgment. Our purpose is to have the addressee follow our judgment as a recommendation. Expressing the judgment to him in that context is giving him a piece of advice; the whole point of our utterance is to help him decide upon a course of action. When a person is trying to decide what make of car to buy, for example, and we say to him "*N* is a good car," we are guiding his choice. The parallel with prescribing is here very close. To express the value judgment "*N* is a good car" in such circumstances is not much different from uttering the prescription, "You ought to buy *N*." The purpose of either sentence (assuming it is uttered in earnest and is affirmed by the speaker) is to have the addressee give his sincere assent to what is being said. And this involves his setting himself to do certain acts and having a pro-attitude toward doing them. Both sentences are uttered in a context in which the addressee is seeking advice or guidance, and has placed himself in the position (or frame of mind) to allow the speaker's utterance to influence his conduct. Whether we address to him a value judgment of an object (the car) or prescribe to him the doing of certain acts (buying the car), the effect will be same. If he decides to follow our advice, he will buy the car. We simply give him the same advice in two different ways: by evaluating or by prescribing.

What, then, is the difference in this context between expressing a value judgment and prescribing? It may be made clear by seeing how each provides an answer to the question "What should I do?" When we express a value judgment of one of the alternatives confronting the questioner, we answer his question indirectly. When we prescribe one of the alternatives, we answer his question directly. In asking the question he wants to be told what he ought to do. He is not asking for *reasons* for doing one thing rather than another. When we prescribe to him, we simply tell him what he ought to do without giving him a reason for doing it. When we express a value judgment, on the other hand, we are giving him a reason for (or against) doing one thing rather than another. When we answer the question "What should I do?" by expressing the value judgment "*X* is the best thing to do," we are not saying that the person ought to do *X*. Rather, we are giving him a sufficient reason for his doing *X*. Of course a person ought to do something whenever he has a sufficient reason for doing it. (Not to do it would be to do an unjustified act.) But prescribing to a person is not giving him a reason, sufficient or otherwise, for doing something. It is merely telling him that he ought to do it, as we saw in the last chapter. The prescription can only answer the question "*What* should I do?" and not the question "*Why* should I do it?" One can always answer the latter question by saying "Because it is the best thing to do." One cannot answer by saying "Because you ought to do it." For in asking "Why ought I to do this?" the questioner already knows what he has been told to do. He is now demanding a justification for his doing it.

To prescribe an act to someone, then, is not to give a reason for his doing it, whereas to express a positive value judgment about an alternative open to him is to give a reason for choosing it. Value judgments serve to justify acts, prescriptions do not. Value judgments may in fact serve to justify prescriptions themselves. We must now examine the logical relation between prescribing and evaluating in order to see why this is so.

B. *The logical relation between prescribing and evaluating*

We express a value judgment as the result of a disposition to give a certain answer to the question "What is the value of object X?" This disposition was formed or acquired when we came to a decision about the value of the object. The decision was a verdict reached in consequence of a process of evaluation. Now an act of prescribing what someone ought to do is an act of uttering a prescriptive sentence. Behind this act there must be a disposition to perform it, since it is not spontaneous, involuntary, or accidental. Just as a disposition to express a value judgment lies behind the uttering of an evaluative sentence, so a disposition to prescribe an act to someone lies behind uttering a prescriptive sentence. The former disposition is the outcome of a process of evaluation. I now intend to show that the latter disposition is likewise the outcome of a process of evaluation.

The disposition to prescribe an act to an agent is formed when the prescriber comes to a decision about which of the alternatives open to the agent ought to be chosen by him. The decision is arrived at through the process of deliberation. This, as we saw in Chapter 1, is a process of evaluating the various alternatives and ranking them in comparison with one another. As an outcome of this process, we are disposed to prescribe one alternative to the agent as that which he ought to choose. Thus both a value judgment and a disposition to prescribe result from processes of evaluation. The difference between the use of the evaluation process in these two situations is twofold. First, the class of comparison in the case of prescribing is always limited to the alternatives open to the agent's choice. And second, the decision to prescribe an act is always arrived at in the context of the agent's present or future situation of choice. Thus we may carry out a process of evaluation for either or both of two purposes—to arrive at a value judgment (i.e., to decide what the value of something is), or to prescribe an act to an agent.

Suppose we carry out an evaluation for the second purpose and arrive at the prescription "You ought to do X." Our prescription then contextually implies a value judgment, namely that act X is the best of the alternatives confronting the agent. Every prescription occurs in a context of deliberation in which the alternatives are evaluated, and the prescribed act is the alternative which has been ranked as better than any other alternative. Professor Baier has argued in *The Moral Point of View* (Chapter 3) that the question "What shall I do?" has the same meaning as "What is the best thing to do?" It would follow from this that the answer to the one question ("You ought to do X") means the same as the answer to the other question ("X is the best thing to do"). But these statements are not equivalent. One is a prescription and the other is the expression of a value judgment. The prescription *contextually implies* the value judgment, but it does not *mean the same thing as* the value judgment. The reason for this should be clear from my discussion of the differences between prescriptions and evaluative sentences in Section A of this chapter. When we say "You ought to do X," we are not giving a reason for doing X. But when we say "X is the best thing to do," we are giving a reason, and a sufficient one, for doing X. Although the act of prescribing contextually implies the value judgment, the two cannot be identified.

In order to justify doing an act, we must show that it is the best thing to do in a given situation of choice. We justify doing an act on the ground of an evaluation, not by prescribing it. Similarly, we may give reasons against doing an act by evaluating the act (as wrong or bad, or simply as less-than-the-best of the alternatives confronting a person)—not by prescribing that one ought not to do it. It is my present task to show that such value judgments not only provide reasons for (or against) *doing* the act, but also provide reasons for (or against) *prescribing* it. In every prescription we find both the act of prescribing and the act prescribed. I shall try to establish two points: first, that *both* of these acts are justified on the basis of value judgments, and second, that the justification of the act prescribed is part of, but not the whole of, the justification of the act of prescribing.

If the doing of an act is to be justified to a person in a situation of choice, the act must be shown to be the best alternative open to him. This is because in such a context "the best act" simply means "the most justified act." Assuming that the value judgments according to which the different alternatives are ranked are themselves justified, to claim that alternative X is better than alternative Y means that a person is more justified in choosing X than in choosing Y. To say in this context "X is the best thing to do," then, is to justify the agent's *doing X.* Is it also to justify the *prescribing* of act X to the agent? My answer is that it is to justify it in part, but not wholly.

We must distinguish two questions here. 1. Is it better to prescribe act X than to prescribe any other act open to the agent? 2. Is it better to prescribe act X at this time, in this place, in this manner, under these conditions, than at any other time, in any other place, in any other manner, under any other conditions? Question 1 concerns the content of the prescription, question 2 concerns the manner and circumstances of the act of prescribing. If we are to justify the act of prescribing completely, we must answer both questions in the affirmative. The first question is answered in the affirmative when the act prescribed is shown to be the best of the alternatives open to the agent. To do this is partly to justify the act of prescribing it. Prescribing any other act than the best would amount to prescribing an act which the agent was less justified in doing, *and such a prescription would not be the best possible prescription open to the prescriber.* The purpose of prescribing is to have the addressee give his sincere assent to the prescription and accordingly set himself to do the act prescribed, or at least have a pro-attitude toward doing it. Corresponding to each of the alternative acts open to the addressee there is an alternative prescription open to the prescriber. If the alternative acts are X, Y, and Z, the alternative prescriptions are "You ought to do X," "You ought to do Y," and "You ought to do Z." Now the best prescription will be the prescribing of the best act. Otherwise the prescriber would be justified in prescribing an act—and so influencing an agent to do an act— which the agent was not justified in doing. If an act of prescribing is to be fully justified, it must be shown that the prescribed act is the best of the alternatives confronting the agent.

The alternative acts of prescribing open to a prescriber may vary in other respects than in their content (i.e., in respect of the acts prescribed in them). The alternatives concern not only what is prescribed but also the time, the place, the manner (including the linguistic form of a prescription), and the surrounding conditions of the act of prescribing. The complete justification of an act of prescribing must include reasons that show it to be the best alternative open to the prescriber in all these respects. To determine the best time, place, manner, and circumstance for prescribing requires an evaluation of the alternative times, places, manners, and circumstances open to the prescriber. Even when he has decided upon what act to prescribe to the agent, the prescriber must then come to a decision about these other matters in order to arrive at the best prescription available to him. And it is only if his prescription is the best available to him that it is justified (both to himself and to the agent).

The logical connection between prescribing and evaluating should now be clear. An act of prescribing is justified on the basis of a set of value judgments, according to which the act prescribed is the best of the alternatives open to the agent, and the time, place, manner, and circumstance of prescribing is the best time, the best place, the best manner, and the best circumstance open to the prescriber. All of these value judgments are in turn justified by the fourfold method of verification, validation, vindication, and rational choice. Whatever is true of justifying value judgments is also true of justifying prescriptions, since justifying prescriptions consists in justifying a set of value judgments. Nothing in principle differentiates the evaluation of the act prescribed from the evaluation of the time, place, manner, and circumstance of the act of prescribing. Both evaluations presuppose a set of standards or rules being appealed to. Both are made within a given class of comparison (in the one case, the class of acts open to the agent; in the other, the class of acts of prescribing open to the prescriber). Both consist in the ranking of alternatives in an order of desirability. And in both cases, the desirability or undesirability of each alternative is determined by its good-making or bad-making characteristics.

In order to justify a prescription, then, we must justify not only *what* to prescribe but also *when* to prescribe, *where* to prescribe, *how* to prescribe, and *in what circumstances* to prescribe. We accomplish this multiple task when we justify a set of value judgments in which alternative acts of prescribing are ranked in these various respects. It is to be noted that the evaluation of the act prescribed and the evaluation of the time, place, manner, and circumstance of the act of prescribing together form the *sufficient conditions* for a complete justification of an act of prescribing. All the possible ways in which acts of prescribing can differ are covered by these evaluations. They consequently exhaust all the possible alternatives open to a prescriber's choice. Since the most justified prescription is the best alternative in all these respects, no further justification need be given once these evaluations are themselves justified. Indeed, no further justification would be possible.

C. Hypothetical and categorical prescriptions

Since the logic of prescribing and evaluating is the same, it is clear that we may prescribe according to standards or according to rules. There is nothing in the prescriptive use of "ought" that limits it to the latter. We prescribe an act according to a standard when the value judgment, which justifies the act as the best alternative open to the agent, is itself justified by appeal to a standard. When it is justified by appeal to a rule, the act is prescribed according to that rule. This helps to clarify the distinction between hypothetical and categorical prescriptions.

When we justify a prescribed act by appeal to a standard, the standard may be one of inherent value, of instrumental value, or of contributive value. (A combination of such standards may also be appealed to.) Standards of intrinsic value are excluded because the evaluatum is an act, not an immediately felt quality of experience. The prescribed act is judged in comparison with all the alternative acts in the agent's situation of choice. The verification of the prescription is the process of determining whether the prescribed act is in fact the best thing for the agent to do, according to the given standard or set of standards. The prescription is verified when it is ascertained that the prescribed act fulfills the given standards more completely than any other act in the class of comparison.

We may say that the difference between categorical and hypothetical prescriptions lies in the fact that we sometimes prescribe an act because we think it ought to be done "for its own sake," and other times we prescribe an act because we think it ought to be done "for the sake of something else." In that case, the kind of standard we appeal to in justifying (verifying) our prescription determines whether it is categorical or hypothetical. When the standard is one of inherent value only, the prescription is, in this sense, categorical. To say that the agent ought to do the act is to claim that *in doing it* the agent will have more satisfying or enjoyable experiences than he will have in doing any of the alternative acts open to him. A hypothetical prescription is one which is verified by appeal either to standards of instrumental value or to standards of contributive value. If we prescribe an act because it will have better consequences than any alternative act, or because the whole of which it is a part is more valuable than any whole of which an alternative act is a part, then the prescription is hypothetical. We think the agent ought to do the prescribed act as a means to certain ends or as a part of a certain whole, not because he will enjoy doing the act itself.

This way of distinguishing categorical and hypothetical prescriptions allows for the possibility of a prescription's being both categorical and hypothetical at the same time. This would occur when the standards appealed to included standards of inherent value as well as standards of instrumental or contributive value. Such a prescription would state that an act ought to be done both for its own sake and for the sake of something else. Suppose the prescription "You ought to do X" is of this kind. When reasons are demanded for accepting this prescription, the speaker would reply,

"Not only will you find more enjoyment in doing X than in doing any alternative act, but doing X will also bring about more good things (or is a part of a better whole) than any alternative act."

There are, then, three possibilities according to this way of understanding the terms. A given prescription may be categorical only, hypothetical only, or both categorical and hypothetical. This classification applies to prescriptions made according to standards rather than rules. In order to justify such prescriptions, we must verify the value judgment that the prescribed act is better than any alternative by appealing to the given standards. A *complete* justification of a hypothetical or categorical prescription would require the validation of the standards appealed to, the vindication of a value system which contains those standards, and a rational choice of a way of life of which that value system is a part.

There is a second way of distinguishing between hypothetical and categorical prescriptions. It applies to prescriptions verified by appeal to rules rather than standards. To verify a prescription by appeal to a rule is to show that the act prescribed falls under the rule and is in accordance with it. When this is done we might say that a particular prescription has been shown to be an instance of a universal prescription. In Section B of the last chapter, the following argument was analyzed: "You ought to do X because anyone in circumstances C ought to do acts of kind K, you are in circumstances C, and act X is an act of kind K." This is a case of justifying the prescription of a particular act by appeal to a general rule of conduct which covers the act in its range of application. The particular prescription "You ought to do X" is justified as an instance of the universal prescription "One ought to do acts of kind K in circumstances C." If the speaker were then to be asked to justify the universal prescription or rule, he could give any of three replies. 1. He could validate the rule in terms of some higher or more general rule. 2. He could validate the rule in terms of a standard. The standard appealed to might be a standard of inherent value, of instrumental value, or of contributive value. (The standard would be used to judge the goodness or badness of the consequences of acting in accordance with the rule in question.) 3. He could accept the rule as a supreme norm of a value system he has adopted.

A hypothetical prescription may now be distinguished from a

categorical prescription as follows. If a particular prescription is justified by appeal to a rule (or general prescription) and if the rule is validated by either method 1 or method 2 above, both the particular prescription and the general prescription (or rule) are hypothetical. If a particular prescription is justified by appeal to a rule and if the rule is accepted according to method 3 as part of the decision to adopt a certain value system, then the particular prescription and the rule (or general prescription) are categorical.

When Kant spoke of the "categorical imperative," he meant among other things that all moral justification consists in the appeal to *one rule* and that the decision to adopt that rule as the test of the rightness or wrongness of any act is the decision to adopt the only value system that can properly be called "moral." If a person does not appeal to that rule in judging acts, he is not looking at his own or others' conduct from the moral point of view. When a person takes the moral point of view he appeals to the one "imperative" of morality in prescribing or evaluating any act. This "imperative" is "categorical" in the sense that its justification requires no reference to any standard or rule beyond itself. We must simply adopt the "imperative" as the sole guide to our conduct. This is what it means to take the moral point of view, according to Kant. To act morally is to act in accordance with a rule or universal prescription (the categorical imperative) to which we are committed by our "practical reason." The decision to follow such a rule is an act of our rational (and hence autonomous) will. We take the moral point of view in the very act of deciding to follow the rule. Kant thought that the justification for taking the moral point of view lay in the concept of rationality itself. To be rational in our conduct *is* to take the moral point of view. This is not the conception of justifying (vindicating) a moral value system which I have set forth in Chapter 5. But the point of agreement with Kant to be noticed here is the identification of a categorical "ought" with a rule or rule-justified prescription that is accepted as an integral part of the decision to adopt a whole value system.

A prescription is categorical, then, in virtue of the fact that it is justified by appeal to a rule which is not itself validated by reference to any higher standard or rule. We accept the rule unconditionally (categorically) because it is a supreme norm of a value system we have adopted. The rule underlying a categorical prescription can only be vindicated (as part of a whole value system); it cannot be validated. A hypothetical prescription, on the other hand, is justified by appeal to a rule that can be validated. There are always higher standards or rules to appeal to, and these provide reasons for deciding to follow the given rule or for accepting the hypothetical prescription itself. The prescription is "hypothetical" in the sense that our acceptance of it is conditional upon our acceptance of the higher standards or rules.

I conclude that hypothetical and categorical prescriptions may be distinguished in two ways, depending on whether they are verified by appeal to standards or to rules. In either case their justification consists in the justification of a value judgment, namely the judgment that the prescribed act is the best of the alternatives confronting an agent. This value judgment must be verified by appeal to a standard or rule which in turn must be justified either by validation or by vindication. The conclusion I wish to emphasize in this chapter is that no new factors are introduced when we turn from the justification of value judgments to the justification of prescriptions. To justify an act of prescribing is to justify a set of value judgments. Most important is to show that the act prescribed is the best act for the agent to do in his situation of choice. This is necessary whether the prescription is hypothetical or categorical. Other value judgments concerning the best time, the best place, the best manner, and the best circumstance in which to do the act of prescribing must also be justified, and this is accomplished by the same fourfold method that is used for any value judgment, namely verification, validation, vindication, and rational choice.

"Ought" and "is"

9

A. The naturalistic fallacy

What has been said up to this point about prescribing and evaluating throws some light on what is often called the problem of the relation between facts and values. This problem consists of a number of related questions. First of all, there are questions about the way evaluative and prescriptive terms function in normative assertions, in contrast with the way empirical terms function in factual assertions. Secondly, there are questions as to the validity or invalidity of arguments in which normative conclusions are drawn from factual premises. Thirdly, there are questions about the use of scientific knowledge in justifying normative assertions. In this chapter I shall consider these various questions in light of the foregoing analysis of prescribing and evaluating. At the end of the chapter I shall try to elucidate the concept of the "autonomy" of normative discourse.

When words like "good" and "bad," "right" and "wrong" are employed in the expression of value judgments, they do not refer to empirically determinable properties of things, in the way that descriptive terms refer to such properties in factual assertions. In a factual assertion we claim that something has certain properties which can be discovered by empirical procedures. In a value judgment we claim that something has a certain value, but its value is not an empirically determinable property. Yet there is always a set of empirically determinable properties *contextually implied* by a value judgment. These properties are the good-making and bad-making (or right-making and wrong-making) characteristics of the evaluatum. In order to justify a value judgment we must show that the evaluatum has these properties, for these are the properties *in virtue of which* it possesses value or disvalue. If a value judgment were fully justified when these properties were found to characterize the evaluatum, then the justification of value judgments would be identical in method with the (empirical) justification of factual assertations. To say that something was "good" or "bad" would be like saying that it was green or round. Normative words would have the same function as descriptive words: to designate the empirically determinable properties of things. But this is not the case. To show that the evaluatum has certain good-making or bad-making characteristics is not sufficient for the justification of a value judgment. For a value judgment does not claim that something has these properties. It claims that something has value or disvalue in virtue of having these properties. This claim can be made *only if one has adopted a standard or rule according to which a certain property is good-making or bad-making*. A value judgment cannot be justified without appealing to the standard or rule according to which the evaluatum is being judged.

It is for this reason that no prescriptive term is ever the equivalent of a descriptive term. We use prescriptive terms ("ought," "must," etc.) to tell a person what he is to do. In prescribing an act for him to do we are not describing the act. We would describe it only if he did not understand what it was we were telling him to do. Our *description* of an act is correct when the act has the empirical properties which we assert that it has. Our *prescription* of an act is correct (i.e., justified) only if the empirical properties of the act which are good-making or right-making make it better than any alternative act open to the agent. We can only know which properties are good-making or right-making if we know which standard or rule is being used in ranking the act in comparison with its alternatives.

A standard or rule of evaluation is thus implicitly referred to whenever we utter a value judgment or prescription. This standard or rule is what transforms an empirical property into a good-making or bad-making (right-making or wrong-making) characteristic. We know whether a value predicate is properly attributable to a subject when we know the good-making and bad-making characteristics of the subject. In order to know these we must know what its empirical properties are *and* what standard or rule determines that its properties are good-making or bad-making. No knowledge of its empirical properties alone can tell us whether it is a good thing or a bad thing.

Let us take some examples. We cannot say that a child knows it is wrong to steal if *all* he knows is that he is taking something which belongs to someone else without his permission. The child must also know that there is a rule of conduct which forbids this sort of act. Again, I do not know that a painting is a bad painting merely because I know that the artist chose his colors haphazardly and used no restraint in smearing paint over the canvas. I have no right to argue that because the painting was done in this manner the result is a bad painting. I have the right to argue this only if I accept the controlled choice of color and application of paint as an appropriate standard of good painting. Given the appropriateness of this standard (which must be established by the processes of validation, vindication, and rational choice) and given the facts about how the work was painted, however, I can then legitimately claim to know that it is a bad painting. For it is the standard which renders empirical facts about how the painting was done as evidence of its badness. In other words, it is the fact that the method of painting failed to fulfill the standard that makes it a bad-making characteristic of the painting. Without a standard, neither the goodness nor the badness of the painting can be known, no matter how much empirical knowledge about the painting a person might have.

It is these considerations that explain why the naturalistic fallacy is a fallacy, or more accurately, why the various errors which Professor G. E. Moore collectively titled "the naturalistic fallacy" are errors. I shall try to show that this is so by considering three different versions of the naturalistic fallacy. For convenience we may call them the definitional error, the deductive error, and the disagreement error.

The definitional error consists in the view that every normative term (value predicate or prescriptive term) is equivalent to some empirical or descriptive term or a set of such terms. The name "naturalism" is sometimes given to this view, and different "naturalistic" theories in ethics are distinguished according to the particular empirical term (or set of terms) which is claimed to define a normative term. Thus one naturalistic theory holds that "good" means "pleasant," another that "good" means "generally approved of in this society," another that "right" means "required by law or custom," another that "desirable" means "leads to the satisfaction of human needs," and so on. There are various ways of demonstrating the error committed by all theories of this sort. I shall give what seems to me the two clearest, using the accounts of the naturalistic fallacy presented by other philosophers. Each of these accounts is derived from Professor Moore's original exposition of the fallacy in his *Principia Ethica*.

The first way is the use of the self-contradiction test. I quote from Bernard Mayo's account of Moore's proof.

If x means the same as y, then it will be self-contradictory to say that something is x but not y; if it is not self-contradictory to say so, then x cannot mean the same as y. Now even if it is true that what is good is always pleasant and *vice versa*, yet it is certainly not self-contradictory, in the normal usage of words, to say that something good is unpleasant, or something unpleasant good; therefore good and pleasant cannot mean the same, as they must if one defines the other. And the same argument holds against all other possible definitions of 'good' in terms of something else. (B. Mayo, *Ethics and the Moral Life*, p. 71.)

Why does the same argument always hold? The answer is that a normative (evaluative or prescriptive) term does not function in a sentence in the same way that a descriptive term functions in a factual assertation. The normative term does not name a property or set of properties, while the descriptive term does. The source of the definitional error of naturalism is in thinking of all adjectives as names of properties, and all declarative statements as attributions of properties to objects. This simply overlooks the radical difference in our employment of expressions when we make normative assertions and when we make descriptive assertions. When a normative term is predicated of a subject, the subject is not being described as having certain properties. We have seen that judging the value of something is not a simple matter of attributing empirical properties to it. Prescribing an act is likewise not attributing empirical properties to the act. It is true that in judging the value of something or in prescribing something, it is judged or prescribed *because* it has certain empirical properties. But the judgment or prescription is not logically entailed by the fact that the thing has those properties. It is logically entailed by that fact *plus* the acceptance of a certain standard or rule, in the light of which we have a pro-attitude, a con-attitude, or a neutral attitude toward the thing.

A second way of revealing the definitional error in naturalism is by the use of the senseless question test. This is stated in Professor Paul Edwards' account of the naturalistic fallacy.

. . . Consider *any* suggested definiens of 'good.' Let x be the suggested definiens. Then construct questions of these two types:

(1) Is goodness good?
(2) Is x good?

If the definiens is really synonymous with 'good' then (2), no less than (1), should be a senseless or self-answering question. . . . But in fact an investigation of any definiens that has ever been or could ever be suggested shows that (2) is not a senseless or self-answering question. 'Is happiness good?,' 'Is obedience to the will of God good?,' 'Is aiding the struggle for survival good?'—none of these is a self-answering question. (P. Edwards, *The Logic of Moral Discourse*. Glencoe, Ill.: The Free Press, 1955, p. 209.)

Here again the explanation of why no naturalistic definiens will work for the term "good" is that reference to a standard or rule of evaluation must always be made to show that the word "good" is correctly (justifiably) ascribed to the subject of an evaluative sentence. "Good" is a *grading* or *ranking* word in this context and as such is radically different from any word or set of words which merely performs the job of describing. The only possible substitutes for "good" in an evaluative sentence would be other positive grading or ranking terms, such as "worthy," "excellent," or "desirable." And the same argument which holds for "good" also holds for these terms. No descriptive words or phrases can be made equivalent in meaning to them.

Professor Richard B. Brandt has argued that the self-contradiction test and the senseless question test only tell us when two expressions are not *overtly* synonymous. They are not adequate tests for "covert" synonymity. According to Professor Brandt two terms are overtly synonymous when

. . . the person, for whose usage they are overtly synonymous, thinks after the briefest reflection (if the question is put to him) that the two terms are merely different verbal devices for saying the same thing; he recognizes them intuitively as alternate, freely interchangeable expressions . . . (R. B. Brandt, *Ethical Theory—The Problems of Normative Ethics.* Englewood Cliffs, N. J.: Prentice-Hall, Inc., 1959, p. 163.)

Thus the statement "X is good but is not approved of by my society" may not appear to a person to be self-contradictory at first glance. In this case "being good" and "being approved of by my society" are not overtly synonymous. But they might still be covertly synonymous. That is, they might actually be synonymous, but this might not be obvious to the person himself. Similarly, the fact that a person thinks it is sensible to ask "Is what is approved of by my society good?" only shows that the two terms are not overtly synonymous. The senseless question test does not exclude covert synonymity. And if the two terms *were* covertly synonymous, then "being approved of by my society" would be a correct definition of "being good," and the alleged error of defining a normative expression in empirical terms would not actually be an error. Consequently the self-contradiction and senseless question tests are not sufficient for disclosing the naturalistic fallacy. The definitional error is an error only if normative expressions can never be either overtly *or covertly* synonymous with empirical expressions.

This argument is correct as far as it goes. But there is a simple way to amend the self-contradiction and senseless question tests so as to include covert as well as overt synonymity. That is to require that the person *reflect carefully* about whether he would be willing to say that the given statement was self-contradictory or whether the given question was senseless. If, after careful reflection about how he ordinarily uses the two expressions, about what he applies them to and what he does not apply them to, and about the way he verifies (justifies) statements in which the expressions occur as predicates, he is willing to assert confidently that the given statement is *not* self-contradictory and the given question is *not* senseless, then the alleged definitional error is not an error, since the two expressions would be *covertly* synonymous. (Actually what had been covertly synonymous would now have become overtly synonymous.) On the other hand, all that we have to do to show that the definitional error is a genuine error is to show that no normative expression is covertly synonymous with a set of empirical expressions under these conditions. We would have to show that the more a person reflects carefully about his use of the empirical terms which are proposed as the definiens of a normative term, the less he will be inclined to say that a sentence which predicates the definiendum of something and denies the definiens (or vice versa) is self-contradictory. Similar considerations would hold for the senseless question test. From what has already been said, it is clear that this always would happen. For the more a person reflected about his use of normative terms the more he would come to understand how they function in evaluating and prescribing, and consequently how they differ from his use of empirical terms.

So far I have been concerned with the definitional version of the naturalistic fallacy. This is logically connected with the deductive version of the naturalistic fallacy, which claims that a normative conclusion can be deduced from empirical premises alone. To show that this is a fallacy, it has been argued that the relation between any set of facts and a value judgment (or a prescription) is never analytic. No contradiction is ever involved in accepting the facts and denying the value judgment (or prescription). Thus even if I accept the fact that an act will be harmful both to myself and to others, I can consistently deny the wrongness of the act. Such wrongness is not *logically entailed* by the facts about its harmful effects. I might be perverse enough to adopt a standard such that an act having harmful effects to myself and others fulfills the standard. Such a "perversion" is not an *intellectual* or *logical* error.

Sometimes the case against the deductive version of the naturalistic fallacy is stated as follows: No argument which has a value judgment or prescription as its conclusion can be valid unless there is at least one value judgment or prescription among its premises. R. M. Hare makes this point in the rule: "*No imperative conclusion can be validly drawn from a set of premises which does not contain at least one imperative."* (Hare, *The Language of Morals,* p. 28. Hare says that this rule is the point behind Moore's refutation of naturalism. *Ibid.,* p. 30.) Thus it is claimed that we cannot draw the conclusion "You ought to do *X*" from such a premise as "Doing *X* will help to alleviate the suffering of others." The prescriptive conclusion will only follow, it is said, if we add a prescriptive (imperative) premise such as "You ought to alleviate the sufferings of others" or an evaluative premise such as "It is right to alleviate the sufferings of others." For, it is argued, unless a prescription or value judgment were included in the premises, a person could consistently accept the (factual) premise and yet deny the (normative) conclusion.

I should like to suggest that this way of putting the case against the naturalistic fallacy is too strong. For it is possible to have a valid argument whose conclusion is a value judgment or prescription and whose premises do not include any value judgment or prescription. What the premises must include in that case is a decision-statement expressing the adoption of a standard or rule. An argument with a normative conclusion may be valid, in other words, under either of two conditions. At least one of the premises must be a value judgment or a prescription, or at least one of the premises must be a decision-statement expressing the adoption of a standard or rule. The standard or rule so adopted must be applicable to whatever is evaluated or prescribed in the conclusion. In the example given in the preceding paragraph, instead of including a value judgment or prescription among the premises, either of the following decision-statements may be included: "I adopt the alleviation of human suffering as an appropriate standard for judging act X and its alternatives," or "I adopt the rule: 'One ought to alleviate human suffering' as covering act X and its alternatives." The justification of any such decision-statement consists in showing that the standard or rule being adopted is an appropriate standard or rule for judging whatever is evaluated (or prescribed) in the conclusion. This would require the validation or vindication of the standard or rule, as stated in Chapters 3 and 5.

It will be noticed that whether the premises of an argument with a normative conclusion include a value judgment, a prescription, or a decision-statement, they must always include at least one statement whose justification requires going beyond empirical verification. We may then formulate our opposition to the deductive version of the naturalistic fallacy as follows: An argument whose conclusion is a valued judgment or a prescription is not valid if all its premises are empirically verifiable. Stated affirmatively: An argument with a normative conclusion is valid only if at least one of its premises must be justified by means of the processes of validation, vindication, and rational choice. This brings to light what is perhaps the most striking difference between normative and factual assertions. The truth of normative assertions depends on human decisions; the truth of factual assertions does not. A factual assertion is true if it corresponds to the way the world is, regardless of whether we want the world to be that way. (Of course we may decide to bring about certain changes in the world. But then our factual assertions concerning those things are true only if they correspond to the changes which actually have taken place. Our decisions do not *make* the assertions true.) A normative assertion is true, on the other hand, only because we have decided to adopt a standard or rule as applicable to what we are making the assertion about. Unless we make such a decision our assertion has no truth or falsity. And the way the world is does not logically determine what decision we must make. Our adoption of a standard or rule on which the truth or falsity of our assertion depends does not itself depend on the way things are. We must *decide* what ought to be the case. We cannot *discover* what ought to be the case by investigating what is the case.

A normative assertion cannot properly be said to be true, however, unless the decision to adopt a certain standard or rule is itself justified. We do not make a normative assertion true merely by deciding to adopt a standard or rule. The assertion is true only when there are *good reasons* for adopting the standard or rule and for applying it to what is being prescribed or evaluated in the assertion. These good reasons ultimately rest on a human decision (though not an arbitrary one). This is the decision to commit oneself to a whole way of life, in terms of which the value system containing the standard or rule is vindicated. This ultimate decision is not arbitrary because it must be made under the conditions of rational choice, as set forth in Chapter 6. We make a normative assertion true only when we adopt a standard or rule which is justified, and it is justified only when the way of life that involves the adoption of the standard or rule has been rationally chosen. Thus we see that the logical basis of a factual assertion and the logical basis of a normative assertion are essentially different. The first includes no element of decision, whereas the second includes an element of decision at two stages—immediately, in the decision to adopt a standard or rule of evaluation, and ultimately, in the rational choice of a way of life. Perhaps the most fundamental error of naturalism is to overlook or deny this element of decision which underlies all normative assertions.

A third version of the naturalistic fallacy I have called the disagreement error. This is the error of believing that it is possible to resolve a disagreement concerning the value of something, or concerning whether an act ought to be done, solely by appeal to the facts about the thing or act in question. No one believes that *every* normative disagreement can *actually* be settled in this way. But the philosophical naturalist believes that this is the method for resolving any such disagreement rationally. His claim is that, assuming the disputants allow their opinions to be governed by the reasons relevant to the case, they would sooner or later come to agreement if they acquired empirical knowledge about the thing in question. Sufficient empirical knowledge might never be acquired in practice, but theoretically there would be a point at which knowledge of facts alone would yield agreement on values.

The error involved here may be seen in light of what has already been said about normative assertions. Let us suppose two people disagree about the value of an object X. Let us further suppose that their disagreement stems from the fact that they apply different standards in judging X. Given one person's standard, X is good. Given the other's, X is bad. Now such a dispute cannot be resolved merely by introducing more facts about the empirical properties of X. For these facts will only reveal to one person more good-making characteristics of X and to the other more bad-making characteristics of X. Each disputant will continue to disagree with the other's value judgment of X, even when both of them agree on all the facts about X, for each appeals to a different standard. Before one can hope to resolve their dispute by introducing more facts, it is necessary to obtain their agreement on the standard to be applied in evaluating X. Since agreement on a standard can be obtained rationally only by a method which goes beyond empirical knowledge (to validation, vindication, and rational choice), knowledge of facts is never sufficient to ensure agreement on values. It is only where there is agreement about a standard (or rule), as well as agreement about the facts, that normative agreement is ensured. Agreement about what is the case, therefore, never by itself entails agreement about what ought to be the case.

The three versions of the naturalistic fallacy discussed so far are all concerned with the meaning and justification of value judgments and prescriptions. The underlying principle which each version of the fallacy overlooks is that empirical knowledge about what is evaluated or prescribed does not by itself provide justification of a value judgment or prescription. There must always be, in addition, the justification of a decision to adopt a certain standard or rule. Speaking broadly, science can only tell us the facts about things, not their value or worth. Knowledge of the empirical world, no matter how complete, is never knowledge of good and evil. In order to know what is good and evil *in* the world, we must bring standards and rules *to* the world. But, we may go on to ask, is it not possible that standards and rules themselves may be discovered *in* the world? If this *were* possible, then philosophical naturalism would be saved. For it would mean that empirical knowledge is sufficient to ensure rational agreement on values. If we acquired enough knowledge of the world, we would finally be able to discover the true standards and rules that apply to the things we wish to evaluate or the acts we wish to prescribe. Knowledge of good and evil would be empirical knowledge and hence philosophical naturalism would be shown to be true. But this attempt to save naturalism must fail, if the account I have given of normative discourse is correct. To say that standards and rules can be discovered *in* the world is to commit the naturalistic fallacy at a higher level. The naturalistic fallacy, in other words, can be applied not only to the justification of value judgments and prescriptions but also to the justification of standards and rules. We have seen that no value judgment or prescription can be deduced from factual statements alone, since we must always appeal to a standard or rule in justifying the judgment or prescription. It must now be shown that no standard or rule can be deduced from factual statements alone and that the attempt to do so commits the naturalistic fallacy at this second level.

The error in trying to base standards and rules on purely empirical grounds becomes clear when we recall how standards and rules are justified. Their justification does not consist in some sort of empirical confirmation, but in the threefold process of validation, vindication, and rational choice. Value judgments and prescriptions themselves can be empirically verified *if* we accept a standard or rule. (This "if" is the key to understanding why the naturalistic fallacy at the first level is a fallacy.) When we ask further whether the standard or rule itself can be empirically verified, we have already gone a step beyond the verification of a value judgment or prescription. That verification can take place only under the assumption that a certain standard or rule is applicable, and we are now questioning the grounds for this assumption. That the grounds for this assumption cannot consist in empirical statements alone should be clear from the analysis of justifying standards and rules set forth in Chapters 3, 5, and 6. A standard or rule must be validated in terms of a value system we have adopted, or else it must be vindicated as a supreme norm of the system. Adopting the system as a whole can only be vindicated in terms of a way of life. Empirical verification cannot be used at this level. A way of life must in turn be justified by a rational choice, and here again we must go beyond empirical verification. It is therefore erroneous to believe that a standard or rule can be based on empirical grounds alone. No standards or rules can be discovered in the world. We must already have adopted them in order to evaluate or prescribe things in the world, and our adoption of them is not justified by reference to the way the world is.

After considering all these ways in which the naturalistic fallacy may occur, it will perhaps be thought that scientific knowledge has little or nothing to do with our knowledge of good and evil. In order to obtain a more balanced perspective on the true role of the sciences in our evaluative and prescriptive knowledge, I shall consider in the next section those aspects of the justification of normative assertions which are dependent upon the kind of enlightenment which only the sciences can give us.

B. Values and scientific knowledge

What is the role of the sciences in the justification of value judgments and prescriptions? Let us begin with the first step in the fourfold process of justification. Here we are already given a standard or rule and all that we need to find out is to what extent something fulfills or fails to fulfill the standard, or whether an act is in accordance with or violates the rule. Usually the knowedge we have gained from everyday experience and the techniques of thinking we use to solve everyday problems are sufficient for this purpose. We do not require the specialized knowledge and techniques of the sciences to determine, for example, the extent to which a house we plan to buy fulfills our standards of comfort and convenience, nor do we have to depend on the sciences to decide whether a person's action is in accordance with or violates the rule of keeping one's promises.

Still, there are at least two important kinds of standard whose application often requires us to use scientific knowledge and techniques. The first kind are standards of instrumental value applied in judging the effectiveness of means to certain ends. If our end is recovery from a serious disease, for example, we must rely on the doctor's judgment of the best remedy. This in turn depends upon the findings of such sciences as chemistry and physiology. Judging the instrumental value of means to "technological" goals also requires the use of scientific knowledge and techniques. To judge the best location for building a dam which will provide electricity and also prevent floods in a certain area requires a knowledge of physics, geology, meteorology, and other sciences. An engineer's value judgment that certain materials are best for building the dam directly or indirectly makes use of the findings and methods of a number of sciences. When we are trying to determine the best means for achieving long range social ideals—such as establishing international peace, ending racial discrimination, or providing a high standard of living for all mankind—we must again rely on many different sciences, including the "human" or "behavioral" sciences of psychology, sociology, anthropology, political science, and economics.

Standards of contributive value are the second kind of standard whose application sometimes requires the use of scientific knowledge and techniques. If one were to judge the contributive value of a certain part of a machine to the successful functioning of the whole, technical knowledge might well have to be obtained. Similarly, various "human" sciences would be required for the verification of a judgment concerning the contributive value of an individual soldier's decisions as part of an entire military operation. There are, of course, judgments of contributive value whose verification does not depend on scientific knowledge, such as judging the aesthetic contribution of sculpture to the overall beauty of a cathedral, or judging the importance of impartiality as an element in the moral life.

Whether it is obtained from science or from common sense, however, knowledge of facts is sufficient for the verification of value judgments and prescriptions. For it is an empirical question whether a given object fulfills or fails to fulfill a given standard, or whether a given act complies with or violates a given rule. It is only when the standard or rule itself is brought into question that we must go beyond empirical verification. Let us next consider the place of scientific knowledge in the *validation* of standards and rules.

In Chapter 3, I presented three methods by which the task of validation may be accomplished. What role does scientific knowledge have in these methods? It is often helpful and sometimes indispensable in the second and third methods. Method II, we recall, is used to determine whether a standard or rule includes in its range of application the class of comparison of a given value judgment. This is done by judging the effects of fulfilling a standard or acting in accordance with a rule, as compared with the effects of failing to fulfill a standard or violating a rule. In the case of a standard, it is necessary to predict the probable consequences that would follow if it were adopted by many people and they tried to fulfill it. Such prediction may require the employment of procedures in the behavioral sciences and may rely on the findings of these sciences. Similarly, in order to judge the effects of people's generally following a rule or their generally violating it, one must make predictions and the behavioral sciences again can be of help here. When we wish to justify social practices by Method II, scientific knowledge and techniques become very important. The rules which define a social practice are judged by their instrumental value or disvalue to a given end, and extremely complex predictions must be made of the effects of an individual's or a society's engaging in the social practice. The ethical theory of restricted utilitarianism operates on this principle, and in so far as scientific knowledge and techniques are needed to make accurate predictions of the consequences of social practices, this ethical theory depends upon the sciences (though not *solely* upon the sciences) for the justification of moral rules.

The use of scientific knowledge and techniques for predicting the consequences of human acts is also a part of Method III. When this method is used for deciding whether an exception to a rule can legitimately be made, the effects of following the rule in a given set of circumstances are evaluated as being better or worse than the effects of violating the rule in those circumstances. Here the sciences may be needed to make accurate predictions of these effects.

One can now readily understand the place of science in the third step of justifying value judgments and prescriptions, namely vindication. We saw in Chapter 5 that vindicating a value system consists in showing that the consequences of a person's adopting the system would be in basic harmony with the ideals of a rationally chosen way of life and that the system itself was part of that way of life. Scientific knowledge and techniques can enable us to make accurate predictions of the consequences of a person's adopting a value system and so make it easier for us to determine its instrumental and contributive value in realizing the ideals of a way of life.

The role of the sciences in the rational choice of a whole way of life has already been explicitly considered in Chapter 6. There the necessary and sufficient conditions of a rational choice were given, and we saw that the second condition, that of enlightenment, included a complete and accurate description of the ways of life among which the choice is being made, a complete and accurate prediction of the effects of living according to them, and a complete and accurate account of the necessary means for bringing them about. In order to obtain this intellectual enlightenment, the findings of the sciences have to be relied upon. Scientific knowledge, however, is not sufficient. Philosophical knowledge is also required, as well as "imaginative" and "practical" knowledge of the different ways of life.

The sciences function in the justification of value judgments and prescriptions, then, as a helpful and sometimes necessary instrument for successfully carrying out the different steps of verification, validation, vindication, and rational choice. But neither the whole four-step process nor any of the individual steps is *solely* dependent upon the procedures and findings of the sciences. (The first step is solely dependent upon *empirical* procedure and findings, but these need not all be scientific.) Thus it is misleading to say that value judgments and prescriptions can be "based on" the sciences. And it is certainly false to say that knowledge of what is good or bad and of what we ought or ought not to do is scientific knowledge. Yet, as I have tried to show in this section, the grounds of our value judgments and prescriptions do very often include empirical statements established by the sciences. These statements do not logically entail the value judgments or prescriptions for which they are grounds, since the process of reasoning by which value judgments and prescriptions are justified is not pure deduction. Furthermore, scientific statements alone are not sufficient for such justification. The naturalistic fallacy is not committed when the grounds of value judgments and prescriptions are scientifically established in the aforementioned ways.

C. The autonomy of normative discourse

In the remainder of this chapter, I wish to point out that the logic of normative discourse is independent of the logic of factual and other kinds of discourse. When we consider the general nature of normative discourse, we see that it is "autonomous" in four respects. I shall refer to these as follows: (1) the autonomy of normative reasoning, (2) the autonomy of normative statements, (3) the autonomy of normative truth, and (4) the autonomy of normative meaning.

1. By the autonomy of normative reasoning, I mean the fact that the rules of inference (or canons of valid reasoning) that govern the justification of value judgments and prescriptions are *sui generis*.

They set up a realm of discourse which, taken as a whole, is distinct from other realms of discourse—such as those of the sciences, of mathematics, of history, and of metaphysics and theology. The rules according to which we give good reasons for (or against) a value judgment or a prescription are logically independent of the rules governing the justification of other kinds of statement. It is true that some of the ways of reasoning which are appropriate in other realms of discourse are also appropriate in normative discourse, but the *over-all structure* of normative thinking is both different from and independent of other systems of thought.

We have seen how empirical knowledge can enter into the justification of normative statements and how we must sometimes rely upon such knowledge in carrying out the steps of verification, validation, vindication, and rational choice. But the total justificatory process remains unique and distinct. To engage in it is to engage in a certain kind of practice (which is both a social activity and a thought activity), defined by certain rules. These rules are the canons of valid reasoning which determine the appropriateness or inappropriateness of different ways of thinking in the context of normative discourse. When we engage in the practice by following the rules, we thereby separate ourselves as thinkers from other "engagements." We commit ourselves to normative reasoning rather than to scientific, mathematical, or some other kind of reasoning. Consequently to engage in normative reasoning is not to engage in scientific reasoning, even though from time to time we must rely on the latter in carrying out some particular step of our normative reasoning.

2. The second trait of normative discourse that constitutes a sign of its independence from factual discourse is the autonomy of normative statements, that is, the autonomy of value judgments and prescriptions themselves. By this I mean that the *premises* (as distinct from the rules of inference) of a deductive argument with a normative conclusion may not consist solely of factual statements. As we saw in discussing the deductive version of the naturalistic fallacy, no normative statement is logically entailed by a factual statement or set of factual statements.

3. The third sense in which normative discourse is autonomous concerns the truth of normative statements. Here its autonomy con-

sists in the fact that no normative statement is empirically verifiable
(or falsifiable). Procedures of empirical verification may be used in
justifying a value judgment or prescription in any of the four steps
of justification, and all value judgments and prescriptions can be
verified empirically by reference to a given standard or rule. But
neither of these points allows us to say without qualification that
normative statements are empirically verifiable. The first point
already implies that empirical verification does not constitute the
whole of the justification of a normative statement, and the second
point explicitly states that only when a standard or rule is given can
a normative statement be verified at all. We have seen that it is
always appropriate to question the justifiability of accepting a
standard or rule; this is not the case with empirical or factual statements.

All three of these senses of the "autonomy" of normative discourse
are closely related to each other. The autonomy of the rules of
reasoning that govern the justification of normative statements
accounts for the second and third instances of "autonomy." Thus
we know that a normative statement cannot be deduced from
factual premises alone, because we know that this kind of inference
is excluded by the rules of reasoning governing normative discourse.
Similarly, it is in light of the entire process of justifying normative
statements, as defined by those rules of reasoning, that we see that
normative statements are not empirically verifiable.

4. The fourth sense in which normative discourse may be said to
be autonomous concerns the meaning (or use) of normative terms
rather than the truth of normative statements or the methods by
which they are justified. The autonomy of normative meaning refers
to the fact that the jobs for which normative language is ordinarily
and correctly employed are fundamentally different from the jobs
for which factual language is ordinarily and correctly employed.
Our typical use of such evaluative terms as "good," "right," "desirable," "excellent," and our typical use of such prescriptive terms as
"ought" and "must," are clearly distinct from our typical use of
words in describing, reporting, predicting, or explaining something.
The use of evaluative terms in expressing value judgments was
examined in Chapter 2, and the use of "ought" sentences for the
purpose of prescribing was examined in Chapter 7. We saw that

expressing a value judgment is a matter of telling someone how we grade or rank an object as a result of our evaluation of it. We may or may not be making a recommendation to the person or guiding his choice when we utter the evaluative sentence. In the case of prescriptive terms, on the other hand, we are always recommending that an act be done and so directly guiding a person's choice. In none of these evaluative or prescriptive uses of words are we asserting a matter of fact or merely conveying information about the empirical properties of things. We are playing a different "language game." Normative discourse is thus distinguishable from descriptive discourse, not only by the logical rules governing the justification of statements, but also by the semantical rules governing the proper or correct employment of the typical words which constitute such discourse.

The *proper* or *correct* employment of expressions in any realm of discourse is determined by the normal use of such expressions. When words are used in such a way that the hearer (or reader) is not misled or confused, and he has learned the "language game" in which the words normally function, then such usage is proper or correct. In the next chapter I shall consider in greater detail what a language game is and how it helps to elucidate the concept of the proper or correct use (meaning) of a term. For our present purposes it is sufficient to point out that the rules which define the language game in which words and sentences are used for evaluative and prescriptive purposes are different from those which define the language games in which we use words and sentences for descriptive or explanatory purposes. To learn how to play one game is not to learn how to play the others, since the rules are different in each case. Indeed, we do not first have to learn how to play any non-normative language game in order to learn how to play the normative language game. Or to put it another way, we do not first have to know how correctly to employ expressions for descriptive purposes in order to know how correctly to employ expressions for uttering a value judgment or prescribing an act to someone. It is in this sense that normative discourse is autonomous with regard to its meaning.

These, then, are four ways in which the autonomy of normative discourse may be understood. It should be noted that I have been speaking of normative discourse as a whole. I have not been concerned with the differences between moral discourse, aesthetic discourse, political discourse, religious discourse, and other "universes" of normative discourse. All of these different languages are normative in so far as they are ordinarily used in expressing value judgments and prescriptions and in reasoning for or against value judgments and prescriptions. As such, they are all autonomous in the four ways discussed above. Their autonomy is something which they have in common with one another and which differentiates all of them from the various kinds of nonnormative discourse. But according to what criteria is each of these normative languages or "universes" of discourse differentiated from the others? This is a question which will concern me in the next part of this book. I have already dealt with it briefly in Chapter 4, but incompletely so. My next task will be to take a new look at the distinction among normative languages and to fill in some gaps in my previous account.

Part III

NORMATIVE LANGUAGE

Wittgenstein's conception of language

10

A. *Language as a set of social practices*

Normative discourse is characterized by those features that are common to the language of morals, the language of aesthetic criticism, the language of politics, and all other languages in which we make and justify value judgments and prescriptions. Each of these languages I call a normative language, and it is the task of this chapter and the next to make clear what a normative language is. I shall use the concept of a normative language for further clarification of the concept of a point of view, which was introduced in Chapter 4. My claim is that *rules of relevance and rules of valid inference, which constitute the canons of reasoning that set the framework of a point of view, are the rules which govern our use of a normative language.* Thus different points of view are defined according to different normative languages, and *taking a certain point of view is deciding to use a certain normative language.* This decision will be shown to be a decision to engage in a certain social practice. In order to elucidate the concept of a normative language, it is first necessary to answer the question, What is a language? The philosopher who has made the most incisive and careful attempt to answer this question is, in my opinion, Ludwig Wittgenstein. I therefore begin with a summary of the main points in Wittgenstein's investigations into the nature of language.

There are two basic characteristics of language that Wittgenstein emphasizes. These may be summed up in two statements. A language is a set of social practices. A language is a set of instruments. I shall discuss each characteristic in turn.

In Chapter 3 we saw that a social practice is defined by a set of rules and that a person's act cannot be described in terms of a social practice unless it is conceived as falling under the practice-defining rules. To say that a language is a set of social practices is to say that there are sets of rules specifying how certain acts shall be done in certain circumstances, and that a person cannot be said to be speaking a language (that is, uttering words *in* the language) unless his acts are done in accordance with the rules. A person may open his mouth and emit sounds, or take up his pen and make marks on paper, but these acts cannot be described as utterances in a language unless they are understood as falling under the rules which state how the language is to be used. This is so even if the sounds (or marks) which the person makes are, from a purely auditory (or visual) standpoint, just like the sounds we make when we say "It is raining" (or the marks we make when we write the same sentence).

This point is made by Wittgenstein whenever he compares languages with games, or whenever he speaks of, and constructs in his imagination, different "language games." A clear example of an act falling under a practice (and hence being describable in terms of a set of rules) is an act performed as part of the playing of a game. Wittgenstein puts it this way: ". . . A move in chess doesn't consist simply in moving a piece in such-and-such a way on the board . . . but in the circumstances that we call 'playing a game of chess,' 'solving a chess problem,' and so on." (L. Wittgenstein, *Philosophical Investigations,* tr. by G. E. M. Anscombe, p. 17e. Copyright 1953 by the Macmillan Company and used with their permission. Reprinted with permission, also, of Basil Blackwell, Oxford, England.) Such an act is comparable to making utterances in a language: "Can I say 'bububu' and mean 'If it doesn't rain I shall go for a walk'?—It is only in a language that I can mean something by something." (*Ibid.*, p. 18e, note.) Thus we cannot call anything a word or a sentence unless it is part of that kind of a rule-governed practice which we ordinarily call a language. A direct comparison between languages and games is made in the following passage:

> We are talking about the spatial and temporal phenomenon of language, not about some non-spatial, non-temporal phantasm. . . . But we talk about it as we do about the pieces in chess when we are stating the rules of the game, not describing their physical properties.
>
> The question 'What is a word really?' is analogous to 'What is a piece in chess?' (*Ibid.*, p. 47e.)

To know what a word is to know what the practice is which makes it correct for us to call the emitting of a sound (or the writing of a mark) a word. And to know what the practice is is to know what the rules are which define it. Wittgenstein points out four basic characteristics of a practice-defining rule in his discussion of language. Since a language is a set of practices defined by rules, his analysis of these four characteristics of rules provides an elucidation of the concept of a language. The four characteristics may be stated as follows: (1) A practice-defining rule functions as a norm or criterion of conduct; it may be appealed to in judging whether something is done correctly or incorrectly. (2) The application of a practice-defining rule must in principle be intersubjectively knowable. (3) A practice-defining rule is always universal; it applies to a class of acts, never to a single act. (4) A practice-defining rule must be teachable, that is to say, it must be possible to train people to act in accordance with it. Let us see how Wittgenstein's account of each of these features of practice-defining rules helps to clarify what we mean by a language.

1. The difference between someone's merely manifesting a *regularity* in his behavior and his following a *rule* is this: only in the latter case does it make sense to ask, "Is he doing it correctly?" The pronoun "it" refers here to a certain kind of act or a certain way of acting which is specified by a rule. The question means "Is he following the rule or is he violating it?" To violate a rule is not merely to do something unusual or irregular, something which one does not ordinarily (i.e., "as a rule") do in a given set of circumstances. It is to make a mistake, to be at fault, to be subject to

correction. Thus we cannot learn how to engage in a practice simply by watching how others behave in certain circumstances. Their behavior must include the possibility of making a mistake and being corrected for it, and we must be able to recognize that a certain kind of act was a mistake, or a certain kind of treatment was corrective. This follows from the fact that a practice is rule-governed behavior. Wittgenstein points this out in the following way.

One learns the game by watching how others play. But we say that it is played according to such-and-such rules because an observer can read these rules off from the practice of the game—like a natural law governing the play.—But how does the observer distinguish in this case between players' mistakes and correct play?—There are characteristic signs of it in the players' behaviour. Think of the behaviour characteristic of correcting a slip of the tongue. It would be possible to recognize that someone was doing so even without knowing his language. (*Ibid.*, p. 27e.)

But this is not the only way to learn how to engage in a practice. We may learn by being taught the rules themselves. And to be taught a rule is to be taught what one is *supposed* to do in certain circumstances. The rule functions as a guide or regulator of correct (rule-obeying) behavior. ". . . We look to the rule for instruction and *do something*, without appealing to anything else for guidance." (*Ibid.*, p. 86e.)

That a rule can serve to guide us does not require that it tell us in *every* situation how we are supposed to act. Wittgenstein compares a rule to a signpost, to bring out this point. The signpost gives direction, but it is not the case that it leaves no doubt about where a person is to go after he has passed it.

A rule stands there like a sign-post.—Does the sign-post leave no doubt open about the way I have to go? Does it shew which direction I am to take when I have passed it; whether along the road or the footpath or cross-country? (*Ibid.*, p. 39e.)

The rules defining the correct uses of a word in a language will specify clear-cut cases of correct usage and will allow us to infer clear-cut cases of incorrect usage, but there will always be a set of doubtful cases. These are often the cases which give rise to philosophical puzzlement and require philosophical "therapy." (*The*

Blue and Brown Books and *Philosophical Investigations* are full of examples of these.)

2. The analogy between a practice-defining rule and a signpost not only holds with regard to the fact that a rule acts as a criterion of correct behavior (still allowing for some doubtful cases); it also holds with regard to the fact that the application of a rule, at least in principle, must be intersubjectively knowable. Suppose there were no *convention* as to how a signpost is to be interpreted. Suppose each individual interpreted it in his own way, one reading the arrow as pointing in the direction from its tail to its head, another reading it as pointing in the opposite direction, another reading it as pointing in a line perpendicular to its axis, and so on. The signpost would not then have the capacity to function as a guide. It would not be a signpost at all. ". . . A person goes by a sign-post only in so far as there exists a regular use of sign-posts, a custom." (*Ibid.*, p. 80e. Sections 199-208 of Part I of *Philosophical Investigations* are especially concerned with this aspect of rules.)

This raises an important question. Does it mean that a person cannot play a game by himself, or cannot make up his own rules for a private game which he alone knows how to play? Does not a child set up his own practice-defining rule when he resolves not to step on any crack in the sidewalk on his way to school? The answer is that the intersubjective convention about how a rule is to be applied is a requirement only in principle. That is, it must be theoretically *possible* for more than one person to learn how to follow the rule. The rules of a private practice (as distinct from a social practice) are genuine rules because, though not publicly known, they are publicly knowable. Mr. Peter Winch has made this point clear in his excellent discussion of Wittgenstein's analysis of rules.

A mistake is a contravention of what is *established* as correct; as such, it must be *recognisable* as such a contravention. That is, if I make a mistake in, say, my use of a word, other people must be able to point it out to me. If this is not so, I can do what I like and there is no external check on what I do; that is, nothing is established. . . . It is, of course, possible, within a human society as we know it, with its established language and institutions, for an individual to adhere to a *private* rule of conduct. What Wittgenstein insists on, however, is, first, that it must be in principle possible for other people to grasp that rule and judge when it is being correctly followed; secondly, that it makes no sense to suppose anyone capable of establishing a purely personal standard of behaviour *if* he had never had any experience of human society with its socially established rules. (P. Winch, *The Idea of a Social Science and Its Relation to Philosophy*. London: Routledge and Kegan, 1958, Paul Ltd. and New York: The Humanities Press, pp. 32-33. The point is elaborated on pp. 33-39.)

The rules which govern the use of a language, then, must be such that it is possible for more than one person to know how to apply them and how to follow them. Otherwise the rules could not be said to have the capacity to regulate behavior and so could not be considered genuine rules at all. Thus this second feature of a practice-defining rule is necessary if the first feature is to hold. For if a rule lacked the capacity to regulate behavior it would also lack the capacity to function as a criterion or norm of correct behavior.

3. In a note on the meaning of the expression "to obey a rule" Wittgenstein says: "It is not possible that there should have been only one occasion on which someone obeyed a rule." (*Op. cit.*, p. 81e.) A rule tells us to do an act of a certain kind (or to act in a certain way) in certain circumstances. If we know the rule we do not have to ask what we are supposed to do each time we find ourselves in those circumstances.

One does not feel that one has always got to wait upon the nod (the whisper) of the rule. On the contrary, we are not on tenterhooks about what it will tell us next, but it always tells us the same, and we do what it tells us. (*Ibid.*, p. 86e. See also Part I, Sections 237-238.)

Thus to be in the position of following (obeying) a rule is to be in the position of having our decisions guided by a universal principle of conduct.

In this light we see that a rule is necessarily general or universal. It must be applicable to a *class* of acts and it must apply to *anyone* who is an agent with regard to those acts. These features of a rule were pointed out in Section B of Chapter 7, where I discussed universal prescriptions and rules. I said there that the basic function of a rule is to regulate the conduct of people in general and that the statement of a rule is a statement that one is to do an act of a certain kind in certain circumstances. The rule applies to anyone in those circumstances who can do the kind of act in question. No practice-defining rule, therefore, can be followed in only one instance by only one person, in the way that a particular prescription ("You ought to do X") could be fulfilled by a single act of an individual (namely, by the addressee's doing act X). Professor Bernard Mayo has argued that there is a point in saying that prescriptions *guide* behavior but rules *regulate* behavior:

Regulation suggests something which guidance does not, namely the application of a system of rules or principles. A guide may lead us to a destination which we should have failed to reach without him, but he may not employ any rules or principles. He may just know the country 'like the back of his hand.' . . . A morally untutored and untutor-able man could live an outwardly exemplary life if he were in constant touch with a moral adviser whose instructions [i.e., particular prescrip-tions] he implicitly obeyed; but he could not live a moral life. For he could not take any decisions in the light of moral principles; his actions are guided but not regulated. (B. Mayo, *op. cit.*, pp. 19-20.)

A rule, then, can regulate behavior only in so far as it is universal or general.

This feature of a rule is closely connected with the two features already discussed, as well as with the fourth feature to be discussed. In its function as a regulator of behavior (in Mayo's sense) a rule also serves as a criterion of correct behavior. A person behaves in-correctly or improperly when his particular acts are of the kind forbidden by a rule; when his acts are of the kind permitted or required by a rule, his conduct is correct. And the fact that a rule is universal gives point to the fact that its application must be publicly knowable. For a rule states that an act of a certain kind is to be done by *anyone*, whenever *anyone* is in a certain set of circumstances. Only one person may ever in fact be in those circumstances, but this does not deny the theoretical possibility of the rule's applying to the acts of anyone who may be in those circumstances. There would be no point in stating that an act is to be done by anyone in certain circumstances if there was only one person who could pos-sibly know this.

4. The fourth characteristic of a practice-defining rule is brought to our attention by Wittgenstein in the following way. He first asks

us to imagine an unknown country where people *seem* to employ a language in carrying on the usual human activities. He then asks how we would go about finding out whether they did in fact have a language. How would we discover whether, in emitting sounds or making marks, they were doing such things (engaging in such practices) as making statements, giving orders, asking questions, and so on? One sign which would indicate they had a language would be: "If we watch their behavior we find it intelligible, it seems 'logical'." (L. Wittgenstein, *op. cit.*, p. 82e.) But then suppose, Wittgenstein continues, that ". . . when we try to learn their language we find it impossible to do so. For there is no regular connection between what they say, the sounds they make, and their actions. . . . There is not enough regularity for us to call it 'language'." (*Ibid.*) The point here is that if it is impossible to learn what appears to be the language of a group, there is actually no language, however similar in appearance to linguistic behavior its behavior may be. Unless there is some way to *train* a person to *use* an alleged language, we cannot say that it is a language. More generally, if there is to be a social practice defined by rules, there must be some way of learning (or of teaching) how to engage in the practice or follow the rules. This is part of what we mean by a social practice. Thus Wittgenstein contrasts acting according to a rule with acting according to inspiration.

Let us imagine a rule intimating to me which way I am to obey it; that is, as my eye travels along [a] line, a voice within me says: 'This way!'—What is the difference between this process of obeying a kind of inspiration and that of obeying a rule? For they are surely not the same. In the case of inspiration I *await* direction. I shall not be able to teach anyone else my 'technique' of following the line. Unless, indeed, I teach him some way of hearkening, some kind of receptivity. But then, of course, I cannot require him to follow the line in the same way as I do. (*Ibid.*, p. 87e. See also, Part I, Section 237.)

What makes a rule capable of being learned (or taught) is the fact that following it implies a regularity of behavior and, in addition, the satisfying of a criterion or test of correct behavior. If one acts in accordance with a rule, it must make sense to say "Here he is doing the *same* thing as he did before," and also to say "Here he is doing the *correct* thing, there he is not." The rule specifies which acts will count as being the same as other acts, and which acts are to be counted as correct. Unless both factors are stated, it would not be possible to learn or to teach what it is to follow (and also to break) the rule. One would not be able to know whether, in a given set of circumstances, the act which one was doing was an act of the kind required or forbidden by the rule, or whether such an act was the correct thing to do.

Learning how to follow rules is gaining mastery of a technique; it is acquiring a skill. *Teaching* someone how to follow rules is training him in a technique; it is developing in him a skill. *Knowing how* to follow rules is having a skill; it is being able to engage in a practice. All of this is true of learning, teaching, or knowing a language, in Wittgenstein's view. "To understand a language means to be master of a technique." (*Ibid.*, p. 81e.) When we learn a language, however, we learn not only one technique but a whole complex set of techniques. To speak a language is not just to engage in one practice, but to engage in many different practices. For every time we learn the meaning of a word we learn a new technique, the technique of using the word correctly. To be taught a language is to be taught how to use the language, and this means to be taught a great many uses of words for a great many purposes. One might say that a language is a composite practice made up of a number of practices, each of which is a (correct, established) use of a word. The rules of a language are then seen to be the rules governing the correct uses of words. Learning a new word in a language (or learning a new use of an old word) thus involves learning to follow a new set of rules. The multiplicity and variety of the practices (word-uses) which constitute a language are emphasized by Wittgenstein in the series of "language games" which he constructs in *The Blue and Brown Books* and in *Philosophical Investigations.* Each "language game" presents a different use of words, that is, a different set of rules governing the use of words. Each "language game" accordingly is a social practice.

B. Language as a set of instruments

The second basic feature of language which is analyzed by Wittgenstein is its function as an instrument or set of instruments.

With regard to any practice it is always possible to ask, What is the point of it? In other words, for what purpose do people engage in it? It is true that we do not usually ask this question about playing games, but that is only because we all know the purpose for which games are ordinarily played, namely either for the entertainment of the players, or (if they are professionals) for monetary reward. However, we may sometimes wonder how certain practices which are part of a game are to be understood in terms of the point of the game as a whole. We wonder what purpose is served by these practices. Wittgenstein constructs some imaginary rules for chess in order to raise this kind of question.

The game, one would like to say, has not only rules but also a *point*. . . . But, after all, the game is supposed to be defined by the rules! So, if a rule of the game prescribes that the kings are to be used for drawing lots before a game of chess, then that is an essential part of the game. What objection might one make to this? That one does not see the point of this prescription. Perhaps as one wouldn't see the point either of a rule by which each piece had to be turned round three times before one moved it. If we found this rule in a board-game we should be surprised and should speculate about the purpose of the rule. ('Was this prescription meant to prevent one from moving without due consideration?') (*Ibid.*, pp. 150e-151e.)

Once we see how a game is played by understanding what is involved in following the rules, we can raise a question about the point of (i.e., the purpose served by) any particular rule of the game.

We may do the same thing for any practice, including the practice of a language. The rules for the employment of linguistic expressions may define many different sorts of practices (games). "Think of the tools in a toolbox: there is a hammer, pliers, a saw, a screw-driver, a rule, a glue-pot, glue, nails and screws.—The functions of words are as diverse as the functions of these objects." (*Ibid.*, p. 6e.)

Sentences as well as words may be understood as tools or instruments. When we become confused about the sense of a sentence, Wittgenstein offers us the following advice.

Look at the sentence as an instrument, and at its sense as its employment. (*Ibid.*, p. 126e.)

Ask yourself: On what occasion, for what purpose, do we say this? What kind of actions accompany these words? (Think of a greeting.) In what scenes will they be used; and what for? (*Ibid.*, p. 137e.)

It is in this way that we come to see how words and sentences are instruments used to accomplish certain purposes. In each case we come to understand the *point* of a practice which constitutes part of a language.

But there is no single point of the practice of a language as a whole. Speaking a language has many purposes. It has all the purposes for which words and sentences are used in the language. Wittgenstein lists a few of these purposes early in *Philosophical Investigations.*

Giving orders, and obeying them—
Describing the appearance of an object, or giving its measurements—
Constructing an object from a description (a drawing)—
Reporting an event—
Speculating about an event—
Forming and testing a hypothesis—
Presenting the results of an experiment in tables and diagrams—
Making up a story; and reading it—
Play-acting—
Singing catches—
Guessing riddles—
Making a joke; telling it—
Solving a problem in practical arithmetic—
Translating from one language into another—
Asking, thanking, cursing, greeting, praying. (*Ibid.*, pp. 11e-12e.)

Immediately following this list Wittgenstein adds this significant remark:

—It is interesting to compare the multiplicity of the tools in language and of the ways they are used, the multiplicity of kinds of word and sentence, with what logicians have said about the structure of language. (Including the author of the *Tractatus Logico-Philosophicus.*) (*Ibid.*, p. 12e.)

In this criticism of logicians, he is warning us against oversimplifying our concept of language as a practice and as an instrument. It is not one practice or one instrument, having one essential function and serving one essential purpose. We must take Wittgenstein's own statement "Language is an instrument" (*Ibid.*, p. 151e.) as a summarizing of the idea that language has various uses for many different purposes. He himself qualifies this statement by saying, "Its concepts are instruments." He adds this, I think, in order to prevent us from taking him to mean that language is one tool serving one purpose (*the* purpose of language) rather than a collection of tools serving a variety of purposes.

Wittgenstein frequently refers to the various ways of using language as "language games," and he speaks of the different language games as forming a "family resemblance." In Sections 65-110 of Part I of *Philosophical Investigations,* he argues that it is a "superstition" to search for the essence of language. If we understand the question, "What is language?" as asking for such an essence, it cannot be answered. But if we examine the way words in a language are actually used and the purposes for which they are used, we see that a language is a collection of partly resembling activities. In this respect the concept of a language is like the concept of a game.

Consider for example the proceedings that we call 'games.' I mean board-games, card-games, ball-games, Olympic games, and so on. What is common to them all?—Don't say: 'There *must* be something common, or they would not be called "games" '—but *look and see* whether there is anything common to all.—For if you look at them you will not see something that is common to *all,* but similarities, relationships, and a whole series of them at that. To repeat: don't think, but look!—Look for example at board-games, with their multifarious relationships. Now pass to card-games; here you find many correspondences with the first group, but many common features drop out, and others appear. When we pass next to ball-games, much that is common is retained, but much is lost. . . . And we can go through the many, many other groups of games in the same way; can see how similarities crop up and disappear.

And the result of this examination is: we see a complicated network of similarities overlapping and criss-crossing: sometimes over-all similarities, sometimes similarities of detail. (*Ibid.*, pp. 31e-32e.)

If the concept of language is in this respect like the concept of game, have I not been mistaken in saying that a language is a set of practices and a set of instruments? For I seem to be trying to define the essence of language. But this is not the case. I am only pointing out certain very general features ("over-all similarities") in respect of which all languages resemble one another. *These are the very features which Wittgenstein himself discloses as fundamental to our understanding of the nature of language.*

Suppose one were to object that Wittgenstein has not told us what the distinguishing feature of language is, that he has specified only the genus, not the differentia, of language. Such an objection would miss the point of Wittgenstein's discussion. It is quite true that there are many social practices and instruments which are not languages, and that one can legitimately ask: What is it that makes a practice a linguistic practice? What is it that makes an instrument a linguistic instrument? But one cannot expect these questions to be answered in the way that we answer such a question as: What makes a government a monarchy? This last can be answered by stating the property or combination of properties which all monarchies possess and only monarchies possess. A person who did not know what the word "monarchy" means (but did know what a government is) could then be taught that a monarchy is a certain form of government. He could be taught this by means of a definition *per genus et differentiam*. But the answer to the question "What is a language?" must be of a different sort.

A language is a set of practices defined by certain rules, namely the rules which govern all the various uses of words in the language. This is a circle, but not a vicious one. In the first place, we all know what it is to use words in a language. In the second place no explanation would be of any help to a person who did not know what it is to use words in a language, since every explanation would be itself a use of words in a language. In this situation we can only give examples of different ways of using words (as Wittgenstein does in imagining and describing various language games). There is nothing illogical about this. Our enlightenment comes with noticing certain features of language which we did not notice before, although we did know, in a pre-analytic way, what a language is before these features were brought to our attention. As we think of more and more uses of words for different purposes in an increasing variety of circumstances, we gradually come to a clearer grasp of the nature of language. We discover how wide a range of practices make up a language, but we discover no boundaries by which to mark off a linguistic from a nonlinguistic practice.

Wittgenstein makes a sharp attack upon logicians who wish to give a *precise* definition of "language." In continuing his comparison between languages and games, he says:

> For how is the concept of a game bounded? What still counts as a game and what no longer does? Can you give the boundary? No. You can *draw* one; for none has so far been drawn. (But that never troubled you before when you used the word 'game.')
> 'But then the use of the word is unregulated, the "game" we play with it is unregulated.'—It is not everywhere circumscribed by rules; but no more are there any rules for how high one throws the ball in tennis, or how hard; yet tennis is a game for all that and has rules too. (*Ibid.*, p. 33e.)

We can know what a word (such as "language") means, and so have a clear understanding of a concept, even when there is no neat demarcation of the meaning of the word. Most of the words we use in everyday talk are like this. Most of our concepts have "blurred edges."

> One might say that the concept 'game' is a concept with blurred edges.—'But is a blurred concept a concept at all?'—Is an indistinct photograph a picture of a person at all? Is it even always an advantage to replace an indistinct picture by a sharp one? Isn't the indistinct one often exactly what we need? (*Ibid.*, p. 34e.)

This does not mean that it is always a mistake to try to make our concepts sharper by drawing boundaries. Wittgenstein repeats a number of times that it is sometimes useful, *for a particular purpose,* to stipulate our own definitions by making clear lines of differentiation among our concepts. But doing this is justified only by a special purpose.

> How should we explain to someone what a game is? I imagine that we should describe *games* to him, and we might add: 'This *and similar things* are called "games." ' And do we know any more about it ourselves? Is it only other people whom we cannot tell exactly what a game is?—But this is not ignorance. We do not know the boundaries because

none have been drawn. To repeat, we can draw a boundary—for a special purpose. Does it take that to make the concept usable? Not at all! (Except for that special purpose.) (*Ibid.*, p. 33e.)

In Wittgenstein's view there is nothing wrong in ". . . giving prominence to distinctions which our ordinary forms of language easily make us overlook." (*Ibid.*, p. 51e.) To reform language in this way may be necessary to prevent misunderstandings.

Such a reform for particular practical purposes, an improvement in our terminology designed to prevent misunderstandings in practice, is perfectly possible. (*Ibid.*)

In the next chapter I shall make such a linguistic reform in defining "normative language," but this discussion of the nature of language in general has not included a boundary-drawing definition of "language." There was no special purpose which would have justified such a definition. At one point in *Philosophical Investigations*, Wittgenstein states that "the great question that lies behind all these considerations" is not the question of what a language is, but the question of what sort of answer can be given to this question. He explicitly presents the issue in terms of the denial of a search for the essence of all languages.

Here we come up against the great question that lies behind all these considerations.—For someone might object against me: 'You take the easy way out! You talk about all sorts of language-games, but have nowhere said what the essence of a language-game, and hence of language, is: what is common to all these activities, and what makes them into language or parts of language. So you let yourself off the very part of the investigation that once gave you yourself most headache, the part about the *general form of propositions* and of language.'
And this is true.—Instead of producing something common to all that we call language, I am saying that these phenomena have no one thing in common which makes us use the same word for all,—but that they are *related* to one another in many different ways. And it is because of this relationship, or these relationships, that we call them all 'language.' I will try to explain this. (*Ibid.*, p. 31e.)

Wittgenstein then proceeds to a discussion, part of which I have quoted, of the similarities and differences among the many kinds of games. The concept of language, like the concept of game, is understood not in terms of an essence, but in terms of a "family resemblance."

It is clear that in this account of Wittgenstein's conception of language I have been interested more in the "over-all similarities" among languages—the general characteristics in respect of which the family resemblances are most striking—than in the important differences among them. In the next chapter I shall be interested in one group of languages, namely normative languages. My purpose in this chapter has been to lay a groundwork for constructing a clear concept of normative language. This concept, although drawn with sharp boundaries, will nevertheless conform to the general nature of language as analyzed by Wittgenstein.

The concept of a normative language

11

A. What is a normative language?

In light of Wittgenstein's analysis of language, a normative language may be viewed as a set of social practices defined according to certain rules governing the use of the language. There are two basic types of rules that define a normative language. Together they set the framework of a universe of normative discourse. The first type govern the use of words in expressing value judgments and in prescribing. The second type govern the use of words in giving reasons for or against value judgments and prescriptions. We carry on moral discourse, for example, when we pronounce moral judgments and utter moral prescriptions according to the first type of rules and when we justify moral judgments and prescriptions according to the second type of rules. In both cases the particular rules that set the framework of moral discourse define the language of morals. Other normative languages may be defined in the same way.

My thesis in this chapter will be that each universe of normative discourse corresponds to a point of view, and that both are determined by the rules of a normative language. To *take a certain*

279

point of view is to be disposed to *use a certain normative language,* that is, to be disposed to *carry on our reasoning within the framework of a particular universe of normative discourse.* The first type of rules that govern the use of a normative language, namely those for the proper expression of value judgments and prescriptions, are the same for all normative languages. Such rules were explicated in Chapters 2, 7, and 8, where I examined what it means to express a value judgment and to prescribe an act to someone. The second type of rules govern the logical relations among evaluative and prescriptive sentences on the one hand and the sentences in which we give reasons to justify value judgments and prescriptions on the other. The latter can be subdivided into rules of relevance and rules of valid inference. They are the very same rules that make up the canons of reasoning for each point of view, as stated in Chapter 4. To do our thinking in terms of these canons (and hence to take a certain point of view) is to use a normative language in accordance with such rules. This is another way of expressing the main thesis I wish to defend in this chapter.

Of the two types of rules that define a normative language, each may be thought of as governing a different type of language game. Thus rules of the first type govern the language games of expressing value judgments and prescribing. To know how to use sentences correctly for these purposes is to know how to play these language games (by following the first type of rules). The sentences whose use is governed by these rules are evaluative and prescriptive sentences, which I shall call "normative sentences" for short.

Which language games are governed by rules of the second type, that is, by the rules of relevance and of valid inference? There are two sorts of sentences governed by them, which I shall call "verification sentences" and "validation sentences" (to contrast them with "normative sentences"). Verification sentences are sentences in which we state the good-making or bad-making (right-making or wrong-making) characteristics of something in the context of verifying a value judgment or prescription. The rules which govern our use of verification sentences define the language games in which we give reasons for or against a value judgment or prescription by appealing to a standard or rule of evaluation. Validation sentences, on the other hand, are the expressions we use in giving reasons for or against the standard or rule which is appealed to when something is being evaluated. In Chapter 3 we saw that giving such reasons consists in various kinds of appeal to higher standards or rules.

A normative language, then, consists of normative sentences, verification sentences, and validation sentences. The use of normative sentences is governed by the first type of rules and the use of verification and validation sentences is governed by the second type of rules. Within the second type, what distinguishes rules of relevance from rules of valid inference? Rules of relevance tell us what specific verification and validation sentences go with a given normative sentence, while rules of valid inference tell us that a verification sentence must express good-making or bad-making characteristics and that a validation sentence must express an appeal to higher standards or rules. If our use of verification and validation sentences complies with the rules of relevance, then the reasons we give by means of such sentences are relevant reasons. If our use of verification and validation sentences (which are already known to be relevant) complies with the rules of valid inference, then the reasons we give by means of such sentences are good reasons. This does not mean, of course, that using verification and validation sentences consists of two separate acts, i.e., giving relevant reasons and giving good reasons. To utter a verification sentence is to assert (when it is uttered in earnest and affirmed by the speaker) that an object or act has a set of good-making or bad-making, right-making or wrong-making characteristics. The point of making such an assertion is to give a reason for a value judgment or prescription. This reason will be a good reason only if the sentence expresses a relevant reason, that is, it "goes with" the normative sentence in question, and at the same time what is says is true. We decide whether the sentence expresses a relevant reason by reference to the rules of relevance governing the universe of discourse in which the sentence is uttered. We decide whether what the sentence asserts is true by verifying it according to the rules of verification. (If the sentence is a validation sentence, we decide whether what it asserts is true by verifying it according to the rules of validation.) Thus the rules governing our use of verification and validation sentences are the canons of reasoning which set the framework of a point of view.

I claimed in Chapter 4 that rules of valid inference are the same in all normative points of view and that rules of relevance are what differentiate one point of view from another. I now repeat this claim in another way by saying that rules of valid inference are common to all normative languages and that rules of relevance are what differentiate one normative language from another. To follow one set of rules of relevance is to carry on normative discourse in one universe of discourse; to follow another set is to carry on normative discourse in another universe of discourse. The rules of valid inference, on the other hand, are common to all universes of normative discourse. They are the rules which govern the ways of reasoning analyzed in Chapter 3. In that chapter I was actually making explicit the rules of valid inference which define the verification and validation of a value judgment—*any* value judgment, whether it be moral, aesthetic, political, or of some other kind. We also saw, in Chapter 8, that these same rules govern the justification of prescriptions. They do not vary in accordance with the type of prescription involved. Consequently they do not differentiate a moral judgment or prescription from an aesthetic, a political, or a religious one.

What does differentiate one kind of judgment or prescription from another are the rules of relevance governing its justification. *Rules of relevance constitute the unifying principles of a normative language.* They are what bind together the three types of sentence (normative sentences, verification sentences, and validation sentences) which make up a single universe of normative discourse. They have the capacity to do this in virtue of the fact that they tell us what verification and validation sentences "go with" a given normative sentence. Thus if I utter a moral judgment or prescription in a normative sentence, certain reasons will be relevant to its verification and validation and other reasons will not. Reasons which are relevant to a moral judgment or prescription may not be relevant to an aesthetic one. In each case the normative sentence in which the judgment or prescription is expressed will "go with" those verification and validation sentences that express relevant reasons and will not "go with" those that express irrelevant reasons. What determines whether a given verification or validation sentence "goes with" a given normative sentence, therefore, is a rule of relevance.

If one sentence "goes with" another then both sentences belong to the same normative language. This is what is meant by speaking of "the same normative language." The rules of relevance governing all the verification and validation sentences which "go with" a given normative sentence define the whole normative language to which the sentence belongs. What does it mean to say that one sentence "goes with" another (i.e., that both sentences belong to the same normative language)? The answer may be stated in the following definition. A verification or validation sentence, V, goes with a normative sentence, N, if—and only if—a person who knows what V means and what N means (i.e., who knows how to make sense by using such sentences) has implicitly or explicitly adopted a set of rules of relevance such that the assertion expressed by V will be accepted by him as a reason for or against (i.e., as relevant to the verification or validation of) the value judgment or prescription expressed by N. Let us designate the particular set of rules of relevance so adopted R. Then we may define the whole normative language to which N belongs as follows: The normative language to which N belongs is the whole set of normative sentences (including N) and the whole set of verification and validation sentences (including V) which rules R allow to go with those normative sentences.

To use one normative language rather than another, then, means to follow three sets of rules—the rules which govern the correct use of normative sentences, the rules of relevance which tell us which particular verification and validation sentences go with which particular normative sentences, and the rules of valid inference which govern the processes of verification and validation. The rules of relevance vary from one normative language to another, and it is only when one set of such rules (defining one universe of normative discourse) is being followed that we can say a person is using *one* normative language.

Let us consider some examples showing this function of rules of relevance. I take as my first example the judgment that a novel is a good novel, as expressed in aesthetic language, in moral language, and in political language. When the judgment is expressed in aesthetic language, only certain reasons will be accepted as relevant to its justification. In other words, only certain verification and validation sentences will be accepted as properly going with the normative sentence "This is a good novel." Suppose that the verification sentence "The writer draws his characters with great skill" is accepted as expressing a good-making characteristic of the novel. We would then have *prima facie* evidence that the value judgment is an aesthetic one, that it belongs to the universe of discourse of literary criticism. For the verification sentence which goes with the normative sentence expresses a reason of a sort that is typical of literary criticism. Let us suppose, furthermore, that the verification sentence "The style is loose and at times obscure" is accepted as stating a relevant reason *against* the judgment that the novel is a good one. We would then have further, confirmatory evidence that the normative language is aesthetic. This hypothesis is still further confirmed if we find that, when the standards of evaluation being used in the foregoing verification sentences are brought into question, a validation sentence like the following is considered relevant: "Appropriate standards for evaluating a novel are such that any novel which fulfills them conveys to the reader a clear imaginative grasp of human motivation and character." Evidence that the normative language being used is not aesthetic would be the fact that such a validation sentence as the following was considered relevant: "A standard for evaluating a novel must be such that, when it is fulfilled, a novel has the power to make the reader a better man or woman than he or she was before reading it." If the standards of a writer's skill in presenting human character and the clarity of his style were validated in this way, we would begin to think that the original value judgment of the novel was not intended as an aesthetic judgment but as a moral one. The rules of relevance which define an aesthetic normative language in this example would include such statements as "A writer's skill in presenting human character is relevant to evaluating a novel," and "Characteristics of the writer's style are relevant to evaluating a novel."

The normative sentence "This is a good novel" is uttered in the universe of moral discourse when such verification sentences as the following are accepted as relevant: "The writer succeeds in arousing the reader's indignation concerning vicious behavior." "No indecent act is allowed to go unpunished." "The general effect of the story is to strengthen our moral convictions." If these are taken to be relevant reasons in support of the judgment that the novel is good, we have *prima facie* evidence that the normative language involved is moral, not aesthetic. Similarly, we have *prima facie* evidence that the judgment of the novel is being made in the universe of political discourse when the following reasons are considered relevant: "The hero of the novel is the leader of our party." "The writer condemns reactionary groups which struggle to gain control of the state." The final victory in the story belongs to our fatherland."

In the foregoing example I have merely tried to indicate the *sort* of evidence which would give us good reasons for saying that the normative language was of one kind rather than another. I have not tried to state the particular features of a rule of relevance that make it defining of aesthetic discourse, moral discourse, or political discourse. This is a complicated and difficult task, as many recent studies of the differentiae of moral, aesthetic, and political discourse show. But as I pointed out in Chapter 4, it is a task that goes beyond the scope of this book, since I am concerned here only with elucidating the concept of a normative language in general.

My second example shows how the prescribing of an act may take place in three different normative languages. Suppose a friend of ours is going to buy a new suit but cannot decide which suit to select among various possibilities. We then say to him "You ought to buy the brown one." If we consider as a relevant reason for his buying the brown suit that it is well worth the price being charged for it, then our prescription is in the universe of *economic* discourse. Our prescription is in the universe of *aesthetic* discourse if we consider as a relevant reason the fact that the style and color of the suit look well on our friend. We use the language of *prudence* when we consider such reasons as the following—the suit is comfortable; it will wear well; it is proper dress for the purposes our friend has in mind; our friend needs a new suit; and so on. In all three universes of discourse, the relevant reasons are expressed in verification sentences, and the relevance of the reasons allows the verification sentences to go with the normative sentence which we utter.

If any of the standards or rules which we implicitly appeal to in evaluating the brown suit are themselves brought into question, they must be validated. Both rules of relevance and rules of valid inference will govern such validation, but only the rules of relevance will tell us which normative language the original prescription belongs to. Thus if the validation sentence "Any standard according to which the economic value of the brown suit is measured is a valid standard" is allowed to go with the normative sentence "You ought to buy the brown suit," then we have evidence that the normative sentence belongs to the universe of economic discourse. The prescription is made in the universe of aesthetic discourse if the following validation sentence is considered relevant: "A standard for judging the suit is appropriate when it pertains to the appearance of the suit." In the case of the universe of prudential discourse, a relevant validation sentence would be: "Any standard is valid whose fulfillment would further the self-interest of the buyer of the suit." The rules of relevance that are followed whenever one of these sentences is made to go with the given prescription determine the normative language to which the prescription belongs.

It may be seen in both of these examples that one and the same normative sentence may belong to more than one normative language. It is quite possible that a novel is good for both aesthetic reasons and moral reasons, or for both moral reasons and political reasons. Similarly, we may prescribe to our friend that he ought to buy the brown suit not only from an economic point of view but also from an aesthetic point of view or from the point of view of prudence. Thus it may be said that universes of normative discourse sometimes overlap. (This corresponds to my claim in Chapter 4 that points of view sometimes overlap.)

Just as there may be normative sentences which are common to more than one universe of discourse, so also may there be verification and validation sentences common to more than one universe of discourse. For example, the verification sentence "The brown suit fits you well" may occur in the language of aesthetic discourse and also in the language of prudence, since the fact that the suit fits well may be a good-making characteristic both from the aesthetic point of view and from the prudential point of view. If all we know is that the verification sentence is given as a relevant reason for buying the suit, we do not know which universe of discourse or normative language is being used. A similar ambiguity would occur in the case of a validation sentence such as "This rule of conduct is valid because the effect of its being followed in society is to further the common welfare." For such an appeal may be made in the universe of moral discourse or in the universe of political discourse. The same standards and rules may thus be shared by different points of view. It is only when we know the *whole set* of rules of relevance governing the validation of a standard or rule that we know which universe of discourse it belongs to. There is no feature inherent in the standard or rule itself which tells us whether it is a moral one, an aesthetic one, or of some other kind. Once we know the whole set of rules of relevance governing verification and validation, we know which verification and validation sentences go with a given normative sentence and thereby know in which universe of discourse the normative sentence (and its relevant verification and validation sentences) occurs. The whole set of rules of relevance *define* the universe of discourse.

I shall now consider four corollaries to my thesis that it is rules of relevance which differentiate normative languages. 1. Normative languages cannot be distinguished according to their uses and purposes. 2. Normative languages cannot be distinguished according to who is competent or qualified to use them. 3. Normative languages cannot be distinguished according to the methods of justification appropriate to them. 4. Normative languages cannot be distinguished according to the cultures in which they are used.

1. What makes a language a normative language? The answer lies in the fact that it is used for expressing value judgments, for prescribing, and for justifying value judgments and prescriptions. These uses or purposes are common to all normative languages, since they are what *make* them normative. Consequently they cannot serve as the basis for differentiating one normative language from another. When we express a moral judgment and when we express an aesthetic judgment we are playing the same language game, namely expressing a value judgment. We are using two different languages in the same way for the same purpose. What occurs here is *one use of language,* not *the use of one language.* In like manner, an act of prescribing is one use of normative language, though many different normative languages may be so used. To utter a moral prescription, an aesthetic prescription, or a political prescription is to perform the same linguistic act within the framework of three different universes of discourse. A similar argument holds for justifying value judgments and prescriptions in different universes of discourse. To utter a verification or validation sentence for the purpose of giving reasons

for (or against) a value judgment or prescription is to perform a certain kind of linguistic act. It is to use language in a certain way for a certain purpose. Which particular language we in fact do use in this way is not to be discovered in the nature or purpose of the linguistic act itself.

One might object that the purposes for which we use moral language are different from the purposes for which we use aesthetic language. Well, what is this difference? Must we not say that we use moral language to guide the *moral* conduct of people, or to make a *moral* appraisal of their character, or to give them *moral* advice, or to educate them *morally?* What is this but to say that in guiding the conduct of people (or in appraising their character, or in giving them advice, or in educating them) we appeal to moral standards and rules rather than to aesthetic, political, or prudential standards and rules? And what makes a standard or rule a moral one rather than some other kind? Here I submit that we must refer to the kinds of reasons considered relevant in justifying value judgments and prescriptions used in the guidance, appraisal, advice, or education. What determines whether reasons are relevant is the set of rules of relevance implicitly assumed in the process of guiding, appraising, advising, or educating. So it is misleading to say that we use moral language for purposes different from those for which we use aesthetic language. Moral advice is advice given by means of moral language; aesthetic advice is advice given by means of aesthetic language. But giving advice, whether by means of one language or another, is still giving advice. It is using language for one kind of purpose in one kind of situation. To say that a person is giving moral advice rather than aesthetic advice is to say that he is carrying on normative discourse in the universe of moral discourse rather than in the universe of aesthetic discourse. Of course we might want to say that giving moral advice is giving advice from the moral point of view and giving aesthetic advice is giving advice from the aesthetic point of view. And this is perfectly correct. But it is not saying anything different from what has already been said. For the canons of reasoning that define each point of view are the rules of relevance that differentiate one universe of discourse from another.

2. In his essay "Ordinary Language" (*Philosophical Review*, LXII, 2; 1953), Professor Gilbert Ryle makes the distinction between the

phrases "the use of ordinary language" and "ordinary linguistic usage." To talk about the use of ordinary language is to talk about language that is common or colloquial, used by everyone in the ordinary affairs of everyday life. It is not to talk about a specialist's use of his technical language. Ordinary language is thus to be contrasted, for example, with the language of physicists. Professor Ryle points out that no sharp dividing line can be drawn between ordinary and nonordinary language.

There is no sharp boundary between 'common' and 'uncommon,' 'technical' and 'untechnical' or 'old-fashioned' and 'current.' Is 'carburetor' a word in common use or only in rather uncommon use? Is 'purl' on the lips of Everyman, or on the lips only of Everywoman? What of 'manslaughter,' 'inflation,' 'quotient' and 'off-side'? On the other hand, no one would hesitate on which side of this no-man's-land to locate 'isotope' or 'bread,' 'material implication' or 'if,' 'transfinite cardinal' or 'eleven,' 'ween' or 'suppose.' The edges of 'ordinary' are blurred, but usually we are in no doubt whether a diction does or does not belong to ordinary parlance. (*Ibid.*, pp. 167-168.)

In contrast to the use of ordinary language, the ordinary use of a linguistic expression refers to a standard, typical or normal use of a word or phrase, aside from whether the word or phrase is a part of ordinary language. Thus there can be a nonordinary use of a word found in ordinary language, and an ordinary use of a word found in technical language.

Whether an implement or instrument is a common or a specialist one, there remains the distinction between its stock use and non-stock uses of it. If a term is a highly technical term, or a non-technical term, there remains the distinction between its stock use and non-stock uses of it. If a term is a highly technical term, most people will not know its stock use or, *a fortiori*, any non-stock uses of it either, if it has any. If it is a vernacular term, then nearly everyone will know its stock use, and most people will also know some non-stock uses of it, if it has any. (*Ibid.*, p. 168.)

In discussing the use of normative language I have been discussing both the use of ordinary (nontechnical) language and the ordinary (stock) use of expressions (such as "good" and "ought"). All normative languages are part of the ordinary language we use in everyday life. One does not have to be trained in a specialty or possess technical knowledge in order to be able to use at least some of the language of morals, of art criticism, or of politics. Nevertheless, all normative languages shade off into technical languages. Thus ordinary moral discourse shades off into the technical discourse of moralists, the ordinary language of art criticism shades off into the sometimes highly technical jargon of professional critics and scholars, and so for the other universes of normative discourse. In each case it would be an arbitrary act to separate ordinary normative language from technical normative language. For much of the vocabulary of evaluative and prescriptive terms that have stock uses in everyday life will also have the same stock uses in the reflective discourse of specialists.

We cannot define a normative language in terms of the technical training and competence of those who know how to use it. In this respect normative discourse differs from the discourse of physics or electrical engineering. One can plausibly define these universes of discourse in terms of the qualifications a person must have in order to be competent in them. But we cannot say simply that the language of morals is the language of moralists, in the way that we can say that the language of physics is the language of physicists (i.e., the language they use *as* physicists). Aesthetic discourse cannot be *identified* with the discourse of art critics, but the discourse of electrical engineering can be identified with the discourse which electrical engineers carry on *qua* electrical engineers. It is true that the discourse of electrical engineering overlaps with the discourse of physics, but this fact can be accounted for in terms of overlapping education and training in the two fields. The overlapping of normative languages cannot be accounted for in this way because they are not languages used only by people educated or trained in special skills.

In general, any technical language can be defined as the language which is used by a certain group of people when they are communicating with one another about a common field of interest and are using skills they have acquired through special education and training. Knowing how to use the technical language correctly is, of course, one of those skills. An ordinary language, whether normative or nonnormative, cannot be so defined, since the very fact that it is an ordinary language implies that there is no special skill required for using it correctly. This holds both for the ordinary (standard, stock) uses of expressions and for nonordinary (unusual, nonstock) uses of expressions.

3. My third point is that normative languages cannot be distinguished according to the *methods* which are appropriate for carrying on rational discourse in each language. The reason for this is that the methods of rational discourse used in morals are the same as those used in art criticism, in politics, in religion, and in any other universe of normative discourse. Which *particular assertions* will count as relevant and good reasons in each universe of discourse will vary, but the *methods* of reasoning are governed by rules of valid inference and these rules are the same in all normative languages. They are the rules which define the processes of verification and validation. To verify a value judgment or prescription is to reason in a certain way, and when we reason in that way we are carrying on (with others or with ourselves) normative discourse. It does not matter in which universe of discourse such reasoning is done. The logical pattern of discourse remains the same. Similarly, the method of validation remains constant regardless of what kinds of standards or rules (moral, aesthetic, political, or other) are being validated. The method is defined by certain rules of inference and these govern the validation of standards and rules in all universes of normative discourse.

Rules of relevance, on the other hand, do not define one basic method of reasoning common to all universes of normative discourse. They tell us which particular verification and validation sentences go with which particular normative sentences. In virtue of this fact they comprise the unifying principles of a normative language. Different rules of relevance demarcate different normative languages and as such are to be contrasted with the methods of verification and validation common to them all. However, these rules of relevance are not entirely unconnected with the methods of verification and validation. Their connection can be made clear by considering the question: When a reason is offered in justification of a value judgment or a prescription, under what conditions is it a good reason? The answer is that a reason is a good reason under two conditions—when it is expressed in a verification or validation sentence that is *relevant*, and when what is said in the sentence is *true*. The relevance of the sentence is determined by the rules of relevance of the normative language concerned. The truth of the sentence is determined by the methods of verification and validation, as analyzed in Chapter 3. Thus although rules of relevance vary from normative language to normative language while rules of valid inference remain constant, both sets of rules must be appealed to in deciding whether a reason is a good reason. The differentiae of a normative language are based on certain features of a reason which make it a good reason in the given universe of discourse. (They are the features which make the reason a *relevant* one.) Common to all normative languages are the features which make a reason a verifying or validating reason, according to the rules of valid inference which define the methods of verification and validation. A good reason in morals is not necessarily a good reason in aesthetics, but what makes a reason in morals a verifying or validating reason is the same thing that does so in aesthetics.

4. I turn now to a fourth corollary of the principle that rules of relevance differentiate normative languages. The same set of rules of relevance may be followed in many different societies or cultures. The concept of a universe of normative discourse is a cross-cultural concept. All sorts of cultures, for example, may use the language of morals. Their moral codes (i.e., their moral value systems) may differ. But if people in the various cultures follow the rules of relevance that define the universe of moral discourse when they try to justify value judgments and prescriptions, they all have a moral language (and a moral code). Similarly, they all carry on aesthetic discourse, no matter how diverse may be their arts and their attitudes toward the arts, if they reason about judgments of art according to the rules of relevance that define the language of aesthetics. The same considerations hold for the language of politics, the language of religion, the language of custom or etiquette, and for the other universes of normative discourse. It is a major mistake to define "realm" *ethnocentrically,* that is, to define it in such a way that only the morality of one's own culture is truly a morality, only the arts of one's own culture are genuine arts, etc. Such ethnocentric definitions would make it absurd to talk about the moralities, the arts, the

political systems, the religions, or the codes of etiquette of different societies. But it is clearly not absurd to talk this way, if we are willing to follow common usage. It is in order to account for this common usage that I define each "realm of value" in terms of a particular universe of normative discourse, distinguished from all other universes of normative discourse by a unique set of rules of relevance.

B. Normative languages and points of view

This analysis of normative language provides us with a further clarification of the concept of a point of view. I said in Chapter 4 that taking a certain point of view involves a disposition to reason according to certain canons of reasoning, and that these consist of rules of relevance and of valid inference. We now see that the canons of reasoning are actually rules governing the use of a normative language. They define a certain universe of discourse in which we express value judgments and prescriptions and give reasons for or against them.

Given this correlation of points of view with normative languages, what is the relation between a point of view and the value systems which belong to it? Two or more value systems belong to the same point of view when the same normative language is used in justifying the standards and rules which occur in them. As people try to live by each system, and as they make judgments and prescribe conduct in accordance with it, they carry on normative discourse according to certain rules of relevance and rules of valid inference. It is the rules of relevance which tell us which particular universe of discourse is involved. The value systems may be made up of different standards and rules arranged in different hierarchies of relative precedence. But as long as their validation is carried out in one universe of discourse, the value systems all belong to one point of view. Thus two dissimilar sets of standards and rules may both constitute *moral* codes if it is the language of morals which people use when they try to justify them or justify applying them to particular cases. What makes a language the language of morals are the rules of relevance that determine which verification and validation sentences go with which normative sentences. To follow them is to take the moral point of view, regardless of which standards and rules make up the value system belonging to it.

In light of this account of points of view, how is the relative precedence of value systems belonging to different points of view to be understood? In Section A of Chapter 6 the relative precedence of value systems was defined as follows. One value system V takes precedence over another value system V' if and only if, according to a given way of life, it is better to live in accordance with V than in accordance with V', whenever the two systems conflict. A way of life consists of many different value systems arranged in an order of relative precedence. Each system belongs to a different point of view, so that conflicts between systems may be thought of as conflicts between points of view, and the precedence of one system over another may be thought of as the precedence of one point of view over another. If we correlate points of view with normative languages, what does it mean to say that two points of view are in conflict or that one point of view takes precedence over another?

To say that two points of view are in conflict is to say, first, that there are reasons both *for* and *against* a given value judgment or prescription, and second, that the reasons *for* belong to one universe of discourse and the reasons *against* belong to another. To say that one point of view takes precedence over another (according to a given way of life) is to say that the reasons belonging to one universe of discourse *weigh more heavily* than the reasons belonging to another. A person who is living that way of life must act in accordance with the value system that takes precedence. This means that the reasons *for* his acting in a certain way outweigh the reasons *against* it. The reasons *for* consist in verification and validation sentences of the normative language corresponding to the point of view to which the superior value system belongs. The reasons *against* are reasons stated in the normative language of the opposing value system. Each set of reasons is given in a different universe of discourse. Suppose that a way of life includes both a moral value system and a prudential value system and that when the two systems are in conflict the way of life stipulates that the moral system shall take precedence. According to such a way of life, moral reasons outweigh reasons of prudence whenever it is the case that to act morally is not to act in one's own interest and to act in one's own interest is to do what is immoral. Anyone who intends to live that way of life must allow moral reasons to make a stronger claim to his assent than reasons of prudence, whenever both sorts of reasons are relevant and are in opposition to each other. In such a way of life, we might say that the universe of moral discourse "takes precedence over" the universe of prudential discourse.

When a person commits himself to a way of life, then, he commits himself doubly. He commits himself to *living* in accordance with those value systems that take precedence over others (in situations where they conflict), and he commits himself to *thinking* in such a way that reasons in one universe of discourse are given greater weight than reasons in another universe of discourse. In stating what a person's way of life is, we may speak in terms of living according to certain sets of standards and rules, or we may speak in terms of carrying on discourse according to certain sets of canons of reasoning. In cases of conflict, these must always go together. If it is better for a person to live in accordance with value system V rather than value system V', then it is better for him to allow reasons offered in the first universe of discourse to outweigh opposing reasons offered in the second.

What is the principle by which we determine whether reasons of one sort are to weigh more heavily than reasons of another sort? It is the same principle as that by which we determine the order of relative precedence among value systems in a way of life. In Section A of Chapter 6 I pointed out that when we commit ourselves to a certain way of life, we *decide* that one value system *shall* take precedence over another when the two are in conflict. That one value system takes precedence over another is simply one of the principles to which a person subscribes in the act of choosing a way of life. By choosing that way of life he *makes* one value system take precedence over another. In like manner a person's commitment to a certain way of life is his decision to have reasons belonging to one universe of discourse count more heavily than reasons belonging to another. This decision is simply part of the person's *ultimate normative commitment.* We cannot give *reasons* to show why moral reasons, for instance, ought to outweigh reasons of prudence, when they are in opposition to each other. We can only say we have chosen a way of life which involves placing greater weight on moral reasons than on those of prudence. Another way of life will involve placing greater weight on reasons of prudence. In order to determine whether moral reasons are "really" superior to reasons of prudence, we must find out whether the whole way of life to which we are committed is justified. And as we saw in Chapter 6, this requires our investigating whether it would be preferred to others under conditions of a rational choice.

It may be the case, of course, that as choices among ways of life become more and more rational, there will be more and more agreement that one way of life is to be preferred to all others. Let us suppose that this does occur, and that the way of life in question is such that its moral value system takes precedence over all its other constituent value systems. We may then claim that, whenever moral reasons are opposed to other sorts of reasons, the moral reasons "really" outweigh the others. If someone were to challenge this claim, only the appeal to a rational choice among ways of life could serve as a reply. There is nothing in the universe of moral discourse itself which shows that moral reasons outweigh all others. Nor is there any higher principle outside all universes of normative discourse which requires that moral discourse take precedence over other kinds of discourse. That reasons of one sort are to outweigh reasons of another sort is precisely something we decide upon when we choose a way of life. The only further question that can legitimately be raised here concerns the justifiability of this choice, and this question can only be answered in terms of the concept of a rational choice.

"Realms of value"

12

A. *How values may be classified*

In Chapter 1, I considered briefly the meaning of the verb "to value," which is approximately synonymous with "to hold precious or dear." A person values something when he has a certain sort of pro-attitude toward it. When the word "value" occurs as a noun, it may be used either to designate the concept of desirability (goodness, rightness, valuableness) or it may be used as a substantive. It is in the first sense that we speak of the value *of* something; it is in the second sense that we speak of a person's (or group's, or society's) values. In this chapter I shall be using the noun "value" in this second sense.

When "value" is used as a substantive and we talk of a person's "values," I suggest that the word refers to three sorts of things—the value judgments and prescriptions accepted by the person as being justified (whether or not he has ever in fact tried to justify them); the standards and rules which the person would appeal to *if* he were asked to justify his value judgments and prescriptions; and all other standards and rules which constitute the value systems the person has adopted, consciously or unconsciously. Thus a person's values include all the standards and rules which together make up his way of life. They define his ideals and life goals (to fulfill the standards; to follow the rules). They are the standards and rules according to which he evaluates things and prescribes acts, as well as the standards and rules he tries to live by, whether or not he is aware of them. When we speak of the values of a whole culture, a society, or a subcultural group, we refer to the value judgments, prescriptions, standards, and rules widely accepted by persons in the culture, society, or group.

Now suppose the values of a person or society are divided into different sorts, such as moral values, aesthetic values, religious values, and so on. Or suppose it is said that the values of a person or society belong to different "realms of value." According to what criteria is one sort of value or one realm of value distinguished from another? One answer that immediately comes to mind is that different realms of value correspond to different universes of normative discourse. Each sort of value would then belong to a particular point of view. But this is not the only way of classifying values or realms of value. In this chapter I shall examine some other ways of classifying them.

Criteria for classifying values or realms of value are not to be confused with criteria for classifying value *systems* or value *theories.* Different value *systems* may be classified, for example, according to their overall structures. Such classification would be required for a detailed analysis, within each point of view, of the value systems belonging to it. Thus we have the breakdown of value systems belonging to the moral point of view into teleological (or utilitarian) systems and deontological (or formalistic) systems. Value *theories* have been classified in many different ways. Examples of such classifications are to be found in the following three lists of alternative theories: "The Objective Approach," "The Subjective Approach," and "The Imperative Approach" (S. E. Toulmin); "Ethical Skepticism," "Approbative Theories," "Process Theories," "Psychological Value Theories," "Metaphysical Theories," and "Intuitive Theories" (T. E. Hill); "Law Theories," "Moral Fact Theories," "Response Theories," and "The Emotive Theory" (K. Baier). These are different classifications of philosophers' views concerning the meaning and truth (or justifiability) of value judgments. When limited to moral judgments, they are sometimes called "meta-ethical theories." In this chapter I shall consider how various sorts of value judgments, prescriptions, standards, and rules are differentiated. I shall not be concerned with the structure of value systems, nor shall I be concerned with theories about the meaning and truth of value judgments.

How values are to be classified depends on what *feature* of a value judgment, prescription, standard, or rule is selected as a basis of comparison. The following are nine features that may be used for this purpose.

1. The *point of view* to which the value belongs.

2. When the value is a judgment or a standard, whether the value is *intrinsic or extrinsic,* and if extrinsic, whether it is *inherent, instrumental, or contributive.* When the value is a prescription or a rule, whether it is *categorical or hypothetical.*

3. When the value is a standard or a rule, the *range of application* of the value. When the value is a judgment or prescription, the *class of comparison* of the value.

4. The *extent of acceptance* of the value.

5. The *relative strength* of the value.

6. The *relative precedence* of the value.

7. The *relative importance* of the value.

8. The *degree of explicitness* with which the value is held.

9. The *degree of rationality* with which the value is held.

The purpose of this chapter is to investigate what classification of values results when each of these features is used as a criterion. The resultant classification in cases 2 through 9 will also be compared with the resultant classification in case 1.

B. Nine ways of classifying values

1. What it means to classify values according to the points of view to which they belong has been examined in Chapters 4 and 11. The realms of value that emerge from such classification are universes of normative discourse corresponding to different points of view. In all civilized cultures there are eight points of view (or realms of value) that may be designated as "basic." We call them basic because of two factors. First, they *pervade* the culture, in the

sense that the conduct of any given individual in the culture is always subject to a value system belonging to at least one of them and is usually subject to value systems belonging to more than one of them. Second, they are the *dominant* points of view in a culture, in the sense that they set the values of the major social institutions and activities which carry on the civilization of the culture. These major social institutions and activities are the moral code, the arts, the pure and applied sciences, the religion or religions, the economic, political, and legal systems, the customs and traditions, and the educational institutions. The eight basic points of view corresponding to these institutions and activities are the moral, the aesthetic, the intellectual, the religious, the economic, the political, the legal, and the point of view of etiquette or custom. There is no single point of view corresponding to the educational institutions of a society, since education is a process which may take place within *any* point of view. Thus there is moral education, aesthetic education, intellectual education, religious education, and so on.

Value systems belonging to the eight basic points of view are embodied in the organizations and institutions of a society. Thus the purpose of a social organization may be to fulfill *standards* which belong to one or another of them. Or else it may be governed by *rules* which belong to one or another of these points of view, and to carry on the organization's activities is to follow these (practice-defining) rules. A church as an organized social institution, for example, exists to further goals defined by religious values, and to practice a religion is to act in accordance with the rules of religious conduct (worship, ritual, prayer). Accordingly it is appropriate to judge a church from the religious point of view. In a similar manner it is appropriate to judge the activities of an art museum from the aesthetic point of view, the activities of a college or university from the intellectual point of view, and the activities of a political party from the political point of view. In all of these cases, however, it is also appropriate to judge the organizations from both the moral and the legal points of view, since their purposes are to achieve certain goals or to pursue certain ends *without* violating the moral code of the society and *without* breaking the society's laws.

In addition to the eight basic points of view or realms of value, every culture includes many nonbasic points of view or realms of value. Each of these corresponds to a particular *group interest* in the culture. One may speak of the military point of view, for example, as the universe of normative discourse or realm of value which is appropriate for judging the activities and policies of an army. The value system belonging to the military point of view contains as its supreme norm the standard of winning a war or defending a society against attack. An army as a social institution exists for these specific and clearly defined purposes and can legitimately be judged according to its ability to accomplish them. Similar considerations hold for all other social organizations with specific and clearly defined purposes, such as a professional baseball team, a hospital, a city's fire department, a local organization to preserve racial segregation (e.g., a White Citizens' Council in a southern state), or a national organization to abolish racial segregation (e.g., the National Association for the Advancement of Colored People). In all such cases, it is appropriate to judge the organization in terms of its *group interest*, that is, in terms of the purposes of the group as a whole (as distinct from the *self-interest* of each member of the group). It is also appropriate to judge the organization in terms of whatever basic points of view its purposes belong to. Thus an army may be judged not exclusively from the military point of view, but also from the moral, political, economic, and legal points of view. In fact all the organizations just mentioned may legitimately be judged from the legal point of view, since they seek to achieve their purposes without breaking the society's laws. The same cannot be said concerning all social organizations, however. The organization of a juvenile street gang, for example, may have purposes that run counter to the law, and there are some organizations, such as gambling syndicates and "dope rings," whose purposes are explicitly illegal.

To say that it is not legitimate to judge the activities of a juvenile street gang or of organized crime from the legal point of view is to speak as a member of the group concerned. When we place ourselves outside the group and speak as a member of the society at large, then the legal point of view becomes relevant. We are then judging the group interest as a whole according to more basic standards or rules (i.e., according to standards or rules belonging to a more basic point of view). This brings out the fact that regarding any social organization, two types of evaluation are possible.

One is an evaluation of the activities and policies of the organization within the framework of the group interest itself. Here we ask: How well do these activities and policies serve the purposes which define the goals of the group? How closely do they accord with the rules adopted by the group? The other type of evaluation is made outside the framework of the group interest. Here we ask: How good or bad, right or wrong are the activities and policies of the group according to standards and rules *not* included in the value systems adopted by the group? The distinction between these two types of evaluation is an instance of the distinction (discussed in Chapter 3) between evaluating something within the framework of a given social practice and judging the social practice as a whole.

When we make value judgments of the second type (i.e., evaluating the activities and policies of an organization from a standpoint outside the organization), there is one point of view that is applicable to *all* organizations, namely, the moral point of view. Every culture embodies a moral code which is concerned with the welfare of the individuals in the culture; and since the activities and policies of every social organization affect, for better or worse, the welfare of at least some individuals in the culture, the culture's moral system is applicable. What is not so obvious is that the moral point of view is relevant to all social organizations even when we restrict ourselves to the first type of evaluation (i.e., judging the activities and policies of an organization within the framework of its group interest). For the activities and policies of any organization are at least in part *moral* activities and policies. They are moral in so far as the furthering of the organization's purposes affects the welfare of individuals who are members of the organization and who participate in its activities. It might at first be thought that the activities of a juvenile street gang or a White Citizens' Council can be judged from the outside according to the moral code of the society at large, but cannot be so judged from the inside, since such organizations lack a moral code. But this is to confuse the moral *point of view* with particular moral *value systems*. Every organization has at least a rudimentary moral value system. (In the case of a juvenile gang or a White Citizens' Council, the moral system may be highly developed, with clearly defined rules and standards of right conduct, and with strict duties and obligations supported by strong sanctions.) It is true that a juvenile gang or a White Citizens' Council may have adopted a moral system which is in conflict with the moral system of the society at large. This would occur whenever acting in accordance with the moral rules of the group involves violating the moral rules of the society at large. To say that the moral point of view applies to all such organizations is to say that the rules of relevance which govern the *reasoning* of those who seek to justify value judgments, prescriptions, standards, and rules within the organization are the rules of relevance that define the moral point of view.

The eight basic points of view and the nonbasic points of view of different group interests are all to be distinguished from the point of view of *self-interest*. The basic points of view are those of society at large. The nonbasic points of view are those of subcultural groups or institutions. The latter are to be contrasted with the self-interest of each member of a group. An individual may participate in various groups and often he will adopt the group interests as his own. That is, he will take their points of view and try to live by their value systems. But he also has his self-interest to pursue and he may consider his group activities either wholly or in part from the point of view of prudence. This point of view is defined by those rules of reasoning according to which an appeal to one's self-interest is always relevant to the justification of a value judgment and any other appeal is always irrelevant.

So far I have considered values (classified according to points of view) as they are embodied in social institutions and activities. I now wish to consider three ways of classifying values, each of which is reducible to the classification of values according to points of view. I shall try to show that whenever values are classified according to (a) different kinds of attitudes or interests, (b) the inherent properties of different standards and rules, and (c) different value predicates, the criterion of classification in each case is a point of view (or universe of normative discourse).

(a) It is sometimes claimed that the difference between moral values, aesthetic values, and religious values, for example, is based on the difference between the moral attitude, the aesthetic attitude, and the religious attitude. It is said that we know directly from our experience of life that moral approval is different from aesthetic appreciation, and that both are distinct from the unique attitude which is religious worship or devotion. This qualitative difference in attitudes is used to distinguish the various kinds of value in the following way. When the pro-attitude ("positive interest") or con-attitude ("negative interest") that accompanies a value judgment or prescription is of a certain kind, the value judgment or prescription is of the same kind. Thus a moral value is a judgment or prescription accompanied by a moral attitude, an aesthetic value is a judgment or prescription accompanied by an aesthetic attitude, and so on. Different standards and rules are also determined in this way. Thus a moral rule is a rule which we apply in judging an action when we take a moral interest in, or adopt a moral attitude toward, the action. An aesthetic standard is a standard according to which we evaluate something when we take an aesthetic interest in, or adopt an aesthetic attitude toward, the thing. And so on. Consequently if we could delineate all the various kinds of attitudes which people can take toward anything, we could exhaustively list all the kinds of value there are.

According to this proposal, then, the criterion for classifying different kinds of value is the criterion by which different kinds of attitude are distinguished. But what is this criterion? To classify values according to a classification of attitudes does not enlighten us unless the basis of the latter classification is made clear. I suggest that when this is done, that basis turns out to be nothing but the concept of a point of view (or universe of normative discourse).

What does it mean to say that we adopt a certain kind of attitude toward something, or that we take a certain kind of interest in something? It means that we are disposed to like, approve of, favor (dislike, disapprove of, disfavor) the thing *on certain grounds*. Professor Baier makes the point this way: ". . . morally approving and disapproving is being for or against something on *moral* grounds: it is nonsense to say 'I morally disapprove of war though I have only selfish reasons for my disapproval.'" (K. Baier, *op. cit.*, p. 27.) The grounds on which one takes a certain attitude toward something are the reasons one would give in justifying an evaluation of the thing. The *kind of attitude* one takes is determined by the *kind of reasons* one would accept as good reasons. Now a reason is accepted as a good reason only if it is considered to be a relevant reason, and we decide whether a reason is relevant by reference to the rules of relevance of a particular point of view. *It is only when we know which rules of relevance govern our reasoning about the value of something that we know which kind of attitude we are taking toward it.* Thus to take a moral attitude toward an action is to be disposed to approve or disapprove of it on moral grounds. And what are moral grounds? They are grounds whose relevance is determined by the rules of relevance that define the moral point of view. Similarly, to take an aesthetic attitude toward something is to be disposed to like it (or dislike it) on aesthetic grounds. Just as one must take the moral point of view in order to have a moral attitude, so one must take the aesthetic point of view in order to have an aesthetic attitude. To have an aesthetic attitude toward a work of art is to have a certain disposition, namely, the disposition to favor or disfavor, to praise or condemn, on the basis of *aesthetic* merits or demerits. What are *aesthetic* merits or demerits? They are the good-making or bad-making characteristics of a work as determined by the rules of reasoning definitive of the aesthetic point of view.

When attitudes or "interests" are classified in this manner, we must not think of them as feelings which we can differentiate by careful introspection. No doubt we ordinarily have certain feelings when we morally approve or disapprove of something (though it is not necessary that we have them), and normally such feelings are different from the feelings that accompany our aesthetic, religious, or intellectual attitudes. But the feelings are not the attitudes, nor can they serve as the basis for distinguishing among the kinds of attitude. In defense of this point I quote Professor Baier's argument.

Some followers of the response theory would, of course, maintain that moral approval is not the attitude of being in favor of something on moral grounds, but is a certain characteristic feeling or response. But what is the *characteristic* of this feeling or response? How do we make sure that it is *characteristically moral?* Plainly we cannot tell in the way in which we tell that a particular feeling we now have is a tickle rather than pins and needles. Feelings such as these are indeed immediately recognizable by their characteristic 'feel'; they are caused by something; we can suddenly find ourselves experiencing them without knowing what caused them, and we may try to discover their causes. . . . Moral approval and disapproval, however, are not such feelings. It would be quite absurd to say, 'I wonder what is causing that moral disapproval of war of mine' or 'I must do something to experience again that moral approval of keeping promises' or 'I suddenly found myself having that feeling of moral approval of kindness.' (*Ibid.*, p. 28.)

This is not to deny that certain feelings may typically be associated with or accompany our moral attitudes, and that characteristically different feelings may be associated with or accompany our aesthetic attitudes. But it would be logically possible (if not psychologically possible) for the same feelings to be associated with or to accompany both kinds of attitude, without making us doubtful whether the attitudes were of one kind or another. If on the other hand we did not know what reasons to consider relevant to justifying our value judgments, prescriptions, standards, or rules, we would not be able to say whether such values were moral, aesthetic, religious, or of some other kind. It is our point of view—the universe of rational discourse in which we defend our values or attack those of others— that tells us what kind of attitude we are taking.

(b) Similar considerations hold for the attempt to classify values according to the inherent characteristics of standards and rules. What makes a standard or rule a moral one is not some distinctive moral quality which inheres in it and which can be identified by direct inspection of it. Nor is there a unique aesthetic quality which makes a standard or rule an aesthetic one. A moral standard is *any* standard which is justified by appeal to the rules of relevance defining the moral point of view. The same standard may also function as an aesthetic standard, a religious standard, or an intellectual standard, depending on whether it is justified within the framework of the aesthetic, the religious, or the intellectual point of view. Of course a given standard or rule which belongs to one point of view may never *in fact* occur in another point of view, but this is not a logical necessity.

That the same standard or rule may belong to more than one point of view can be shown by the following examples. Take the value judgment that an act is wrong because it violates the Income Tax Law. Here the set of rules which make up the Income Tax Law are the justificatory grounds for the judgment. These rules may belong to the moral point of view, the legal point of view, or the economic point of view. It all depends on the context of rational discourse in which we would answer the question, "Why is it wrong to break the Income Tax Law?" We might give moral reasons, or legal reasons (simply the fact that the Income Tax Law is the duly established and administered law of the land), or economic reasons. It is only when we know which reasons will be accepted as relevant in such a context that we know to which point of view the rules belong. Nothing inherent in the rules themselves will tell us this. We must see, in other words, which universe of normative discourse is involved when the value judgment is justified. What is true of rules is also true of standards. Consider the case of judging a cathedral according to the standard of the appropriateness of its form to its function. This may be an aesthetic standard or a religious standard, depending on the context of the value judgment. If we are speaking of the cathedral as a work of architecture, the standard would be an aesthetic one, applicable to any building. If we are speaking of the cathedral as a place of worship, the same standard is a religious one, and is not applicable to any building. In each case the appeal to the standard is made within a different rational framework. The cathedral is being judged from two different points of view, though it is being judged according to the same standard. How do we know which point of view is involved? We must find out which reasons are considered relevant when the use of the standard is challenged, or when anyone attempts to justify the application of the standard in the given case. That is, we must see which normative language is used in making and justifying the given value judgment.

The difference between two kinds of standards or rules, then, does not depend on any inherent characteristics of the standards or rules themselves. The difference between them is like the difference between two kinds of value systems, which was discussed in Chapters 4 and 11. There we saw that many different value systems may belong to the same point of view. It is perfectly proper, for example, to speak of the various moral codes or moral systems of different societies as "moral," and so distinguish them from the customs, the laws, the political systems, and the economic systems of those societies. Now value systems are simply sets of standards and rules arranged in an order of relative precedence or superiority. If points of view serve to differentiate one kind of value system from another, by that very fact they also serve to differentiate one kind of standard or rule from another.

(c) The concept of a point of view is also the criterion underlying the classification of different "value predicates." A value predicate designates a property attributed to an object in a value judgment. Typical value predicates are moral rightness, aesthetic excellence, holiness, politeness, economic efficiency, legality, and prudence. Value judgments are thought to be classifiable according to their predicates. Corresponding to the predicates just listed would be moral judgments, aesthetic judgments, religious judgments, judgments of etiquette, economic judgments, legal judgments, and judgments of prudence. The various value predicates are often spoken of as different kinds of value; moral rightness, for instance, is a different kind of value from aesthetic excellence. To make a value judgment (i.e., to judge the value of something) is conceived of as an assertion that something possesses a certain kind of value. The assertion is taken to be the attributing of a property to an object, the property being a value of a certain kind. Different properties are thus seen to constitute different kinds of value.

(It should be noted that here the noun "value" shifts from its substantive to its attributive use. That is, we are now speaking, not of a person's values, but of the value of something. Different kinds of value are not different kinds of judgments, prescriptions, standards or rules, but different kinds of properties attributable to things that are evaluated or prescribed.)

The first question to be raised is this. How do we distinguish one value property (or predicate) from another? Unless an answer is provided for this question, we do not really understand the criterion of classification that allows us to speak of different kinds of value. I submit that the answer to this question is to be found in *the criteria of application of the words which serve as value predicates.* The question "How is one value predicate (and hence one kind of value) to be distinguished from another?" becomes, in clearer light, the question "By what criteria do we apply a given value term to an evaluatum?" In his analysis of the value term "good," R. M. Hare distinguishes between the meaning of the word and the criteria for its application. The meaning of "good" is constant in all value judgments, no matter what class of comparison or what standard or rule of evaluation is presupposed. The criteria of application of the word, on the other hand, varies from class of comparison to class of comparison and from standard to standard.

We can teach the criteria for applying the word 'good' within a particular class; but this does not teach the meaning of the word. A man could even learn to tell good augers from bad, without in the least knowing what 'good' meant; he could, that is to say, learn to sort out augers into piles, good and bad, and do this quite correctly, but still not realize that this classification was for the purpose of selecting some augers *in preference* to others. (R. M. Hare, *op. cit.*, p. 103.)

The *meaning* of "good" is its use as a term expressive of a pro-attitude toward the object to which it is applied. The *criteria* for applying the term, on the other hand, are the standards or rules appealed to in evaluating the object.

Now suppose we understand "good" as the name of a property, goodness, and a value judgment ("X is good") as the attributing of this property to an object. We may then begin to speak as if different kinds of value judgments correspond to the different kinds of goodness attributable to an object. We may speak of a moral judgment as a judgment about the moral goodness of something, an aesthetic judgment as a judgment about the aesthetic goodness of something, and so on. But what is the differentia here? It cannot be what Hare refers to as the "meaning" of the word "good," since this does not vary between moral judgments and aesthetic judgments. Nor can the answer be that we just "sense" the difference between the moral meaning of "good" and the aesthetic meaning of the word. If that is the case, how did we learn to "sense" this difference, other than by means of learning some criterion by which to tell the difference? The same objection holds for the claim that we "just know" the difference between two simple properties, moral goodness and aesthetic goodness. This does not get rid of our perplexity, for we immediately want to know *how* we came to "just know" the difference. An intuitive recognition of a qualitative difference would not explain how we did so, since such recognition must itself be preceded by a learning process in which a person acquires the capacity for it.

We can answer our question and at the same time avoid all these difficulties if we drop the idea that the word "good" is the name of a property, goodness. Instead of asking ourselves, "What is the difference between moral goodness and aesthetic goodness?" we now ask, "What different criteria of application of the word "good" do we use in moral judgments and in aesthetic judgments?" So-called value predicates are not names of properties but *words whose criteria of application are the standards and rules we appeal to in evaluating things*. The difference between the moral "meaning" (use) of "good" and the aesthetic "meaning" of the word lies in the difference between moral standards of evaluation and aesthetic standards of evaluation. And *that* difference, we have seen, is a matter of the particular universe of discourse or point of view within which the value judgment is made and justified. Here again we have an instance of the classification of values in terms of points of view. Let us now consider other ways of classifying values.

2. The second way of classifying values mentioned in Section A is based on whether the value is intrinsic or extrinsic, or categorical or hypothetical; extrinsic values are themselves classified as inherent, instrumental, or contributive. This classification is perfectly compatible with the one we have just considered. There are two ways in which we might go about combining them.

(I) A. Moral values
    1. Moral standards and value judgments
        a) Intrinsic
        b) Extrinsic
            (1) Inherent
            (2) Instrumental
            (3) Contributive
    2. Moral rules and prescriptions
        a) Categorical
        b) Hypothetical
  B. Aesthetic values
    1. Aesthetic standards, etc.
(II) A. Standards and value judgments
    1. Intrinsic
        a) Moral
        b) Aesthetic, etc.
    2. Extrinsic
        a) Inherent
            (1) Moral
            (2) Aesthetic, etc.

    b) Instrumental
     (1) Moral
     (2) Aesthetic, etc.
    c) Contributive
     (1) Moral
     (2) Aesthetic, etc.
 B. Rules and prescriptions
  1. Categorical
   a) Moral
   b) Aesthetic, etc.
  2. Hypothetical
   a) Moral
   b) Aesthetic, etc.

The mutual independence of the first two ways of classifying values implies that it is logically permissible to make any combination of a class from one with a class from the other. For example, there is nothing *logically* wrong in talking about aesthetic standards of instrumental value. It may be the case that the aesthetic point of view does not actually include such standards, but it is not self-contradictory to speak of this possibility. The only thing that prevents us from saying that aesthetic standards may be standards of instrumental value is the *empirical* fact that the rules of relevance implicit in the universe of aesthetic discourse do not allow the application of such standards to be relevant. This is just the nature of the use of aesthetic language. By the same argument is it not logically necessary to limit moral prescriptions (as Kant does) to categorical prescriptions. It may be the case that moral discourse excludes hypothetical prescriptions. Whether it does or not can only be discovered by explicating the rules of relevance implicit in our use of moral language. The issue cannot be decided *a priori*, without reference to the way people do in fact carry on moral discourse.

 3. A third way of classifying values is based on their range of application (if they are standards or rules) and on their class of comparison (if they are value judgments or prescriptions). The range of application of a standard is the class of things which it is considered appropriate to evaluate according to that standard. The range of application of a rule is the class of all acts which fall under the rule. The scope or breadth of standards and rules varies accord-

ing to the number and variety of things included in their range of application. Thus standards and rules belonging to the eight "basic" points of view mentioned in connection with classification 1 are all broader in scope than standards and rules belonging to nonbasic points of view. But even among basic points of view there is some variation in scope. In most societies, for example, moral rules are given a wider range of application than legal rules (the laws). In our own society people apply economic standards to more things and to a greater variety of things than aesthetic standards. Such differences in range of application may vary from society to society. There may be societies in which the laws cover more kinds of acts than do moral rules, and in which aesthetic standards are applied to more things than economic standards. Classification of standards and rules according to their range of application, in other words, is independent of their classification according to points of view.

The total *range of application* of a standard or rule corresponds to the *classes of comparison* of all value judgments and prescriptions made by reference to the standard or rule. Just as standards and rules may be classified according to the scope of their ranges of application, so may value judgments and prescriptions be classified according to the scope of their classes of comparison. The judgment that someone is a good man is broader in scope than the judgment that he is a good chess player. In the former judgment the class of comparison is the class of all human beings; in the latter it is the class of chess players. Similarly, the prescription "You ought to become a doctor" (said to a college student) is broader in scope than the prescription "You ought to take organic chemistry this semester" (also said to a college student). The class of comparison in each case is the set of alternatives open to the agent in his situation of choice. In the first case these alternatives are presumably all possible careers which the student may pursue, while in the second case the alternatives are limited to the courses which are offered that term and for which the student is qualified.

Since the range of application of standards and rules is not determined by the point of view to which they belong, and since the scope or breadth of value judgments and prescriptions corresponds to range of application, the classification of judgments and prescriptions according to their scope or breadth is independent of their classification according to points of view. Moral judgments are not necessarily broader in scope than, say, political judgments or legal judgments, although in a given culture or even in all cultures this may be empirically true. Furthermore the scope of judgments and prescriptions made from different points of view may be the same. This would occur if different judgments or prescriptions had the same class of comparison. The class of automobiles, for instance, may constitute the identical class of comparison for a moral judgment (in which an automobile is evaluated with regard to its effect on the safety and health of the public), an aesthetic judgment, an economic judgment, a legal judgment, a prudential judgment, and so on. The class of comparison implicitly referred to in the prescription "You ought to buy the brown suit" (where the alternatives consist in the addressee's buying any other suit within a certain price range) remains the same whether the prescription is made from the aesthetic point of view, the economic point of view, or the prudential point of view.

4. To classify values according to their breadth or scope is not to classify them according to how widely they are accepted. Thus to speak of the degree of "generality" or "specificity" of a value is ambiguous. On the one hand it may mean the degree to which the class of comparison or the range of application of the value is wider or narrower than that of other values. On the other, it may mean the extent to which the value is accepted in a given culture or throughout the world. In the latter sense, the most general values would be universal values, that is, judgments, prescriptions, standards, or rules accepted by everyone everywhere. Whether there have actually been such universal values in all periods of history and in all civilizations is highly doubtful. What cannot be doubted is that values vary with regard to the extent of their acceptance, both within a culture and cross-culturally. Some values may be accepted only by a single individual. Others may be shared by the members of a group. Indeed, a group may be organized for the express purpose of fulfilling these shared values. Other values may be accepted widely throughout a whole culture. Still others may be found in more than one culture. Thus values may be arranged in an order of

increasing extent of acceptance—personal or idiosyncratic values, group values, social or cultural values, cross-cultural values, and panhuman or universal values.

The classification of values according to how widely they are accepted is logically independent of their classification according to breadth or range of application. A "narrow" value may be widely accepted and a "broad" value may be accepted only by a few. Thus everyone throughout a culture may adopt a rule which has a very restricted range of application (for example, the rule in football which allows the point after touchdown to be made either by a place kick or by a run or a pass). On the other hand a small group may accept very broad values. Thus an esoteric society having very few members may adopt its own aesthetic standards which its members apply to all works of art in all cultures.

The classification of values according to the extent of their acceptance is also independent of the classification of values according to points of view. Values belonging to one point of view are not necessarily more widely accepted than values belonging to another. Religious values, for example, may be cultural or subcultural or cross-cultural. It is even possible for an individual to have his own religion with a unique value system. In like manner, there may be different moralities in different cultures, and indeed different moralities within a culture (such as the morality of a juvenile street gang, the morality of business executives, the morality of organized crime, and so on). Thus there can be values which vary from culture to culture or from group to group, all of which are properly called moral values. They all belong to the moral point of view because they are all justified in the universe of moral discourse. The rules of relevance that define that universe of discourse are "universal" only in the sense that they make no reference to how many people must accept them. The same is true of the rules of relevance that define other points of view. In no case must a value system be adopted universally or even cross-culturally for it to be correctly placed within a particular point of view. The closest relationship between classifying values according to points of view and classifying them according to the extent of their acceptance lies in the empirical fact that values belonging to the eight basic points of view tend to be more widely accepted throughout a culture than values belonging to nonbasic points of view.

Finally, the classification of values according to *extent* of acceptance is logically independent of their classification according to *depth* of acceptance. To this way of classifying values I now turn.

5. All the values held by a given individual, group, or society may be arranged according to their relative strength. This is measured by the depth of the individual's, group's, or society's commitment to them. The deeper the commitment, the more strongly is the value held. It is necessary to explain the meaning of "depth of commitment." In order to do this, I shall distinguish between personal commitment and social commitment. There are three criteria for determining depth of personal commitment: (a) general conformity of a person's conduct to the value, (b) the extent to which the person strives to attain the value when there are difficulties and obstacles to be overcome, and (c) the extent of self-blame and dissatisfaction in cases of failure to attain the value. Let us look at these criteria more closely.

(a) How deeply a person is committed to a standard or rule is reflected in the extent to which his conduct is actually governed by the standard or rule. A person cannot be said to be deeply committed to a standard which he seldom tries to fulfill, even when there is plenty of opportunity for him to do so. The extent to which a person violates a rule in circumstances in which it is not especially difficult to follow it is a measure of the relative weakness of his commitment to the rule. Again, if a person merely gives lip service to a value judgment or prescription, but seldom acts in accordance with its demands, his commitment is weak. The strength of a person's values is directly proportionate to the extent to which his conduct is guided by them.

(b) The second criterion of depth of commitment provides a further indication of the strength of a person's values. When we find that the person continues to act in accordance with his values even when he must exert considerable will power and self-control to do so, and when he displays great determination, perseverence, and courage to accomplish his goals in difficult and frustrating circumstances, we have reliable evidence of the depth of his commitment. On the other hand if a person gives up any attempt to live by his proclaimed values whenever considerable effort is required to do so, or whenever doing so involves unpleasantness for him, we consider his commitment to be shallow.

(c) A third test for determining the depth of one's own or another's commitment is the intensity of self-blame that is experienced when one is responsible for failing to live in accordance with a value. The extent to which a person feels dissatisfied with himself in these cases is a measure of the depth of his commitment to the value in question. Of course the fact that his conduct does not conform to a given standard or rule or the fact that he does not feel self-blame in cases of failure may not tell us anything about the depth of his commitment. For we may be referring to situations to which the person does not believe the given standard or rule is applicable. It is only where a standard or rule is thought to be applicable by the person in question that any of the aforementioned criteria can tell us how deeply he is committed.

Social commitment is the commitment of a group or society to a set of values. The criteria for determining depth of commitment here would include the three criteria for personal commitment, applied now to all members of the group or society. They also include three additional criteria—(d) the presence of sanctions to support the value, (e) the strength or severity of the sanctions, and (f) the consistency with which the sanctions are administered and enforced. A society as a whole is deeply committed to a value not only to the extent to which each member of the society has a deep personal commitment to the value, as defined by criteria (a), (b), and (c), but also to the extent to which the society has well established sanctions which reward those who live by the value and punish those who do not. The sanctions themselves may take many forms. Social approval or disapproval (public honor and disgrace), economic rewards and penalties, legal sanctions, religious sanctions (the rewards and punishments of a supernatural power) would all be examples. The greater the rewards and the more severe the punishments, the higher the praise and the heavier the blame, the deeper is the social commitment.

We may now say of two values, both of which are accepted by a person or society, that one is stronger than the other when the person or society is more deeply committed to the first than to the second. Theoretically, all the values accepted by a person or society can be arranged in a graduated order of increasing strength. Such an order is what I mean by the classification of values according to the depth of their acceptance. It should now be clear that such a classification is logically independent of the classification of values according to the extent of their acceptance. Highly unconventional or idiosyncratic values may be held by an individual with greater strength than those values which he shares with others. On the other hand, the most widely accepted values in a society are not necessarily the society's strongest values. There may be many standards and rules accepted by practically everyone in a society to which hardly more than lip service is given.

Is there any logical connection between the relative strength of a person's or society's values and the points of view to which they belong? Again I think the answer is in the negative. It is not part of the definition of a moral value (or a religious value, or an aesthetic value) that it be held with a deeper commitment than that with which another kind of value is held. There are some people whose moral values are stronger than, say, their etiquette values, but the reverse is true of others. We might want to say that people whose etiquette values have greater strength than their moral values have a "distorted sense of values." (What we mean by this phrase will be discussed in connection with the next classification of values.) But we do not say that etiquette turns into morality for such people. Similarly, the religious values of one society may have greater strength than its political values, but the opposite may be the case in another society. The nature of the values does not change when their relative strength changes. Nor does the severity of sanctions supporting a value determine the kind of value it is, that is, the point of view to which it belongs. It is only an empirical fact that in most societies moral and religious values are supported by stronger sanctions than aesthetic or etiquette values.

6. Another way of classifying values is according to their relative precedence. The relative precedence of values may occur either within a value system or among value systems. In Chapter 3, we saw how the validation of standards and rules reflects their relative precedence within a value system; in Chapter 6, relative precedence

among different value systems was shown to define a way of life. When there is a conflict between standards or rules within a value system, to say that one takes precedence over another is to say that the first makes a higher claim upon us than the second. Accordingly we are justified in following the first at the cost of violating the second. It is also by appeal to higher standards and rules that we justify making exceptions to a given standard or rule. Thus the extent to which a person feels justified in making exceptions to a value is in inverse proportion to its relative precedence.

The relative precedence of values within a system applies only to values of one kind, since they all belong to one point of view. Accordingly, this classification of values has nothing to do with their classification according to different points of view. But what of relative precedence among different value systems? Here each value system belongs to a different point of view, and all the value systems that constitute a way of life are arranged according to their relative precedence. Is there any logical connection between the points of view to which value systems belong and their relative precedence in ways of life? The answer is no, because different ways of life allow for different hierarchies of relative precedence. In one way of life, for example, a moral system will take precedence over a political system, while in another way of life (such as that embodied in the ideology of a totalitarian state) the political system will take precedence over the moral. In the latter case, one's political duty is considered to be superior to one's moral duty; one's obligations to the state make a higher claim than one's obligations to family or friends. The fact that both ways of life are possible (though one may be more justified than the other by the test of a rational choice) implies that it is not part of the *definition* of "moral value" that it take precedence over political value and that it is not part of the *definition* of "political value" that it take precedence over moral value. If the former were the case, it would be self-contradictory to speak of a way of life in which political values were supreme. If the latter were the case, the ideology of a totalitarian state would turn out to be a logical entailment of the definitions of "political value" and "moral value." Both of these consequences are absurd, and I think the same sort of argument can be given for every other case in which ways of life differ according to the relative precedence of their value systems. In no instance would the description of a way of life be either self-contradictory or tautological. My conclusion, then, is that *it is not part of the definition of any point of view that its values must take precedence over those of any other point of view.* This is simply another way of saying that the classification of values according to the criterion of relative precedence is logically independent of their classification according to the criterion of points of view.

It is important not to confuse the relative precedence of values with their relative strength. Each may vary independently of the other. It is possible for a person (or a society) to hold one value with greater strength than another value and at the same time accept the second as taking precedence over the first. Such a discrepancy between relative strength and relative precedence is a mark of irrationality in the person's (or society's) commitment to values. A rational person would be most deeply committed to those values which make the highest claim upon him and less deeply committed to those making a lower claim. He would be willing to make exceptions to the lower values sooner than to the higher ones; and he would be more strongly inspired and motivated by his higher values than by his lower ones. Ideally, relative strength ought to be determined by relative precedence, since a person is never *justified* in choosing to fulfill a lower value when a higher value is in conflict with it.

But the possibility of discrepancy between the relative precedence of a person's values and the relative strength with which they are held implies that relative precedence cannot be *defined* in terms of relative strength. By definition, a person always has a more intense pro-attitude toward those things which fulfill his stronger values than those things which fulfill his weaker values. Similarly, he always has a more intense con-attitude toward those things which fail to fulfill his stronger values than those things which fail to fulfill his weaker values. When a person must choose between having one thing or another, knowing he cannot have both, his choice will always reflect the relative intensity of his pro-attitudes and con-attitudes and accordingly will reflect the relative strength of his values. For this reason we cannot define a person's supreme (highest) values in terms of what he is unwilling to sacrifice for anything else. This only reveals the values to which he is most deeply committed, that is, his strongest values. But his strongest values are not necessarily his highest.

A person's highest values are those to which he ought to be most deeply committed, not those to which he is most deeply committed. They are the values which he believes are *justified* in taking precedence over all others, as far as his rational thinking goes. In any given case the degree of depth of his commitment and the corresponding degree of intensity of his pro-attitude or con-attitude might be at variance with his reasoning. He might find one thing emotionally more attractive than another and so sacrifice the second for it, even though in reflective moments he would acknowledge that the second is superior to the first (and accordingly makes a higher *claim* upon his choice). A very common case of such discrepancy between relative precedence and relative strength occurs when someone seeks to fulfill his short-range interest at the expense of his long-range interest.

We are now in a position to make clear what it means to say that a person (or group) has a "distorted sense of values." What we refer to by this phrase, I suggest, is not only a discrepancy between the relative precedence and the relative strength of a person's values, but also a discrepancy between the relative precedence of his values and the relative precedence of the values of a rationally chosen way of life. When we say that someone has a distorted sense of values, we do not mean merely that his hierarchy of values is different from our own. Nor do we mean that he holds values with degrees of strength which do not correspond to the degrees of strength with which we hold similar values. (In these instances we tend to say only that the other person's sense of values *differs* from our own.) To speak of a *distorted* sense of values implies two things—that the person's pro-attitudes and con-attitudes are not in accord with the relative precedence of his values, and that his values are false (that is, cannot rationally be justified). This twofold test also applies to the claim that a person has a "good" or "proper" sense of values. We make this claim about someone only if the relative strength of his values is in direct proportion to their relative precedence, and at the same time his values are arranged hierarchically in accordance with a rationally chosen way of life. Since the relative strength of a person's values is reflected in his decisions and conduct, a person could not be said to have a proper sense of values according to this definition unless he actually lived in accordance with a rationally chosen way of life, or at least was striving to live that kind of life.

7. In addition to classifying values by their relative strength and relative precedence, it is possible to classify them by what might be called their relative importance. There are two criteria of the importance of a value—whether it is indispensable to the fulfillment of another value, and, if it is not indispensable, the extent of its effectiveness in fulfilling another value. Suppose a person or a society has adopted the standard of benevolence as a moral ideal. Causally related to this standard are certain other standards, such as generosity, honesty, and forgiveness; and certain rules, such as helping others in need, obeying the law, and treating others fairly. The causal relation between the standard of benevolence and these other standards and rules is such that by fulfilling or acting in accordance with the latter people tend to fulfill the standard of benevolence. Indeed, the fulfillment of some of these standards and rules is absolutely indispensable for fulfilling the standard of benevolence. One cannot possibly be benevolent, for example, if one is unwilling to forgive others or if one does not help others in need. Being honest and obeying the law, on the other hand, are not indispensable means to benevolence, at least in many circumstances, though the ideal of benevolence is furthered in a society where people generally are honest and do obey the law. Let us distinguish, then, between a *necessary means* to the fulfillment of a standard and an *effective means*. If a standard S' will fail to be fulfilled unless another standard S is fulfilled or unless a rule R is followed, then S and R are necessary means to S'. If on the other hand it is possible to fulfill S' without fulfilling S or without acting in accordance with R, and yet if S' tends to be fulfilled the more a person fulfills S and acts in accordance with R, then S and R are effective means to S'.

The relative importance of a value (a standard or rule) is determined by whether it is a necessary means or an effective means to the fulfillment of other values (standards). Assuming that a person or a society has adopted a standard S', then a given standard or rule is of greater importance than another standard or rule if either (1) it is a necessary means to S', while the other is an effective, but not a necessary, means to S', or (2) it is an effective means to S' while the other is neither a necessary nor an effective means to S'.

To this concept of *positive* importance we may readily contrast the concept of *negative* importance. The latter applies whenever two or more values are in conflict. We have seen that one standard is in conflict with another if it is the case that the extent to which something fulfills one it fails to fulfill the other. Thus as commodities are produced more cheaply (and so tend to fulfill the economic standard of low cost) they tend to lose whatever "prestige" value they might have. One rule is in conflict with another if it is the case that to act in accordance with one is to violate the other. Now one standard or rule has negative importance in relation to another with which it is in conflict when it is either a *sufficient dismeans* or an *effective dismeans* to the other. It is a sufficient dismeans to the other when its fulfillment is sufficient to prevent or destroy the fulfillment of the other. It is an effective dismeans when its fulfillment is harmful or detrimental to, but does not completely prevent or destroy, the fulfillment of the other.

One can see from these definitions that positive and negative importance are cases of instrumental value and disvalue, as defined in Chapter 1. Thus we can view the classification of values according to their relative importance as a subdivision of classification 2 above (where the three kinds of extrinsic value—instrumental, contributive, and inherent—were distinguished from intrinsic value). I have considered relative importance separately here in order to bring out its difference from relative precedence and relative strength. For just as it is possible to arrange *all* the values of a person or society in an order of increasing strength or in a hierarchy of relative precedence, so it is possible to arrange them in an independent order of relative importance, each value being assigned a certain place according to the degree of its importance to all the other values of the given set. Let us see how this can be done.

If a person has adopted a standard whose fulfillment is a necessary means to the fulfillment of not only one, but of many other of his values, it has far greater importance to him than a standard whose fulfillment is a necessary means to only one of his values. And even the latter has greater importance to him than a value which is a necessary means to none of his other values. Again, if one value is a more effective means than another to the realization of the person's ideals, the first has a greater degree of importance than the second. Similarly, one value has a greater degree of negative importance than another when it is a sufficient dismeans to more of the person's values than is the other, or when it is a more effective dismeans to the same values than is the other. Accordingly, the degree of importance of a value to a given person or society may be defined as follows. A value increases in positive importance to the extent that the number and positive importance of other values, to which it is a necessary means, increases, and to the extent that its degree of effectiveness increases when it is an effective but not a necessary means to other values. ("Degree of effectiveness" is in turn defined as the extent to which the fulfillment of the effective means tends to bring about the complete fulfillment of the value or values to which it is a means.) According to these definitions, the most important of a person's values are those without which he cannot achieve his other values and those which make the greatest contribution to his achieving his other values. Except for individuals who have decided to commit suicide, the most important values of people are the "biological necessities," that is, those things without which they cannot live. Similarly, except for those societies (if there be any) which seek their own destruction or dissolution, the most important values of a society are those things which are indispensible for its survival as a society.

With regard to negative importance, the most important of a person's values are those which he should be most concerned with controlling or avoiding. They are those values which so conflict with his other values that if he fulfills them he cannot fulfill the others. Ordinarily they would include such things as his self-interest when it conflicts with his moral obligations, or his immediate pleasure when its pursuit is harmful to his health. A society's most important values, in the negative sense, would be those institutions and policies which people in the society approve of, but which work against the long-range welfare of the society as a whole.

It is theoretically possible to place all the values of a person or society in one order, going from the highest degree of positive importance, through lesser degrees of positive importance, to lesser degrees of negative importance, and terminating with the highest degree of negative importance. I now wish to compare such an order, first with the order resulting from relative precedence of values, and second with the classification of values based on points of view. To take up the first point, is there a correlation between degree of importance and level of precedence? There does not appear to be any logical ground for such a correlation. We certainly cannot maintain that the higher a value is in the order of relative precedence the greater is its positive importance. The highest standards a person appeals to in validating his other standards are seldom such that their fulfillment is a necessary or effective means to the fulfillment of his lower standards and rules. If anything, the reverse seems to be the usual relationship. Let us suppose, for example, that an individual seeks to fulfill a standard of good health. If asked to justify that standard, he might appeal to any number of other ends to which having good health is an indispensable means, such as having a happy family life, being a useful member of society, enjoying the beauties of nature, and so on. These higher values are not a necessary means and are not always an effective means to his health, but his health is a necessary means to all of them. Furthermore, each of the higher values may not be indispensable for achieving all the other values of his life, whether higher or lower. But good health is such an indispensable means. Hence good health is more important than any one of the other values, though it is lower in relative precedence.

The reason why the relative importance of values and their relative precedence may vary independently of each other is that relative importance is a causal property whereas relative precedence is a logical property. Relative importance is determined by the cause-effect relations holding among the actual values accepted by individuals and groups. Whether the fulfillment of one value is a necessary or effective means to the fulfillment of another depends upon its effects, which in turn depend upon the nature of the values involved, the psychological and social conditions surrounding their fulfillment, and the physical nature of the world. Relative precedence, on the other hand, is determined by the reasons which people give in justifying their values. Although these reasons often take into consideration causal relations among values, they do not wholly consist in the appeal to such relations. The giving of reasons, as we have seen, is a much more complex process than making statements of causal properties. It is for the same reason that relative importance is not correlated with points of view. For the classification of different kinds of values according to points of view is a logical classification, dependent upon the rules of relevance that govern the reasoning people use in justifying their values. That a certain standard accepted by a person is a moral standard, for example, is not sufficient for claiming that it is of greater or lesser importance than a non-moral standard accepted by the person. Even if we know that the person has adopted a way of life in which moral values take precedence over, say, aesthetic values, we still do not know that a particular moral standard has greater importance in the person's way of life than a particular aesthetic standard. We must know whether the fulfillment of the moral standard is indispensable for the fulfillment of other values in the way of life, or we must know how effective it is, when compared with the aesthetic standard, in fulfilling the other values in the way of life. In one way of life a moral standard may have greater relative importance than an aesthetic standard, but in another way of life the reverse may be the case. Indeed, even if two people accepted the same way of life, the relative importance of a moral and an aesthetic standard might still differ as a result of psychological differences between the two people.

8. Values may be classified not only according to their logical and causal properties, but also according to the manner in which they are held. Thus people may accept values either explicitly or implicitly, and either rationally or irrationally. These "modes of acceptance" are independent of *which* values are accepted, or how they are logically or causally related. I have already considered one mode of acceptance in the concept of the relative strength of values. We saw that relative strength depends upon how deeply committed is the person who accepts the values. The deeper the commitment, the greater the strength of the value. In this and the following section, I shall deal with two other modes of acceptance— how explicit or implicit the acceptance is, and how rational or irrational the acceptance is. In both cases, we are dealing with a matter of degree. There is a continuous gradation from extreme explicitness of acceptance to extreme implicitness, and from extreme rationality

to extreme irrationality. I shall consider the explicit-implicit continuum first.

A value is held explicitly by someone when he knows that he holds it, implicitly when he does not know that he holds it. This distinction applies to standards and rules rather than to value judgments and prescriptions, since a person cannot judge the value of something or prescribe an act to someone without being aware of what he is doing. But he may not be aware of the standards or rules he is applying in each case. Furthermore, a person may not know that he has adopted certain standards and rules which are reflected in his conduct and feelings. Such a person cannot answer the questions: What standards are you trying to fulfill? What rules have you adopted? He has accepted his values implicitly, as the result of a gradual process of acculturation, beginning in early childhood with the "introjection" of the values of his parents. We can discover what values he has implicitly accepted by observing his behavior, learning about his upbringing, becoming aware of the circumstances in which he feels pride or guilt, noticing the goals he tends to seek and the situations he tends to avoid, and so on. The one thing we cannot do is simply to ask him about his standards and rules. If he could answer us, his values would be held explicitly, not implicitly.

People who are articulate about their standards and rules are, to that extent, explicit in their acceptance of them. Of course a person may be articulate about some of his values and inarticulate about, or even unaware of, others. A religious person, for example, may be articulate about his religious and moral values, but inarticulate about his aesthetic values. If we knew enough about a given individual and his way of life, we would theoretically be able to arrange all the standards and rules which constitute that way of life in an order of increasing explicitness (or decreasing implicitness), depending on the degree to which the individual could identify clearly and correctly the standards and rules he had adopted.

How explicit or implicit are the values of an individual or society has nothing to do with how justified they are. A person may be wholly articulate about a way of life which nevertheless cannot be justified under conditions of a rational choice. On the other hand, a person may have adopted a value system of which he is unaware, yet which can be vindicated in terms of a rationally chosen way of life. Degree of explicitness or implicitness, however, does have an important bearing on how rationally a person has *accepted* his values. I shall discuss this relationship in the next section.

Is there any connection between the explicit-implicit mode of acceptance and the classification of values according to points of view? In the first place, there is no logical connection between them. There is nothing in the definition of any point of view which requires that the standards or rules belonging to it be accepted explicitly. Whether a person accepts a moral system implicitly or explicitly has no bearing on the fact that it is a moral system and not some other kind. Even intellectual standards and rules (of truth, validity, etc.) may be accepted implicitly. Indeed, most people are quite unaware of their intellectual standards and the rules of reasoning in which they have been trained. In the second place, there seems to be no psychological connection between the acceptance of a value of a particular kind and the degree of explicitness of its acceptance. The values which people accept explicitly vary according to their different professional or vocational interests and their different social roles. The literary critic has explicit aesthetic values; the minister or priest has explicit religious and moral values; the politician has explicit political values; the businessman has explicit economic values; the scholar has explicit intellectual values; and so on. Thus there is nothing in the points of view themselves which tells us that the values belonging to them must be held explicitly. Nor does explicitness of acceptance vary with the relative strength of values. A person may not be aware of values to which he is deeply committed and yet be quite articulate about values to which he gives but lip service.

9. Besides holding values with varying degrees of strength and with varying degrees of explicitness, it is possible to hold values with varying degrees of rationality. Whether values that are held irrationally tend to be held with greater strength than those held rationally is a question of psychology which I leave open here. But I do wish to emphasize that there is no *logical* connection between depth of commitment to a value and the degree of irrationality of the commitment. It is not self-contradictory to say that the values which a person holds most strongly are those for which he can give good reasons. On the other hand there is a logical connection be-

tween the degree of explicitness with which values are held and the degree of rationality with which they are held. In order to show this, I must first make clear what it means to accept values rationally or irrationally.

The degree of rationality with which a value is held is the degree to which the person who holds it can justify his holding it. Degree of rationality here refers to subjective rationality, not objective rationality. That is to say, it is measured by the degree to which the person himself is able to give good reasons for his values, not by whether there are in fact good reasons (which could be given by someone else) for his values. A person might not be able to give good reasons for his values even though they exist. In such a case, his values would be objectively rational but not subjectively rational. The values would be justifiable, *but they would not be held with a high degree of rationality*. They would in fact be held irrationally, since the person would be unable to give good reasons to justify his holding them.

A value judgment or a prescription is objectively rational if it can be verified. It is subjectively rational if the person who does the judging or prescribing can verify his own judgment or prescription. Similarly, a standard or rule is subjectively rational (i.e., it is accepted with a high degree of rationality) if the person who accepts it can validate it. Ideally, the standard or rule is accepted with the highest degree of rationality when the person is able not only to validate it but also to vindicate the entire value system of which it is a part by appeal to a way of life which is preferred by people under conditions of a rational choice. (He need not have made such a rational choice himself, though ideally he would know that his way of life would be preferred by anyone under conditions of a rational choice.) Thus the degree of rationality with which a value is held is *not* determined by how closely the value does in fact correspond to a value in a rationally chosen way of life. Instead it is determined by how well the person who holds the value can verify or validate it, although ideally he must be able to show that it can be vindicated in terms of a rationally chosen way of life. To the extent that the person cannot do this his values are held irrationally (i.e., held without good reason), even if they do in fact correspond to those of a rationally chosen way of life.

It is now easy to see the connection between the explicit-implicit mode of acceptance and the rational-irrational mode of acceptance. A person cannot justify his values unless they are explicit, that is, unless he is fully aware of them and can accurately state (at least to himself) what they are. In order to verify a value judgment or prescription, the judgment or prescription must be stated in explicit form. But this can always be done, since there is no such thing as an implicit value judgment or prescription. The implicit-explicit distinction, as was pointed out above, applies only to standards and rules. It is here that degree of explicitness and degree of rationality are logically connected. For a person would not be able to validate a standard or rule, and so could not be said to accept it rationally, unless he could state what the standard or rule was. He must know what it is he is to validate. If a person has accepted a standard or rule implicitly and so does not know that he has accepted it, he is unable to justify his acceptance of it. The implicitness of an acceptance thus precludes its rationality. The explicitness of an acceptance, on the other hand, does not guarantee its rationality. A person may be very articulate about his values and still be unable to give good reasons for them.

Whether a value is accepted rationally or irrationally has nothing to do with what kind of a value it is. Although different kinds of values are distinguished on the basis of points of view, and points of view are distinguished on the basis of rules of reasoning appropriate to them, one does not have to *follow* such rules of reasoning in order to *adopt* the values belonging to a point of view. One may adopt moral rules (of conduct), for example, and not be able to justify them according to the rules of reasoning that define the moral point of view. They are moral rules and not political, economic, or religious rules, because *if* they were to be justified by anyone moral rules of reasoning would govern the argument. Similarly, an aesthetic standard is a standard whose adoption is justified from the aesthetic point of view, but this does not mean that everyone who adopts such a standard can in fact justify his adopting it. This is true also of intellectual values. It is perfectly possible to accept such values irrationally. This occurs whenever a person decides to believe an assertion or accept an argument on the basis of certain standards of truth and certain rules of inference, without being aware that he is using such standards and rules. He accepts them implicitly and is therefore unable to give good reasons for doing so. Indeed, it is quite rare for a person to examine his intellectual standards and rules in order to see whether they can be justified. Only the logician and the epistemologist carry out such an examination carefully and systematically, and it takes a high level of intellectual sophistication even to be aware of the problem. But standards of truth and rules of validity are used by everyone in everyday life. Most people are simply unaware of them and accept them uncritically. This is not to say that the standards and rules so accepted are false (unjustifiable). They may well be *objectively* rational. It is only to say that they are not *accepted* rationally, that is, that their mode of acceptance is irrational.

The distinction between objective and subjective rationality enables us to see more clearly what is involved in the classical ideal of "the examined life." It would appear that if there is such a thing as the most justified way of life and if we know what it is, the ideal is to have everyone in the world live that way of life. In order to bring about such an ideal as quickly as possible, it would seem that the best thing to do would be forcibly to control all societies in the world and indoctrinate everyone to accept automatically the values of the most justified way of life. In this manner, everyone's values would become objectively rational. Of course they would not be subjectively rational, but why should this bother us? If everyone is living what we know to be the good life, why deplore the fact that they have accepted that life irrationally? Indeed, if irrational acceptance can make people more deeply committed to their values than rational acceptance, there would seem to be every reason to *prevent* people from trying to justify their values rationally and so becoming critical and reflective about them.

Is this a legitimate conclusion to draw from the general theory of value presented in this book? I think not, for three reasons. In the first place, it rests on a mistaken conception of the nature of a rational choice among ways of life. In the second place, it does not take into account how conditions of a rational choice can be realized. In the third place, it overlooks the possibility that subjective rationality itself may be a part of the rationally chosen way of life. I shall consider each of these points in turn.

The concept of a rational choice among ways of life is the concept of an ideal. No one ever makes such a choice in practice. The concept merely gives meaning to the idea that one way of life is more justified than another; it does not tell us which way of life is the most justified. Indeed, if there were to be widespread disagreement among those who made a rational choice, no way of life could be claimed to be superior to all others. But even if we assume that one way of life would be preferred to all others under the ideal conditions of a rational choice, this still does not warrant our imposing by force any known way of life upon everyone. For no one knows, or ever will know, what that way of life is. If the conditions of a rational choice were approximated to a fair degree, we might be able to make claims with some degree of probability. But even these claims would have to remain open to future revision or rejection. The conditions of a rational choice are simply too ideal to allow us to have any confidence in decisions reached under conditions that we can now approximate in this world.

If this is the case, then our only reasonable hope is to be able gradually to increase the probability of our guess as to what the most justified way of life is. This process of a gradual approach to the truth requires that the conditions of a rational choice (freedom, enlightenment, and impartiality) be approximated more and more closely in the future. How can this be done? The answer lies in developing a kind of society in which everyone is not only permitted but is actually encouraged to make free, enlightened, and impartial choices, as described in Chapter 6. Any attempt to impose one way of life upon everyone would automatically preclude the possibility of anyone's making such a choice. For a *free* choice demands absence of external constraint. *Enlightened* choice demands imaginative as well as intellectual knowledge of many different ways of life; this would be impossible if everyone were forced to live the same way of life. *Impartiality* demands that a person not choose between the way of life in which he was brought up and another way of life. It also demands that the person himself not be indoctrinated from childhood in one way of life, which is the very thing that would happen under the conditions in question. The point is that no one really knows which values are objectively rational and the only way to find out is by having an "open" society throughout the world, which tolerates and even encourages great diversity in ways of life and the freedom to choose among them.

There is a third reason why the critical examination of one's own life is compatible with the general theory of value presented in this book. There is the possibility that subjective rationality may itself be an integral and basic aspect of a rationally chosen way of life. It is not *logically* necessary that a free, enlightened, and impartial choice be the choice of a way of life which includes freedom, enlightenment, and impartiality. Nevertheless, the possibility that this would be the case must be left open. If it were to be the case, those values that were objectively rational would have to be subjectively rational as well. That is, they would constitute a way of life which required that people be able to give good reasons for their value judgments, prescriptions, standards, and rules. Such good reasons ultimately would involve the appeal to a rationally chosen way of life (though not everyone would be expected to make such a choice himself). Thus critical and reflective acceptance of values would be a part of the objectively rational way of life. It might even be the case that such a rational mode of acceptance would be one of the fundamental principles of a rationally chosen way of life. In living this way of life *it would be more important that people be able to give good reasons for their values than that they should accept a particular set of values.* Indeed, diversity and even conflict among the values accepted by people would become an essential aspect of that way of life. Tolerance would have to accompany such diversity and conflict, however, if the conditions for rational acceptance of values were to be maintained.

The classical ideal of the examined life is not antithetical to the theory of value presented in this book. Critical reflection upon the values of one's own society is absolutely necessary if a person is to seek a way of life that is rationally chosen. Even if it were the case that the way of life of his own society happened to be the way of life which would be preferred by everyone under conditions of a rational choice, he would not be able to *know* this unless he questioned the justifiability of all the values of his society. Only then would he know whether his society's value judgments and prescriptions could be verified, whether his society's standards and rules could be validated, and whether the value systems embodied in the structure and functioning of his society could be vindicated. To have everyone in a society make such a critical examination of his own values would require a whole educational process directed toward the rational acceptance of values as its basic goal. This is, indeed, what a liberal education means. Liberal education may be viewed in this light as a complex method for seeking the most justified way of life. In seeking the objectively rational as its end it must develop subjective rationality as its means. The educated man would be the one who steadily and impartially investigates the rational basis of his own and others' values, in order to discover those values (if there be any) which can be shown to be more justified than all others.

It may be the case that if we could know with certainty what the most justified way of life was, it would turn out to be a way of life which excludes the development of subjective rationality. But this is an idle question. We actually never can know with certainty which way of life is most justified. There is therefore every reason to develop and further the highest degree of subjective rationality we are capable of. Only in this way can we hope to attain a reasonable guess about the ideal way of life. Developing the capacity for subjective rationality, whether in everyone or in oneself alone, is an "open" commitment. The Socratic quest is a lifetime's endeavor for each individual, and each individual's pursuit of the quest is merely part of a task for humanity which has no end. The quest is a search for wisdom, and the final goal, which can never be reached, is knowledge of the good.

Bibliography

Books and articles which are concerned with the logic of evaluating and prescribing, but which are not limited to the field of moral philosophy or ethics:

Aiken, H. D., "Evaluation and Obligation: Two Functions of Judgments in the Language of Conduct," *Journal of Philosophy,* XLVII, No. 1 (1950), 5-22.

Baylis, C. A., "Grading, Values, and Choice," *Mind,* LXVII, No. 268 (1958), 485-501.

Braithwaite, R. B., "Critical Notice on *The Language of Morals* by R. M. Hare," *Mind,* LXIII, No. 250 (1954), 249-62.

Campbell, C. A., "Moral and Non-Moral Values: A Study in the First Principles of Axiology," *Mind,* XLIV, No. 175 (1935), 273-99.

Carritt, E. F., *Ethical and Political Thinking.* Oxford: The Clarendon Press, 1947.

Dewey, J., "Theory of Valuation," *International Encyclopedia of Unified Science,* Vol. II, No. 4. Chicago: University of Chicago Press, 1939.

Diggs, B. J., "A Technical 'Ought,'" *Mind*, LXIX, No. 275 (1960), 301-17.

Edwards, Paul, *The Logic of Moral Discourse.* Glencoe, Illinois: The Free Press, 1955.

Falk, W. D., "Goading and Guiding," *Mind*, LXII, No. 246 (1953), 145-71.

Frankena, W. K., "The Naturalistic Fallacy," *Mind*, XLVIII, No. 192 (1939), 464-77.

Glasgow, W. D., "On Choosing," *Analysis*, XVII, No. 6 (1957), 135-39.

Hall, Everett W., *What Is Value?* London: Routledge and Kegan Paul, Ltd., 1952.

Hampshire, Stuart, *Thought and Action.* London: Chatto and Windus, Ltd., 1959.

Hare, R. M., *The Language of Morals.* Oxford: The Clarendon Press, 1952.

Harrison, B., "Some Uses of 'Good' in Criticism," *Mind*, LXIX, No. 274 (1960), 206-22.

Hilliard, A. L., *The Forms of Value.* New York: Columbia University Press, 1950.

Isenberg, A., "Critical Communication," *Philosophical Review*, LVIII, No. 4 (1949), 330-44.

Johnson, C., "Commending and Choosing," *Mind*, LXVI, No. 261 (1957), 63-74.

Kennick, W. E., "Does Traditional Aesthetics Rest on a Mistake?" *Mind*, LXVII, No. 267 (1958), 317-34.

Knight, H., "The Use of 'Good' in Aesthetic Judgments," *Proceedings of the Aristotelian Society*, XXXVI (1935-36), 207-22.

Köhler, Wolfgang, *The Place of Value in a World of Facts.* New York: Liveright Publishing Corporation, 1938; and New York: Meridian Books, Inc., 1959.

Ladd, J., "Value Judgments, Emotive Meaning and Attitudes," *Journal of Philosophy*, XLVI, No. 5 (1949), 119-28.

Laird, John, *The Idea of Value.* Cambridge, England: Cambridge University Press, 1929.

Lamont, W. D., *The Value Judgement*. Edinburgh: University of Edinburgh Press, 1955.

Lepley, Ray, *Verifiability of Value*. New York: Columbia University Press, 1944.

———, ed., *Value: A Cooperative Inquiry*. New York: Columbia University Press, 1949.

———, ed., *The Language of Value*. New York: Columbia University Press, 1957.

Lewis, Clarence Irving, *An Analysis of Knowledge and Valuation*. La Salle, Illinois: The Open Court Publishing Company, 1946.

Macdonald, M., "What Are the Distinctive Features of Arguments Used in Criticism of the Arts?" *Proceedings of the Aristotelian Society*, Supplementary Vol. 23 (1949), 183-94.

Matthews, G. M., " 'Evaluative and Descriptive,' " *Mind*, LXVII, No. 267 (1958), 335-43.

Nowell-Smith, P. H., "Choosing, Deciding and Doing," *Analysis*, XVIII, No. 3 (1958), 63-69.

Osborne, H., *Foundations of the Philosophy of Value*. Cambridge, England: Cambridge University Press, 1933.

Parker, Dewitt H., *Human Values*. New York: Harper & Brothers, 1931.

———, *The Philosophy of Value*. Ann Arbor: University of Michigan Press, 1957.

Pepper, Stephen C., *A Digest of Purposive Values*. Berkeley and Los Angeles: University of California Press, 1947.

———, *The Sources of Value*. Berkeley and Los Angeles: University of California Press, 1958.

Perry, Ralph Barton, *General Theory of Value*. New York: Longmans, Green and Company, 1926.

———, *Realms of Value*. Cambridge, Mass.: Harvard University Press, 1954.

Pitcher, G., "On Approval," *Philosophical Review*, LXVII, No. 2 (1958), 195-211.

Prall, D. W., "A Study in the Theory of Value," *University of California Publications in Philosophy*, Vol. III, No. 2. Berkeley: University of California Press, 1921.

Rice, Philip Blair, *On the Knowledge of Good and Evil.* New York: Random House, 1955.

Smith, James Ward, "Should General Theory of Value Be Abandoned?" *Ethics,* LVII, No. 4, Part I (1947), 274-88.

——, "Senses of Subjectivism in Value Theory," *Journal of Philosophy,* LXV, No. 15 (1948), 393-405.

——, *Theme for Reason.* Princeton: Princeton University Press, 1957.

Timur, M., "Better as the Value-Fundamental," *Mind,* LXIV, No. 253 (1955), 52-60.

Urban, W. M., *Valuation: Its Nature and Laws.* New York: The Macmillan Company, 1909.

Urmson, J. O., "On Grading," *Mind,* LIX, No. 234 (1950), 145-69.

Winch, Peter, *The Idea of a Social Science and Its Relation to Philosophy.* London: Routledge and Kegan Paul Ltd., and New York: The Humanities Press, 1958.

Wittgenstein, Ludwig, *Philosophical Investigations.* New York: The Macmillan Company, 1953.

Zink, S., "Objectivism and Mr. Hare's *Language of Morals,*" *Mind,* LXVI, No. 261 (1957), 79-87.

Some books and articles in moral philosophy and ethics which contain important material bearing on problems in general theory of value:

Adams, E. M., *Ethical Naturalism and the Modern World-View.* Chapel Hill: University of North Carolina Press, 1960.

Baier, Kurt, *The Moral Point of View.* Ithaca, N. Y.: Cornell University Press, 1958.

Bennett, J., "Moral Argument," *Mind,* LXIX, No. 276 (1960), 544-49.

Brandt, Richard B., "The Status of Empirical Assertion Theories in Ethics," *Mind,* LXI, No. 244 (1952), 458-79.

——, *Hopi Ethics.* Chicago: University of Chicago Press, 1954.

——, "The Definition of an 'Ideal Observer' Theory in Ethics," *Philosophy and Phenomenological Research,* XV, No. 3 (1955), 407-13.

————, "Some Comments on Professor Firth's Reply," *Philosophy and Phenomenological Research*, XV, No. 3 (1955), 422-23.

————, *Ethical Theory*. Englewood Cliffs, N. J.: Prentice-Hall, Inc., 1959.

Broad, C. D., *Five Types of Ethical Theory*. London: Kegan Paul, Trench, Trubner and Co. Ltd., 1930.

————, "Is 'Goodness' the Name of a Simple Non-Natural Quality?" *Proceedings of the Aristotelian Society*, XXXIV (1933-34), 249-68.

————, "Some Reflections on Moral-Sense Theories in Ethics," *Proceedings of the Aristotelian Society*, XLV (1944-45), 131-66.

Cavell, S. and Sesonske, A., "Moral Theory, Ethical Judgments and Empiricism," *Mind*, LXI, No. 244 (1952), 543-63.

Ewing, A. C., "Subjectivism and Naturalism in Ethics," *Mind*, LIII, No. 210 (1944), 120-41.

————, *The Definition of Good*. London: Macmillan & Company, Ltd., 1947.

————, *Second Thoughts in Moral Philosophy*. London: Routledge and Kegan Paul, Ltd., 1959.

Feigl, H., "Validation and Vindication: An Analysis of the Nature and Limits of Ethical Arguments," *Readings in Ethical Theory*, eds. Wilfred Sellars and John Hospers. New York: Appleton-Century-Crofts, Inc., 1952.

Firth, R., "Ethical Absolutism and the Ideal Observer," *Philosophy and Phenomenological Research*, XII, No. 3 (1952), 317-45.

————, "Reply to Professor Brandt," *Philosophy and Phenomenological Research*, XV, No. 3 (1955), 414-21.

Geach, P. T., "Good and Evil," *Analysis*, XVII, No. 2 (1957), 33-42.

Gilman, E., "The Distinctive Purpose of Moral Judgments," *Mind*, LXI, No. 243 (1952), 307-16.

Hampshire, S., "Fallacies in Moral Philosophy," *Mind*, LVIII, No. 232 (1949), 466-82.

Hare, R. M., "Geach: Good and Evil," *Analysis*, XVII, No. 5 (1957), 103-11.

Harrison, J., "Can Ethics Do Without Propositions?" *Mind*, LIX, No. 235 (1950), 358-71.

Hart, H. L. A., "Positivism and the Separation of Law and Morals," *Harvard Law Review*, LXXI, No. 4 (1958), 593-629.

Hartland-Swann, John, *An Analysis of Morals*. London: George Allen and Unwin, Ltd., 1960.

Henson, R. G., "On Being Ideal," *Philosophical Review*, LXV, No. 3 (1956), 389-400.

Hill, Thomas English, *Contemporary Ethical Theories*. New York: The Macmillan Company, 1950.

Hospers, John, *Human Conduct*. New York: Harcourt, Brace and World, Inc., 1961.

Ladd, John, *The Structure of a Moral Code*. Cambridge, Mass.: Harvard University Press, 1957.

MacBeath, A., *Experiments in Living*. London: Macmillan & Co. Ltd., 1952.

Mayo, Bernard, *Ethics and the Moral Life*. London: Macmillan & Co. Ltd., 1958.

McNeilly, F. S., "Competing Criteria," *Mind*, LXVI, No. 263 (1957), 289-307.

Monro, D. H., "Are Moral Problems Genuine?" *Mind*, LXV, No. 258 (1956), 166-83.

Moore, G. E., *Principia Ethica*. Cambridge, England: Cambridge University Press, 1903.

———, *Ethics*. London: Oxford University Press, 1912.

———, *Philosophical Studies*. London: Routledge and Kegan Paul, Ltd., 1922. Chapter 8: "The Conception of Intrinsic Value" and Chapter 10: "The Nature of Moral Philosophy."

Nielsen, K., "Justification and Moral Reasoning," *Methodos*, IX (1957), 1-35.

———, "Speaking of Morals," *Centennial Review*, II, No. 4 (1958), 414-44.

———, "The 'Good Reasons Approach' and 'Ontological Justifications' of Morality," *Philosophical Quarterly*, IX, No. 35 (1959), 2-16.

————, "Can a Way of Life Be Justified?" *Indian Journal of Philosophy*, I, No. 3 (1960), 164-74.

Nowell-Smith, P. H., *Ethics*. Harmondsworth, England: Penguin Books Ltd., 1954.

Perry, O. L., "The Logic of Moral Valuation," *Mind*, LXVI, No. 261 (1957), 42-62.

Prior, A. N., *Logic and the Basis of Ethics*. Oxford: The Clarendon Press, 1949.

Rawls, J., "Outline of a Decision Procedure for Ethics," *Philosophical Review*, LX, No. 2 (1951), 177-97.

————, "Two Concepts of Rules," *Philosophical Review*, LXIV, No. 1 (1955), 3-32.

Rees, W. J., "Moral Rules and the Analysis of 'Ought,'" *Philosophical Review*, LXII, No. 1 (1953), 23-40.

Ross, W. D., *The Right and the Good*. Oxford: The Clarendon Press, 1930.

————, *Foundations of Ethics*. Oxford: The Clarendon Press, 1939.

Sharp, F. C., "Voluntarism and Objectivity in Ethics," *Philosophical Review*, L, No. 3 (1941), 253-67.

Sidgwick, Henry, *The Methods of Ethics*, 6th ed. New York: The Macmillan Company, 1901.

Singer, M. G., "Generalization in Ethics," *Mind*, LXIV, No. 255 (1955), 361-75.

————, "Moral Rules and Principles," in *Essays in Moral Philosophy*, ed. A. I. Melden. Seattle: University of Washington Press, 1958.

Stace, W. T., *The Concept of Morals*. New York: The Macmillan Company, 1937.

Stevenson, Charles L., "Moore's Arguments against Certain Forms of Ethical Naturalism," *The Philosophy of G. E. Moore*, ed. P. Schilpp. Evanston, Illinois: Northwestern University Press, 1942.

————, *Ethics and Language*. New Haven: Yale University Press, 1944.

Tomas, V., "Ethical Disagreements and the Emotive Theory of Values," *Mind*, LX, No. 238 (1951), 205-22.

Toulmin, S. E., *An Examination of the Place of Reason in Ethics.* Cambridge, England: Cambridge University Press, 1950.

Westermarck, Edward, *Ethical Relativity.* London: Routledge and Kegan Paul, Ltd., 1932, and Paterson, N. J.: Littlefield, Adams and Co., 1960.

Appendix

In accordance with Ludwig Wittgenstein's wish that translations of his works be accompanied by the original German, all direct quotations which have been taken from his *Philosophical Investigations* (*Philosophische Untersuchungen*) are given here in the original German. For the reader's convenience, they are placed in the order of their occurrence in Chapter 10 above.

. . . ein Schachzug nicht allein darin besteht, dass ein Stein so und so auf dem Brett verschoben wird, . . . sondern in den Umständen, die wir nennen: "eine Schachpartie spielen", "ein Schachproblem lösen", und dergl. [Page 264]

Kann ich mit dem Wort "bububu" meinen "Wenn es nicht regnet, werde ich spazieren gehen"?—Nur in einer Sprache kann ich etwas mit etwas meinen. [Page 264-65]

Wir reden von dem räumlichen und zeitlichen Phänomen der Sprache; nicht von einem unräumlichen und unzeitlichen Unding. . . . Aber wir reden von ihr so, wie von den Figuren des Schachspiels, indem wir Spielregeln für sie angeben, nicht ihre physikalischen Eigenschaften beschreiben.

Die Frage "Was ist eigentlich ein Wort?" ist analog der "Was ist eine Schachfigur?" [Page 265]

Man lernt das Spiel, indem man zusieht, wie Andere es spielen. Aber wir sagen, es werde nach den und den Regeln gespielt, weil ein Beobachter diese Regeln aus der Praxis des Spiels ablesen kann,— wie ein Naturgesetz, dem die Spielhandlungen folgen.—Wie aber unterscheidet der Beobachter in diesem Fall zwischen einem Fehler der Spielenden und einer richtigen Spielhandlung?—Es gibt dafür Merkmale im Benehmen der Spieler. Denke an das charakteristische Benehmen dessen, der ein Versprechen korrigiert. Es wäre möglich, zu erkennen, dass Einer dies tut, auch wenn wir seine Sprache nicht verstehen. [Page 266]

. . . wir nur auf den Mund der Regel schauen und *tun*, und an keine weitere Anleitung appellieren. [Page 266]

Eine Regel steht da, wie ein Wegweiser.—Lässt er keinen Zweifel offen über den Weg, den ich zu gehen habe? Zeigt er, in welche Richtung ich gehen soll, wenn ich an ihm vorbei bin; ob der Strasse nach, oder dem Feldweg, oder querfeldein? [Page 266]

. . . sich Einer nur insofern nach einem Wegweiser richtet, als es einen ständigen Gebrauch, eine Gepflogenheit, gibt. [Page 267]

Es kann nicht ein einziges Mal nur ein Mensch einer Regel gefolgt sein. [Page 268]

Man fühlt nicht, dass man immer des Winkes (der Einflüsterung) der Regel gewärtig sein muss. Im Gegenteil. Wir sind nicht gespannt Sieht man ihrent Treiben zu, so ist es verständlich, erscheint uns immer dasselbe, und wir tun, was sie uns sagt. [Page 268]

Sieht man ihrem Treiben zu, so ist es verständlich, erscheint uns 'logisch'. [Page 270]

Versuchen wir aber, ihre Sprache zu erlernen, so finden wir, dass es unmöglich ist. Es besteht nämlich bei ihnen kein regelmässiger Zusammenhang des Gesprochenen, der Laute, mit den Handlungen. . . . Zu dem, was wir "Sprache" nennen, fehlt die Regelmässigkeit. [Page 270]

Nimm an, eine Regel gebe mir ein, wie ich ihr folgen soll; d.h., wenn ich der Linie mit den Augen nachgehe, so sagt mir nun eine innere Stimme: "Zieh *so!*"—Was ist der Unterschied zwischen diesem

Vorgang, einer Art Inspiration zu folgen, und dem, einer Regel zu folgen? Denn sie sind doch nicht das Gleiche. In dem Fall der Inspiration *warte* ich auf die Anweisung. Ich werde einen Andern nicht meine 'Technik' lehren können, der Linie zu folgen. Er sei denn, ich lehrte ihn eine Art des Hinhorchens, der Rezeptivität. Aber dann kann ich natürlich nicht verlangen, dass er der Linie so folge, wie ich. [Page 270]

Eine Sprache verstehen, heisst eine Technik beherrschen. [Page 271]

Das Spiel, möchte man sagen, hat nicht nur Regeln, sondern auch einen *Witz*. . . . Das Spiel soll doch durch die Regeln bestimmt sein! Wenn also eine Spielregel vorschreibt, dass zum Auslosen vor der Schachpartie die Könige zu verwenden sind, so gehört das, wesentlich, zum Spiel. Was könnte man dagegen einwenden? Dass man den Witz dieser Vorschrift nicht einsehe. Etwa, wie wenn man auch den Witz einer Regel nicht einsähe, nach der jeder Stein dreimal umzudrehen wäre, ehe man mit ihm zieht. Fänden wir diese Regel in einem Brettspiel, so würden wir uns wundern und Vermutungen über den Zweck der Regel anstellen. ("Sollte diese Vorschrift verhindern, dass man ohne Überlegung zieht?") [Page 272]

Denk an die Werkzeuge in einem Werkzeugkasten: es ist da ein Hammer, eine Zange, eine Säge, ein Schraubenzieher, ein Massstab, ein Leimtopf, Leim, Nägel und Schrauben.—So verschieden die Funktionen dieser Gegenstände, so verschieden sind die Funktionen der Wörter. [Page 272]

Sieh den Satz als Instrument an, und seinen Sinn als seine Verwendung! [Page 272]

Frage dich: Bei welcher Gelegenheit, zu welchem Zweck, sagen wir das?

Welche Handlungsweisen begleiten diese Worte? (Denk ans Grüssen!) In welchen Szenen werden sie gebraucht; und wozu? [Page 273]

Befehlen, und nach Befehlen handeln—
Beschreiben eines Gegenstands nach dem Ansehen, oder nach Messungen—

Herstellen eines Gegenstands nach einer Beschreibung (Zeichnung)—
Berichten eines Hergangs—
Über den Hergang Vermutungen anstellen—
Eine Hypothese aufstellen und prüfen—
Darstellen der Ergebnisse eines Experiments durch Tabellen und Diagramme—
Eine Geschichte erfinden; und lesen—
Theater spielen—
Reigen singen—
Rätsel raten—
Einen Witz machen; erzählen—
Ein angewandtes Rechenexempel lösen—
Aus einer Sprache in die andere übersetzen—
Bitten, Danken, Fluchen, Grüssen, Beten.

—Es ist interessant, die Mannigfaltigkeit der Werkzeuge der Sprache und ihrer Verwendungsweisen, die Mannigfaltigkeit der Wort- und Satzarten, mit dem zu vergleichen, was Logiker über den Bau der Sprache gesagt haben. (Und auch der Verfasser der *Logisch-Philosophischen Abhandlung.*) [Page 273]

Die Sprache ist ein Instrument. Ihre Begriffe sind Instrumente. [Page 274]

Betrachte z.B. einmal die Vorgänge, die wir "Spiele" nennen. Ich meine Brettspiele, Kartenspiele, Ballspiele, Kampfspiele, usw. . . . Was ist allen diesen gemeinsam?—Sag nicht: "Es *muss* ihnen etwas gemeinsam sein, sonst hiessen sie nicht 'Spiele' "—sondern *schau,* ob ihnen allen etwas gemeinsam ist.—Denn, wenn du sie anschaust, wirst du zwar nicht etwas sehen, was *allen* gemeinsam wäre, aber du wirst Ähnlichkeiten, Verwandtschaften, sehen, und zwar eine ganze Reihe. Wie gesagt: denk nicht, sondern schau!—Schau z.B. die Brettspiele an, mit ihren mannigfachen Verwandtschaften. Nun geh zu den Kartenspielen über: hier findest du viele Entsprechungen mit jener ersten Klasse, aber viele gemeinsame Züge verschwinden, andere treten auf. Wenn wir nun zu den Ballspielen übergehen, so bleibt manches Gemeinsame erhalten, aber vieles geht verloren. . . . Und so können wir durch die vielen, vielen anderen Gruppen von Spielen gehen. Ähnlichkeiten auftauchen und verschwinden sehen.

Und das Ergebnis dieser Betrachtung lautet nun: Wir sehen ein kompliziertes Netz von Ähnlichkeiten, die einander übergreifen und kreuzen. Ähnlichkeiten im Grossen und Kleinen. [Page 274]

Wie ist denn der Begriff des Spiels abgeschlossen? Was ist noch ein Spiel und was ist keines mehr? Kannst du die Grenzen angeben? Nein. Du kannst welche *ziehen:* denn es sind noch keine gezogen. (Aber das hat dich noch nie gestört, wenn du das Wort "Spiel" angewendet hast.)

"Aber dann ist ja die Anwendung des Wortes nicht geregelt; das 'Spiel', welches wir mit ihm spielen, ist nicht geregelt."—Es ist nicht überall von Regeln begrenzt; aber es gibt ja auch keine Regel dafür z.B., wie hoch man im Tennis den Ball werfen darf, oder wie stark, aber Tennis ist doch ein Spiel und es hat auch Regeln. [Page 276]

Man kann sagen, der Begriff 'Spiel' ist ein Begriff mit verschwommenen Rändern.—"Aber ist ein verschwommener Begriff überhaupt ein *Begriff?*"—Ist eine unscharfe Photographie überhaupt ein Bild eines Menschen? Ja, kann man ein unscharfes Bild immer mit Vorteil durch ein scharfes esetzen? Ist das unscharfe nicht oft gerade das, was wir brauchen? [Page 276]

Wie würden wir denn jemandem erklären, was ein Spiel ist? Ich glaube, wir werden ihm *Spiele* beschreiben, und wir könnten der Beschreibung hinzufügen: "das, *und Ähnliches,* nennt man 'Spiele' ". Und wissen wir selbst denn mehr? Können wir etwa nur dem Andern nicht genau sagen, was ein Spiel ist?—Aber das ist nicht Unwissenheit. Wir kennen die Grenzen nicht, weil keine gezogen sind. Wie gesagt, wir können—für einen besondern Zweck—eine Grenze ziehen. Machen wir dadurch den Begriff erst brauchbar? Durchaus nicht! Es sei denn, für diesen besondern Zweck. [Page 276-77]

. . . Unterscheidungen *hervorheben,* die unsre gewöhnlichen Sprachformen leicht übersehen lassen. [Page 277]

So eine Reform für bestimmte praktische Zwecke, die Verbesserung unserer Terminologie zur Vermeidung von Missverständnissen im praktischen Gebrauch, ist wohl möglich. [Page 277]

Hier stossen wir auf die grosse Frage, die hinter allen diesen Betrachtungen steht.—Denn man könnte mir nun einwenden: "Du machst dir's leicht! Du redest von allen möglichen Sprachspielen, hast aber nirgends gesagt, was denn das Wesentliche des Sprachspiels, und also der Sprache, ist. Was allen diesen Vorgängen gemeinsam ist und sie zur Sprache, oder zu Teilen der Sprache macht. Du schenkst dir also gerade den Teil der Untersuchung, der dir selbst seinerzeit das meiste Kopfzerbrechen gemacht hat, nämlich den, die *allgemeine Form des Satzes* und der Sprache betreffend."

Und das ist wahr.—Statt etwas anzugeben, was allem, was wir Sprache nennen, gemeinsam ist, sage ich, es ist diesen Erscheinungen garnicht Eines gemeinsam, weswegen wir für alle das gleiche Wort verwenden,—sondern sie sind mit einander in vielen verschiedenen Weisen *verwandt*. Und dieser Verwandtschaft, oder dieser Verwandtschaften wegen nennen wir sie alle "Sprachen". Ich will versuchen, dies zu erklären. [Page 277]

INDEX

Index